_28 48_

UNDERSTANDING
SOCIAL PROBLEMS

Albert Schaffer
Ruth C. Schaffer
Gladys L. Ahrenholz
Charles S. Prigmore

All of the University of Alabama
Tuscaloosa, Alabama

CHARLES E. MERRILL PUBLISHING COMPANY

Columbus, Ohio   A Bell & Howell Company

70964

MERRILL SOCIOLOGY SERIES

Under the editorship of

Richard L. Simpson

University of North Carolina,
at Chapel Hill

International Standard Book Number 0-675-09331-7

Library of Congress Catalog Card Number: 73-115332

1   2   3   4   5   6   7   8   9   10—74   73   72   71   70

PRINTED IN THE UNITED STATES OF AMERICA

PREFACE

Among the difficult tasks confronting authors is the selection of material and an approach. The broad scope of social problems complicates decisions on inclusion and exclusion of certain areas. Since an effort to treat comprehensively all of the important social problems in America would lead either to a multivolume work or to inadequate coverage, the authors decided upon a more intensive analysis of a limited number of problems. We selected problems which appeared especially significant in terms of

1. the degree to which each involved strategic units and large numbers of persons;
2. the degree to which each had engaged the resources of the nation for some time; and
3. the likelihood that in the coming decade ameliorative efforts on each would have far reaching consequences for the structure of American society.

Our analysis of social problems has three main objectives. The first is concerned with the description of the main dimensions of each problem, the features of American society contributing to its existence, and the problem's impact on various social units. The authors seek to help students understand the connections between the main features of society and the problem. Second, relationships between the problem and features of social stratification are emphasized wherever relevant. Third, the efforts being made to alleviate the problem or the applied phase of social problem analysis indicative of the society's adaptive capabilities, and sources of resistance to problem reduction are discussed at length.

In emphasizing the management of social problems, attention is given to certain changes in ideas on the nature of government and the law which made possible a wider range of responses to problems than had hitherto occurred. The emphasis on the political sector as an important factor in problem management requires a concern for the role of interest groups and interest group conflict. Attention also focuses on the relatively recent emergence of social scientists as advisors to decision makers, and the tools which they employ—especially those pertaining to systematic collection and interpretation of information through the medium of social indicators and social forecasting. The volume concludes by comparing the utility of these two strategies of problem management, the involvement of interest groups and the use of information systems to guide decision making.

Since the authors held many discussions on content and approach, it is difficult to single out the contribution of each. It will suffice to say that Albert Schaffer wrote chapters 1, 2, 8, and 9, and with Ruth C. Schaffer,

iii

chapter 10; in addition to chapter 10 Ruth C. Schaffer wrote chapters 3 and 5; Charles Prigmore wrote chapters 4 and 6; and Gladys Ahrenholz wrote chapter 7.

The authors wish to express their appreciation to Richard L. Simpson for his thoughtful suggestions, a number of which have been reflected in the final draft of this book. We are especially grateful for the skilled assistance of Jean and Raymond Rayfield and Jennie S. Flowers, research librarian.

Albert Schaffer

Ruth C. Schaffer

Gladys L. Ahrenholz

Charles S. Prigmore

To

Edie, Barbara, Glenn, Philip

CONTENTS

Chapter

CHAPTER ONE

UNDERSTANDING SOCIAL PROBLEMS

Since the mass media continually explore a number of social problems, many college students have some acquaintance with this subject area. Urban riots, campus rebellions, crime in the streets, varieties of drug abuse, sexual aberrations and accounts of "underworld" organizations frequently are presented by movies, newspapers, magazines, and television. The tendency of the mass media to emphasize extreme forms of deviant behavior—to underscore the harsher and more bizarre features of particular social problems—in order to catch the attention of the audience, often causes misleading impressions of the nature and complexity of the phenomena.

Sociological understanding of social problems requires an approach quite different from that generally found in the mass media. In many cases when considering conditions which are general and widespread, such as the circumstances within a ghetto or the impact of a standard school curriculum on the achievement of minority group children, commonplace facts prove indispensable for an understanding of the situation. Analysis of a social problem generally must go beyond popular explanations, such as laziness, to account for the circumstances of the poor.

Effective explanation requires the application of one or more theoretical frameworks, which specify causes and their relationships and connections to the problem condition. These theories emphasize social and social psychological rather than psychological and environmental processes.

Study of the efforts to overcome a social problem can also be enlightening. The manner by which society seeks to cope with social problems reveals the nature and vitality of its adaptive capacities and its potential for accomplishing those changes in social structure which measurably reduce the level of disorganization. Knowledge of these elements of societal behavior enables the sociologist to differentiate between societies with extensive and those with limited adaptive powers.

Since research findings often contribute to the formulation of remedial programs,[1] the sociological enterprise is part of society's adaptive capabilities. Sociological knowledge of social structure and social process can assist leaders to recognize a problem and to choose between alternative strategies of remedial action. Use of social science knowledge in this manner leads to more intelligent choices and to outcomes more consistent with the basic values of American society. Sociologists occasionally advise officials and leaders seeking to solve a problem situation.[2] The degree to which a society copes with social problems depends partly on the relevance and use made of sociological knowledge. For these reasons, our approach emphasizes an understanding of the causes of social problems and of societal reactions.

3

LEVELS OF ANALYSIS

A complex society may be viewed as one total unit whose parts interconnect in definite ways, constituting modes of organization. Two societies may differ not in the nature of component units but in the structure of connecting links. The federal form of government, for example, is characterized by performance of somewhat different functions at each level—national, state and local. The latter two levels thus possess a measure of autonomy from the national government, and each depends on the others. This arrangement binds local and national units together in a distinct pattern which can be distinguished both in theory and practice from more centralized forms in other societies.

The concept of level of organization involves several ideas.[3] First, the concept maintains that each level of organization represents a unit of organization found throughout a society and is characterized by structures and activities which may not be found elsewhere. The unique properties of each level permit it to be differentiated from the others. Second, levels can be thought of as varying from a "lower" to a "higher" plane of organization, as each successive level has activities and structures not found on a "lower" level. At the same time, a "higher" level has processes found on each of the "lesser" levels. Certain social processes, such as interaction and socialization, occur on all levels of a society and in all groups and organizations. Third, each "higher" level has social units which serve a larger territory and population than those at "lower" levels.

The number of levels which can be delimited depends on the scope of the study. Our purposes require delimitation of three levels, interpersonal, community and societal. The first involves various forms of social interaction, the interdependence of groups and the psychic attributes of members. On this level one examines, first, how interaction becomes organized into stable forms, such as the primary group, and second, how groups and the personalities of members interact upon each other. At the second level organization of social activities within a fairly large territory, often but not necessarily coexistent with the legally defined boundaries of a municipality, characterizes the community. Many local activities are organized spatially and temporarily to facilitate movement of people and goods between the sites where various events occur, such as commuting between home and work. In addition, the community serves to connect activities on the interpersonal level with those on the societal level through communication, transportation and government. Programs enacted by the Congress, such as education and housing, are often implemented by community agencies and organizations.

Structures on the societal level, especially government, organize relations internally and externally, between levels within the nation and with other societies. Top officials of the federal government pursue the "national interest" in transactions with leaders of other governments and in making decisions which are felt throughout society. The annual budget, for example, prepared by the President and his major advisors, reflects the priorities assigned to domestic and international programs. The amount and type of resources available for handling domestic problems greatly influence the adaptive capabilities of the nation.[4]

The several levels of social organization are involved in the study of social problems as arenas in which difficulties occur and as environments which generate remedial efforts. Where problems occur solely in a few social settings on a "lower" level, whether community or interpersonal, the conditions responsible may also be specific to the environment. Organizations on the societal level may not become involved, and compensatory actions may be taken in the arena where the trouble is located. Friction in the family or peer group will occur to some degree in every community, partly as a response to atypical factors, such as personality quirks, or temporary events, such as illness. In many instances, adaptive modes of behavior will confine the conflict to tolerable intensities. If, however, the conflict occurs in units throughout a level of organization, the sources of the trouble may lie in relations between levels. Under these circumstances, remedial programs may have to be developed and enacted on the community and societal level.

Deaths and injuries caused by automobile accidents illustrate relationships between the several levels of social organization. A high accident rate in a community may result from local factors: bad roads and a shortage of policemen for patrolling the highways. Correction of these conditions, by action of local officials, probably would reduce but not eliminate vehicular accidents as an important cause of death. Other causes, which operate throughout society, also may become involved. National policies which favor construction of highways and freeways at the expense of facilities for mass transit promote the use of the automobile. The number of automobile accidents could be reduced if more drivers relied on mass transit facilities for travel to and from work. A successful attack on automobile accidents requires coordination of the efforts of agencies on each of the three levels of organization.

The factors responsible for the existence of social problems in America generally involve all levels of social organization. This circumstance results from the long-term trend toward increased interdependence of the parts of society. This derives from several factors: development of a nationwide system of transportation and communication which link all regions and communities to each other; industrial development which exposes most communities to such side-effects as pollution and technological unemployment; the increased involvement of the nation in world affairs, which makes great demands of all citizens and social organizations. The effects of problem conditions will extend to all levels of an interdependent society. The rise of the welfare state in America can be viewed as a long-term response to this trend which provides more central direction for efforts at problem management. Legislative programs in a variety of areas, such as health, education, housing and civil rights, allocate resources of the total society to problem solving agencies in each level of American society.

Controversy on the relative contribution and importance of each level to problem solving remains a debatable question despite the growing importance of the state. Two opposing theories receive consideration in this volume. The first theory, social pluralism, maintains that compensatory actions emanate primarily from the local level.[5] These actions include the mobilization of persons who are sufficiently bothered about some condition to take the time and trouble to make their feelings known in a concerted and disciplined fashion. Formation of interest groups or a social movement on the local level informs societal level leaders that the time has come to consider carefully compensatory actions. The second strategy, based on the information theory, maintains that certain agencies on the societal level play a vital role in detecting and coping with social problems.[6] The complexity of social structure and process requires an elite group, social scientists, operating on the societal level to detect the existence and define the parameters of a social problem. Performance of this intelligence function requires a system of gathering information about all levels of society. Social scientists would use this knowledge in advising national leaders on how best to cope with the problem situation. An elite group on the societal level would possess considerable influence over problem management. These two views on problem management, that of social pluralism and of information, are discussed more fully later in this chapter.

SOCIAL PROBLEMS DEFINED

The few examples of social problems mentioned in the previous section offer some clues concerning the nature of this phenomenon. Automobile accidents deprive victims and their families of precious resources —life, health and property. Absence of one or all of these conditions interferes with the operation of certain social units, especially the families of the persons involved. Similarly, chronic family dissension often warps the personalities of children. Serious psychic disturbances can prevent a person from functioning properly in his social roles. In both examples the victims and persons close to them lose some vital resource. Since items of value appear to be involved in the existence of a social problem, an understanding of the value concept should precede consideration of the concept of a social problem. Robin Williams defines values as:

> . . . those *conceptions of desirable states of affairs* that are utilized in selective conduct as *criteria* for preference or as *justifications* for proposed or actual behavior. . . .[7]

Values refer to those ideas which indicate the conditions or concrete situations which are worthwhile and significant. They focus the attention, interest and behavior of individuals and groups on objects or relationships whose attainment is considered to be rewarding. People thus expend thought, time, energy and other resources in the quest for obtaining or for preserving particular values. Possession of values enables men, both individually and collectively, to be selective in activity, to choose between objects of different merit, and to choose between conditions of varying importance.

To influence behavior the meaning of particular values must be connected with specific objects, either material, social or symbolic. Otherwise values cannot orient men to their surroundings. "Education," for example, offers less assistance for action when its meaning is vague than when people associate it with a particular type of schooling. The latter provides concrete targets which can be attained by arranging social relationships in specific configurations, *e.g.,* establishing a public school system. One transformation which values undergo in society involves acquisition of more precise meanings.[8] Values which experience this pattern of change generally exercise considerable influence over individual and group behavior.

Values do not become attached to organizations and groups by random or chance processes. The decision to adopt, drop or modify one or more values has far-reaching consequences for a social unit. Since values refer to worthwhile conditions or resources, a change in values involves a modification of the particular features of the environment, social or otherwise, which the organization will pursue. For example, a decision to either place the value of containing communism in Viet Nam ahead of the value of social justice for minority groups at home, or to reverse the order of preference, will determine the kinds and amounts of resources allocated to each sphere of activity. This, in turn, will influence the nation's power and prestige on the world scene and the degree of its internal cohesiveness. The values of a group or society have a close connection to its most vital interests, those of stability or instability, growth or decline, effectiveness or ineffectiveness, strength or weakness. A group's values influence both its internal structure and operations and its relations with other groups and organizations.

Since an organization's selection of values has serious consequences for its present and future vitality, value conflicts between groups can be bitter and divisive. For numerous reasons the resolution or alleviation of a social problem often requires those in positions of authority to choose between the values of various groups—a situation which many political leaders prefer to avoid if possible.

The Concept of Social Problem

The problems in this chapter have at least one feature in common— the operation of a social unit becomes impaired by the inability of many persons to obtain needed amounts of top-rated values. If this condition becomes widespread and many people and organizations cannot obtain adequate amounts of socially approved values despite legitimate and repeated efforts within the social order, they will be receptive to plans and schemes for extensive social change. An entire society may be regarded as unstable when leaders and citizens no longer accept its rules as legitimate.

To cite a few examples, those who burglarize and murder deprive their victims of valuable resources, namely wealth and life itself. A less obvious example concerns organized gambling syndicates which provide services to people who willingly pay for them. Those who play the numbers, for example, derive certain satisfactions from indulging in a wager which offers the prospect of a sudden and large windfall. In what sense are these persons deprived of values? Since the odds are usually rigged to reduce the amount of the payoff, the bettor is cheated. However, the bettor often receives satisfaction from the mere anticipation of winning—wagering provides him with a prospect of riches which he otherwise may not have. Gambling, however, finances many illicit activities sustained by organized gangs, such as trafficking in drugs, protection rackets, and gaining control over legitimate businesses. The profitability of the numbers racket strengthens organized crime in America making the syndicate a threat to the vitality and effectiveness of several institutions, notably the economy and government.[9]

The example of gambling suggests that the victims of illicit activities may not be disturbed by the loss of valued resources. If this is the case, can gambling be classified as a social problem in the sense that a high rate of homicide or of burglary constitutes a social problem? From a sociological standpoint, *a social problem exists whenever many or even a few strategic groups undergo major deprivations of highly valued items.* If, for one reason or another, the members of these groups are not troubled by this circumstance, the tensions in society remain low, and the problem condition exists largely in the minds of the analysts of social processes—sociologists and other intellectuals. Under these conditions, the social problem remains "latent."[10] Where public awareness of a problem situation spreads throughout a community or society and demands build-up for remedial action, the latent social problem becomes "manifest," with its main features finally recognized and proposals for action considered. These conditions constitute prerequisites for efforts to eliminate or reduce the severity of the particular problem.[11]

Changing a "latent" to a "manifest" social problem, a critical step in the reduction of distress, may not occur easily or quickly. The beliefs of society usually provide explanations of value deprivation which many members readily accept.[12] These beliefs include the traditionalist argument that "things have always been this way," a religious explanation that suffering constitutes punishment for sins, or the belief of optimists that the condition is merely temporary.[13] In some cases, those who define the situation as a problem may remain inert due to a belief in the impossibility of reform—"you can't fight city hall." The process by which these evaluations are changed and people begin to define deprivation as a problem, believing in the prospect of social change, merits careful investigation. This process is, in effect, the change from a "latent" to a "manifest" social problem. One might hypothesize that the shorter the time required for this change, the greater the probability that the severity of the social problem will be substantially reduced in an orderly fashion.

Neither widespread awareness of a problem nor a desire for change assures the success of change efforts. In many cases, certain groups or organizations derive certain benefits from the conditions causing the value deprivations of other groups. Organized gangs in the United States take in billions of dollars annually from the public.[14] These syndicates fight doggedly against efforts to eliminate the profitability of organized crime. Bribery of public officials and policemen frequently blunts the edge of law enforcement by giving officials a vested interest in the continuation of criminal activities.

Proposals designed to improve the socioeconomic condition of minority groups are often opposed by those groups which fear that such changes will damage their standing in society. Economic groups often oppose plans which call upon government to provide some service or commodity usually produced by a private organization. The federal government often provides some type of subsidy to private firms for producing the commodity, as in the case of public housing for low income families. If the firms cannot be persuaded to participate by this type of inducement, the government program often is ineffective. Finally, certain groups may refuse on ideological grounds to participate in a government-sponsored program for coping with a social problem. This state of affairs existed in America between the stock market crash of 1929 and the election of Franklin Delano Roosevelt. Although many of Hoover's advisors considered mounting unemployment to be a social problem, their belief that the self-regulating character of the economy would correct the situation minimized direct government action.[15] The depression deepened and suffering continued until, with the election of Roosevelt, an alternative view of social reform became the basis for direct government intervention. If remedial action on a large scale had been taken in 1930 and 1931, the depression might have ended prior to the onset of the Second World War.

In summary, a social problem exists where many organizations, groups and people experience serious value deprivations resulting from the inability of institutions to fulfill the aspirations of these varied social units. Whether or not these conditions persist or abate depends on the following:

a. degree to which the conditions are defined as unsatisfactory by members of society;
b. willingness of persons and organizations to commit resources to an attack on the problem situation;
c. ability to develop effective remedies;
d. ability to obtain agreement on the desirability of specific courses of action;
e. availability of resources required for implementation of the program.

The study of social problems involves the nature of value deprivation, the conditions responsible and the factors influencing the degree of persistence of these circumstances.

SOCIAL STRATIFICATION AND SOCIAL PROBLEMS

No single factor or specific set of factors could be regarded as decisive in causing or eliminating social problems. Any effort to specify a particular social structure as more influential or significant than others would be misguided. Nevertheless, organized patterns of inequality, social stratification, usually are involved as causes of and in efforts to manage a social problem. This condition may be attributed in part to the continuing tension between equalitarian values and the factors which perpetuate the class hierarchy.

The negative reaction of many people to varied manifestations of inequality provides a chronic source of discontent and energy for social change. The notion that one should not aspire to a level of reward or achievement beyond his "station," which is common in societies with rigid class systems is alien in America, where the "rags to riches" and "log cabin to the White House" themes continue to have broad appeal. Where every man considers himself equal to others, the tendency will be to aim high for material, social and political goals. Since few people will attain goals that are unrealistic, dissatisfaction will be chronic. In addition, the efforts of corporations to expand markets by publicizing their latest products and the availability of credit through installment buying provides a steady upward thrust on the standards for a suitable style of life.[16]

The influence of equalitarian values and traditions in America and in other western, democratic nations can be seen from the long-term evolution of the status of citizen. According to the analysis by T. H. Marshall, two major trends have occurred.[17] First, status has been broadened to include diverse types of rights, civil, political and social. Second, possession of this status has been gradually extended to groups previously denied this right—those who own little or no property and, in America, black Americans. The history of modern nations can be interpreted by viewing the process in which the emerging classes were included within the political framework and allowed rights equal to those of the more powerful classes.[18] In other words, the historical record can be seen as an account of the conflict between groups committed to equality of citizenship and to those advocating the privileges of aristocracy.[19]

There is little prospect that all of the major sources of inequality can be abolished. Bureaucracies of all types will outbid rival firms for the most talented and well-trained persons. The resultant inequalities in wealth and prestige will continue to produce variations in opportunities and political influence.[20] Those persons and groups committed to equalitarian beliefs will maintain their efforts to raise the economic and social standing of the bottom class and to maximize the opportunities for advancement available to all citizens. At the same time, those members of the middle class who take the equalitarian ethos seriously will strive to improve their style of life, their social standing, and possibly their political and economic rank.

On occasion, technological progress aggravates the conditions of the working class. The long-term trend in America toward increased technological complexity and automation has greatly reduced the proportion of unskilled workers needed in the labor force.[21] Workers with little or no training have been reduced in status to that of the unemployed or underemployed. Many of these are black Americans living in urban ghettos or white Americans living in Appalachia and other rural areas.

The most serious discontinuity between equalitarian values and patterns of social stratification in America concerns the elements of caste which trap many black Americans in the lowest level of the class hierarchy. Discrimination and prejudice against black Americans condemn many of these citizens to live in extreme poverty in substandard housing, with little or no access to effective medical care and education. Many serious tensions in America surround the efforts of black Americans to gain all the rights of citizenship.

Efforts to cope with these and related problems are often complicated when members of a higher class oppose proposals which seem to weaken their position and strengthen that of lower social classes. Members of "higher" classes tend to favor measures which consolidate their position and strengthen the barriers which impede mobility from the classes below. Several examples of these divergent class interests are considered in this volume. Chapter 8, which examines housing, shows that national housing policies, until recently, played a critical part in segregating the white middle class from the black ghettoes in the central city. These policies assisted many white families while preventing most black families from buying new homes in the suburbs. Chapter 2 discusses race relations and describes the efforts of some labor unions to protect the economic position of members by restricting the employment of minority group members, especially Negroes.

Since the middle classes generally possess greater political influence than the lower classes, its leaders have been able, at times, to modify the objectives of programs initially adopted to aid the lower classes. The public housing program, discussed in Chapter 8, exemplifies this situation.[22] Originally intended to provide better housing to low income families than that available on the open market, the program has served to confine many black families to the ghetto. The program has protected urban patterns of racial segregation. As another example of the differential benefits of government programs, Chapter 4 considers public assistance programs, which are intended to provide financial aid to families in great distress. A large proportion of such families receives no aid at all, and those who do receive amounts considerably below that required for even a minimal standard of living. To receive financial help, the poor family often endures indignities from personnel in welfare agencies that middle class citizens would not tolerate in comparable situations.

These few examples suffice to indicate the sizable impact of the policies and programs of complex organizations in both private and public arenas on the opportunities of various class members. Employment, income, housing, education, and health are among the concerns involved in efforts to influence the activities of these organizations. Ultimately the issue concerns the probability that a family will change its class position.

The conflict between the classes takes a number of different forms. The rivalry can be political, where members of a lower class seek to replace elected officials from a higher class with their own candidates. In other instances the members of a higher class may have to share some of their resources with those from a lower class. This takes place, for example, when a formerly white school admits Negro students or when Negro families move into a white neighborhood. One common class issue concerns the method of financing programs intended to aid the poor and, of even greater importance, the overall tax structure of a community or of society. The levying of a graduated income tax and the steepness of the rate has a great bearing on the possibility of redistributing income from the wealthy to the poor. Financing programs by raising the level of the income or property tax or by levying a sales tax likewise influences the weight of the tax burden on various classes. Inevitably, plans for combatting many social problems encounter resistance from those classes and strata which fear adverse consequences. Where this resistance is supported by skilled leadership, effective organization and considerable wealth, progress may be slow and conflict prolonged.

PROBLEM MANAGEMENT

Where the vital interests of various classes are directly involved in the continuation of and efforts to change conditions underlying social problems, conflict between these units could become divisive. The violence which has erupted in many of the nation's cities in recent years signifies one type of disorder which can occur when more orderly processes of conflict resolution operate ineffectively or not at all.[23] Processes by which social problems could be eliminated or alleviated in a relatively peaceful but effective manner are indispensable for the continuity of a democratic society. Consequently, efforts to cope with social problems receive considerable attention in this volume. To a large degree, such efforts include those on the societal level which involves agencies of the federal government that try to cope with problems existing on the other levels of social organization. As indicated earlier, many of these programs can be subsumed under the concept of the welfare state.

The term "problem management" as used in this volume refers to certain types of problem solving procedures. First, it refers to those efforts involving the exercise of governmental powers including those enacted by private organizations receiving assistance from public agencies. Second, the term applies to collective rather than individual efforts to cope with a disturbing situation. Substantial reduction in the severity of a problem usually requires concerted efforts by a variety of groups and organizations over an extended time period. Social change and action directed at problems has always been the work of individuals and groups who plan, organize, manipulate, and influence. These people are in a social, economic, and political position to effect change. What may appear to be a major social change at a specific point in history is usually the result of a cumulative process of minor changes over a prolonged time period which have synthesized into a significant development. For example, the Civil Rights movement of the sixties may be traced to a large number of highly specific social, political, and especially economic changes in the forties and fifties. Likewise, the creation of the federal Social Security program during President Franklin Roosevelt's administration was not the brainchild of the President, but reflected a series of minor changes and ideas which dated back over a forty-year period.[24] This is not, however, to deny the role of individual leaders in accelerating change when enabling conditions are present.

Third, the term "problem management" signifies the growing effort in America to direct the forces and processes of change in a planned, rational manner. Using the resources of science and technology to attack social problems can improve society's capacity for controlling these conditions. The theories and data provided by the social sciences need to be integrated with the policy making activities of public and private organizations. Improving the working relationship between social scientists and society's leaders can assist the location and definition of social problems as well as development of effective strategies of social change.

Interest Groups and Problem Management

Expression of concern over particular social conditions by groups representing specific classes and strata plays a vital part in transforming a latent problem into a manifest one. The information provided by conferences, reports, lobbying for or against legislation, the publicity given rallies, demonstrations and other means of expressing a position on important matters helps to create the widespread awareness which constitutes the first and perhaps most important step toward coping with a problem situation. The groups and associations from various classes must be prepared to engage in prolonged political conflict to play a constructive role in the process of solving social problems in America.

A brief rundown of some major interest groups indicates their diversity and role in politics.[25] Thousands of associations endeavor to protect and further the interests of members whenever possible.[26] Innumerable organizations represent industries such as banking, insurance, and automotive, steel and textile manufacturers, while several associations cut across industry boundaries—The National Association of Manufacturers and the Chamber of Commerce. Labor has its organizations, principally unions, and farmers are represented by the Grange, Farmers' Union and American Farm Bureau Federation. Professional groups also have associations to express and defend their viewpoints. Among the more familiar are the American Medical Association, American Bar Association, National Education Association and the American Federation of Teachers. This listing can be extended endlessly to include organizations representing public employees,—city managers and city planners, policemen and firemen, and on the local level, organizations of realtors, merchants, property owners, civic associations, and major political parties. Nor should we overlook the organizations representing various minority groups, whether racial, religious or ethnic. Some of these organizations, especially the National Association for the Advancement of Colored People, The Urban League and the Southern Christian Leadership Conference, to name but a few, have spearheaded the Civil Rights Movement.[27]

Many of the associations mentioned above have a fairly long history, a record of accomplishment, and an acceptance in political circles as being legitimate. A variety of other groups are committed to extremist political programs and are regarded as somewhat disreputable. These include, among others, radical student organizations, militant organizations of black people, Yippies, the various Klan groupings, the Minutemen, and the John Birch Society. Some of these groups manifest a willingness to use force to obtain their objectives. While such tactics threaten the stability of the social and political order, the threat of violence often focuses attention on the existence and sources of discontent. Student revolts at Berkeley, Columbia, San Francisco State and elsewhere called into question long neglected features of the university.

By criticizing and defending certain features of the social environment, interest groups perform a number of vital functions for problem management.[28] First, the leaders of these pressure groups inform officials of anticipated or actual consequences created by the existing programs or activities of private organizations which they consider to be detrimental. Officials of government or private organizations might have been unaware of these matters or their significance. Planners, lawmakers, economists and other specialists engaged in directing the activities of government cannot anticipate all the ways in which particular laws and programs will affect various groups and classes. Nor can they predict or control the activities of private organizations—economic, professional, religious, etc., which also affect the different social classes. Second, by criticizing the on-going activities and policies of an organization, interest groups provide feedback to those responsible for the programs. Officials are constrained to review and re-examine past actions and to consider modification of them. Third, in stating their case, alternative programs or procedures often are suggested. By so doing, leaders may examine courses of action which initially received insufficient consideration. Fourth, the intensity of the views put forth and the resources expended by the various organizations provide indications of the severity of the problem, the dangers of inaction, and the degree to which the objectives of the various factions should be satisfied. Therefore, the interaction between public bodies and interest groups represents one mechanism whereby policy makers receive the information required for bringing the activities of institutions closer to the values of these groups and of society. At the same time, the efforts of groups representing the various classes constrain the organizations of the total society to operate in ways which benefit diverse sections of the citizenry and not just the more privileged groups.

This discussion implies that government mediates the conflicting claims of interest groups and develops compromises which each can accept. Government plays other important roles in the management of social problems and in the accomplishment of social change. Governmental agencies both on the federal and local levels, possess and utilize the capacity to direct the total energies of society toward the greater realization of basic values. Government must therefore be regarded as an instrument for social change and for coping with social problems.

Public and Private Sectors and Problem Management

The constructive role which partisan groups play in problem management signifies both communication and the exercise of influence from the "lower levels" of the stratification hierarchy to the topmost elements, the chief policy makers in federal and state governments. The degree to which interest groups influence policy decisions does not depend solely on the soundness of the views presented, but on the amount of influence exercised by the group in behalf of its objectives. To state this obvious axiom implies that America's power arrangements are not concentrated in the hands of a small clique of men who refuse to recognize the needs and interests of the masses of people. The view expressed here implies a substantial dispersion of power between the several levels of government and between various institutions and social classes.[29] Since a more detailed discussion of the American power structure is taken up in Chapter 9, no further discussion is warranted, with one exception. The crucial role of interest groups in problem solving efforts demonstrates the dependence of political institutions on groups representing the non-governmental sphere of society, the so-called private sector.

Throughout the history of America private groups and organizations greatly influenced the total society in resolving various problems. The activities of the abolition movement prior to the Civil War exemplifies the influence that can be exercised in a democratic polity by organized groups committed to definite objectives. The social gospel movement of the Protestant Church, discussed in Chapter 7, laid the groundwork for a broad and continuing attack on the excesses of our industrial and urban civilization. The social gospel movement made America more aware of her teeming slums, the impoverished condition of their inhabitants, the recently arrived immigrants of many nationalities, and of the inhuman conditions which existed in most factories and workshops. The social gospel movement, which originated within the religious sector, helped to launch the welfare state.[30]

Many communities in the United States have private organizations combatting a multitude of problem situations, such as alcoholism, juvenile delinquency, family instability, various illnesses and aid to the sick, the elderly, and the poor. Many of these organizations belong to the United Fund, a centralized planning, fund-raising and allocating agency. In recent years, nationwide organizations have been created to cope with problems of great complexity. The Urban Coalition, consisting of representatives from hundreds of the nation's wealthiest corporations, seeks to combat a number of urban problems.[31] In other instances existing organizations initiate programs designed to alleviate problem situations, such as the program of a large retailing firm to assist and advise black businessmen on merchandising problems.[32] Other corporations with financial assistance from the federal government have undertaken to train disadvantaged men and women with few if any employable skills.[33] These and related activities illustrate the efforts of the "private sector" of American society to cope with a variety of social problems.

The private sector consists of citizens and organizations to which members voluntarily commit their resources and from which they can resign at any time. Organizations in the private sphere enjoy a measure of freedom in establishing rules and policies, which apply solely to members, while rules of government apply to all citizens. In the final analysis, the private sector of society refers to a sphere of activity over which the individual and the organization enjoy a substantial measure of autonomy from the regulatory activities of government.

While voluntary organizations, foundations and corporations have played and continue to play significant roles in attacking social problems, the private sector has a number of significant limitations. Only two need concern us. First, certain problems can be overcome only through the establishment of programs and rules of behavior on a national basis. Had the registration of black Americans as voters in southern communities been left to local officials, progress toward equality of political rights would still be infinitesimal. Laws requiring equality in many social spheres with appropriate machinery of enforcement are indispensable conditions for social change.[34] Second, progress in areas such as poverty, slum housing, unemployment, to name but a few, requires resources in amounts far beyond the capacity of municipalities or states. For these and other reasons, the legislative acts of Congress, the rulings of judicial bodies and agencies of the federal government constitute essential agents of social change.

Although both separately and jointly public and private sectors of society have long been involved in efforts to solve social problems, the role most appropriate to each has not yet been defined and remains hotly contested. Over the years, especially since the New Deal, the necessity of the federal government to maintain a steady and growing economy free of the "boom and bust" cycle and to extend the rights of citizenship to all citizens irrespective of race or other ascriptive characteristics has led to considerable expansion of its responsibilities, structures and resources. As the federal government has for many years played a large part in the attack on a number of social problems, evaluations of its varied programs have been made. Progress in some areas, for example poverty among black Americans, has occurred slowly, leading some experts to conclude that the federal bureaucracy cannot effectively cope with certain social problems.[35] Some industry leaders, on the other hand, contend that business firms can make a satisfactory profit by providing goods and services for the poor, and urge their colleagues to reconsider customary activities with this end in mind. At the same time, proposals for increasing the responsibilities of the states to attack social problems also are under review. One proposal calls on the federal government to provide block grants to the states to be used as state officials deem best. The current re-examination of the activities and responsibilities of the various levels of government and of diverse private organizations for managing social problems will lead in the future to further changes in the relationships of these structures to each other. Hopefully whatever changes occur will reflect greater effectiveness in solving the multitude of grave problems confronting America.

Information, Planning, and Problem Management

Current efforts to co-ordinate more effectively the functions of gathering information on social problems and of policy making will modify relations between public and private organizations. If successful, these plans would enable public agencies to formulate more dynamic programs and to play a more influential role in problem management. The plans call for improving procedures for gathering the information needed to understand social structure and change, and for improving the channels of communication between social scientists and government decision-makers. Considerable concern exists over how these objectives can be achieved while preserving the integrity of particular types of private organizations and persons, especially of citizens in general and of various social scientists.

Some social scientists now consider it possible to systematize and routinize the collection and interpretation of data on the "well-being" of American society.[36] Establishment of national data banks would provide for the periodic collection and storage of information from a multitude of private and public organizations and from the American people as a whole. This would enable social scientists to determine the performance level of all social institutions and to assess the physical and mental well-being of the citizenry. The social scientists could report on such important and diverse matters as the health of the people, the incidence of mental illness, the distribution of wealth, the extent and severity of poverty, the degree of participation in the polity, and the degree of commitment to democratic ideals, to name only a few.[37] Since, wherever possible, trends of change on each variable would be ascertained, it would be possible to specify the time at which favorable and unfavorable change took place, and to anticipate, on the basis of past performance and future conditions, the occurrence of major disturbances. These predictions would enable program planners to prepare contingency plans and to take remedial action prior to eruptions of riots and other forms of violence rather than after these occur.

While these innovations may appear rational and necessary, implementation requires the solution of technical and political difficulties. Problems of a technical nature include selection of organizations in both the private and public sectors which will periodically transmit selected data and organization of reporting units into an information network. Establishment of data banks raises certain legal issues, namely the privacy of citizens and safeguards against the misuse of the collected information.[38] A third set of problems pertains to relationships between those who collect and interpret the information, the social scientists, and those exercising political power. This issue involves the question of whether or not social scientists should hold office in government or in a private organization. One proposal, which is discussed in the final chapter, calls for the establishment of a Council of Social Advisors in the Office of the President which would be comparable to the Council of Economic Advisors.[39]

Critics of this proposal contend that the social scientists will succumb to political pressures and issue reports which are biased in favor of particular government agencies. To preserve a neutral viewpoint, social scientists should serve in private organizations which gather and interpret data. Such an arrangement, however, cannot compel top government leaders to use the reports of the social scientists, in developing agency programs.

Whatever procedures are adopted for handling these matters, the development of central data banks and the use of social science information for developing public programs signifies the growing interdependence between social science and government. This developing partnership also stimulates the trend toward central planning based on the most recent and comprehensive information currently available. Nevertheless, interest groups representing the several classes and diverse organizations must still perform the indispensable function of criticizing the collected data along with the various proposals for action, and for expressing the needs and concerns of their constituents. The views of social scientists cannot substitute for those who represent special interests since these persons are accountable for their actions to the persons who support or elected them.

CONCLUSION

This volume concentrates on social problems in American society. Each chapter analyzes various parameters of a specific problem, the factors which have influenced its development, and the efforts made to cope with the situation. These efforts are conditioned by the structure of society, especially by the prevailing distribution of power and definitions of class interests. The final two chapters focus on certain aspects of problem-solving, namely the welfare state and the systematic organization and use of knowledge.

Selected Readings

Bendix, Reinhard and Seymour Martin Lipset, eds. *Class, Status, and Power: Social Stratification in Comparative Perspective,* 2 ed. (New York: Free Press, 1966).

Conot, Robert. *Rivers of Blood, Years of Darkness* (New York: Bantam, 1967).

Cressey, Donald R. *Theft of the Nation: The Structure and Operations of Organized Crime in America* (New York: Harper & Row, 1969).

Etzioni, Amitai. *The Active Society* (New York: Free Press, 1968).

Hammond, Phillip E., ed. *Sociologists at Work* (New York: Basic Books, 1964).

Horowitz, Irving Louis. *Professing Sociology* (Chicago: Aldine, 1968).

Liebow, Elliot. *Tally's Corner: A Study of Negro Street-corner Men* (Boston: Little, Brown, 1967).

Nisbet, Robert A. *The Sociological Tradition* (New York: Basic Books, 1966).

Merton, Robert K., Leonard Broom and Leonard S. Cottrell, eds. *Sociology Today* (New York: Basic Books, 1959).

U.S. Department of Health, Education, and Welfare. *Toward A Social Report* (Washington, D.C.: U.S. Government Printing Office, 1969).

Williams, Robin M. Jr. *American Society,* 2 ed. (New York: Knopf, 1967).

Notes to Chapter 1

¹ For works which elaborate this viewpoint, see the following: Amitai Etzioni, *The Active Society* (New York: The Free Press, 1968); Raymond A. Bauer, *Social Indicators* (Cambridge, Mass.: M.I.T. Press, 1966); Karl W. Deutsch, *The Nerves of Government* (New York: The Free Press of Glencoe, 1963). For a series of articles on a major change in procedures of decision making in important federal agencies, see "PPBS: Its Scope and Limits," *The Public Interest,* 8 (Summer, 1967), pp. 3-48. For articles on measuring features of society pertinent to solving social problems, see Bertram M. Gross, *ed., The Annals of the American Academy of Social and Political Science,* 371 (May, 1967), 373 (September, 1967).

² Merton and Lerner examine the financial and prestige rewards of social scientists in relation to type of involvement with business and government and explore the relations of the social sciences to problems of policy formulation. Robert K. Merton and Daniel Lerner, "Social Scientists and Research policy," in Daniel Lerner and Harold D. Lasswell, eds., *The Policy Sciences* (Stanford, Calif.: Stanford University Press, 1951), pp. 282-307. Bruce Smith provides an interesting case study of the role of social science information in changing policies of the Air Force on location of bases in Bruce L. R. Smith, *The Rand Corporation* (Cambridge, Mass.: Harvard University Press, 1966), pp. 195-240. Loren Baritz explores the applications of social science theories and information to various fields of industry, such as advertising, recruitment of personnel, counseling and the human relations approach to management. Loren Baritz, *The Servants of Power* (Middletown, Conn.: Wesleyan University Press, 1960).

³ The concept of level was implied by Marx, who differentiated the modes of production in a society as the "infrastructure" from which emerged a "suprastructure" of culture and belief. Karl Marx and Friedrich Engels, *The German Ideology, Parts I and II* (New York: International Publishers, paperback, 1963), pp. 12-16.

The concept level has been useful for efforts to delimit the proper scope of sociology and to set it apart from other disciplines. The fight against reductionism waged by Durkheim and others may be viewed in terms of defining sociological processes as a level different from psychological and environmental factors and requiring methods of investigation and laws appropriate to the features of these variables. Emile Durkheim, *The Rules of Sociological Method,* Sarah A. Solvay and John H. Mueller, trans., George E. G. Catlin, ed. (Glencoe, Ill.: The Free Press, 1938), pp. 1-46.

As applied to society, the concept of level of analysis involves a basic sociological question, how does one study a social unit? Two general approaches are available, to concentrate on the total unit and study the parts within a holistic context, or to concentrate on the parts and see the total unit as emerging from the interaction between the parts. For a discussion of these orientations, see Percy S. Cohen, *Modern Social Theory* (New York: Basic Books, 1968), pp. 13-15; Werner Stark, *The Fundamental Forms of Social Thought* (New York: Fordham University Press, 1963), pp. 1-13.

The concept level permits one to classify in a general way the parts of a social system without becoming involved in the question of which type of variable is more or less influential than others. The concept helps the analyst to keep in mind that questions appropriate for one level may be inappropriate for another, due to variation in kinds of processes. Recognizing the differential location of variables by level aids clarity of analysis.

Peter Blau analyzes the structure of society in terms of the macrostructure and microstructure, each of which represents a distinct level. He says, for example, "The interdependence between the macrostructure and its substructures can be further analyzed by tracing the interrelations among three facets of social structure-integration, differentiation, and organization—on these two levels. . . ." Peter M. Blau, *Exchange and Power in Social Life* (New York: Wiley, 1964), p. 289. By differentiating levels as units of society, the analyst raises a basic question, that of modes of interrelationships. For two contrasting views, see *Ibid.*, pp. 289-94; Robert Dubin, *Theory Building* (New York: Free Press, 1969), pp. 122-25.

For a general analysis of the concept of level which considers its meaning in social thought, sociological theory and as a unit in social structure, see Abraham Edel, "The Concept of Levels in Social Theory," in Llewellyn Gross, ed., *Symposium On Sociological Theory* (New York: Harper & Row, 1959), pp. 167-95.

⁴ For studies of the budgetary process and decision making, see Aaron Wildavsky, *The Politics of the Budgetary Process* (Boston: Little, Brown, paperback, 1964). Committee on Government Operations, Subcommittee on National Policy Machinery, U.S. Senate, *Organizing for National Security: The Budget and the Policy Process*, 87th Congress, 1st Session (Washington, D.C.: U.S. Government Printing Office, 1961); Aaron Wildavsky, "Political Implications of Budgetary Reform," *Public Administration Review*, XXI (Autumn, 1961), pp. 183-90; Edward C. Banfield, "Congress and the Budget: A Planner's Criticism," *The American Political Science Review*, XLIII (December, 1949), pp. 1217-27.

⁵ For relevant bibliography, see footnotes 23 through 26 in this chapter.

⁶ See footnote 1.

⁷ Robin M. Williams, Jr., "Individual and Group Values," *The Annals*, 371 (May, 1967), p. 23. For a more detailed discussion of values, see Robin M. Williams, *American Society*, 2 ed. (New York: Knopf, 1960), pp. 397-470. For discussions of the relations between values and the organization of society see the following: Clyde Kluckhohn, "Values and Value Orientations In The Theory Of Action," in Talcott Parsons and Edward A. Shils, *eds., Toward A General Theory Of Action* (New York: Harper & Row, Torchbook, 1962), pp. 388-433; Edward A. Shils, "Centre and Periphery," in *The Logic of Personal Knowledge: Essays Presented to Michael Polanyi on His Seventieth Birthday* (London: Routledge & Kegan Paul, 1961), pp. 117-30; William L. Kolb, "The Changing Prominence of Values in Modern Sociological Theory," in Howard Becker and Alvin Boskoff, *eds., Modern Sociological Theory* (New York: Dryden, 1957), pp. 93-132. For a comprehensive analysis of changes in American values, see Clyde Kluckhohn, "Have There Been Discernible Shifts In American Values During The Past Generation?" in Elting E. Morison, *ed., The American Style: Essays in Value and Performance* (New York: Harper, 1958), pp. 145-217. See also the following journal articles: Harold Fallding, "A Proposal For The Empirical Study of Values," *American Sociological Review*, 30 (April, 1965), pp. 223-33; Charles Perrow, "The Analysis of Goals in Complex Organizations," *American Sociological Review*, 26 (December, 1961), pp. 854-866; Franz Adler, "The Value Concept In Sociology," *The American Journal of Sociology*, LXII (November, 1956), pp. 272-79.

⁸ Williams describes ten different types of changes which values undergo. Robin M. Williams, Jr., "Individual and Group Values," *op. cit.*, pp. 29-30.

⁹ President's Commission On Law Enforcement and Administration of Justice, *The Challenge Of Crime In A Free Society* (Washington, D.C.: U.S. Government Printing Office, 1967), pp. 187-209. For a critical examination of the existence and nature of "organized crime" see Gordon Hawkins, "God and the Mafia," *The Public Interest*, 14 (Winter, 1969), pp. 24-51.

¹⁰ For a discussion of manifest and latent social problems, see Robert K. Merton, "Social Problems and Sociological Theory," in Robert K. Merton and Robert A. Nisbet, *eds., Contemporary Social Problems* (New York: Harcourt, Brace & World, 1961), pp. 708-09.

¹¹ Merton views social problems in a manner similar to but not identical to the one presented above. He writes: "The first and basic ingredient of a social problem consists of any substantial discrepancy between socially shared standards and actual conditions of social life. . . ." Robert K. Merton, *Ibid.*, p. 702. This

definition of social problems stresses the differences between particular social conditions and people's expectations of how matters ought to be arranged. Our definition, in contrast, stresses the discrepancy between values and the outcomes of social behavior.

Cuber and his associates use a definition which emphasizes the psychological reaction of subjects. ". . . Until or unless a sizable or influential group becomes convinced that some social condition is 'really' undesirable, then that condition cannot be considered a social problem. . . ." John F. Cuber, Robert A. Harper and William F. Kenkel, *Problems of American Society: Values in Conflict,* 3rd ed. (New York: Henry Holt, 1956), p. 29.

The editor of a recent volume on social problems uses a definition of social problems which also stresses subjective evaluation of social conditions as undesirable. This definition, first formulated in 1941 by Fuller and Myers, asserts: . . . *social problems are what people think they are* and if conditions are not defined as social problems by the people involved in them, they are not problems to those people, although they may be problems to outsiders or to scientists. . . .

Richard C. Fuller and Richard R. Myers, "The Natural History of a Social Problem," quoted by Howard S. Becker, *ed.,* "Introduction," *Social Problems: A Modern Approach* (New York: John Wiley, 1966), p. 2. Becker also recognizes the importance of objective social conditions for the existence of a social problem.

Our definition places greater emphasis on certain elements of social organization and less on the psychological reaction of subjects. The strong linkage between the values and operations of organizations frequently leads to a serious disturbance when goal attainment falls short of expectations. Since this condition alone does not suffice to produce a social problem, our discussion examined additional ingredients and used Merton's distinction between latent and manifest social problems.

Since each of the definitions cited above rely to greater or lesser extent on the viewpoint of the actor, inevitably the reader gains the impression that the existence of a social problem is deplorable. Horowitz takes note of this factor when he contends that the occurrence of social problems may portend the imminence of changes which further the development of the society. He writes: ". . . the increase in so-called social problems may in fact mean an increase in social development. Therefore, the existence of social problems may be good. . . ." Irving Louis Horowitz, *Professing Sociology* (Chicago: Aldine, 1968), p. 85. Horowitz therefore reminds the reader of the importance of society as a variable in the study of social problems.

[12] In an examination of the factors which weaken the influence of class on the political behavior of the lower classes, Lipset says: "The normative system inherent in all stratified societies reduces the political effectiveness of the lower strata. To a very high degree, lower classes throughout history have acceded to the societal values that define them as being, in various respects, inferior to those of higher status. . . ." Seymour Martin Lipset, "Class, Politics, and Religion in Modern Society," in *Revolution and Counter-revolution* (New York: Basic Books, 1968), p. 160.

[13] In their study of Middletown during the height of the depression, the Lynds considered the optimistic view of the business classes that the period of economic stagnation was temporary, an unusual rather than characteristic feature of capitalism, as hindering social change. Robert S. Lynd and Helen Merrell Lynd, *Middletown In Transition* (New York: Harcourt, Brace, 1937), pp. 470-73. Some students of American value patterns regard this optimistic outlook as an important national characteristic. Robin Williams views optimism as closely associated with faith in progress. Robin M. Williams, Jr., *American Society, op. cit.,* pp. 431-33. Cora Du Bois finds the optimistic outlook manifested in the "never say die" spirit, the continuing faith in the efficacy of individual effort in the face of insuperable odds. See Cora Du Bois, "The Dominant Value Profile of Ameri-

can Culture," in Edgar A. Schuler, *et. al., Readings In Sociology,* 2 ed. (New York: Crowell, 1960), pp. 642-43.

The optimistic outlook and faith in progress leads those experiencing serious value deprivation to believe that society itself, without direct intervention, will change conditions for the better. These orientations discourage the organization of change efforts.

[14] One respected criminologist offers the following estimate of income from illegal gambling. Cressey wrote: ". . . there is a consensus among law-enforcement officials that illegal betting on horse races, lotteries, and sporting events totals at least $20 billion a year. Cosa Nostra members take about one-third of the gambling gross as their share, so if that gross is in fact $20 billion, they acquire some $6 to $7 billion annually. . . ." Donald R. Cressey, *Theft of the Nation* (New York: Harper & Row, 1969), pp. 74-5.

The monetary cost to the public of Cosa Nostra activities is suggested by the following: ". . . We are concerned because millions of Americans are, in hundreds of minor ways, already paying ransom to organized criminals . . . the housewife who must pay a few cents extra each day to have her trash hauled by a company controlled by criminals . . . the teen-ager who pays a few cents more for a hamburger and a glass of milk because the vendor must buy his supplies from companies controlled by criminals . . . . all the other citizens who are required to spend a quarter here and a dollar there because someone, somewhere in the chain from raw material to finished product, must pay a tribute to criminals. . . ." *Ibid.,* pp. 5-6.

[15] Stephen Kemp Bailey, *Congress Makes A Law* (New York: Random House, Vintage Books, originally published in 1950), p. 6.

[16] The influence of material values and of installment buying are reflected in the following statistics for families with annual incomes under $3,000:

79% own a television set
51% own both a television set and a telephone
73% own a washing machine
19% own a home freezer
65% have a dwelling unit that is not dilapidated and has hot running water
      and a toilet and a bath for their exclusive use
14% bought a car last year

Herman P. Miller, "Major Elements For A Research Program For the Study of Poverty," in Task Force on Economic Growth and Opportunity, *The Concept of Poverty,* (Washington, D.C.: Chamber of Commerce of the United States, 1965), p. 122.

[17] T. H. Marshall, *Class, Citizenship and Social Development* (Garden City, N.Y.: Doubleday, Anchor Book, 1965), pp. 71-134.

[18] Seymour Martin Lipset, "Issues in Class Analysis," in *Revolution and Counterrevolution, op. cit.,* pp. 134-35. In the same volume, see "The Modernization of Contemporary European Politics," pp. 214-15.

[19] Lipset and Zetterberg expressed this idea as follows:
. . . many of the major political problems facing contemporary society are, in part, a consequence of the conflict and tensions resulting from the contradictions inherent in the need for both aristocracy and equality.
Seymour Martin Lipset and Hans L. Zetterberg, "A Theory of Social Mobility," in Reinhard Bendix and Seymour Martin Lipset, *eds., Class, Status, and Power,* 2 ed. (New York: Free Press, 1966), p. 570.

[20] The functionality and inevitability of social stratification has been a lively subject of controversy among sociologists for several decades. For articles expressing various positions on this issue, see "The Continuing Debate on Equality," in *Ibid.,* pp. 47-72.

[21] U.S. Bureau of the Census, *Statistical Abstract of the United States: 1968* (Washington, D.C.: U.S. Government Printing Office, 1968), p. 226; U.S. Bureau

of the Census, *Historical Statistics of the United States: Colonial Times to 1957* (Washington, D.C.: U.S. Government Printing Office, 1960), p. 74.

[22] The considerable disproportion of the benefits of the government's housing program to the well-to-do and to the poor are evident in the following statement: . . . Closer examination shows that the subsidy is heaviest for the largest incomes. . . . In 1962, the federal government spent 820 million dollars to subsidize housing for poor people—roughly 20 percent of the population. For the uppermost 20 percent (with incomes over $9,000) the federal subsidy was 1.7 billion dollars. A family in the uppermost fifth got about twice as much, on the average, as a poor family. Alvin L. Schorr, *Explorations in Social Policy* (New York: Basic Books, 1968), p. 275.

[23] Racial rioting tended to occur in cities whose leaders and governmental agencies failed to respond constructively to the many signs of grievances and dissatisfaction increasing in the black community. National Advisory Commission On Civil Disorders, *Report* (New York: Bantam Books, 1968), pp. 117, 138-39.

[24] For several studies of the development of Social Security, see the following: Roy Lubove, *The Struggle for Social Security, 1900–1935* (Cambridge, Mass.: Harvard University Press, 1968); Arthur Joseph Altmeyer, *The Formative Years of Social Security* (Madison, Wisc.: University of Wisconsin Press, 1966).

[25] For an exhaustive analysis of the activities, objectives and influence of interest groups in the American political system, see David B. Truman, *The Governmental Process* (New York: Knopf, 1965).

[26] The studies cited below concern either a particular interest group or the activities of one or more interest groups in various types of political campaigns. Raymond A. Bauer, Ithiel de Sola Pool and Lewis Anthony Dexter, *American Business and Public Policy* (New York: Atherton, 1967); Samuel E. Lawrence, *United States Merchant Shipping Policies and Politics* (Washington, D.C.: The Brookings Institution, 1966); Allan S. Everest, *Morgenthau, the New Deal, and Silver: A Story of Pressure Politics* (New York: King's Crown Press, 1950); Louis C. Kesselman, *The Social Politics of FEPC: A Study in Reform Pressure Movements* (Chapel Hill, N.C.: The University of North Carolina Press, 1948); Oliver Garceau, *The Political Life of the American Medical Association* (Cambridge, Mass.: Harvard University Press, 1941); E. Pendleton Herring, *Group Representation Before Congress: Public Administration and the Public Interest* (New York: McGraw-Hill, 1936); Peter H. Odegard, *Pressure Politics: The Study of the Anti-Saloon League* (New York: Columbia University Press, 1928).

[27] For studies of the civil rights movement, see the following: Lewis M. Killian, *The Impossible Revolution?* (New York: Random House, 1968); Lerone Bennett, Jr., *Confrontation: Black and White* (Baltimore: Penguin, 1965); Alan F. Westin, ed., *Freedom Now: The Civil Rights Struggle in America* (New York: Basic Books, 1964); Louis Lomax, *The Negro Revolt* (New York: Harper, 1962); Kenneth B. Clark, "The Civil Rights Movement: Momentum and Organization," *Daedalus*, 95 (Winter, 1966), pp. 239-67.

[28] Most of these functions are discussed by Edward C. Banfield, *Political Influence* (New York: The Free Press of Glencoe, 1961), pp. 331-41.

[29] For a variety of viewpoints on national power elites, see the following: Arnold M. Rose, *The Power Structure: Political Process in American Society* (New York: Oxford, 1967); R. Joseph Monsen, Jr. and Mark W. Cannon, *The Makers of Public Policy: American Power Groups and Their Ideologies* (New York: McGraw-Hill, 1965); William V. D'Antonino and Howard J. Ehrlich, eds., *Power and Democracy in America* (Notre Dame, Ind.: University of Notre Dame Press, 1961); Floyd Hunter, *Top Leadership, U.S.A.* (Chapel Hill, N.C.: The University of North Carolina Press, 1959); Arthur Kornhauser, ed., *Problems of Power In American Democracy* (Detroit: Wayne State University Press, 1957); C. Wright Mills, *The Power Elite* (New York: Oxford University Press, 1956).

[30] Sidney Fine, "The General-Welfare State in the Twentieth Century," in Charles I. Schottland, *ed., The Welfare State* (New York: Harper & Row, Torchbook, 1967), p. 47.

[31] *The New York Times* (September 26, 1968).

[32] *Action Report,* I (Summer, 1968), p. 1.

[33] *Time* (January 24, 1969), p. 28.

[34] Albert Schaffer and Ruth C. Schaffer, "Law, Faculty Desegregation and Social Change," *Phylon,* XXXI (1970); Yehezkol Dror, "Law and Social Change," in Rita James Simon, ed., *The Sociology of Law* (San Francisco: Chandler, 1968), pp. 663-80; Lynn W. Eley and Thomas W. Casstevens, *eds., The Politics of Fair-Housing Legislation* (San Francisco: Chandler, 1968); Leon Mayhew, *Law and Equal Opportunity: A Study of the Massachusetts Commission Against Discrimination* (Cambridge, Mass.: Harvard University Press, 1968); Morroe Berger, *Equality By Statute,* rev. ed., (Garden City, N.Y.: Doubleday, 1967); Paul H. Norgren, "Fair Employment Practice Laws-Effects, Prospects," in A. M. Ross and Herbert Hill, *eds. Employment, Race, and Poverty* (New York: Harcourt, Brace and World, 1967), pp. 541-70.

[35] James Q. Wilson, "The Bureaucracy Problem," *The Public Interest,* 6 (Winter, 1967), pp. 3-9.

[36] Carl Kaysen, "Data Banks and Dossiers," *The Public Interest,* 7 (Spring, 1967), pp. 52-60; *Report of the Task Force on the Storage of and Access to Government Statistics* (Washington, D.C.: Bureau of the Budget, 1966).

[37] For a conceptual framework which establishes a basis for a comprehensive, quantitative analysis of American society, see Bertram M. Gross, "The State of the Nation: Social Systems Accounting," in Raymond A. Bauer, *ed., Social Indicators* (Cambridge, Mass.: The M.I.T. Press, paperback, 1967), pp. 154-271.

[38] Alan F. Westin, *Privacy and Freedom* (New York: Atheneum, 1967); John Lear, "Whither Personal Privacy," *Saturday Review* (July 23, 1966), pp. 36, 41.

[39] S.843 (Washington, D.C.: 90th Congress, 1 Session, 1967).

CHAPTER TWO

THE CRISES OF THE CITY: THE RACE PROBLEM

TYPES OF PROBLEMS

Since the founding of America, her inhabitants have congregated increasingly in urban communities. Cities, large and small, are home for close to three out of every four Americans. The steady growth of population concentration in central cities and adjacent satellite communities has persisted despite the threat of nuclear warfare in the postwar era. Increasingly, the quality of social life in America depends on characteristics of the urban environment. Conditions which affect the health and welfare of urban inhabitants touch the lives of most Americans. Disruptions and interruptions in the activities of the urban economy reverberate throughout the nation and many parts of the world. In the decade ahead preservation or radical change in American institutions will depend on the nature of their responses to urban problems.

Historically, cities were established at sites suitable for certain commercial, manufacturing, political, military or religious functions. Whether for defense against enemy attack, the lure of religious ceremonies, or opportunities of employment, workers and their families have taken up residence in cities. With the rise of the industrial technology and manufacturing processes in the western world, cities require thousands of workers. In America, a host of economic opportunities and amenities have induced people to leave the countryside and migrate to urban centers. This trend has persisted from the late eighteenth century to the present time. The majority of immigrants from Europe settled in cities, thereby adding considerably to the diversity of cultures and the complexity of problems in intergroup relationships. The rate of population growth, which at times has been considerable, places extra burdens on the adaptive capacities of urban leadership and institutions. Finally, the ideology to which most urban and national leaders have usually subscribed discourages long range planning for the development of the total city. On the contrary, laissez-faire principles of economics and government have resulted in the subordination of the city to the needs of manufacturing and commercial organizations. The requirements of the community as a whole and of many population groups have often been neglected. A host of problems have received scant attention for many years. These problems include the pollution of the urban environment and atmosphere, obsolescence of buildings and entire sections of the city, the monotony of the gridiron plan and of the overall architectural design of the city, the depletion of vacant land within the city suitable for recreation, the migration of middle class white families to the suburbs, and the traffic congestion. As cities grow in population—in diversity of minority groups and structural complexity—the problems and disturbances multiply with dismaying rapidity. In recent years the leaders of the nation discovered the "crises of the cities," a complex of problems which does not yield readily to ameliorative programs and which diminishes the usefulness of urban communities by its existence.

Two general categories of urban problems will be discussed. One category concerns specific characteristics of particular population groups adjusting to life in the city while the second category housing, is considered in chapter 8.

RACE RELATIONS AND THE CITY

The traditional basis of race relations in America developed in the South. Slavery provided the type of labor force—large, inexpensive and tractable—preferred by an agricultural institution unique in this country. This was especially true for the larger units specializing in the production of a few cash crops. A caste system took the place of slavery and functioned effectively to subordinate black Americans in the latter half of the nineteenth and the early decades of the twentieth century. The majority of Southern Negroes have remained impoverished, tied to farms which, in most cases, they did not own and deprived of basic political rights.

To escape these conditions, large numbers of black Americans began to leave the South at the time of World War I. Although the rate of out-migration fell during the depression, it rose considerably in the early forties and remained at a high level until recently. A slight majority of America's black citizens still resided in the South in 1969.

The southern Negro left his native region to escape the harshness of rural life, tenant farming and sharecropping. He moved to the cities to find employment in nonagricultural activities and to escape the poverty which had trapped him for generations. This urban migration represented the search of still another minority group for fulfillment of the promises of equality, freedom and material comfort which had brought millions of immigrants to these shores.

The growing concentration of black Americans in the cities challenges the institutions of these communities and of the nation to terminate racism, which has existed for three hundred years in America. Can millions of black Americans be integrated into the life of the city with the rights, responsibilities, opportunities and rewards available to all other citizens?

The issue presently remains in doubt. In moving to the city, many Negroes exchanged rural for urban poverty—a shack in the country for an undersized apartment in a decaying tenement building, the barrenness of the land for the overcrowded ghetto. Conflict with the police and prolonged rioting have become standard outlets for frustration and rage. City governments struggle to provide essential services while the rate of increase of tax revenue lags behind the rising demands. Whatever the influence of slavery in creating the framework of white-black relationships, the future of race relations will be determined by forces operating throughout metropolitan America.

It is necessary to understand the nature of these forces and to assess prospects for racial integration. The redistribution of black Americans from the rural South to the cities, their socioeconomic characteristics and a brief review of the history of race relations must be studied by those who seek to tackle this problem.

THE URBAN NEGRO

Redistribution has largely placed Negroes in metropolitan areas in both the North and South. While in 1910 virtually all black Americans lived in the South, 89 percent,[1] by 1968 only slightly more than half, 53 percent, remained in this region.[2] From 1940 to 1966 the South had a net loss of more than 3.7 million nonwhite inhabitants.[3] Most Negro migrants went to the cities. The same percentage of blacks, 73 percent, who, in 1910 lived in rural communities, lived in urban places in 1960.[4] Furthermore, the Negroes did not scatter to all cities but preferred to live in the areas of greatest urban development—the metropolitan communities. While in 1910, 29 percent of the nation's Negroes resided within Standard Metropolitan Statistical Areas,[5] by 1968, 69 percent resided there. This contrasts with 64 percent of the white population.[6] Negro migrants located in the central city of metropolitan communities rather than in the suburbs. In 1968, 42 percent of the nation's Negroes in contrast to 34 percent of the white population lived in metropolitan communities having a million or more inhabitants.[7] The majority of the country's black citizens, 54 percent, lived in the central city with only 15 percent in the suburban ring. The corresponding figures for the white population are 26 and 38 percent, respectively.[8] In terms of numbers of people, more than 15 million black Americans lived in metropolitan communities in 1968, and 11.8 million lived in central cities.[9]

If the trend of the early sixties in the increase of black population continues for the coming decade, racial problems will increase. Between 1960 and 1966, virtually all of the increase in the nation's black population, 88.9 percent, took place in central cities.[10] Based on this rate of growth, the black population of central cities should reach 17.7 million by 1980. A more conservative estimate, based on natural increase and not including immigration, provides a figure of 15.6 million black residents.[11]

If either of these projections prove correct, many large cities soon will have a majority of black people. The cities listed below are expected to have a majority of black residents at the time specified.

New Orleans	1971	St. Louis	1978
Richmond	1971	Detroit	1979
Baltimore	1972	Philadelphia	1981
Jacksonville	1972	Oakland	1983
Cleveland	1975	Chicago	1984[12]

The difficulty of accomplishing racial integration in urban institutions under this condition is suggested by data on school enrollment. In almost all of the cities listed above, Negro children presently constitute a majority of those enrolled in public elementary schools. St. Louis, for example had a population in 1965 that was 36 percent black, but enrollment in public schools showed that 63 percent were black.[13]

As the number of black people in an area inhabited by whites increases, the latter generally search for techniques of reducing and avoiding social contact. In the case of the schools, many white parents place their children in private or parochial institutions. Exodus to the suburbs provides an escape from an integrated neighborhood and contributes to the increase of spatial segregation of the races. A number of studies indicate the prevalence of racial segregation in urban areas.

Table 1 shows the percentage change within recent years of Negroes in twelve cities living within census tracts with varying proportions of Negro inhabitants.[14] The data for these twelve cities suggest the changes which are occurring throughout America in urban centers of less than half a million residents. With only a few exceptions, census tracts with the largest proportion of black inhabitants increased their share of black residents while those declining had the smallest proportion. Residential segregation of the Negro increased in these cities between 1960 and 1964.

Further corroboration for this conclusion comes from a study which compared segregation for blacks in ten cities between 1930 and 1950 with that for native whites and for foreign-born whites.[15] In each of the ten cities, segregation of foreign-born whites decreased in relation to native whites in the twenty year period. Negroes had the opposite experience. Black segregation increased relative to native whites in eight of the ten cities and it increased relative to foreign-born whites in all but one city.[16]

TABLE 1

PERCENT OF ALL NEGROES IN SELECTED CITIES LIVING
IN CENSUS TRACTS GROUPED ACCORDING TO PROPORTION
NEGRO IN 1960 AND 1964-1966*

	Year	All census tracts	75 percent or more Negro	50 to 74 percent Negro	25 to 49 percent Negro	Less than 25 percent Negro
Cleveland, Ohio	1960	100	72	16	8	4
	1965	100	80	12	4	4
Phoenix, Ariz.	1960	100	19	36	24	21
	1965	100	18	23	42	17
Buffalo, N.Y.	1960	100	35	47	6	12
	1966	100	69	10	13	8
Louisville, Ky.	1960	100	57	13	17	13
	1964	100	67	13	10	10
Rochester, N.Y.	1960	100	8	43	17	32
	1964	100	16	45	24	15
Sacramento, Calif.	1960	100	9	—	14	77
	1964	100	8	14	28	50
Des Moines, Iowa	1960	100	—	28	31	41
	1966	100	—	42	19	39
Providence, R.I.	1960	100	—	23	2	75
	1965	100	—	16	46	38
Shreveport, La.	1960	100	79	10	7	4
	1966	100	90	—	6	4
Evansville, Ind.	1960	100	34	27	9	30
	1966	100	59	14	—	27
Little Rock, Ark.	1960	100	33	33	19	15
	1964	100	41	18	22	19
Raleigh, N.C.	1960	100	86	—	7	7
	1966	100	88	4	2	6

* Selected cities of 100,000 or more in which a special census was taken in any of the years 1964–1966. Ranked according to total population at latest census.
− Represents zero.
Source: U.S. Department of Commerce, Bureau of the Census. Published in United States Department of Labor and United States Department of Commerce, *Social and Economic Conditions of Negroes in the United States,* BLS Report No. 332. Current Population Reports, Series P-23, No. 24. October 1967.

A study of residential segregation in cities between 1940 and 1960 found evidence of a slight decline. Segregation increased for almost all of the 109 cities studied between 1940 and 1950. The degree of residential segregation of the Negro between 1950 and 1960 declined slightly in northern and western cities but remained high in southern cities.[17]

Despite the decline, a high level of residential segregation of Negroes existed in 1960 for almost all 207 cities in the sample. Using an index that varied from 0 to 100, with the latter value indicating total segregation, the Taeubers found that "half the cities have values above 87.8 and a fourth above 91.7." In contrast, only 8 cities had scores below 70. Elimination of racial segregation in three-fourths of America's cities would require resettlement of approximately 90 percent of the black inhabitants.[18]

A study by Farley and Taeuber of racial segregation during the sixties in thirteen cities in all parts of the nation found a reversal of the desegregation trend of the fifties.[19] Slight increases in the degree of residential segregation in eleven of the cities combined with continued increases in the size of the black population strengthened segregation in urban areas. As the number of Negroes living in cities increased, more whites moved to the suburbs. Inevitably, the size of the black ghetto and the number of segregated institutions increased. In relating these findings to the earlier study of segregation by the Taeubers, the authors stated:

> . . . there is strong evidence that the pervasive pattern of residential segregation has not been significantly breached. . . . Stability in segregation patterns has been maintained despite . . . marked advances in Negro economic welfare, urban renewal . . . high vacancy rates in many of the worst slums. . . .[20]

These findings on spatial segregation of the two races confirm the conclusions of the National Advisory Commission on Civil Disorders.

> Three critical conclusions emerge from this analysis:
> 1. The nation is rapidly moving toward two increasingly separate Americas.
> Within two decades, this division could be so deep that it would be almost impossible to unite:
> *a white society principally located in suburbs, in smaller central cities, and in the peripheral parts of large central cities; and
> *a Negro society largely concentrated within large central cities. . . .[21]

A Brief History of Race Relations in America

The black migrant to the city has been forced to live in neighborhoods segregated by race partly because of an income which does not permit a wide selection of housing. This circumstance can be attributed in part to a number of carry-over effects from the Southern caste system and to factors associated with the timing of the heavy migration of blacks to the cities, which followed, rather than preceded, the migration of European whites.

Of all the minority groups in the United States, only the black had been enslaved. Neither oriental minority groups nor the American Indian received this extreme type of treatment. In subsequent decades, the ideological basis of slavery in Southern states, for various reasons, influenced the legal status of the Negro in the nation as a whole.

During the early settlement period in the United States, many whites served as indentured servants, a status which differed little from that held initially by blacks. Many Southern colonies later passed laws prohibiting racial intermarriage and classified the offspring of interracial alliances as Negro. Other laws deprived Negroes of the right to vote, testify, and bring suit in court. By 1800 a significant differentiation in status of whites and of blacks had developed.[22]

When the plantation system expanded early in the nineteenth century, the subordination of the Negro had reached a stage which made classification as a slave logically and economically functional. The antebellum South developed an elaborate legal foundation for slavery. Stampp discussed the legal codes in *The Peculiar Institution*:

> In the customary phraseology of the antebellum codes, South Carolina's slaves were "deemed, held, taken, reputed and adjudged in law to be chattels personal, in the hands of their owners and possessors and their executors, administrators and assigns, to all intents, constructions and purposes whatsoever." Slaves had the attributes of personal property everywhere, except in Louisiana (and Kentucky, before 1852) where they had the attributes of real estate. . . .[23]

To rationalize and justify slavery in a nation founded on the Judaic-Christian tradition of brotherhood and the dignity of man, leaders of the antebellum South fostered an ideology of racial difference. This ideology proclaimed the idea that the racial factors which differentiated Caucasian and Negroid included mental and emotional differences. The Negro was inherently and for all time biologically inferior to the white man. Since he was deficient in mental ability, he could not function adequately in social positions other than those which were most subordinate and least demanding of his mental powers—positions which involved few complex responsibilities. Furthermore, the Negro would always need the guidance and assistance of the white man. The institution of slavery was ideally suited to the inferior capacities of the Negro.

Paternalistic plantation owners and their overseers stood ready to provide the instruction which the slave needed.[24]

Although the institution of slavery was not established north of the Mason-Dixon line, the supporting ideology was disseminated far and wide. The historian, C. Vann Woodward, reports that discrimination against the Negro was widespread throughout the North in the mid-nineteenth century. Many states "carved" from the Northwest Territory had barriers against the admission of Negroes and by 1861, the major political groups in the North had taken positions favoring white supremacy and racial segregation—positions endorsed by Abraham Lincoln.[25]

Although some improvements in race relations were made in the South in the Reconstruction Period, the trend was reversed in the final years of the nineteenth century with the adoption of Jim Crow laws. These laws, together with regulations disenfranchising the Negro, laid the legal basis for a rigidly segregated society. Fifty years after the end of the Civil War, the subordination of the Negro in the South did not differ greatly from the condition of slavery.

The dogma of innate inferiority of the Negro achieved its greatest triumph in a series of decisions by the United States Supreme Court from about 1873 to the middle of the twentieth century. In 1883 the Supreme Court of the United States ruled unconstitutional those provisions of the Civil Rights Act of 1875 which prohibited discrimination in public accommodations for reasons of race.[26] Another far-reaching decision was handed down in *Plessy v. Ferguson*, concerning Jim Crow practices in railroad cars. By ruling constitutional the system of racial segregation, many of the concurring Justices revealed the extent to which they accepted the doctrine of the biological inferiority of the Negro. After stating that racial segregation did not "stamp the colored race with a badge of inferiority," Justice Brown wrote:

> If the two races are to meet upon terms of social equality, it must be the result of natural affinities, a mutual appreciation of each other's merits and a voluntary consent of individuals. . . . If the civil and political rights of both races be equal one cannot be inferior to the other civilly or politically. *If one race be inferior to the other socially, the Constitution of the United States cannot put them upon the same plane.*[27]

In the years that followed, *Plessy v. Ferguson* provided the basis for a number of rulings which reinforced segregation. Of particular relevance to the condition of the urban black in the twentieth century was the decision in 1926 which upheld real estate covenants excluding blacks from ownership of residential property.[28] For more than thirty years this ruling allowed government agencies to support the efforts of realtors and builders to maintain black segregated neighborhoods.

Between *Plessy v. Ferguson* in 1896 and *Brown v. Board of Education* in 1954, the United States Supreme Court and the government agencies which followed its rulings reinforced and strengthened patterns of racial segregation throughout America.[29] The highest judicial body in the United States legitimized racial segregation in sensitive and critical areas of social life from voting to use of public accommodations. The Supreme Court thereby approved practices of caste in America. The fact that these decisions occurred over a period of fifty years suggests that many justices of the court reflected and expressed the opinions and prejudices on race held by most Americans. This result must be seen as a victory for the racial ideology which explained, justified and supported both slavery and the caste system. By the time the Supreme Court backed away from the philosophy underlying these decisions, in the forties, the heavy migration of white Europeans to America's cities had ended. As the Negro organized the drive in the fifties to acquire his share of America's respect and riches, competition and resistance from many members of these ethnic minority groups presented a formidable obstacle to progress. Had the Supreme Court reversed itself early in the century and had the Negroes initiated their urban migration long before the first World War, the problems of urban adjustment in the final third of this century might have been simpler.

One of the most lasting and important results of the caste institution has been the inflexible association in the minds of white Americans between the Negro and the lowest prestige positions. Belief in the necessary conjunction of these two traits leads many white citizens to view with concern and fear the desegregation of the institutions of their neighborhoods—housing, schools and playgrounds. Fearing that the in-migration of even a few black families will lead to a swift devaluation of the prestige rating of their locality and to racial friction at gathering places, white residents often put up unyielding resistance. Frequently such behavior proves to be a self-fulfilling prophecy, a statement which is false but comes true since the blacks remain confined to the lowest status neighborhoods. The long-run solution to the race problem requires elimination of the belief in the inevitable conjunction between inferior social positions and black incumbents.

A second derivative of slavery and caste pertains to the economic condition of Negroes who migrated to the cities. Had the majority of black workers held positions of skill and responsibility in the southern economy, they would have been well equipped to compete for middle class jobs in the urban economy. Since the majority of black adults performed unskilled work, and since few had been able to gain more than the bare fundamentals of learning in one-room country schools, the urban economy offered few opportunities other than unskilled employment. The largest number of black migrants entered the urban labor force, if they entered it at all, at the bottom.

This circumstance distinguishes the Negro from those minority groups, such as the Jews from western Europe, whose members had had extensive experience with trade, commerce and various other learned professions. A substantial number of these Jewish immigrants entered middle class occupations and once in these positions, employed many co-religionists. They also organized a variety of associations devoted to assisting the less fortunate members of their faith. Similarly, the Irish displayed considerable talent for politics and by the end of the nineteenth century had become a major force in the political organizations of the larger cities. Many Italian immigrants were attracted to construction activities since these were similar to the pattern of work experiences in their native land. The more successful Irish politician and Italian contractor, like their Jewish counterparts, created jobs for many members of their own groups, and thereby accelerated the mobility rate of members from the minority community into the middle class. The black community, on the other hand, with few prosperous business and professional men, lacked the resources for promoting the economic and educational advancement of its members. The necessity of gaining assistance from the white community strengthened the dependency of the Negro on whites and his subordination in the social system. A weak middle class hindered the organization of the movement to abolish racial segregation from American society.[30]

Several features of the timing of black migration to the cities proved disadvantageous. Large numbers of Negroes did not arrive in the urban centers of the nation until America entered World War I. The rate of migration declined during the depression and revived during and after World War II. In contrast however, the peak of migration from Europe had ended by the twenties. Consequently, members of these white minority groups had a considerable headstart over the black in the struggle for economic and social advancement in the urban social system. During the postwar era, many of the superordinate positions in urban institutions were held by members of minority groups who only recently had moved from the ghettos.[31] For many of these persons, the escape from economic

insecurity and low prestige positions was too recent and too well re-
membered to permit a calm and rational view of the Negro's efforts to
duplicate the process. The status anxiety of members of these ethnic
groups often has been a source of stubborn resistance to measures for
improving the economic and social conditions of Negroes.

The late arrival of the Negro in the urban centers put him at a disadvantage for another reason. Manpower requirements in the forties and
fifties differed greatly from those of the eighteen-eighties and nineties. In
the interval, the bottom rungs of the occupational ladder had become
much smaller. The opportunity to enter the urban labor force at the only
level open to the majority of black workers, unskilled factory work, was
far less than when the migration from Europe reached its peak, between
1901 and 1910. This circumstance combined with inadequate education
contributed to high unemployment and even higher rates of underemployment for urban Negro males. Another factor which reduced employment opportunities in manufacturing establishments in the postwar era
has been the trend for new factories to be built in the hinterland of the
metropolis. Too often, inadequate mass transit facilities and the inability
to purchase an automobile prevented unemployed Negroes living in the
central city from commuting to the plants in the hinterland.

A number of factors brighten prospects for the maintenance of a
sustained trend in the improvement in the economic condition of the
poor black and white families in the cities. For almost twenty years the
Supreme Court has refused to support racial segregation. By serving as a
major force for the attainment of racial equality, the Court has en-
deavored to undo the consequences of many of its earlier decisions. A
second and equally important consideration—one which did not exist
prior to the New Deal—pertains to the acceptance by the federal government of responsibility for maintaining a stable economy, one that no
longer experiences the "boom and bust" cycles which plagued the nation
for much of its history. The federal government also seeks to encourage
a substantial rate of economic growth and minimal rates of unemployment. In the final analysis, improvement of the economic condition of
the nation's poor requires a stable and prosperous economy. While this
condition by itself does not suffice, without it progress would be impossible. These characteristics of the recent history of America may be
regarded as advantages for low income groups which comparable
minorities did not possess in 1900.

Inevitably, the move from the country to the city for many blacks
resulted not in the discovery of the promised land, but in exchanging the
hardships of southern, rural life for the poverty and insecurity of urban

slums. At the same time, the successes scored by the Civil Rights movement have brought substantial economic and prestige advances to those black men and women with a college education or vocational skills.

The Economic Condition of Blacks

Some Negroes have made impressive economic advances in recent years. The proportion of black wage earners employed in white collar occupations and earning more than $7,000 per year increased substantially. Many Negroes who bettered their economic status moved from the slums into neighborhoods with attractive housing and into apartments with adequate living space. Conditions improved for the black families who managed to reach the middle levels of the class system. On the other hand, very little progress has been made by families subject to high unemployment and underemployment—the members of the "underclass." The distance between these two strata in the black community appears to have increased in recent years.[32]

Evidence of the improvement noted above can be seen from statistics on occupation for whites and nonwhites. Between 1950 and 1966, the proportion of nonwhites[33] employed in white collar occupations[34] increased from about 10 to approximately 21 percent. Since the proportion for whites increased from 40 to 48 percent in that period, it can be seen that the black is slowly catching up in this respect.[35] Nevertheless, the 21 percent of blacks in white collar occupations for 1966 falls considerably below the figure for whites in 1950, a time gap of more than sixteen years.[36]

A decline in the proportion of nonwhites engaged in menial occupations also indicates an economic gain. The proportion of nonwhite farm workers dropped from 18 percent in 1950 to 6 percent in 1966; the corresponding figures for laborers are 14 and 12 percent, a much smaller drop. The black labor force appears now to be experiencing the upward occupational redistribution which has been occurring in the white labor force for the past seventy years.

Data on the proportion of nonwhite families earning more than $8,000 indicate improvement in black economic status. Between 1947 and 1967 this proportion rose from 5 to 27 percent and for white families, from 18 to 53 percent.[37] The margin of difference between white and nonwhite dropped from better than three to two to one. On the other hand, much progress remains to be made by black families. The proportion of nonwhite families in 1967 with an income greater than $8,000, 27 percent, had been reached by white families in 1955, a time lag on this index of twelve years.

Middle class Negroes do not fare well in at least one major way. Their efforts to succeed do not seem to be as productive as those made by white persons with comparable education. Data on estimated lifetime earnings for white and nonwhite males show that the income gap widens as years of schooling increase. Lifetime earnings of nonwhites with less than eight years of education was 61 percent of that for whites. For persons with four years of college, the ratio dropped to 47 percent. In 1959, $191,000 was the estimated lifetime earnings of white males with only eight years of education, while that earned by nonwhites with from one to three years of college training was $162,000.[38]

Negroes with college training have less opportunity to acquire positions commensurate with their education and skills; white persons often receive preference despite an inferior educational background. A college education does not usually provide an economic payoff for blacks comparable to that for whites. On the basis of these data, one can understand why many black youths lack faith in higher education as the strategic route to economic advancement. Their apathy toward education often results from a realistic appraisal of job opportunities. On the other hand, assessment of discrimination in employment at the hiring stage based on the number of years of education is extremely complex. While the gap between black and white education in formal terms continues to narrow, it is difficult to determine what has happened in the quality of that education. Alan Batchelder indicated that in the 1950's, the quality dilution in educational attainment "exceeded quantitative gains for Negroes in the North and West."[39] While major differences between the level of white vs black education remain and are perpetuated, employment patterns will not change radically.

Paul Siegel recently calculated in monetary terms the "cost" of being a Negro.[40] He divided the mean difference in white–nonwhite earnings into several components and found that two-fifths of the difference, or slightly more than a thousand dollars, represented the cost in earnings of racial discrimination. The remainder of the difference, roughly $1,800, was attributed to differences in the regional, occupational and educational backgrounds of white and black workers. While continued migration from the South and gains in education and occupation would raise black income, the persistence of discrimination perpetuates a sizeable income differential. On the average Negroes still would be paid considerably less than whites performing the same tasks.

Discriminatory practices may partially account for the long-term persistence of the sizeable discrepancy between white and nonwhite median income, despite the economic gains registered by blacks. From 1950 to 1965 the nonwhite median income has been about 55 percent of that for whites. In 1967 the proportion rose to 62 percent.[41] The picture brightens when one takes region into consideration. Excluding statistics from the South increases the ratio for 1967 to over 70 percent. In the South the median black income in 1967 was 54 percent of that earned by whites.[42]

Another dimension of the economic status of black families concerns those classified as below the poverty level. This concept, developed by the Social Security Administration, takes into account a number of factors other than income—family size, number of children and farm-nonfarm residence. The poverty level for a nonfarm family of 7 or more persons is placed at $5,440 while for a nonfarm family of 4, it is $3,335. Between 1959 and 1967 the proportion of nonwhite persons below the poverty level fell from 55 to 35 percent. Despite this impressive improvement in a brief time span, the proportion of nonwhites living in poverty in 1967 exceeded that of whites by more than three times.[43] In terms of numbers, 25.9 million Americans lived in poverty in 1967 and 8.3 million were nonwhite.[44]

High Negro unemployment accounts for much of the poverty. From 1949 to 1967, virtually the entire postwar period, the nonwhite unemployment rate has been twice that of the white. Although married men have lower unemployment rates than the unmarried, the two to one differential by race persists.[45] Nonwhite unemployment is even more serious than that indicated by these facts since Negroes tend to be unemployed for long periods of time. In 1964, for example, nonwhites represented only 11 percent of the labor force, but they accounted for almost a forth or 23 percent of those who were out of work for fifteen weeks or longer, and 25 percent of those unemployed for over half a year.[46] To add to the problem, a higher proportion of employed blacks than of employed whites experience temporary layoffs and work part-time. Fein reports that for persons engaged in nonagricultural industries in 1963, 81 percent of the whites and 74 percent of the nonwhites worked full time.[47] The proportion of nonwhites engaged in part-time work was three times greater than that for whites, 9.6 percent and 3.1 percent, respectively.[48]

Underemployment is much more prevalent for black than for white workers.[49] Many of the nation's more important cities have a high proportion of "underemployed" black men.[50] The proportion ranges from 23 percent in slum areas of Boston and San Francisco, about 27 percent for two black ghettos in New York City, and 34 per cent in Philadelphia, to 38 percent in St. Louis and 45 percent in New Orleans. When one adds the high unemployment rate for black youth—approximately 25 percent in 1966 for teenagers 16 to 19 years of age of both sexes[51]—one can readily understand the despair and frustration which exists in many Negro areas of the central city.

Recent census statistics on black neighborhoods in Cleveland provide some insight into the difficulties of improving the economic status of certain black families. Households with a female head have little chance for obtaining higher incomes. This circumstance helps to explain the deterioration in income of many of Cleveland's black families. In the nine neighborhoods which make up the poverty area of Cleveland, the incidence of poverty between 1959 and 1964 among the black residents remained fairly stable, 26 and 25 percent, respectively. In the Hough area the proportion rose from 31 to 39 percent. In the four neighborhoods in the area with the highest concentration of Negroes, the average median family income also declined. In contrast, the incidence of poverty among the black families outside this area declined from 18 to 10 percent. Another difference between the poverty area and nearby sections inhabited by Negroes provides an explanation. In the poverty area the proportion of families with a female head increased between 1959 and 1964 from 58 to 64 percent and declined in the other neighborhoods from 53 to 25 percent.[52] Many of the black families with a male head improved their incomes during the period and moved to better housing outside the poverty area. The stability of the black family and its economic status are closely connected. Unquestionably, the unemployment and the underemployment of the black male has led to the disorganization of the black family and the increase in broken homes. Moynihan has stated:

> . . . the most pressing question for American social policy is whether the essential first step for resolving the problem of the Negro American is to provide such a measure of full employment of Negro workers that the impact of unemployment on family structure is removed.[53]

Discrimination and Negro Employment

Several explanations for the relatively poor economic condition of black people have been suggested. The continued development of the economy has considerably reduced the proportion of workers needed for unskilled work. Since lack of education and training prevents black workers from competing for the expanding numbers of skilled and white collar positions in industry, they experience unemployment and underemployment. These circumstances also contribute to the high proportion of Negro families which are broken by the separation of husband and wife. This mires the family even deeper in poverty.

A third explanation pertains to job discrimination. A report by the Office of Equal Opportunity in Manpower Programs of the Department of Labor provides information on the mechanics of discrimination against black persons eligible for white collar positions. State employment agencies engage regularly in a variety of practices which handicap Negro applicants. The first annual report of the Office of Equal Employment declared:

> Negro applicants were consistently assigned occupational classifications for low-skilled traditional jobs despite their qualifications for other work, while white applicants with the same or inferior qualifications were assigned higher classifications. . . .[54]

The report listed other discriminatory practices: referrals to employers on the basis of race, minority group members receiving fewer referrals than majority group members, and qualified Negro applicants seldom being referred for positions in retail stores, banks, finance and loan firms and other business enterprises.[55] Negro applicants were referred not for white collar but for more menial positions. These practices, if carried out by private and public employment agencies, would play an important role in the misallocation of black workers. That Negroes with the requisite training and education would generally not apply for white collar vacancies in corporations was a condition found to be prevalent, by a study discussed in more detail later in the chapter, of the hiring practices of corporations in fifteen metropolitan areas.[56] Instead, they would be encouraged to seek positions for which they were overtrained. These conditions would keep a disproportionately large number of black workers in low wage occupations.

Certain types of labor unions also engage in job discrimination. Many craft unions refuse to accept black persons as members and exclude them from apprenticeship programs. While a large number of industrial unions admit Negroes, they often confine them to segregated locals and to the lowest paying jobs. Those unions of both types which admit Negroes usually have rules which greatly reduce the likelihood of a Negro running for elected office. Generally the policies of labor unions are made and administered by white officials.

Negroes have been systematically excluded from many of the country's most powerful unions—plumbers, carpenters, electricians, printers, metal workers and machinists. Arthur M. Ross, Commissioner of the Bureau of Labor Statistics, cited a study of the percentage of black workers required to be employed in various building trade occupations to bring their number up to a level proportionate to their ratio in the labor force. He said:

> ... Negroes would hold 37,000 more jobs as carpenters, 45,000 more as construction workers, 97,000 more as mechanics, 82,000 more as metal craftsmen, and 113,000 more as construction foremen.[57]

An indication of the union practices responsible for these huge deficits in black membership is suggested by the practices of building trade unions in New York City. Herbert Hill, Labor Secretary for the NAACP, reports that unions prefer to bring in white members from outside the city rather than permit companies to employ black workers for local projects when labor is needed for these projects. In this manner the unions prevent black men from becoming members, although the out-of-town union members

> ... travel as much as 120 miles per day from Connecticut and elsewhere ... when the available local union membership supply is exhausted.[58]

These craft unions maintain the color line in two principal ways, by control over hiring and by excluding Negroes from apprenticeship programs. In many cases, the collective bargaining agreement which unions establish with construction firms provide for employment of workers by means of the union controlled hiring hall. The firm responsible for the construction project does not employ the men who will work on the particular project. This rule applies to both municipal and private building projects and often operates in cities which have adopted a fair employment ordinance. In these circumstances, the dominant political machine either tacitly or overtly cooperates with the building trades unions in the subversion of fair employment laws.[59]

Admission to apprenticeship programs operated by various craft unions often serves as a prerequisite for membership in the unions in somewhat the same way that a professional education is a requirement for admission to the bar or for certification as a physician. Many of the craft unions systematically exclude nonwhites from these training programs. Hill reports that

> ... less than one percent of the apprentices in the building and construction industry throughout the United States are Negro. In the ten year period, 1950-1960, in the State of New York, the increase of Negro participation in building trades apprenticeship programs rose from 1.5 percent to 2 percent.[60]

Hill goes on to point out that these practices are responsible for the number of Negroes with Ph.D. degrees exceeding the number of licensed black plumbers or electricians.[61] Young black males who complete their course of training in vocational high schools often cannot find employment suitable for their skill level and are compelled to work in low paying menial jobs. Inevitably, disillusionment and discouragement spreads to the high school-aged youngsters in the community, creating the strong conviction that working hard in school does not provide an economic payoff comparable to that received by white youngsters. Under these circumstances, high dropout rates from school should occasion little surprise.

Although many industrial unions admit Negroes, most restrict them to low paying, unskilled jobs and often segregate black members into separate union locals. Many unions accept lower wage scales for black than for white workers performing comparable tasks and insist upon preferential treatment for the white workers in promotions and layoffs.[62] The agreement which long has existed between U.S. Steel and the United Steelworkers Union for differentiating jobs appropriate for whites and those suitable for Negroes appears to be typical of similar practices by other unions and corporations. For many years in the Fairfield, Alabama plant of U.S. Steel, jobs have been graded from one to fourteen. Negroes were not allowed to rise higher than grade six, crane helpers, while whites could advance to the highest wage job for union members, locomotive cranemen. Subsequent modification of this arrangement has not appreciably improved the promotion opportunities for black workers.[63]

Union discrimination involves more than just the attitudes of officers of particular locals in the South. The building trades unions, which are strongest in the largest cities throughout the nation, maintain strict practices of racial exclusion. Furthermore, the officials of the national union and of the A.F.L.-C.I.O. either approve these discriminatory practices or are unwilling to press for their abandonment. While the A.F.L.-C.I.O. has expelled unions for corruption, "it has never expelled a union for racial discrimination."[64] Furthermore, corporation officials also must share responsibility for the continuation of discrimination in employment. These executives adhere to the rules specifying "white" and "black" jobs and pay scales. Officials of municipalities, states and the federal government are no less responsible when they tolerate discrimination against Negroes on projects and in firms financed by public funds.

The high rates of black unemployment and underemployment cannot be attributed solely to the instability of family life and to inadequate education received in segregated schools. Even where these disadvantages do not exist or have been overcome, black workers often are barred from employment for which they are well-prepared. Widespread discriminatory practices in the economy perpetuate the subordination of black Americans in the class system.

THE BLACK MIDDLE CLASS

Many of the factors which make life precarious for low income Negro families also influence the black middle class. These factors have restricted the size and resources of the black middle class, thereby weakening it as a force for the elimination of caste.

The middle class includes within its ranks a diversity of occupations, the men and women who staff administrative positions in complex organizations, managers and executives, the owners of business enterprises, various types of professional people—doctors, lawyers, engineers, professors, teachers, social workers—and occupations in the "lower" middle class such as sales and clerical activities. Much of the influence these people exercise derives from the positions which they fill in bureaucracies and from participation in community activities. Executives and owners of business organizations can influence the employment policies of their firms, a matter of concern to all minority groups. As participants in local affairs, middle class men and women often are able to modify the policies of the school board, of social agencies and of governmental bodies.[65] Members of the middle class generally have disposable income sufficient for contributions to a variety of "causes." In contrast the small Negro middle class has had few resources to donate to movements to assist other members of the black race. Nor has the Negro community been able to support adequately the self-help and philanthropic organizations which other minority groups, such as the Jews, have established and maintained over the years.

Data on occupations show a large difference in the proportion of white and of black people regarded as middle class. In 1965, 40.5 percent of white men were engaged in white collar occupations (professional, managerial, clerical and sales) in contrast to 16.5 percent of nonwhites.[66] Furthermore, very few Negroes were employed as business proprietors and managers, vital middle class occupations. For example, in 1965 only 3.4 percent of nonwhite but 14.3 percent of white men were engaged in managerial and entrepreneurial occupations.[67] Between 1960 and 1967 nonwhite persons employed in professional occupations increased by 80 percent but by only 17 percent for business occupations.[68]

A survey taken in the late sixties of major employers in fifteen metropolitan areas found that few Negroes were employed in white collar positions. Almost one-fourth of the 434 firms interviewed, 23 percent, employed no Negroes in these positions. Taking the reporting firms collectively, the median proportion of Negro white collar employees was 1 percent. Excluding the firms with no black employees in white collar positions raised the median number to 3 percent.[69]

Black Americans who obtained employment in middle class occupations have less job security than white employees. Unemployment rates for blacks in white collar occupations exceed those for whites. Fein reported:

> . . . 6 percent of white professionals and technical workers with work experience in 1962 were unemployed for some time during the year, but this was true for 11 percent of nonwhites. . . . Twelve percent of white but 18 percent of nonwhite clerical workers were unemployed in 1962. . . .[70]

Rates for part-time employment in white collar occupations also were higher for nonwhites than for whites.

The insecurity of the black middle class also is indicated by data on occupational mobility. Downward mobility from the Negro middle class greatly exceeds that from the white middle class. Of those employed in lower manual occupations the percentage of Negro sons whose fathers occupy higher white collar occupations, was 53 percent, and for sons of men in lower white collar occupations, 69 percent. Comparable figures for whites were 11.9 and 14.6 percent, respectively.[71] Duncan attributes the higher rate of downward mobility from the black middle class to racial discrimination, inferior education and structural weaknesses in the Negro family.[72] Another factor, not cited by Duncan, but which may increase the rate of downward mobility for black middle class families is the difficulty of moving from the poverty neighborhoods.[73] In 1968, 53 percent of the nonwhite families in metropolitan areas with a million or more residents lived in poverty areas. In areas with a population between a million and a quarter of a million this jumped to 63 percent.[74] Low income does not suffice to explain these high concentrations, for the majority of inhabitants of poverty areas had incomes above the poverty level.[75] Many families move out of the poverty area as soon as suitable housing elsewhere can be found.

Inability to escape the ghetto disadvantages middle class families in several ways. The children are compelled to attend schools which often are inferior in curriculum and staff to schools outside the ghetto. The families continue to reside in blighted neighborhoods, which induce apathy and discouragement. Black businesses are often greatly handicapped. Each of these factors, in addition to those mentioned by Duncan, makes the grip of the black family on its middle class position less secure.

Black Business Enterprises

Various factors have been successful in keeping the black business category small and its members deficient in capital and expertise. The failure of earlier efforts to establish viable banks had adverse affects for other types of black enterprises as well. Between 1888 and 1934 Negroes organized a minimum of 134 banks. During one seven year period, from 1899 to 1905, a minimum of twenty-eight banks were launched by black Americans in southern cities. By 1905 only seven of these banks remained in operation.[76] Subsequent efforts met with no greater success since in 1962, in all the United States, there were only ten Negro-owned and operated banks.[77] Some progress occurred in the next six years with the addition of ten banks. However, these banks have limited fiscal resources, since their assets totalled less than 1 percent of the assets, 24 billion dollars, of the nation's largest bank.[78] In comparison to the typical bank, those owned by black businessmen were able to make only small loans.

The inability of black businessmen to succeed in banking has been attributed to several factors: ignorance of banking operations and the nature of the clientele. Due in part to the agrarian and servile antecedents of America's Negroes, and the absence historically of opportunity to participate in a wide variety of business activities, the black community has lacked a strong business and managerial tradition. Furthermore, the market served by black-owned banks offered few opportunities for growth and prosperity. Black businesses usually were small and marginal and black families generally were in the low income category.[79]

Characteristics of black businesses in Philadelphia are probably representative of such establishments in the major cities of the nation.[80] Almost all of the Negro businesses were located in neighborhoods inhabited predominantly by Negroes. Most of the establishments engaged in retail trades and personal services, such as hairdressing and barber shops, restaurants and luncheonettes, and the manufacturing and wholesaling enterprises serving these types of firms. Figures for 1964 on volume of business suggest the weak financial condition of these enterprises.

. . . median sales for a sample of Negro-owned beauty shops were $2,500, for Negro-owned luncheonettes, $6,800, and for barber shops, $4,400.[81]

These facts led Foley to conclude that:

> . . . the Negro in business is . . . a very small businessman—who is generally not a very good businessman, and, frankly, not a very significant factor in the Negro community.[82]

Foley described some of the consequences of these conditions for the black community:

> . . . and there were no Negro Giannini's, Kennedy's, Rosenwald's, or similar great makers of fortunes from immigrant families. The Negro, therefore, had no reason to believe or hope that persistence, thrift, initiative could pay off. . . . Totally limited to a poverty market, the best the Negro could work for was a modest, marginal retail or service operation, hardly an example to cause great dreams or build high hopes. . . .[83]

Black businessmen have many disabilities. Confinement to the ghetto greatly restricts the size and affluence of their market. They have little opportunity to gain a foothold in those industries dominated by white minority groups. The antecedents of servile status still are manifest in a weak entrepreneurial tradition and lack of know-how of business operations. Each of these factors made it difficult for black businessmen to obtain financing from banks and other lending agencies. Under these circumstances, most black businesses were small and marginal. A weak business class handicapped the entire black community in a number of ways. Small firms and enterprises which relied on family labor could generate few employment opportunities for black workers and could not substantially reduce poverty in the ghetto. It provided too little assistance for organizations devoted to civil rights, the welfare of black people and to the termination of caste in America.

A middle class whose families had but a tenuous grip on their class position had few opportunities for moving into such elite groups as top corporate executives, top government officials, intellectuals and artists, scientists and military leaders. Since elites in government, politics, industry, education, and the military are primarily white, knowledge of the black community and its needs are obtained mainly through intermediaries. The scarcity of black persons in elite groups reinforces whatever beliefs on Negro inferiority may be expressed in these circles. Visible symbols of black achievement in important organizations would refute the myth of racial inferiority and persuade many black youngsters that avenues of escape from the ghetto are open.

PROBLEM MANAGEMENT

What has been done in the past and what can be done in the future to accelerate the movement of black Americans out of poverty and the ghetto, into the suburbs of the metropolis and the higher social classes? Strategy would seem to require two general approaches, one pertaining to conditions in the country as a whole and one to particular features of the black community.

National Economic Policy

Negro unemployment has been especially sensitive to national economic trends, rising rapidly in times of recession and falling when the labor market becomes tight. James Tobin, an economist, described this situation when he said

> . . . A tight labor market means not just jobs, but better jobs, longer hours, higher wages. Because of the heavy demands for labor during the second world war and its economic aftermath, Negroes made dramatic relative gains between 1940 and 1950. Unfortunately this momentum has not been maintained, and the blame falls largely on the weakness of labor markets since 1957.[84]

These circumstances reflect the significance of national economic policies for maintaining those conditions which will reduce unemployment rates for minority group members to very low levels. Such conditions involve a steady rate of economic growth and avoidance of excessive inflation or recession. These conditions have been achieved in the past by policies regulating the level of government spending and the availability of credit. High levels of government spending stimulates economic growth and increases the demand for labor, leading to a reduction in unemployment. Unfortunately, these conditions also increase demand for goods and drive prices upward, thus bringing on inflation. Government economists must delineate and maintain a middle course, one which promotes growth but avoids a severe inflationary spiral. Achieving this end involves coordinating domestic and foreign trade, balancing imports and exports, and maintaining the gold value of the dollar. Hence national economic stability entails solution of many complex problems, some of which concern global activities. But, as Tobin insists, these economic matters are closely connected to the economic standing of Negro Americans.

> . . . the connection between gold and the plight of the Negro is no less real for being subtle. We are paying much too high a social price for avoiding creeping inflation and for protecting our gold stock and "the dollar". . . . The interests of the unemployed, the poor and the Negroes are under-represented in the comfortable consensus which supports and confines current policy.[85]

Economic Discrimination

Reducing, if not ending, discrimination in employment of minority group members would provide substantial benefits to black Americans. It would increase the rate of employment, reduce the prevalence of poverty, stabilize the family by increasing the proportion of families with both husband and wife present, strengthen the middle class and provide additional incentives for youngsters to take education seriously. Substantial progress toward the elimination of caste in America cannot be made without a marked reduction in job discrimination.

The federal government and some of the states have moved slowly in recent decades toward strong efforts at overcoming discrimination in employment. The first major step by the federal government took place in 1941 when, in response to pressure from Negro leaders, President Franklin D. Roosevelt established a Committee on Fair Employment Practices. This committee sought to eliminate discrimination in employment by companies and unions engaged in projects financed by government contracts.[86] Although the committee's limited powers handicapped its operations, its establishment signified the commitment of the federal government toward achieving equality of economic opportunity.

Although Congress abolished the F.E.P.C. in 1946, President Truman presented a comprehensive civil rights program two years later, a move which led Dixiecrats to abandon the Democratic Party in that year's election. Although this legislation was not enacted, President Truman ended segregation in the armed forces and ordered the termination of discrimination in federal employment and in economic activities financed by government contract.[87]

Congress did not prohibit racial discrimination in employment until it passed the Civil Rights Act of 1964. Two titles of that act authorized efforts to combat job discrimination. Title VI established an Office of Equal Opportunity in the Department of Labor to help reduce discrimination in such manpower programs as on-the-job training, apprenticeship programs, and employment referral services, among others.[88] Title VII applied to industry. It enjoined discrimination by both employers and unions with 25 or more employees or members. It established an Equal Employment Opportunity Commission to determine the existence and nature of discrimination in employment.[89] If the E.E.O.C. establishes the existence of discrimination, through hearings or other procedures, it may request the Justice Department to file suit against the offending organization.[90] In instances where other government agencies have jurisdiction over the offending organization, their cooperation may be required for ending discriminatory practices.[91]

Progress by unions in industry and even in government financed operations in curtailing job discrimination has been slow. The number of organizations which must be investigated, the time and resources required for collection and the careful examination of the evidence are vast. The process of formulating plans for ending discrimination and for redressing past injustices tends to be complicated and to require considerable time. Federal agencies have been reluctant to terminate defense contracts with firms which practice discrimination, although the threat of such action would appear to be a major deterrent. Such action could be quite costly for the government and taxpayers if other firms could not produce the commodities at the same price as those which have had the contract. Furthermore, the heads of corporations and of unions, especially those engaged in defense production, often enjoy a close relation with the chairman of powerful congressional committees. These senators and congressmen may suggest to the heads of government agencies that demands for ending job discrimination be scaled down.[92]

Recent efforts to end job discrimination in three of the nation's largest textile producers illustrate many of these difficulties. Initiated in January 1967, the processes of investigation and negotiation have taken more than two years. At the plants of one of these corporations, the following conditions were found to exist:

> . . . virtual exclusion of Negro women from clerical jobs; assignment of black males to low paying, low status jobs; . . . In one plant, for example, blacks working for twenty years were in lower paying positions than white employees hired in 1967. . . .[93]

During 1968 while the three companies engaged in these and similar practices, they received federal contracts worth 77.5 million dollars.[94] At the time of writing it was uncertain as to whether and how the companies would end job discrimination.

The E.E.O.C. launched another effort in 1968 to end discriminatory practices in a key industry. Hearings on discrimination in the hiring of motion picture personnel revealed one device for excluding members of minority groups, employment rosters. The film companies hire only those persons listed on the roster, which contains few or no Negroes and Mexican Americans. Consequently fewer than

> . . . one in 10 employees of this key West Coast industry are members of minority groups, though Negroes and Mexican-Americans make up 20 percent of the Los Angeles area population.[95]

The Commission decided that a pattern of job discrimination existed and requested the Justice Department to file lawsuits as an effort to end discrimination in motion picture companies and unions.

Many states also have taken action to curb, if not terminate, discrimination in employment. By the mid-sixties, thirty-four states and the District of Columbia had enacted fair employment legislation. These laws covered about 70 percent of the total population of the nation and 45 percent of the Negro population.[96]

Terminating or substantially reducing discrimination in employment would greatly increase economic opportunities for Negroes and members of other minority groups. However, success in the near future will require more money, larger staffs and possibly a greater determination to achieve this end.

The Population Problem in the Black Ghetto

The complex and varied factors responsible for the concentration of most urban Negroes in the ghetto requires an equally varied strategy for social change. Some of the difficulties result from the size of the black population and from the prevalence of poverty. Both factors result in rising expenditures by public bodies and a growing need for a variety of technical and professional services. Holding down the number of ghetto residents and the number of poor people would help reduce the rate of increase in municipal services and monies needed to assist these people. This can be accomplished by reducing the rate at which black Americans and the poor move to the city from the country. Fostering a high rate of economic growth in the southern region and vigorous enforcement of nondiscriminatory regulations would improve economic opportunities for Negroes. One important incentive for leaving the region would be weakened.[97]

While the logic of this argument is sound, the difficulties of its implementation may be enormous since both national planning and strict government enforcement would be required, conditions which neither exist nor are desirable. Whether present efforts by southern governors and business leaders to achieve a high rate of economic growth produces the desired result remains to be seen.

Hauser has shown that as family size increases, the incidence of poverty also increases. Virtually all black children in families with five or more youngsters are raised under conditions of poverty. He wrote:

. . . Of nonwhite children in families with three or four children, 54 to 68 percent were living in poverty, compared with 15 to 25 percent for white. Of nonwhite children in families with five or more children, 81 to 94 percent were being reared in poverty, as compared to 33 to 48 percent for white. Probably no other facts link high fertility and poverty so dramatically and point up so vividly the plight of the poor and especially the Negro poor in this country.[98]

Reducing the birth rate in poor families requires a considerable expansion of the family planning programs of voluntary associations and governmental agencies. The willingness of poor black and white parents to use knowledge and techniques of family limitation when these are made available at little or no expense has been reported in several studies.[99] These programs presently reach only a small proportion of those in need of their services. Greater federal and state support needs to be allocated to public and private agencies committed to assisting low income families in limiting the number of children.

A second consideration for reduction of the birth rate among the poor is the tendency for the rate of child birth to decline as the class position of the family increases. Educated women in well-to-do families generally have fewer pregnancies than women of lesser education in poorer families. Rapid movement of black families out of poverty and improvement of the educational attainment of black youngsters also would reduce the rate of natural increase in the black ghetto. Maintaining a prosperous

economy and overcoming job discrimination, would contribute to the
reduction of the natural rate of increase.

The Black Ghetto: Enrichment vs. Dispersion

Moving now to conditions within the metropolitan community, a
difficult choice confronts the policy makers, both in private and in public
organizations. Since the black ghettos of the central city have a large
proportion of low income families, substandard housing and poor
schools, it seems reasonable to design programs to improve the living
conditions and economic circumstances of the families inhabiting the
ghetto. Improving living and working conditions in the ghetto makes
the area more attractive to its residents and reduces the rate of out-
migration. Hence spatial segregation of the races persists and along with
it, segregation in the schools, churches, voluntary associations and the
remaining institutions of the community.

The opposite tactic is recommended by Kain and Persky, who urge
the breakup of the large, central city ghettos by facilitating, as a first
step, the formation of newer but smaller ghettos in suburban communities.[100] This can be done through several housing programs discussed
in chapter 8; first, building low income housing projects in the
suburbs, second, increasing the proportion of Negro families able to rent
or purchase dwelling units in white neighborhoods through the rent
subsidy program, and third, vigorously enforcing open housing legislation. Incentive to move out of the ghetto will be strengthened by programs which inform job seekers in the ghetto of positions available in
suburban towns. Providing efficient and inexpensive rapid transit facilities also will enable the ghetto dweller to commute to work. Sooner or
later the commuting employee will endeavor to obtain housing closer to
his place of employment and, if successful, he will move out of the
ghetto. The influence of these factors on the employment of Negroes is
suggested by research findings that noted that the proportion of Negroes
in the labor force of a neighborhood or community varied directly with
the distance from the black ghetto.[101]

To postpone improvement of the ghetto—of economic opportunities,
housing and schools—until many residents had relocated in the suburbs,
might require considerable patience. In the meantime, the low income
families that had been unable to move would remain in dire want.
Despite the risk of stimulating an increase in in-migration of poor blacks
from the rural South, living and working conditions within the ghetto
must be improved.

Employment Programs for the Ghetto Poor

Two strategies for reducing the unemployment rate could be implemented. The federal government could accept the lion's share of responsibility by developing public works programs similar to those used during the depression of the thirties. Thousands of unemployed men could be put to work on projects of considerable benefit to the community, such as construction and improvement of municipal sanitation systems.[102] Presumably many of these jobs would be unskilled or semi-skilled, and would not prepare the workers to enter more technical occupations in industry. Opposition in Congress and elsewhere to this strategy, due in part to its cost, has eliminated it for the time being as a possible remedy.

President Johnson requested corporation leaders to take the initiative in hiring increasing numbers of the "hard core" unemployed. As the private sector's organizational weapon against poverty, business leaders in fifty cities throughout the nation established the JOBS program. Many of the participating corporations developed job training programs for disadvantaged men and women which, in many cases, were financed by federal agencies. Executives of participating corporations promised to employ those persons, many of whom were black Americans, who complete the training program.[103]

The nature of the training program tended to vary from company to company. The program of one chemical company, under contract with the Office of Economic Opportunity, ran from nine to twelve months, paid each trainee $30 per month and offered courses in such subjects as automotive repair, air conditioning, refrigeration and metal working.[104] A program organized by a publishing firm and founded by the Department of Labor, ran for eighteen months and included such basic subjects as arithmetic, English and communication skills. The graduates were employed by the company in responsible positions. The JOBS program reached its initial employment goal of a hundred thousand "hard core" unemployed persons by the target date of June, 1969 and seems likely to provide a half million jobs by the middle of 1971. The "Big Three" automotive companies alone employed 40,000 of the disadvantaged adults in 1968.[105]

The success of the program depends on more than the number of disadvantaged persons who have been employed. Other factors must be considered, such as the length of time these people retain their positions —whether for a few months or for many years—and the degree to which they advance in rank and salary relative to other employees. The motivation and morale of the trainees depends on the type of position which they obtain at the end of the training period. Many trainees have little or no interest in "dead-end" jobs, but prefer positions which offer promotion opportunities. Finally, whether or not these workers retain their positions depends on national economic trends. Since these employees are newcomers to the firms, they have little seniority and are the first to be laid off when production drops. Where layoffs have occurred, as in some automotive companies, the impact has been softened by a variety of measures, such as switching the workers to the training program. These arrangements are merely temporary, however, and could not prevent layoffs if the recession persisted for many months.[106]

A number of companies have followed a different tactic to fight poverty. They have built plants in the ghetto and hired local residents. One company organized and located a manufacturing concern in the Watts section of Los Angeles and employed five hundred local residents after completion of a two week, company operated training course. Another company built a plant in the Roxbury section of Boston and taught two hundred and fifty workers a printing trade in a program funded by the federal government.[107]

The principle of bringing the jobs to the unemployed by constructing factories in the ghetto runs counter to the dominant trend of industrial location, moving industry from the city to the suburbs. It might be expected that the number of new factories built and jobs created in the ghetto will be small. More could be accomplished by bringing the unemployed ghetto dweller to the places of employment in the suburbs.

Assistance for Black Enterprise

Aiding the development of enterprises owned by Negroes also will generate additional employment opportunities in the black community. A number of programs seek to eliminate a circumstance which has seriously hindered the formation and the growth of businesses owned by Negroes, the inability to borrow capital. Few banks and other lending agencies made loans to these establishments, since management often lacked experience and know-how, and the enterprises were marginal. The Economic Opportunity Act of 1964 authorized the Small Business Administration to loan relatively modest sums for as long as fifteen years for the initiation and improvement of a business.[108] This lending authority developed into a "black capitalism" program in the late sixties with a goal of establishing ten thousand small businesses annually. At the time of writing, only half that rate had been achieved and an important feature of the program, technical assistance by industry executives, also has fallen behind expectations.[109]

The federal government also sought to encourage investment in black neighborhoods through a provision of the 1965 Housing and Urban Development Act, which reduced the risk of lending money to black businessmen by guaranteeing their leases. Commercial interests are encouraged to provide mortgage money for the purchase of land and construction of buildings.[110]

Local development funds, which may involve both the federal government and private capital, also encourage the economic development of the ghetto. Development funds may be established either as a profit-making or nonprofit organization, with funds from public and private sources. A local development fund serves as a source of capital designed specifically to encourage new and assist existing enterprises in the black ghetto and in the neighborhoods of other minority groups. The fund assists entrepreneurs in one other important way, by making available the services of corporation experts as advisors to local entrepreneurs.[111]

These measures are designed to assist business establishments in the neighborhoods inhabited by specific minority groups. Consequently they fail to change one circumstance which in the past has handicapped the black businessmen, serving the relatively less affluent market in the ghetto. Encouraging black people to become small businessmen in the ghetto does not suffice as a long-run stimulant to the growth of a black business class. Ghetto boundaries can be crossed by aiding the establishment of black-owned enterprises in white neighborhoods to serve both white and black patrons. Black businessmen should have the same opportunity to serve the white community as white businessmen have had over the years to serve the black community.[112]

Development of a black business and managerial stratum also requires the opportunity to achieve executive status in major corporations, in banks, investment houses, brokerage firms, and insurance companies, where one seldom sees a black face in executive offices. Similar opportunities are required in manufacturing establishments, in the electronic and aerospace industries and throughout the economy. To accomplish these objectives requires equal opportunity in employment and a considerable increase in the proportion of black youngsters attending universities and graduate schools. Vigorous recruitment programs and generous scholarship funds would prove helpful.

Many other programs and activities can be considered part of the problem management efforts of American society. Later chapters will consider measures for assisting those unable to help themselves and programs to improve education. One other matter which cannot be considered here concerns conflict between the ghetto community and law enforcement agencies. Most of the riots which occurred in the past few years were ignited by seemingly minor incidents involving police and residents of the black ghetto. The circumstances responsible and measures for improving relationships between residents of black neighborhoods and local police deserve the attention of the reader.[113]

CONCLUSION

This chapter considered features of social organization in America responsible for the existence of race relations as a serious social problem, —the inability of most black Americans to attain basic goals and values. Chapter 1 defined such a condition, where it pertained to significant groups and large numbers of people, as an essential characteristic of a social problem. Many of the frustrations and inequities encountered daily by many black Americans can be attributed directly or indirectly to racial segregation in the cities, and to the prevalence of the black ghetto. It has become the instrument for transposing the caste system of the South to the cities of the nation. Within ghetto walls, black Americans are isolated from white Americans, restricted to inferior housing, schools and economic opportunities. Many of those who live their entire lives within the black ghetto also feel inferior to those who live outside.

Enabling black Americans to attain the basic goals of American society requires the dissolution of the black ghetto. We have discussed the various programs which can accomplish this end, both those specific to black people and to the nation as a whole. One measure which is crucial for the dispersion of black Americans throughout the metropolis, open housing, is considered in chapter 8.

Selected Readings

Blalock, H. M. Jr. *Toward A Theory of Minority-Group Relations* (New York: John Wiley & Sons, Inc., 1967).

Glazer, Nathan and Daniel Patrick Moynihan. *Beyond the Melting Pot* (Cambridge, Mass.: The M.I.T. Press, paperback, 1964).

Gordon, Milton M. *Assimilation in American Life* (New York: Oxford University Press, 1964).

Myrdal, Gunnar. *An American Dilemma* (New York: Harper & Brothers Publishers, 1944).

Parsons, Talcott and Kenneth B. Clark, eds. *The Negro American* (Boston: Beacon, 1967).

Pettigrew, Thomas F. *A Profile of the Negro American* (Princeton, N.J.: D. Van Nostrand Company, Inc., 1964).

Report of The National Advisory Commission on Civil Disorders (New York: Bantam Books, 1968).

Supplemental Studies for The National Advisory Commission on Civil Disorders (Washington, D.C.: U.S. Government Printing Office, 1968).

Taeuber, Karl E. and Alma F. Taeuber. *Negroes In Cities* (Chicago: Aldine Publishing Company, 1965).

"The Negro Protest," *The Annals of the American Academy of Political and Social Science,* 357 (January, 1965).

van den Berghe, Pierre L. *Race and Racism* (New York: John Wiley & Sons, Inc., 1967).

Notes to Chapter 2

[1] Philip M. Hauser, "Demographic Factors in the Integration of the Negro," *Daedalus,* 94 (Fall, 1965), p. 850.

[2] Department of Labor and Bureau of the Census, *Recent Trends In Social and Economic Conditions of Negroes in the United States, July, 1968* (Washington, D.C.: U.S. Government Printing Office, 1968), p. 3.

[3] Department of Labor and Bureau of the Census, *Social and Economic Conditions of Negroes in the United States, October, 1967* (Washington, D.C.: U.S. Government Printing Office, 1967), p. 6.

[4] Philip M. Hauser, *op. cit.,* p. 851.

[5] *Ibid.,* p. 852.

[6] U.S. Bureau of the Census, *Current Population Reports,* Series P-23, Special Studies (formerly Technical Studies), No. 27, "Trends in Social and Economic Conditions in Metropolitan Areas," (Washington, D.C.: U.S. Government Printing Office, 1969), p. 4.

[7] *Ibid.*

[8] *Ibid.*

[9] *Ibid.,* p. 6.

[10] *Report of the National Advisory Commission on Civil Disorders* (Washington, D.C.: U.S. Government Printing Office, 1968), p. 215.

[11] *Ibid.,* p. 227.

[12] *Ibid.,* p. 216.

[13] *Ibid.*

[14] Bureau of Labor Statistics and U.S. Bureau of the Census, *Social and Economic Conditions of Negroes in the United States, op. cit.,* p. 12.

[15] Stanley Lieberson, *Ethnic Patterns in American Cities* (New York: The Free Press, 1963).

[16] *Ibid.*

[17] Karl E. Taeuber and Alma F. Taeuber, *Negroes In Cities* (Chicago: Aldine Publishing Company, 1965), pp. 37-43.

[18] *Ibid.,* p. 34.

[19] Reynolds Farley and Karl E. Taeuber, "Population Trends and Residential Segregation Since 1960," *Science,* 159 (1 March 1968), pp. 953-56.

[20] *Ibid.,* p. 955.

[21] *Report of the National Advisory Commission on Civil Disorders, op. cit.,* p. 225.

[22] For a discussion of this development, cf. Oscar Handlin, *Race and Nationality in American Life* (Boston: Little, Brown and Company, 1948), pp. 3-28.

[23] Kenneth Stampp, *The Peculiar Institution* (New York: Vintage Books, 1956), pp. 196-7.

[24] *Ibid.,* pp. 6-14.

[25] C. Vann Woodward, *The Strange Career of Jim Crow,* 2 ed. (New York: Oxford University Press, 1966), pp. 18-21.

[26] Irving Brant, *The Bill of Rights: Its Origin and Meaning* (Indianapolis: The Bobbs Merrill Company, 1965), p. 365.

[27] *Ibid.,* p. 371. Authors' italics.

[28] *Ibid.,* p. 373.

[29] For a discussion of the supportive relationship between the ideology of bigotry in general and a high status group in America cf. E. Digby Baltzell, *The Protestant Establishment* (New York: Random House, 1964).

[30] For a discussion of these matters, see Nathan Glazer and Daniel Patrick Moynihan, *Beyond the Melting Pot* (Cambridge, Mass.: The M.I.T. Press, paperback, 1964).

[31] For a study of minority groups in a New England community, see W. Lloyd Warner and Leo Srole, *The Social System of American Ethnic Groups* (New Haven: Yale University Press, 1945).

[32] For a discussion of these trends, see Daniel Patrick Moynihan, "Employment, Income, and the Ordeal of the Negro Family," *Daedalus,* 94 (Fall, 1965), p. 747.

[33] Negroes comprise 92 percent of the nonwhites in America.

[34] This category includes the following occupations: professional, technical and kindred workers; managers, officials and proprietors; clerical and sales.

[35] U.S. Bureau of the Census, *Statistical Abstract of the United States, 1967,* 88th ed. (Washington, D.C.: U.S. Government Printing Office, 1967), p. 231.

[36] *Ibid.*

[37] Bureau of Labor Statistics and U.S. Bureau of the Census, *Recent Trends In Social and Economic Conditions of Negroes in the United States, op. cit.,* p. 8.

[38] U.S. Bureau of the Census, *Income Distribution in the United States, by Herman P. Miller,* A 1960 Census Monograph (Washington, D.C.: U.S. Government Printing Office, 1966), p. 270. Paul M. Siegel also found that the differential between white-nonwhite income increased with higher education of respondents, Paul M. Siegel, "On the Cost of Being a Negro," *Sociological Inquiry,* 35 (Winter, 1965), pp. 48-51.

[39] Alan B. Batchelder, "Decline in the Relative Income of Negro Men," *Quarterly Journal of Economics,* Vol. 78 (November, 1964), p. 538.

[40] Paul M. Siegel, *Ibid.,* p. 56.

[41] Bureau of Labor Statistics and U.S. Bureau of the Census, *Recent Trends In Social and Economic Conditions of Negroes in the United States, op. cit.,* p. 6.

[42] *Ibid.,* p. 7.

[43] *Ibid.,* p. 9.

[44] *Ibid.*

[45] Ibid., p. 11.

[46] Rashi Fein, "An Economic and Social Profile of the Negro American," *Daedalus,* 94 (Fall, 1965), p. 828.

[47] *Ibid.,* p. 829.

[48] *Ibid.*

[49] Explaining these trends in unemployment for married and unmarried men presents a challenge. Professor Richard L. Simpson has pointed out that variation

in education between older and younger age groups suggests that older men should have higher unemployment rates than younger, as the latter age group generally has completed more years of school than the former. The influence of this factor may be offset by preferences of employers for married men, and by a greater willingness of men with families to accept low wage, menial jobs which younger, unmarried men may spurn. These considerations should operate on both white and nonwhite men, and therefore do not explain the consistently higher unemployment rate for nonwhites.

[50] Underemployment refers to unemployment, part-time employment, working full time at less that $60 per week and the addition of half of the able-bodied men not looking for work. Edmund K. Faltermayer, "More Dollars and More Diplomas," *Fortune,* LXXVII, No. 1 (January, 1968), p. 144.

[51] *Ibid.,* p. 144.

[52] U.S. Bureau of the Census, "Changes in Economic Level in Nine Neighborhoods in Cleveland: 1960 to 1965," *Current Population Reports, Series P-23, N. 20* (Washington, D.C.: U.S. Government Printing Office, 1966).

[53] Daniel Patrick Moynihan, "Employment, Income, and the Ordeal of the Negro Family," *op. cit.,* p. 764.

[54] U.S. Department of Labor, *Equality of Opportunity In Manpower Programs* (Washington, D.C.: Manpower Administration, 1968), p. 20.

[55] *Ibid.,* p. 21.

[56] Peter Rossi, et. al., "Between White and Black: The Faces of American Institutions in the Ghetto," *Supplemental Studies for the National Advisory Commission on Civil Disorders* (Washington, D.C.: U.S. Government Printing Office, 1968), p. 119.

[57] Thomas O'Hanlon, "The Case Against the Unions," *Fortune,* LXXVII, No. 1 (January, 1968), p. 170.

[58] Herbert Hill, "Racial Inequality in Employment: The Patterns of Discrimination," *The Annals,* 357 (January, 1965), p. 44.

[59] *Ibid.,* pp. 44-45.

[60] *Ibid.,* p. 37.

[61] *Ibid.,* p. 45.

[62] Thomas O'Hanlon, *op. cit.,* pp. 170-1.

[63] *Ibid.,* p. 188.

[64] *Ibid.,* p. 171.

[65] For a review of the literature of participation in political affairs in America and in other countries, which considers a number of variables, see Lester W. Milbrath, *Political Participation* (Chicago: Rand McNally, 1965), pp. 110-41. For a review of the literature on participation in voluntary associations, see Arnold M. Rose, *The Power Structure* (New York: Oxford University Press, 1967), pp. 213-54.

[66] Bureau of Labor Statistics, *The Negroes In the United States: Their Economic and Social Situation* (Washington, D.C.: U.S. Government Printing Office, 1966), p. 107.

[67] *Ibid.*

[68] Bureau of Labor Statistics and Bureau of the Census, *Recent Trends In Social and Economic Conditions of Negroes in the United States,* July, 1968, *op. cit.,* p. 16.

[69] Peter Rossi, et. al., "Between White and Black: The Faces of American Institutions in the Ghetto," *op. cit.,* pp. 119-120.

[70] Rashi Fein, "An Economic and Social Profile of the Negro American," *op. cit.,* p. 829.

[71] Otis Dudley Duncan, "Patterns of Occupational Mobility Among Negro Men," *Demography,* 5 (1968), pp. 17-19.

[72] *Ibid.,* pp. 19-20.

[73] Poverty areas are those census tracts in metropolitan areas with a population in excess of a quarter of a million which rank high in the following characteristics:

1. family income below $3,000; 2. children in broken homes; 3. persons with low educational attainment; 4. males in unskilled jobs; 5. substandard housing.

[74] Bureau of Labor Statistics and Bureau of the Census, *Recent Trends In Social and Economic Conditions of Negroes in the United States, op. cit.,* p. 25.

[75] *Ibid.,* p. 26.

[76] E. Franklin Frazier, *Black Bourgeoisie* (New York: The Free Press, paperback, 1965, originally published in 1957), pp. 38-9.

[77] *Time* (February 28, 1969), p. 89.

[78] *Ibid.*

[79] E. Franklin Frazier, *op. cit.,* pp. 41-2.

[80] The following discussion relies heavily on material presented by Eugene P. Foley, "The Negro Businessman: In Search of a Tradition," in Talcott Parsons and Kenneth B. Clark, eds., *The Negro American, op. cit.,* pp. 555-92.

[81] *Ibid.,* p. 561.

[82] *Ibid.,* p. 563. For somewhat similar findings on Negro businesses in New York City, see Nathan Glazer and Daniel Patrick Moynihan, *Beyond the Melting Pot* (Cambridge, Mass.: The M.I.T. Press, paperback, 1964), pp. 29-37.

[83] Eugene P. Foley, "The Negro Businessman," in Talcott Parsons and Kenneth B. Clark, eds., *op. cit.,* p. 574.

[84] James Tobin, "On Improving the Economic Status of the Negro," *Daedalus,* 94 (Fall, 1965), p. 880.

[85] *Ibid.,* p. 886.

[86] *Revolution In Civil Rights, 3rd ed.* (Washington, D.C.: Congressional Quarterly Service, 1967), p. 2.

[87] *Ibid.,* p. 3. For studies of the Negro in the armed forces, see the following: Charles C. Moskos, Jr., "Racial Integration in the Armed Forces," *The American Journal of Sociology,* 72 (September, 1966), pp. 132-48; Lee Nichols, *Breakthrough on the Color Front* (New York: Random House, 1954); Paul C. Davis, "The Negro in the Armed Services," *Virginia Quarterly,* XXIV (Autumn, 1948), pp. 499-520.

[88] U.S. Department of Labor, *Equality Of Opportunity In Manpower Programs* (Washington, D.C.: Manpower Administration, 1968), pp. 3-15.

[89] *Revolution In Civil Rights, 3 ed., op. cit.,* p. 76.

[90] *The New York Times,* (March 14, 1969), p. 13.

[91] Barney Sellers, "Packard's Deal with the Textile Big Three," *The New Republic* (March 22, 1969), pp. 9-11.

[92] *Ibid.*

[93] *Ibid.,* p. 10.

[94] *Ibid.*

[95] *The New York Times, op. cit.*

[96] Morroe Berger, *Equality By Statute: The Revolution In Civil Rights,* rev. ed. (Garden City, N.Y.: Doubleday, 1967), p. 160.

[97] John H. Kain and Joseph J. Persky, "Alternatives to the Gilded Ghetto," *The Public Interest,* 14 (Winter, 1969), pp. 83-5.

[98] Philip M. Hauser, *op. cit.,* p. 862.

[99] See the discussion of these programs and studies in Adelaide Cromwell Hill and Frederick S. Jaffe, "Negro Fertility and Family Size Preferences: Implications for Programming of Health and Social Services," in Talcott Parsons and Kenneth B. Clark, eds., *The Negro American* (Boston: Beacon, 1967), pp. 208-14.

[100] John H. Kain and Joseph H. Persky, *op. cit.,* pp. 79-80.

[101] *Ibid.,* pp. 77-8.

[102] This type of project receives a strong endorsement from Roger Starr and James Carson, "Pollution & Poverty: The Strategy of Cross-Commitment," *The Public Interest,* 10 (Winter, 1968), pp. 104-31.

[103] "Employing The Employables," *U.S. News and World Report* (August 12, 1968), p. 49.

[104] *Action Report,* I (Summer, 1968), p. 3.

[105] Robert Dietsch, "Hard-Core Blacks and the Shiny Auto," *The New Republic* (March 1, 1969), p. 10.

[106] *Ibid.*

[107] *Action Report,* I (Winter, 1968), p. 1.

[108] Eugene P. Foley, "The Negro Businessman: In Search of a Tradition," *op. cit.,* p. 575.

[109] *The New York Times* (March 11, 1969), p. 29.

[110] Eugene P. Foley, "The Negro Businessman: In Search of a Tradition," *op. cit.,* p. 577.

[111] *Ibid.,* pp. 577-78: Urban America, Inc., "The Role Of the Private Sector In Urban Problems," in Joint Economic Committee, Congress Of the United States, *Urban America: Goals and Problems* (Washington, D.C.: U.S. Government Printing Office, 1967), pp. 285-86.

[112] Most of the banks in Harlem are branches of "white-owned downtown banks." One large department store and much of the local real estate also are owned by white people who live outside Harlem. Kenneth B. Clark, *Dark Ghetto: Dilemmas of Social Power* (New York: Harper & Row, Torchbook, 1967), pp. 28-29.

[113] *Report of the National Advisory Commission On Civil Disorders, op. cit.,* chs. 1, 2, 11; David J. Bordua, ed., *The Police: Six Sociological Essays* (New York: Wiley, 1967); Robert Conot, *Rivers Of Blood, Years Of Darkness* (New York: Bantam Books, 1967); Tom Hayden, *Rebellion in Newark* (New York: Random House, 1967).

CHAPTER THREE

CONTEMPORARY PROBLEMS IN AMERICAN EDUCATION

Contemporary American Society is so complex that it would be literally impossible to convey all of our cultural heritage to each generation within the confines of the individual family. Our history, our political, social, and economic structure and their functioning, and the scientific development upon which our life is dependent represent so large a body of cultural knowledge that no single individual could learn and teach it all to his children. In addition, a complex society must evolve, year after year, hundreds of new occupational positions, and discard others which have outlived their usefulness. The simple stratification categories used by less complex societies such as age, sex, and inherited status are not versatile enough to create more than a few social classes—not nearly enough to fill the needs of a society such as our own.

The formalization of education into a separate agency for the trans-mission of existing knowledge and the discovery of new knowledge has proved to be an effective way of adapting the socialization of the young to these societal needs. By expanding the stratification categories to include and encourage individual achievement as well as the ascription of status—use of age, sex, inherited position—greater latitude for the filling of new societal positions is permitted. This allows society to utilize many more individuals by providing a legally required learning situation in which, ideally, all children may acquire skills and a knowledge base to fit them for employment and higher education. While the school, in this respect, is a solution to several of society's major problems, as an agent of change it is also faced with a number of serious and consequential problems resulting from internal and external conflicts and strains. Out of a variety of these problems, three have been selected for consideration and analysis: the effect of stratification on American education as it relates to the lower classes and the Negro, the expansion of and re-sistance to the role of the federal government in education, and the problem of increased militancy of teachers as workers within the educa-tional institution.

The first problem involves the application of the American Creed and the rights of man as they have been defined in the United States. It particularly pertains to the development of manpower from all levels of society making effective our system of division of labor. The second problem has proven controversial for several decades. It has become increasingly important with the extension of the federal government's control into a variety of institutional areas such as health, welfare and business, and its use of force to integrate local schools.

While the first two problems involve broad, external concerns of rights, privileges, definitions and functions of education in a free society, the third problem is partially restricted to the institution itself. The struggle of the teacher for status and reward comparable to that of other pro-fessionals began to utilize some of the format of lower status labor organizations in the late sixties. The use of the strike, bargaining and picketing by teachers, created societal conflict and struggle. The management or resolution of each problem area considered could grant many more Americans the opportunity for social mobility through education.

EDUCATION: FOR WHAT?

From the age of five or six, children in our society are legally removed from their families for a large portion of many days each year. These years of childhood, adolescence, and often young adulthood are generally spent in a public, secular school whose function it is to teach our society's cultural heritage of beliefs, knowledge, values, norms, specific skills and technology. With over 55 million young people of school age,[1] an elaborate system of education is required. The United States does not have a unified system of schools housed under a central authority. No standard curricula and organizational form exist. Throughout the 21,697 operating school districts in the United States, controls, textbooks, even aims and methods vary.[2] One would be hard pressed to determine the unifying themes in American education—with one exception. The common framework which cuts across the board is the widespread belief in the *value* of education. This belief is supported on three ideological grounds: only an educated citizenry may participate effectively in a democracy; education provides the individual with the leverage to advance socially and economically; and education provides the individual with the expertise required for steady and rewarding participation in a complex, industrialized economy. A tremendous gulf exists between the enthusiasm for education as a symbol and the practical realities of its high cost to the taxpayer, the economic competition it creates through mass education, and the threat it presents to traditional values and prejudice. Implementation of the ideal of equality of educational opportunity encounters problems of class, race, ethnic background, religion, cost and control of education and educational personnel.

STRATIFICATION AND AMERICAN EDUCATION

Stratification patterns in the United States, different levels of individual and family rank and prestige, have existed since the earliest settlement. Although both federal and state constitutions suggested that the United States was a democracy, inequality existed. In many colonies voters had to be landowners and the holding of public office was almost exclusively delegated to the affluent. In the eighteenth and nineteenth centuries, education, which required free time spent in noneconomic pursuits, was a luxury that few families could afford since children had important economic responsibilities. Only the wealthy family could permit children to attend school for several years. During the latter part of the 19th century, after depression brought mass adult unemployment and after labor leaders gave active support to public education, child labor laws were enacted and compulsory education acts were passed which removed children from the labor market.[3] Passage of state compulsory education laws requiring children to remain in school until 16 years of age followed closely upon the wake of laws establishing 16 years of age as a minimum requirement for industrial employment. Realization that large numbers of people were being deprived of a status symbol or that the American system of education was undemocratic and discriminatory did not foster development of extensive systems of public education. It was part of an economic attempt to withhold a portion of the population from the labor force.

In combination, restrictive child labor laws and large-scale immigration of low status Europeans to the United States fostered recognition of education as a vehicle to a higher class position. Access to more money, better housing, better food, better public and private services was obtainable through education. Since racial, ethnic, and religious background usually influence an individual's position in the stratification system, lower status immigrant groups were cognizant of the structures in American society which permitted economic and social mobility. The Irish, Italian, Polish and Jewish immigrant, to name a few, quickly equated the preservation or partial elimination of their minority group status with educational opportunities. Those who were able to stay in school through high school and, more significantly, through college, were able to acquire some of the prestige and power so unevenly distributed among Americans. Each mobility-oriented group from the Irish in the late nineteenth century to the Negro and Puerto Rican of the late twentieth century recognized and has fought for power and prestige through a principal status-granting structure—education.

The degree to which education has become an important determinant of class position in America can be seen from data on the relation between number of years of formal schooling and lifetime earnings. Income, for our purposes, must be viewed as the means for purchasing other valuable resources. These include the psychological security which an adequate and steady income provides and the ability to satisfy the basic needs of one's family—to provide for the education of one's children and thus assure the future class position of the younger members of the family, satisfactory housing in a "good" environment, and the amenities of recreation, travel and cultural development. In recent years stratification has been based on the distinction between those with many and those with few years of formal education.[4]

Increasingly, employment and economic success in the United States is dependent upon the educational level of the worker. Many different factors undoubtedly contribute to such success including technological and organizational changes. In 1966 men who had completed elementary school could expect to receive, from age 25 to their death, approximately $55,000 more income than men who had less education; a male high school graduate could expect to earn $92,000 more income in his lifetime than the elementary school graduate; and a college graduate could expect to earn $200,000 more than the man who had only completed high school.[5] These figures also indicate that the earning power of men tends to increase with the increase in number of years of schooling. This can be seen from the fact that the ratio of the difference of lifetime earnings between high school and elementary school graduates is 1.7 to 1 while that for college and high school graduates is 2.2 to 1. Undoubtedly a college education is a principal vehicle for a lifetime position in the middle class.

The association between educational levels and the utilization of the labor force is not confined to differences in lifetime income. There is also a direct relationship between level of education and unemployment. Generally, unemployment declines among men and women in all age groups as educational level increases.[6] The black population in the United States, with only 58 percent completing high school compared to 75 percent of the white population, suffers additional handicaps.[7] Slum schools and unequal educational institutions compound the problems. Christopher Jencks put the case succinctly when he stated, "A man's employment prospects are not improved by teaching him ten percent more if, at the same time, all his neighbors are being taught twenty percent more."[8]

Furthermore, with certainty, economic security is one important answer to the question "Education: For What?" in contemporary American society.

For over twenty years—thirty if we include the work of Lloyd Warner in Yankee City—considerable research has been conducted on the relationship of social class and education in the United States. Most of the studies indicate a significant connection between a student's social class and his school history in terms of achievement.[9] This relationship is discussed below in terms of: (a) the affect of a student's cultural and social class background on his test scores, his grades, the curriculum he takes, his extracurricula activities, whether he withdraws or continues his education; (b) the affect of the social class of a child's teacher on the child's successes and failures in school; and (c) the affect of the general social class composition of the particular school attended and the community in which it is located on the child's educational opportunity.

Social Background of the Child

In his classic study of the relationship between social class and the school in the midwest community of Elmtown, August B. Hollingshead found a significant relationship between adolescents' social class and their attitudes toward school, their attendance pattern, and their beliefs about right and wrong.[10] The slum child and the middle class child behave differently. Each has learned from family, friends, and foes, how to act and react in social situations. Each has learned the role he must play and the face he must wear to survive, live, or thrive in his environment. Lower class families do not necessarily place a low value on education. Some research evidence reveals the contrary.[11] The perspective or the culture from which the educational process is viewed differs for the various social classes. The slum youngster daily faces the immediacy of hunger, inadequate clothing, overcrowded and unsanitary living arrangements—the rat infested room with wall-to-wall roaches, too hot in summer and too cold in winter—and sporadic employment or long periods of annual unemployment, never knowing whether or not the family will be able to scrape together next month's rent. Against this backdrop, the middle class value system within the school stressing neatness, cleanliness, order, thrift and planning seem like senseless virtues. Settlement house case records of a number of New York City slum children indicated that in the winter, each child had to collect wood for fuel along the Hudson River before and after school. Without the fuel their families would have suffered immeasurably from the cold. When they were late to school because of these primary responsibilities, they were reprimanded. Punishment for tardiness was unimportant when pitted against the realities of family survival. The teacher who states unequivocally that assignment papers, the child, and his clothing must be neat and clean in order to meet the criteria of respectability often demands the impossible. Soap, water, thread, needles, antibiotics, and insecticides which would permit clean assignment papers and students are luxuries to thousands of families living in poverty. Many of the standards demanded by middle class-oriented schools may only be successfully reached and valued by a child from an economically and socially secure environment.

In general, the lower class family expects the child to fill a position of economic responsibility at the earliest possible moment. Education is often misunderstood or looked upon unfavorably by the family because it does not seem to provide for rapid movement into the labor market, and, on occasion, attempts to focus the child's interest on long range plans for additional education rather than on the assumption of an early adult role.

In 1966 a comprehensive and exciting study of education in the United States—exciting because of the findings and the size of the research project on which they were based—was completed by James S. Coleman and sponsored by the U.S. government.[12] The Coleman Report stated forcefully that the range of student achievement in our schools varied more within particular schools than from one school to another. The report considered the social, economic and educational background provided by the school's students and teachers to be critical. Coleman indicated that the gap between lower and upper class students widen with length of years in school. The longer a disadvantaged child is in school, the greater the influence of his family and his peer groups in comparison with his teachers. In Charles E. Silberman's words,

> To put the case bluntly, we simply do not know how to educate children from lower-class homes. I emphasize "lower class" because the lower achievement of minority youngsters is related primarily to their lower social class, not their race.[13]

In addition, the report revealed a significant amount of racial segregation exists in the North as well as in the South and that considerable differences exist in the achievement levels of racial and ethnic groups throughout the country.[14]

One of the most significant educational questions facing the United States is whether or not it is possible to educate the lower class child into the mainstream of middle class society when the child lives at least three-fourths of his time during the school year, full-time holidays and summers as a functioning member of a subcultural group which may be at odds with the dominant culture. The second question is how! One proposal based on the supposition that the child learns the principal tenets of his culture before the age of five, is to begin public education at a much earlier age. Operation Head Start, which began in the summer of 1965, was an attempt to broaden the preschool experiences of culturally disadvantaged children from low-income families in order to prepare them for formal schooling. Project Head Start was sponsored by the United States government in cooperation with local communities. Professional teachers and volunteer aids trained to assist preschool children were employed in each center throughout the country. Through individual instruction teachers attempted to develop a child's ability to communicate, join in group activities, and adjust to their communities. All children admitted to the program were given medical and dental examinations in order to detect physical defects which might hinder the ability to learn. Head Start has been recognized as the most successful Economic Opportunity Act program.

Since gains achieved from preschool programs are often wiped out later through lack of follow-up, an experimental program developed by New York University's Institute for Developmental Studies extends preschool level through third grade. By utilizing small classes, two teachers for each class, and a battery of curriculum experts, psychologists, social workers and community aides, the emphasis lies in developing a child's self-confidence and motivation.[15] This is an area where we have only begun to consider the possibilities and alternatives.

The Teacher and Social Class

We have emphasized that each of us, overtly and covertly, ranks, measures, and places those with whom we come in daily contact in terms of those class factors which our neighborhood, friends, and community rate high. How many times a month do we casually ask, "What does his father do?" "Is the 'X' family active in the community?" or "Where did he go to college?" Whether we wish to or not, deny it or not, the answers affect our relationship with the individuals involved. They allow us to place ourselves and define the role we play in relation to others. In turn, we pass on to others our conception of deference or superiority of another individual by the way we treat them, by the way we introduce them, by the way we speak of them or refer to them. Since this behavior is part of all our lives, it would be almost impossible not to carry it over into the attitudes and behavior of teachers toward pupils of different social class backgrounds. The social class background of a teacher and the attitudes she has accumulated over her lifetime toward other classes affect her ability to teach and to help children relate to our society.

In *Elmtown's Youth*, Hollingshead indicated the relationship between a child's place in the Elmtown class structure and it's affect on teachers:

> ... New teachers soon learn from their associations with other teachers, townspeople, parents, and adolescents "who is who" and what one

should or should not do to avoid trouble. Trouble, a constant fear among the high school teachers, takes many forms which range from adverse reports by students to their parents to threats in Board meetings to dismiss so-and-so for such-and-such. Teachers, if they are successful, act judiciously in their relations with the children of the powerful; on appropriate occasions they look the other way. Teachers experienced in the system warn newcomers about this boy or that girl. Narratives, gossip, a hint here, a warning there, remarks in faculty meetings, give the teacher some understanding of the situation.[16]

Whether a teacher reacts positively or negatively to some of the factors which make up the class position of a child's family—he will react. A teacher who comes from a lower class background and has embraced middle class culture patterns may exhibit a number of different responses to lower class children. Havighurst and Neugarten suggest that one teacher:

> . . . . for example, tortured by inner feelings of inferiority, may regard his origin as a thing of shame to be lived down. Another, having a powerful identification with father and older siblings, may so conduct himself as to retain and exemplify his family's social rank, and in so doing ally himself with pupils and parents of similar origin. A third, imbued with strong achievement drives, may seek to deny his origin by accepting middle-class standards and by being unusually strict, if not actually punitive, against the children and parents from whose ranks he sees himself as having risen by dint of self-denial.[17]

Combined with the cultural differences between middle and lower class families, the middle class family is often more geared toward educational achievement, is oriented to the future, and may be largely child centered. The lower class family, in comparison, is generally more adult centered, is oriented to the present with an uncertain future, and is likely to hold physical toughness and practicality as virtues. For this reason many teachers and pupils are faced with difficult culture gaps.[18] For example, doctoral students in a University Counseling and Guidance Institute, who were employed in high school systems in four regions of the United States, were requested to submit a list of the most important social problems with which they had to deal. Several which were considered high priority, in addition to school desegregation, were student smoking, and inappropriate student appearance, such as wearing shirts outside of pants or long hair. Although class discussions pinpointed the fact that none of these "violations" were essentially connected with a student's ability to learn, the counselors stressed the importance of conformity.

Their principals and school boards felt appearance and behavior extremely important in the educational process.

Teachers generally rank in the middle class and identify themselves as middle class in terms of styles of life, attitudes, and values.[19] The middle class-oriented teacher may find it extremely difficult to understand lower class or upper class children and their families, and therefore tend to value and reward the middle class child.[20] In the former case, Becker and Winget found that even more than favoritism was involved. The middle class teacher who began his career in a lower class or slum school often found discipline and the morals of the pupils so unacceptable that he transferred to a more desirable school as soon as possible.[21]

Havighurst and Neugarten recognized that the relationship of middle class teachers to lower class children does not provide the only example of the interaction of social origin and teaching. There are teachers, they state, who have just as much difficulty working with upper or middle class children and prefer not to work with the advantaged child.[22] The latter may be as challenging to teach as the disadvantaged child. An additional factor creating problems for teachers of advantaged children may be the upper class parent who often has had more education and societal experience than the teacher, and who may not hesitate to make demands or raise questions which the teacher is unable to meet or answer.

Havighurst and Neugarten contributed further insight into the relationship of social class and the ability to teach by indicating that the social class background of the teacher must be considered in relation to the individual personality. A teacher's social background may not make him ineffective in dealing with children from other class backgrounds.[23] Individual differences are very important and must be considered, but it would be foolhardy to conclude that living in a particular subculture does not color the attitudes of large groups of people toward individuals from different racial, religious, ethnic and economic backgrounds. Persons who argue that men who loiter around the court house and railroad station, or that the urban core are "just born lazy" are not expressing personality differences or scientific conclusions. They express cultural views learned from parents, relatives, and peers.

In conclusion patterns of teacher deference, discrimination, and favoritism toward children often relate to the teacher's own cultural background through which he views the child. On the one hand, the teacher reacts, categorizes, and defines his role as many of us do when we learn the social background about a stranger. Major federal, state and local conflicts are being waged over the issue of whether a child's class position should influence his treatment in a democratic institution.

The Social Class Composition of the School

Contributing to the problems facing American education is the realization of minority group leaders that schools differ in communities large enough to support more than one elementary or Junior/Senior high school. The differences, they feel, are related to a group's opportunities for mobility in American society. In essence, there is considerable truth to the charges of discrimination, albeit, it is not only a racial and ethnic problem but a problem for all lower class families.

The community school has developed at least two major classification patterns based on (1) a child's ability and (2) his social class. Most schools develop either advanced groups within a class or grade, or, when numbers permit, segregate children into grades by ability. Such a system presumably eases the teaching burden and problem. The second pattern, social class, may be closely related to ability in terms of the cultural advantages the middle and upper class child may have in comparison with his lower class classmate. In addition, in larger communities or urban centers with a number of schools, construction and districting, whether based on natural geographic phenomenon or not, usually has been centered around a homogeneous area where the school population is drawn from one or at the most two social classes. In many instances, the schools with parent-teacher organizations concerned with high educational levels for their children often secure more than their share of the educational equipment and programs. Adding to this disproportion of goods is the attempt by teachers to seek transfers to the "better" schools.[24] The slum school, located in a lower class neighborhood, often with high crime rates, with an old, outdated, poorly equipped plant does not represent a particularly attractive work situation to the middle-class-oriented teacher. The child in the last years of the twentieth century who is attending a slum school or a rural one or two-room school is handicapped. In most of these schools the new math, programmed reading, science education with exciting experiments for grades 1-6 are as remote as the moon and often just about as comprehensible.

School Desegregation

Utilizing the educational institution as a spring board or ladder to economic and social success has been a frustrating experience for the American Negro. He did not meet with the successes of other ethnic and religious minorities whose struggles were fortified by various forms of power, even the occasional use of force. The Negro was not able to or did not vote. He was not able to gain low level political office from which

Contemporary Problems in American Education   77

to manipulate further gains. His family was female-centered, lacking the
economic strength to plan and implement educational aims.
In addition, the legion of public school systems in the United States
has been responsive to the major influences within their host communities. The educational policies developed by city, county, and state
boards of education have been conditioned by political and economic
forces, leadership, and pressure groups. Officials responded to the prejudices and social attitudes of many community leaders. As a result, by
the 1960's not only were schools in the South segregated by race but also
hundreds of elementary schools in the northeast had student bodies
composed of more than 60 percent Negroes. Except for some Northern
high schools serving large geographic areas, most blacks in all parts of
the United States went to predominantly black schools.[25] See Table 2.

TABLE 2

PERCENT OF NEGRO PUPILS IN SCHOOLS IN GRADES 1 AND 12
IN WHICH THEY ARE IN THE MAJORITY, BY REGION,[a]
FALL 1965*

Region	Grade	
	1	12
Metropolitan North	72	35
Metropolitan South	97	95
Nonmetropolitan North	70	8
Nonmetropolitan South	92	85
United States	87	66

[a] South includes the States of the old Confederacy and Arizona, Kentucky, New
Mexico, Oklahoma, and West Virginia. All other states are defined as being in
the North.

* Source: James S. Coleman, et. al., Equality of Educational Opportunity
(Washington, D.C.: U.S. Government Printing Office, 1966), p. 40.

Unquestionably the black citizen's demand for full parity has been
severely affected by the two great educational handicaps of segregated
schools and inferior instruction. The two are closely related. As John H.
Fischer has asserted, the school with a predominantly black student body
is "almost universally considered of lower status and less desirable," and
it has an unfortunate psychological effect upon a child to attend a school
in which the students as a group are viewed as "less able, less successful,
and less acceptable than the majority of the community."[26]

The three legal cases[27] in which the Supreme Court ruled that segregated education is unequal education and violates the Fifth and the Fourteenth Amendments of the U.S. Constitution did not bear fruit until a decade later. Between 1954 and 1965, national attention focused largely on the Southern community. In case after case, Negroes insisted that the legal structure which had compelled school segregation for decades be removed and schools reorganized without regard to race. Often black children living in the shadow of a white school had to walk several miles to an all black school.

With the exception of the border states where the dual system of education sometimes represented extreme financial burdens, integration of the Southern schools made little progress between 1956 and 1964.[28] When the Federal Government through the Department of Health, Education and Welfare demanded desegregation plans from Southern school districts and threatened to withhold federal funds, major steps in desegregation were taken. Numerous court actions ordering desegregation and eliminating all feasible alternatives strengthened the tenuous resolve of many local school boards by legitimizing desegregation.

As major gains were made in breaking down *de jure* (legal) school segregation in the Southern community, new drives began in other regions where the problems differed. The attack in the late sixties moved from *de jure* to *de facto* school segregation. *De facto* school segregation usually arises out of residential patterns where people of the same color, nationality, or religion live in the same neighborhood defined as a school attendance district. The causes and problems of *de facto* segregation are exceedingly complex. Their solution, resolution, or management may indeed be the major problem of the next several decades. As *de jure* segregation failed in larger urban centers in the South rapid attempts to develop *de facto* segregation were made. Dilapidated Negro housing was torn down, urban renewal projects were developed which pushed Negroes into all-Negro sections where school attendance could be more effectively controlled. In most of the major cities in the United States, new groups found housing in neighborhoods where rent was cheap. These were usually the oldest areas—the slums, where poverty, disease, disorder, economic and social discrimination, and where dilapidated and congested housing were prevalent.

One of the problems of the slum is the slum school. Outside of the South, school attendance traditionally has been based on geography. School system boundaries within which children must attend school often reflect economic, social, and racial homogeneity. Usually restrictions are made against transfer to schools outside of the residence area.

By the 1960's Negroes made up the largest proportion of slum dwellers. Unlike the white immigrant who moved into the mainstream of

American life, the black faces numerous handicaps. In addition to the problems of higher rates of family disorganization and illegitimacy, he faces discrimination in employment and, regardless of economic resources, encounters further discrimination in his efforts to acquire housing outside of the ghetto. Many Negroes have migrated from southern communities and have further educational and social handicaps. During a decade when major strides had been taken toward school desegregation in the South, the black living in urban centers in other regions vocally and violently expressed his discontent regarding the largely or entirely segregated schools. Protests have demanded increased integration.

Developing integrated schools which satisfy the demands and needs of black and white communities may prove unattainable. Both recognize that teacher-pupil learning is only a small segment of a child's education. What the child learns from his classmates may be equally important. What a child learns from ghetto or slum classmates may prove a liability in later years. On the other hand, the middle and upper class parent looks with disfavor on contacts and learning experiences for his child which will not prove an asset in the critical struggle for wealth and power.

In one of the highly controversial articles Joseph Alsop wrote in *The New Republic*, he summarized the results of the cultural and educational lag for low income Negroes:

> Briefly, 400,000-plus eighteen-year-old Negroes are annually injected into this country's socioeconomic bloodstream; but of these 400,000-plus, hardly 10 percent have the true equivalent of a normal white middle-class high-school education—which means no more than an ordinary blue-collar education! In other words, we annually add to the American body politic no less than 360,000 Negroes of both sexes who are wholly unequipped to get or hold any job in which grossly deficient schooling is a handicap—and that means, more and more with every passing year, just about any job at all! If a malevolent and astute racist were asked to design a system guaranteed to prevent Negro achievement, to promote bitterness, frustration and violence, to perpetuate and even to intensify discrimination, this is the system that he would surely come up with. To reform this system, any outlay, any sacrifice, any effort, however great and however painful, is not merely a moral imperative; it is also a political and social imperative of the most pressing and urgent character. And the system is not going to be reformed, alas, by more desegregation orders.[29]

Sides have been closely drawn in the quest for a solution: some people believe complete integration is the only answer while others state that

substantial integration will never occur and therefore society must
markedly upgrade slum schools. The amount of public support among
power and decision-making groups for the latter is questionable. As
Jencks forcefully concludes in the case of the latter,

> . . . If Washington begins to pour large sums of money into the slums
> to equalize opportunity, middle class areas will respond by pouring
> more money into *their* schools, in order to keep ahead.[30]

Forms of Management

American society requires more fruitful alternatives to both the problem of the slum school and of *de facto* school segregation in the large
urban centers. A number of alternatives have been widely considered:
1) rezoning attendance areas, 2) reclassification of schools, 3) development of new school building programs, 4) planned assignment of
pupils, and 5) the development of education parks.

1) *REZONING ATTENDANCE AREAS.*   Whether school boards
submitted to community pressures over the years isolating lower socioeconomic families and races into different school zones or whether urban
growth was responsible for separating older housing areas from newer
neighborhoods, school zones reflect the socioeconomic status of their
residents. Hopefully, by rezoning school areas to alter the previous class
and racial character, a more heterogeneous school population will result.

2) *RECLASSIFICATION OF SCHOOLS.*   Rather than maintain
schools serving the popular grade levels—1-6 or 1-8—schools would be
reclassified to handle fewer grades and a larger geographic area. One
school might handle all pupils in a large heterogeneous attendance area
from kindergarten through second grade; an adjacent school would
handle grades three through six. Hopefully, the expansion of the school
area would promote integration—at least on the fringe of a segregated
neighborhood.

3) *NEW SCHOOL BUILDING PROGRAMS.*   This solution calls
for revisions in building programs, which are usually planned many years
in advance, in order that new school sites be selected in locations which
will allow for integration on the fringe of a white and black residential
area, both of which would be included in the school district. Essentially
this serves to prevent the construction of schools within the Negro ghetto.

4) *PLANNED ASSIGNMENT OF PUPILS.*[31]   Plans 1 through 3
for rezoning, reclassification, and new buildings promote some integration along the boundaries of segregated neighborhoods. They do not

treat the ills of schools deep in the heart of a segregated neighborhood. Proposals for these situations involve moving some of the children, upon parental request, to less crowded, predominantly white schools in other parts of the city. Since reassignment must be requested by parents and sometimes involves transportation problems, this plan provides service for only the few children whose parents are motivated to seek transfer. The majority will remain in segregated schools.

5) *THE EDUCATION PARK.*[32]   The education park offers the best opportunity for success. The neighborhood school system would be abandoned and a centrally located consolidated campus-style school complex would be constructed to serve as many as 20,000 students. The boundaries of the district would be drawn to include many diverse residential areas. The larger size of the education park would allow greater staff specialization and more effective deployment through a centralized administration.

Most of these proposals represent departures from the traditional character of public schools.[33] Increased verbalized discontent with the segregated school, supported by strikes and riots, will increase the alternatives necessary to develop equality of educational opportunity and system-wide educational excellence in the big city. The attempts which have been made to implement these approaches have created considerable furor and conflict, mostly on a social class basis. Regardless of how liberal they purport to be middle class parents fear that their children may be educationally crippled if thrown into close proximity with large numbers of culturally disadvantaged children and this hinders problem management.

PUBLIC EDUCATION AND THE FEDERAL GOVERNMENT

Over the years, Americans have placed tremendous value on the development and control of education on the local community level. It has been a value held by large numbers of people from different social class levels for what appears to be a variety of complex reasons. In addition to the economic questions involved, there is a legion of concern which has been publicly enhanced by local citizen groups and politicians that education is one of the few remaining areas of local democratic participation and control still reserved by Americans. Its loss, it is felt, would dramatize the bitter struggle between local government and big government above the local level. For others, greater out-of-the-community control would limit the opportunity for disproportionate economic and quality personnel allotment to schools within the same community. As a result of these concerns, education in the United States consists of a complex network of approximately 21,697 separate systems controlled by over 10,000 school board members.[34] The maintenance of control demands that state and local governments carry the major cost of elementary and secondary education. With increased national mobility of population, population growth, and emphasis on education, the costs of elementary and secondary education have risen sharply from approximately 12 billion dollars in 1956 to 31 billion in 1968.[35] As costs rise, the social policy question of who should pay for education is reviewed. While state and local governments may continue to pay the major educational bills, the problems of cost for rapid expansion of new programs, construction, and state and regional economic differences have led to a new interest in federal support to education at all levels.

Historically the schools in the more affluent states have been years ahead of those in the economically disadvantaged ones. For example, while Massachusetts passed a compulsory education law in 1647, in 1870 the average length of schooling in most of the United States was less than 4½ years.[36]

The average annual salary for an elementary and secondary school teacher in less affluent Mississippi is $4,505 and $4,739, respectively. In New York State, elementary and secondary school teachers average $7,900 and $8,500, respectively.[37] Average national per pupil expenditures for public school education is $623 annually; Mississippi spends $346 per pupil while New York spends $982.[38]

Until the nineteen-fifties, attempts to encourage major federal interest in education to raise the quality of programs through adequate financing were cries in the wilderness. Even state control was limited largely to financial and service functions. Local communities enjoyed the advantages derived from control in terms of the availability of political positions and spoils—the school board, appointment of teachers and supervisors, and educational purchases. Education, in most communities, had become a useful political training ground and in many cases a lucrative business enterprise. By the midfifties it became apparent that major differences continued to exist and intensify regionally and from community to community because of local control and inadequate financing on the state and local levels. Since society's ability to conduct its political and economic affairs was directly dependent upon education, it became a national problem, not an exclusively local or state affair. While education was not considered a cure-all for the ills of society, it generally altered man's attitudes toward sickness, toward certain types of crime (exclusive of white collar crime), and toward unemployment. More conclusively, the competition of scientific skills with the Soviet Union, the inability of large percentages of young men from certain areas

to qualify for military service, and the tremendous increase in population mobility in the sixties which dumped large numbers of men and
women with inadequate education on states and communities, made the
control of educational levels and standards a national concern.

For at least thirty years, some educators have balked at and refuted
the expectation that each state could and would provide adequate financing for its own system of education. Only recently have interest groups
in large population-drawing metropolises and Congress echoed this concern. The educational differences between the economic have and have
nots continued to increase, regardless of the high percentage of the local
and state tax dollar appropriated to education. See Table 3. Limited

TABLE 3

STATE EXPENDITURE ON PUBLIC ELEMENTARY AND SECONDARY SCHOOL EDUCATION BY STATE RANK[a]

Rank	*Average Annual Current Expenditure Per Pupil in Average Daily Attendance 1966–1967*	
	State	*Amount*
1.	N.Y.	$912
2.	Alaska	877
3.	N.J.	740
4.	Hawaii	669
5.	Wyo.	668
6.	Mont.	665
7.	Conn.	657
8.	Oreg.	645
9.	Ariz.	635
10.	Nev.	635
11.	Minn.	634
12.	Del.	626
13.	Calif.	613
14.	Wis.	608
15.	Md.	603
16.	Mass.	599
17.	Pa.	597
18.	Mich.	596
19.	R.I.	596
20.	Ill.	591
21.	N. Mex.	586

TABLE 3 CONTINUED

Rank	Average Annual Current Expenditure Per Pupil in Average Daily Attendance 1966–1967	
	State	Amount
22.	Wash.	$581
23.	Ind.	580
24.	Vt.	578
25.	Colo.	570
26.	Iowa	567
27.	La.	567
28.	Va.	556
29.	Kans.	552
30.	Okla.	533
31.	N.H.	523
32.	S. Dak.	521
33.	Mo.	506
34.	Utah	500
35.	N. Dak.	485
36.	Fla.	479
37.	Ohio	468
38.	Nebr.	464
39.	Tex.	449
40.	Ga.	430
41.	Maine	430
42.	Idaho	418
43.	N.C.	411
44.	W. Va.	411
45.	Tenn.	404
46.	Ky.	400
47.	Ark.	393
48.	Ala.	390
49.	S.C.	373
50.	Miss.	335
	D.C.	693
	United States	**569**

ᵃ Source: U.S. Department of Health, Education, and Welfare, Office of Education, Advanced Data, *Fall 1966 Statistics of Public Schools* (OE-20007-66).

resources within a school district have probably been responsible for uneven distribution of funds to schools within a district. The average annual expenditure per pupil or school is often misleading. Most intensive studies of school districts have shown that schools attended by lower class children have lower expenditures per pupil than those attended by middle and upper class children.[39]

Two important factors led to the intervention of the federal government into education: (1) state and local control permitted undemocratic educational opportunities determined by socio-economic class and racial and ethnic origin and (2) the inability of education to compete as successfully for the tax dollar as many nonschool activities. Factually, children from lower income groups and particularly those from the nonwhite, non-English speaking family experienced unequal educational opportunities for decades. Although efforts had been made to alter patterns of educational inequality in the past, the most effective attempts occurred after the midfifties. These were linked with factor (2) above.

By the latter part of the twentieth century, education in the United States had become such a complex and expensive matter that few states could adequately finance their own system. Expectations of "going it alone" were no longer realistic. Expanding communities and the growing population sharply increased the financial demands on state and local governments. State legislators were literally bombarded by financial requests from official, semi-official and private interest groups. There were demands for funding of road building projects, for hospitals, for libraries, and for welfare agencies, each attempting to expand their annual grants, each offering valuable and necessary services to state residents, and each in a continuous and growing "life and growth" competition with education for the tax dollar.

As long as local school boards were assured some state support and competition for funds was limited, local control was assured. Social and economic changes, scientific discoveries and population growth in the space age altered attitudes toward federal support, albeit control of public education. Local school officials, boards, businessmen and community leaders who benefited over the years by their ability to control who became educated and how, found their school systems no longer could survive financially with only local and state aid. The competition from other program areas was far too great. Programs of road building, hospital construction, and welfare were in a more advantageous position to compete for state and local tax dollars because they benefited from matching federal grants. This made them appear to be better business propositions to economy-minded legislators. State allocations to school support bring no added dollars and cents benefit. For example, under some of the federal highway construction programs, a dollar of state money may add eight or nine dollars of federal support.

In comparison with the federal structure, state and local tax structures have proven grossly inadequate for the increased pressure for services. Between 1930 and 1968, national income rose from $86.8 billion to approximately $722.5 billion;[40] state and local government revenues totaled $91,626,000 billion.[41] The federal government has been successful in tapping new revenue for new services over the last forty years while state and local sources have had little success. Until the expansion of federal spending for education in the midsixties, public education continued to rely and still does to a considerable extent, on financial support based on a limited, almost inflexible tax base.

Attempts at Management

The problem of whether or not to accept Federal funding in the local school districts in order to provide a quality education was exceedingly complex and very controversial. Local school boards had several options: (1) Continue to inadequately finance local school programs from the state and local coffer as they had in the past (2) Attempt to alter the state and local tax structures through drastic reforms and (3) Allow the federal government to assume the responsibility for a significant portion of public school support. This problem was further complicated by the increased recognition on the local level that social mobility accrued from education. During the late forties and fifties, returning servicemen, through the use of G.I. educational benefits, were able to acquire education which formerly would have been denied many of them for financial reasons. It allowed thousands to move from a lower to a higher class position.

The increased importance of high school and college accreditation in terms of access to the college or graduate school of one's choice were additional reasons for developing new sources of revenue. Accreditation and the development of enriched academic programs would cost money if adequate staffing, facilities, and equipment were to be acquired. Few school boards or communities would accept the first option as a solution. The second alternative seemed equally unrealistic when the record of consistent attempts by other interest groups to alter state tax structures were reviewed. Cities whose fiscal problems have been precarious have failed for decades to initiate change.

In light of the alternatives available, it appears that if education is to be strengthened, the federal government must participate financially. Nevertheless there has been throughout U.S. history a fear that federal money is synonymous with federal control. Citizens on all levels of society have taken different positions concerning the value of federal participation. Many tag local control of all institutions as good and federal control as evil. Certainly it would be unjust to assume that federal funding should be given to all worthy public programs whether they are aligned with the national ethos or not. The dispersal of most public funds have and ought to have "strings attached" if they are to be spent in the best interest of all of the public from whom they were subscribed. Ironically, amid all the furor favoring local control of educational decision making, it was the inability of state and local governments to adequately finance public education which sabotaged much of the local control of schools. As a result, Congress enacted laws in the midsixties giving the federal government a much larger role in education.

From a monumental but nevertheless unauspicious beginning with the passage in 1917 of the Smith-Hughes Act providing $7 million annually for the promotion of vocational education in agriculture, trades and industry, and home economics, fifty years later the federal government was appropriating billions of dollars annually. Federal spending in public education changed little until 1958. For over forty years it underwent little change compared to other federal spending. With the concern for Soviet space achievements combined with the emergence of the civil rights movement, the situation changed. In 1958 Congress passed the National Defense Act which, with its amendments in 1963, 1964, and 1965, authorized, among other provisions, loans to college students, support to science and liberal arts programs, fellowships to federal colleges, institutes to provide counselor-training, and languages and area study centers for over thirty college and university campuses. In rapid succession came the Area Development Act of 1961 providing millions for vocational training of the unemployed and underemployed in designated "redevelopment areas"; the Manpower Development and Training Act of 1962 and its 1963 amendment to provide training for the hard core unemployed and unskilled workers or those whose skills had become obsolete as a result of technological change; the Vocational Education Act of 1963 which attempted to update the Smith-Hughes and George-Barden Acts by bringing vocational education into a closer harmony with labor market realities; the Higher Education Facilities Act of 1963 to assist in the construction of undergraduate academic facilities; and the Elementary and Secondary Education Act of 1965 to improve the education of children from low-income families and to aid local schools.

In addition, some portions of the Economic Opportunity Act of 1964, the Mental Retardation Facilities and Community Mental Health Center Construction Act of 1963, the Health Professions Educational Assistance

Act of 1963, the Library Services and Construction Act of 1964, the Civil Rights Act of 1964: Titles IV and VI, the Nurses Training Act of 1964, and the Appalachian Aid Bill of 1965 contained some assistance to educational programs.

By 1968 Congress was appropriating over 10 billion dollars a year for public education, more than triple the allocation in 1960. While substantial federal support has been directed toward school/university construction programs and research, large sums have been made available to improve school libraries, purchase equipment and to employ educational specialists unheard of before except in affluent public school systems. The gift-giving has been a mixed blessing to local and state officials. Federal funding has not come without demands and suggestions for rearrangement of local social patterns related to education. Demands for student racial integration, staff integration, racial balance, and stipulations for new building placement have conflicted with many local community and regional culture patterns. Federal demands are geared to give the lower class child equal access to an education which would enable him to become socially and economically mobile. It is an attempt to develop controls over public education which would allow the poor man and the minority group member to participate more fully in the bounties of middle and possibly upper class life in the United States by raising the level of teaching and facilities in all schools. The furor aroused on state and local levels by federal attempts to control, alter, and shape American education is not essentially a reaction to control as such. It is rather local leadership's attempt to determine who shall control education. Education in the United States has never been an autonomous institution. It has been the product of decades of conflict and compromise among dominant institutional groups. It has, in turn, been the product of goals, procedures, and control of the church, the family, and business.[42] In fact, its survival as an institution in American society has been based on its willingness to change goals and structure to adapt to fluctuating circumstances. For example, we will consider briefly two previous institutional controls over education—the church and business. The major difference between these controls and Federal control was the social class groups they attempted to service.

Control of Education by the Church and Business

The early settlement of America was principally, in terms of the Protestant revolt, a middle class struggle against the power of the Church and state in Europe.[43] The aim of the struggle was to provide a government under which middle-class economic interests might thrive. It represented an attempt by mercantile interests to ascend the social class system—not democratize or revolt against the established social class hierarchy! As a consequence, during the Colonial period, churches dominated the school. The primary function of schools was religious, not vocational.[44] The first "public" education act in the United States, the Massachusetts Act of 1647, made public education mandatory and provided the population with vocational training to assist them against delusion by Satan. Let us clarify the fact that the term "public" is very misleading to the twentieth century mind: public was defined as being the members of the established church of that particular region. Universal education did not develop in the United States until the 19th and in many cases until the 20th century.[45]

The transition from church control during the 17th and 18th centuries to business dominated education in the 19th century was related to the similarities in the value systems of these two groups. In *Protestant Ethic and the Spirit of Capitalism*, Max Weber maintained that the Protestant ethic was very similar in ideology to the "spirit of capitalism."[46] It was only a short distance from the preordained salvation of Luther and Calvin to the identification of the saved as those favorably endowed in this world. Both hard work and profit were defined as moral virtues. This definition affected the attitudes of the gainfully and successfully employed middle and upper classes toward the nonworking public welfare recipient.

As the influence of religious ideology was supplemented by the belief one could achieve salvation through material success, religion became a less powerful influence than the commercial motive. Education realized the requirements of a business oriented society. During the early 19th century when child labor was an economic essential, business did not consider education necessary. When labor unrest developed in mid-century, business leaders began to see the importance of the educational institution as an agent of social control. From an educational system which focussed on character building, changes were introduced which indoctrinated children with the business ideology. Business hoped that public education would provide their community with security in the face of growing unrest among the working classes. The business ideology became so completely woven into the curriculum that during the latter part of the nineteenth century, it was supported by educators and by their professional organization, the National Education Association. During the labor disorder of 1877, the president of the NEA stated that schools should teach discipline and respect for property and for the rights of organized industry. The NEA took a firm position against strikes and other forms of resistance to big business.[47]

Just as early education was designed to preserve the position of religion in American society, during the early industrial period in this country schools were expected to preserve the status-quo of the commercial classes. The problem confronting education today in terms of federal control is the fear that the federal government will utilize public education to develop new ideologies and new avenues of social mobility which will alter the status-quo of the "commercial" or middle and upper classes in the United States. They fear that the educational institution which has been a conservative and a preservative force will become a radical and innovative agency. At its 1967 national convention the NEA, whose basic strength has resided in rural and small urban centers where conservatism and traditional control has been strong, urged the federal government to abandon its categorical aid program which earmarked funds for special purposes. It proposed that federal funds be given to the states for use as the local community and states see fit.[48] On the question of whether the federal government should play the role of "partner or patron" in American education, the NEA supported the traditional approach—patron. Whoever wins temporarily and controls public education will manage the educational institution, deciding which problems to solve, who shall be educated, and how.

THE INCREASED MILITANCY OF THE TEACHING PROFESSION

In an educational sociology class consisting almost entirely of education majors, a student asked the instructor how he felt about teachers picketing for higher salaries or better working conditions. The student then proceeded to inform the class that any teacher who joined a union or picketed lost the respect of the community in which he taught and was a disgrace to his profession. All except three students readily agreed. The majority maintained that every fall there seemed to be an increase in the incidence of this "unseemly" behavior. Over the years, with the growth of public education, stereotypes have developed of how teachers ought to behave. For example, Willard Waller describes the role of the teacher in American society in the thirties:

> . . . the school has become almost equally with the church the repository of ideals. The teacher, like the minister, possesses a high degree of social

sacredness. He must be a little better than other men; it is therefore better if he does not smoke, and he certainly must not drink. In fact, he must be the master of all the negative virtues. It is his part to enjoy the finer things of life, literature, art, and the best music. . . . Like the minister, the teacher excites very real reverence. . . .[49]

Four decades later changes had occurred in the social position of the teacher. Substantial increases in the percentage of individuals completing high school and college lowered the status of teachers. As more and more people earned college and graduate degrees, the teacher found he was no longer esteemed as one of the few educated citizens in the community— he was only one of a sizeable, rapidly growing group.[50]

As education became more complex, the men and women attracted to it became more heterogenous—particularly in large urban centers. This heterogeneity will continue to alter the way the teacher sees himself playing the role of teacher and it will necessitate changes in the expectations of the community. For example, a large proportion of interviewers for new teaching positions formally question whether the applicant drinks, smokes, and attends church regularly. These inquiries imply a certain moral/ethical expectation and commitment which may be linked to the views of community leaders of what a teacher ought to be. While stereotypes of teacher roles in terms of behavior patterns have evolved, other expectations have resulted in additional conflict. Many community leaders have expected teachers to dress commensurate with middle class patterns and to participate in "worthwhile" cultural and social endeavors. While these may be justifiable demands, they also are costly in monetary terms. Usually teacher salaries do not permit the fulfillment of these expectations. While teachers have been granted some prestige in American society, they are on a much lower socioeconomic level than most other professional groups.

With the large-scale expansion of public education since 1950, role conflicts for the teacher related to class and status have emerged more clearly. Teacher shortages, teacher dropouts occasioned by recruitment from business and industry, and the increased status of education have done little to increase the teacher's prestige as a professional or raise his income level commensurate with other professionals. Unless blessed with inherited wealth and family position, the teacher is seldom classified above middle class.[51] His new militancy is a result of the teacher's status dilemma based on his identity as both professional and employee. The incompatibility of the latter and the role conflicts they create have prevented the teacher from progressing as either employee or professional in terms of status and ready access to more tangible rewards. As a professional meeting the recognized definition, teachers should be bound by national standards of the educator set by nationwide organizations. Loyalty of a professional is oriented first and foremost to these standards and to professional colleagues largely outside the community. The teacher however is confounded by his employee position which is locally controlled, and whose rules and regulations are locally made and locally enforced. Working conditions, salaries, and the selection of personnel are local responsibilities. The school board or controlling agent is concerned with more than the traditional "sins" of drink, tobacco, and sex. Teachers are expected to refrain from partisan politics, place their student's welfare above that of their own family's economic interests, and seldom make demands for changes in educational programs set by the board.

The multiplicity of teacher roles, particularly those clustered about the employee status versus professional aspirations, has limited professional development. A profession must control its own work, advance economically, and control entree into the profession in terms of education and training. Although specialists in education, teachers seldom lead the drive for innovation in curriculum. Although most teachers consider themselves professionals, they do not control the schools and school systems in which they operate. Unlike physicians who would challenge an inadequate hospital and who have raised the level of medical education and training so that few may enter the profession, the teacher is immobile. He makes few decisions on academic education, employment practices, and school policy. Instead, by the late sixties, unable to secure even a modicum of control from local authorities and unable to increase professional status through educational organizations such as the NEA, teachers have resorted to other methods of increasing salaries and control —the union and union techniques. The use of the strike, bargaining, and picketing, do not solve the basic problem facing the teacher: elevation of the profession. Only control of entree into the profession, control of professional education, and control of the school will solve the problem of low status.

While most Americans would tacitly agree that teacher salaries need to be improved, considerable disagreement exists regarding the role of the teacher in the effort to improve his own status. Many feel that the teacher should apply gentle and invisible pressure, and not play the part of a threatening, picketing, vocal individual whose actions are incompatible with the view of the teacher as a dedicated public servant concerned with the welfare of children.

The average incomes of elementary and secondary school teachers in the United States in 1966 were $6,293 and $6,768, respectively.[52]

Starting salaries in some states were only a few hundred dollars above the $3,000 income level defined as poverty. As professionals, teachers have not benefited as substantially as have other professional groups from the economic progress of the 1950's and '60's. Social status and economic gains for most professionals are usually made through professional organizations. Some of these organizations have records as strong lobbies and as effective agents in producing and preventing changes, such as the American Medical Association. One of the principle reasons for the failure of teachers to progress in their drive for status has been the orientation of the two national teacher organizations: the National Education Association, founded in 1870, which almost a hundred years later has a membership of 1,028,000; and the American Federation of Teachers, founded in 1916, with a membership by the late sixties of 146,000.[53] The NEA's concern for the professional status of the teacher has involved limited lobbying functions. Its early program consisted of an annual convention and a published report of its proceedings. Research into various teacher-welfare problems was begun in 1922.

The National Education Association historically supported whichever group was in power. Amid the struggles of organized labor in the late 19th century, the president of the NEA stated that schools should teach respect for property and for the rights of organized industry.[54] Educators in the eighteen-seventies and eighties rarely sympathized with the struggles of laborers. During the Spanish-American War, which historians feel was based on expansionist motives, the NEA stated it had been "entered upon in the most unselfish spirit and from the loftiest of motives."[55]

The position of the NEA, in oversimplified terms, is to align all persons engaged in the field of education and to work for the improvement of teaching as a profession. In line with this approach, the NEA holds workshops and a variety of other local, state, and national meetings geared to the improvement of educational techniques and the solution of contemporary educational problems such as student and staff desegregation. Few concerted attempts have been made by the NEA to raise teacher salaries commensurate with the needs of professionals attempting to fill middle class positions or to limit local control of education.

At the other end of the continuum the American Federation of Teachers supports the view that classroom teachers could benefit more effectively by regarding themselves as workers. They would affiliate with the organized labor movement in the United States. Early attempts to organize teachers into unions met with little success. In 1904 Margaret Haley, a Chicago classroom teacher and pioneer in the teachers' union movement, urged teachers to unite with other laborers.[56] Educators preferred to utilize other methods. Many argued that union affiliation was the subversion of the welfare of children to the interests of the working class.[57]

Over the last twenty years, there has been an increase in the number of local teacher's unions in large cities. Most of the unions are locals of the American Federation of Teachers. The AFT is affiliated with the American Federation of Labor-Congress of Industrial Organizations (AFL-CIO), and utilizes the techniques, procedures, and other forms of assistance offered by the parent body in the achievement of goals. Walter Reuther, who is interested in the unionization of white-collar workers, has given support to the teacher-labor movement.[58] In general the AFT has been almost entirely concerned with the attainment of higher salaries, released time, sabbaticals, and the acquisition of some degree of governing control over the public schools through the organization and marshaling of militant action when necessary.

The AFT has had some successes in the large cities.[59] With the increase in its efforts in the late sixties, the NEA has been challenged to devise new methods to compete effectively with the AFT. While a large number of AFT members hold membership in both organizations and consider their functions as separate and complementary, continued successes by AFT could alter the membership differences between the two organizations and could result in a major change in the economic level of the teacher. The question of whether professionalization and use of some forms of power such as collective bargaining/coercive action are as incompatible as is currently believed would have to be faced.

Certainly NEA's action at its 1963 national convention when it adopted guidelines for collective pressure applications and supported Florida teacher demands in 1967 were doubtless meant to outflank the union drive.[60] At least in the big cities many teachers have come to feel that economic change will not occur through the traditional approaches of professionalization. While they may be subject to cries of unprofessionalism, unbecoming and "bad" behavior, militancy has been resorted to in several cities—New York, Paducah, Ky., East St. Louis and Detroit. During the twenty year period between 1945 and 1965 there were approximately 100 strikes held by public school teachers. In 1966 there were thirty strikes. By 1967 the number more than trebled. In the fall of 1968 teachers in eleven states were on strike with as many as 400 strikes predicted by the spring of 1969.[61]

During the New York school strike in the fall of 1967, *The New York Times* was outspoken in its criticism and disdain for the actions of the

United Federation of Teachers. In an editorial entitled "Road to Civic Chaos" *The Times* stated:

> The United Federation of Teachers, in disregard of law, reason and responsibility to the city's children, has voted to boycott the opening of schools this morning. The issues underlying the strike impress us as meretricious, but there can be argument on that point. What is not subject to argument—or to civic toleration—is the union's wanton resolve to defy the law and desert the classrooms that represent New York's first line of attack on the frustrations and despair of the slums.[62]

After three weeks fraught with charge and supercharge, the strike ended with major financial benefits for New York teachers and increased conflict within the city's educational structure. Regardless of the financial gains which have been recorded, the basic issue of professionalization and social class position remain unchanged. Teachers have not been offered the means of increasing their control within government employment which forbids strikes and locally controlled school systems of increasing their control or applying their knowledge to the need for change in the educational institution. While making a vital contribution to American society, they are paid less than many people who lack such education. Voters will more often approve a bond issue to build a gymnasium or football stadium than to raise teachers' salaries. Lacking other attributes of professionalization, economic returns have become more significant and the union approach most feasible.

Some see the union approach as another effort to control education. Tom Wicker, in *The New York Times* of September 10, 1967, stated,

> . . . The unions, moreover, may learn to use the strike weapon or the new technique of mass resignations in order to influence school administration, curriculum matters, and other noneconomic questions, in their favor; ultimately, aggressive unions might gain effective control of the public schools.
>
> That kind of unionism would be bad for the school system but so, surely, is the public niggardliness that has forced teachers at last to resort to strikes.

The power struggle between the NEA and AFT, as John Scanlon concluded, will continue and unless other forces operate to offer teachers higher socioeconomic status, society will have to accommodate another potentially hostile power group which will place the educational function in a continually unsolved conflict.[63]

CONCLUSION

The problems facing education in the United States are legion. Certainly the whole history of education in this country has been reflected in its control by first one and then another power group. Public schools presently face three major problems which may profoundly effect their organizational pattern: the increased cost of education and the search for adequate financing; the militancy of the lower class in its view of education as a source of mobility spearheaded by Negro organizations; and militant professionalism within the teaching profession.

Two of these movements are attempts by lower levels of the social structure, teachers and lower class groups, to develop and utilize power. They represent, as does the movement toward federal financing and influencing of education, widespread dissatisfaction with traditional patterns of educational structure, function, and control. All three movements, in some way, seek to change traditional school values and patterns of organization. The economic problem of the ghetto where children are not given the opportunity to acquire marketable skills increases the need of reevaluating American education. Slum dwellers and Negroes, as well as teachers and white "middle-class" parents, are utilizing varieties of activism—boycotts, resignations, counterdemonstrations—in search of instant answers. The impass and civic strife which result are clear indications that social organization in any society is not readily changed.

Selected Readings

Blum, Albert A., ed., *Teacher Unions and Associations* (Urbana: University of Illinois Press, 1969).

Coleman, James S., *et. al.*, *Equality of Educational Opportunity* (Washington, D.C.: U.S. Government Printing Office, 1966).

Conant, James B., *Slums and Suburbs* (New York: McGraw-Hill, 1961).

Curti, Merle, *The Social Ideas of American Educators* (New York: Charles Scribner's Sons, 1935).

Gross, Neal, *Who Runs Our Schools?* (New York: Wiley, 1958).

Havighurst, Robert J., *American Higher Education in the 1960's* (Columbus: Ohio State University Press, 1960).

Havighurst, Robert J. and Bernie L. Neugarten, *Society and Education* 2nd ed. (Boston: Allyn and Bacon, Inc., 1962).

Hollingshead, August B., *Elmtown's Youth* (New York: Wiley, 1949).

Levin, Henry M., "The Coleman Report: What Difference Do Schools Make?" *Saturday Review* (January 20, 1968).

Mayer, Martin, *The Teachers Strike New York, 1968* (New York: Harper and Row, 1969).

Powledge, Fred, *To Change a Child* (Chicago: Quadrangle Books, Inc., 1967).

Warner, W. Lloyd, Robert J. Havighurst, and Martin B. Loeb, *Who Shall be Educated?* (New York: Harper & Row, 1944).

Notes to Chapter 3

[1] U.S. Bureau of the Census, *Pocket Data Book, U.S.A. 1969* (Washington, D.C.: U.S. Government Printing Office, 1969), p. 151.

[2] "States Statistical Supplement," *Britannica Book of the Year* (Chicago, Ill.: Encyclopedia Britannica, Inc., 1967), p. 30.

[3] Merle Curti, *The Social Ideas of American Educators* (New York: Charles Scribner's Sons, 1935), pp. 234-40.

[4] For an analytical and witty treatise on the influence of education on stratification, see Michael Young, *The Rise of the Meritocracy: 1870-2033* (Baltimore: Penguin Books, 1961). For interesting reactions to Young's book, see David Riesman, "Notes on Meritocracy," *Daedalus*, 96 (Summer, 1967), pp. 897-908.

[5] U.S. Bureau of the Census, "Annual Mean Income, Lifetime Income, and Educational Attainment of Men in the United States, for Selected Years, 1956 to 1966," *Current Population Reports*, Series P-60, No. 56. (Washington, D.C.: U.S. Government Printing Office, 1968), Table F.

[6] U.S. Department of Labor, Bureau of Labor Statistics, "Educational Attainment of Workers, March 1967," *Special Labor Force Report No. 92* (Washington, D.C.: U.S. Government Printing Office, 1968), p. 29.

[7] U.S. Bureau of the Census, "Recent Trends in Social and Economic Conditions of Negroes in the United States," *Current Population Reports,* Series P-23, No. 26 (Washington, D.C.: U.S. Government Printing Office, July 1968), p. 18.

[8] Christopher Jencks, "Is the Public School Obsolete?," *The Public Interest,* No. 2 (Winter 1966), p. 21.

[9] See W. Lloyd Warner, Robert J. Havighurst, and Martin B. Loeb, *Who Shall be Educated?* (New York: Harper & Row, 1944); Stephen Abrahamson, "School Rewards and Social Class Status," *Educational Research Bulletin,* 31 (1952), pp. 8-15; Helen H. Davidson and Gerhard Long, "Children's Perception of Their Teachers' Feelings Toward Them Related to Self-Perception, School Achievement and Behavior," *Journal of Experimental Education* (December, 1960), pp. 107-18; and August B. Hollingshead, *Elmtown's Youth* (New York: Wiley, 1949).

[10] Hollingshead, *op. cit.*, p. 9.

[11] Frank Riessman, *The Culturally Deprived Child* (New York: Harper & Row, 1962), p. 10.

98   Contemporary Problems in American Education

[12] James S. Coleman, *et al., Equality of Educational Opportunity* (Washington, D.C.: U.S. Government Printing Office, 1966).
[13] Charles E. Silberman, "A Devastating Report on U.S. Education," *Fortune,* LXXVI, No. 2 (August, 1967), p. 181.
[14] Coleman, *op. cit.,* pp. 3, 40-41, 219, 330-31.
[15] Fred Powledge, *To Change a Child* (Chicago: Quadrangle Books, Inc., 1967).
[16] Hollingshead, *op. cit.,* p. 180.
[17] Robert J. Havighurst and Bernice L. Neugarten, *Society and Education,* 2nd ed. (Boston: Allyn and Bacon, Inc., 1962), p. 472.
[18] Ronald G. Corwin, *A Sociology of Education* (New York: Appleton-Century-Crofts, 1965), pp. 158-62.
[19] See Florence Greenhoe, *Community Contacts and Participation of Teachers* (Washington, D.C.: American Council on Public Affairs, 1941); W. Lloyd Warner, *et. al., Who Shall be Educated,* p. 101; and Wilber B. Brookover, *A Sociology of Education* (New York: American Book Co., 1955), p. 173.
[20] Havighurst and Neugarten, *op. cit.,* pp. 468-73.
[21] H. S. Becker, "Role and Career Problems of the Chicago Public School Teacher," Unpublished Ph.D. dissertation, Department of Sociology, University of Chicago, 1951, and John Winget, "Teacher Inter-School Mobility Aspirations of Elementary Teachers, Chicago Public School System, 1947-48." Unpublished Ph.D. dissertation, Department of Sociology, University of Chicago, 1952.
[22] Havighurst and Neugarten, *op. cit.,* pp. 470-73.
[23] *Ibid.,* p. 470.
[24] Becker and Winget, *op. cit.*
[25] National Association of Intergroup Relations Officials, *New York State Commissioners' Conference on Race and Education* (Albany, N.Y.: State Education Department, 1964); and James S. Coleman, *op. cit.*
[26] John H. Fischer, "Race and Reconciliation: The Role of the School," *Daedalus,* Vol. 95, No. 1 (Winter 1966), p. 26.
[27] Brown vs. Board of Education, Briggs vs. Elliot, Davis vs. County School Board, Gebhart vs. Belton, May 17, 1954 (347 U.S. 483), Bolling et. al. vs. Sharpe et. al., May 17, 1954 (347 U.S. 483), Brown et. al. vs. Board of Education et. al., May 31, 1955 (349 U.S. 294).
[28] *School Desegregation 1966: The Slow Undoing December 1966* (Atlanta, Georgia: Southern Regional Council, 1966).
[29] Joseph Alsop, "No More Nonsense About Ghetto Education!" *The New Republic,* Vol. 157 (July 22, 1967), pp. 21-22. For the other two articles in the series which develop conflicting views concerning the difficulties of eliminating the ghetto school and the possibility of developing an effective learning experience in the slum, see also Thomas Schwartz, Thomas Pettigrew and Marshall Smith, "Fake Panaceas for Ghetto Education," *The New Republic,* Vol. 157, No. 13 (September 23, 1967), pp. 16-19, and Joseph Alsop, "Ghetto Education," *The New Republic,* Vol. 157 (November 18, 1967), pp. 18-22.
[30] Jencks, *op. cit.,* p. 20.
[31] *Report to the Board of Education, City of Chicago by The Advisory Panel on Integration of the Public Schools* (Chicago, March 31, 1964).
[32] Nathan Jacobsen, *ed., An Exploration of the Education Park Concept* (New York: New York City Board of Education Arden House Conference, 1964).
[33] See Jencks, *op. cit.,* pp. 18-27.
[34] *Britannica Book of the Year, op. cit.,* p. 30.
[35] *Pocket Data Book, U.S.A. 1969, op. cit.,* p. 159.
[36] Curti, *op. cit.,* p. 206.
[37] *Pocket Data Book, U.S.A. 1969, op. cit.,* p. 160.
[38] *Ibid.,* p. 159.
[39] Henry M. Levin, "The Coleman Report: What Difference Do Scnools Make?" *Saturday Review* (January 20, 1968), p. 58.

40 *Pocket Data Book, U.S.A. 1969, op. cit.,* p. 191.

41 *Ibid.,* p. 92.

42 Curti, *op. cit.*

43 Newton Edwards and Herman Richey, *The School in the American Social Order* (Boston: Houghton Mifflin, 1947).

44 Corwin, *op. cit.,* pp. 70-72.

45 *Ibid.,* pp. 73-74.

46 Max Weber, *The Protestant Ethic and the Spirit of Capitalism,* trans. by Talcott Parsons (New York: Charles Scribner's Sons, 1950).

47 Curti, *op. cit.,* pp. 80, 83, 218, 330.

48 *The New York Times* (July 9, 1967).

49 Willard Waller, "The Teacher's Roles," in *Sociological Foundations of Education,* J. S. Roucek and Associates, *eds.* (New York: Thomas Y. Crowell Company, 1942), p. 217.

50 Martin Trow, "The Second Transformation of American Secondary Education," in Richard L. Simpson and Ida Harper Simpson, *eds., Social Organization and Behavior* (New York: John Wiley & Sons, Inc., 1964), p. 144.

51 Corwin, *op. cit.,* pp. 162-163.

52 *Britannica Book of the Year, op. cit.,* p. 30.

53 Peter Janssen, "The Union Response to Academic Mass Production," *The Saturday Review,* L (October 21, 1967), p. 64.

54 Curti, *op. cit.,* pp. 219-21.

55 *Ibid.,* p. 225.

56 Margaret Haley, "Why Teachers Should Organize," *NEA Proceedings* (1904), pp. 145-52.

57 *Educational Review,* XXX (November, 1905), pp. 344-74.

58 Walter Reuther, "Reports to the Industrial Union Department of the AFL-CIO," Fifth Constitutional Convention, Washington, D.C., November 7-8, 1963, and Victor Riesel, "New Unionization Program Shoots for Million in Schools and Colleges," *Deseret News* (November 18, 1963).

59 R. Joseph Monsen, Jr. and Mark W. Cannon, *op. cit.,* p. 157.

60 *Guidelines for Professional Negotiations,* and *Guidelines for Professional Sanctions* (Washington, D.C.: National Education Association, November, 1963). See also, *The New York Times* (August 25, 1967), and *The Wall Street Journal* (September 8, 1967).

61 *The New York Times* (September 3, 1968).

62 *The New York Times* (September 11, 1967). Martin Mayer, *The Teachers Strike New York, 1968* (New York: Harper & Row, 1969).

63 John Scanlon, "Strikes, Sanctions and the Schools," *The Saturday Review* (October 19, 1963), p. 51.

CHAPTER FOUR

IN AID OF THE POOR: PUBLIC WELFARE IN THE UNITED STATES

In over three decades, the United States has developed a complex system of public welfare consisting of a number of diverse programs to meet the needs of the poor. While the resulting product is intricate, indeed, it is not comprehensive. Consequently, the assistance offered does not raise the poor above the poverty level and millions of nonrecipients receive no aid. Basic to the development of what are essentially a number of makeshift measures is the value system of our society. Intrinsic to what we consider right or wrong, necessary or irrelevant in aiding the poor, are our attitudes toward them, toward work, toward the causes of poverty, family spending, the "necessities" of life, rights, privileges, charity, illegitimacy, and a host of other concepts. The attitudes toward public welfare which each of us has acquired and those of our parents and friends have been the controlling factor in the problems surrounding aid to the poor in the United States.

This chapter deals primarily with public welfare as a social problem rather than specifically with poverty, since public welfare is a primary and important agency in our society which is undergoing social change and reassessment of purposes and functions. Several of the problem areas which shall be considered in this chapter are: the extensiveness of public assistance in the United States; assistance as a right of citizenship; the effect of social class on attitudes toward public welfare and poverty; and the techniques utilized to ration welfare services, including requirements for eligibility. Suggestive management programs such as income support proposals and the involvement of the poor in program and policy planning are reviewed.

PUBLIC WELFARE PROGRAMS

The American public welfare system consists of three major types of programs based on a family's or individual's labor force status. The first type of programs has been established to offer assistance to those outside the labor force including old-agers and survivors. These programs include disability insurance, pensions for needy veterans, public assistance programs under the Social Security Act, and general assistance for the needy not covered by the Social Security Act but financed by state and local agencies. Second, programs aiding those within the work force include training in salable skills, aid to depressed areas, unemployment insurance, job creation and work relief. Third, programs providing services such as child care, subsidized housing, food distribution and medical services to the poor are based on need without regard to position in the labor force.

The distinction based on labor force status is arbitrary and illogical. A mobile, technologically oriented society would, of necessity, sustain con-

101

tinuous movement in and out of the labor force. Family problems and economic modification in a region or community naturally could create a labor status change. Determining the type of assistance which is to be provided, work or cash, adds a complex dimension.

Recipients and Cost

It is difficult to determine how many poor receive aid from the three types of programs outlined above or to hang an exact price tag on each. By the late sixties approximately 10.7 percent or 5.3 million American families lived on less than $3,000 annually.[1] Yet only a fraction of the poor are actually reached by public welfare. It has been estimated that in 1966, there were 21.7 million persons in the United States with incomes below the poverty level. Only a third of this number received public assistance.[2] The reasons for the gap between need and assistance are complex and range from communication problems on the existence of assistance, fear of stigma, complexity and difficulty of securing assistance, to problems of eligibility. For example, a large segment of the poor live in families with a working but underemployed or submarginally paid male breadwinner. Such families are excluded from Aid to Families with Dependent Children (AFDC) programs.

It has been estimated that nearly 8 million individuals are reached each month by public welfare programs, including 2.8 million under the Old-Age Assistance, Aid to the Blind, and Aid to the Disabled programs, with 3.9 million children served under the Aid to Families with Dependent Children program.[3] An additional 1.3 million parents are reached under the latter program, including over a million mothers and less than 200,000 fathers.[4]

While only a third of the poor received assistance, public welfare represents an increasingly burdensome outlay of public funds. In 1967 almost 9 billion dollars were spent for public assistance compared to $3 billion a decade before.[5] The grants of public welfare today, in terms of large outlays, are Old-Age Assistance, Aid to Families with Dependent Children, and medical assistance. These three programs account for over 84 percent of expenditures. Aid to the Blind, Aid to the Permanently and Totally Disabled, medical assistance for the aged, and general assistance account for the other 16 percent. AFDC grew from a little over half a billion dollars in 1950 to almost 3 billion by 1967. Heavily affected by the movement of nonwhite families to urban ghettos, AFDC shifted from a position claiming 23 percent of all public assistance funds in 1950 to

32 percent in 1966—before the new Medical Assistance program began to represent a substantial percentage of total welfare expenditures.

With the increased affectiveness of insurance programs under Social Security, old age assistance has dropped in comparative size from a commanding 59 percent of the total funds in 1950 to 29 percent in 1966.

Although these amounts may seem huge, they are pitifully small when translated to the level of the welfare recipient. The average monthly payment for Old-Age Assistance in December 1967 was $70, for Aid to Dependent Children $162 per family, for Aid to the Blind $90, for Aid to the Permanently and Totally Disabled $81, and for general assistance $88.[6] The range for Old-Age Assistance was considerable with the average monthly payments going from $38 in Mississippi to $121 in New Hampshire, for Aid to Dependent Children from $35 in Mississippi to $243 in New York, for Aid to the Blind from $46 in Mississippi to $137 in California, for Aid to the Permanently and Totally Disabled from $46 in Mississippi to $127 in Iowa, and for general assistance from $12 in Oklahoma to $138 in New Jersey.[7] The grants for the AFDC program have been considered well below the poverty subsistence level under any standard.[8] The National Advisory Council on Public Welfare has described the national average as little more than half the amount required for assistance and considers it a factor in the perpetuation of poverty.[9]

Public welfare's growing size extends to personnel as well as to outlay for grants. In 1956 there were 107,000 state and local employees in public welfare, with a payroll of $29,800,000.[10] In 1966, on the other hand, there were 182,450 state and local public welfare employees. The total payroll was $81,326,000.[11] The payroll over this ten-year period almost tripled in size and the number of employees almost doubled.

THE CONCEPT OF PUBLIC WELFARE

There have been many approaches in the United States and in other nations, to the solution of poverty. A partial listing includes the protection of the lord of the manor under feudalism, socially-sanctioned mendicancy, theft, migration, punishment in the stocks, imprisonment, and aid from guilds or from private foundations or from the church.[12] In 1531 because of the widespread problem of vagabondage and begging related to the breakdown of feudalism, the first Elizabethan Poor Law was enacted in England. This law and others which followed recognized the responsibility of government for the care of the poor. England began a succession of liberal measures as early as the Workmen's Compensation

Act of 1897, a Pension's Act in 1908, and legislation covering widows and orphans in 1926.[13] In the early decades of the 20th Century, English policy did not consider the social services to be forms of charity. Rather, they were natural benefits such as justice, law and order available to any citizen.[14]

In the United States the most drastic changes in the discharge of this responsibility occurred during the Great Depression of the 1930's, when a sizeable percentage of the work force was unemployed for reasons beyond individual control. The enactment of the Social Security Act and the current public assistance or welfare programs for the aged, children, blind, and disabled, date from the recognition in the mid-1930's that widespread economic depression would have to be met by equally widespread governmental programs. Public welfare has "come to be regarded as part of a battery of instruments available to the modern state in its efforts to maintain economic stability."[15] Public welfare, as we know it today, is a product of the Depression of the 1930's, although its origin reaches further back into history.

Michael Harrington, among others, has stressed that today's poor are not the same kind of people as those who were unemployed in the 1930's.[16] Today's poor are the product of a system which has increasingly cared for middle class persons with hardships, but which has not adequately cared for the minority group member, the migrant laborer, the rejects of automation and changing industry, the aged, the rural poor, the alcoholic, the mentally impaired, the children of families with female heads, or the people who are accustomed to public welfare as a way of life and whose children are born into poverty. Some scholars, in short, see today's poor as a group predominantly born into a culture of poverty.[17]

Public welfare was originally perceived by social workers and labor leaders as a program to alleviate poverty. Economists saw it as a device to prevent future depressions by recirculating some of the nation's wealth. Some industrialists and businessmen have considered it a measure to stave off the possibility of widespread discontent among the disadvantaged and unemployed. As in the case of poverty, the concept of public welfare is not something concrete and stable which is perceived identically by different groups. Rather, it may be examined through entirely different lenses by different people.

For our purpose, public welfare is a system of dispensing tax-derived financial resources and services to disadvantaged individuals, families, and communities, predominantly using the method of determining financial need on an individual basis and then providing economic help along with appropriate social services. Public welfare is exclusive of the Social

Security program and other contributory social insurance provisions. It is found in every city and county in the nation and is typically administered at the local level in compliance with Federal standards. The system uses a combination of local, state and Federal funds.

HISTORICAL BACKGROUND

It may be helpful to review in a little more detail the meaning of public welfare and poverty as our nation has grown and changed. In the eighteenth and nineteenth centuries, poverty signified the difficulties presented by certain disadvantaged groups—orphaned children, the sick, the disabled and the aged without relatives able and willing to care for them. Healthy men were able to find jobs or subsist from the relatively undeveloped land and natural resources of the continent. Able-bodied women found husbands or a source of livelihood in teaching, nursing or other socially acceptable occupations.

Perhaps the first serious cracks in the dike appeared toward the end of the 19th Century and the early 20th Century when urbanization, industrialization and a money economy had advanced to the point that seasonal unemployment, widespread economic depressions, and changing patterns of industrial expansion began to have serious repercussions on the employment and employability of able-bodied men and women. In the United States, economic and political leaders had to consider the responsibility of the state for ensuring that able-bodied people would have jobs and an income when there was a gap between the number of jobs available and those that were needed.[18] Private and church-centered philanthropy historically has never been able to meet widespread crises of unemployment. Before the 1930's, public welfare had developed as a relatively small and weak system in many of the states—some had no public welfare agencies.

The Depression of the 1930's brought the development of a federally administered Social Security System with its social insurance provisions and a universal state-administered public welfare system with federal support provided on a matching basis. Government responded to a widespread poverty condition of unemployment and unemployability with public welfare which included public assistance, aid to dependent children and aid to the blind.

These programs rested on the assumption that temporary provision of a minimal level of subsistence to eligible adults and children would lead to recovery of financial independence. In the meantime, children would be saved from lives of misery, ignorance, poverty, crime and lack of realization of potentialities. The blind would be spared lives as beggars in the streets and shops.

The presence of so many children in the ranks of public welfare clients contributes to the establishment of a secondary goal besides the alleviation of poverty in the public welfare system—strengthening the families affected by temporary conditions of poverty. From the 18th and 19th Centuries the United States has had a heritage of considering the family as the cornerstone of society, and this particular goal was well chosen to solicit and elicit support for public welfare measures in the states and communities. Nobody in the 1930's and 1940's wanted to speak or vote against anything that seemed to strengthen the American family as a social institution.

Social workers and sociologists vigorously supported the spread of public welfare in the 1930's, although its initial expansion at that time was largely engineered by economists, politicians, and political scientists. The latter saw public welfare and social security as several policies among many that would alleviate widespread conditions of poverty and prevent or control any future economic recession or depression.

Although the profession most involved in the application of Social Security, social work generally has only been able in the 1930's, 1940's, and 1950's to conceptualize and act upon a theory of the individual as being more or less passive in the face of biological, psychological and sociocultural forces. This has led to the inability to participate fully in the planning and establishment of the Social Security Act and the public welfare system, as well as in other efforts to modify social institutions and structures.

But time does not stand still, and it seems far more than three decades, in a cultural sense, since 1935. Very few leaders, thinkers, professionals, scientists, or other citizens worry very much about the danger of another economic depression as serious as that of the 1930's. There are too many safeguards: economic, political, and social. Bank deposits, for example, are protected against monopoly, manipulation, panic and collapse. The Federal government has developed a broad range of economic barriers to depression. Political parties and political leaders now are alert to early signs of a recession and usually react with a panoply of solutions.

Today, many no longer consider public welfare to be quite as necessary as it was in the 1930's, 1940's, and 1950's as a safeguard against economic depression. Nor is the family considered to be as all-important a social institution, as we continue to create new services for recreation, religion, education, counseling, friendship and other activities once assumed by the family. Finally, public welfare does not seem as inevitably related to the prevention and control of poverty as it once did, evidenced by the recent development of other community-focused and child-focused programs such as those under the Economic Opportunity Act of 1964.

Today, there is a new ferment about poverty triggered by the civil rights movement, automation, the population explosion, urbanization and industrial developments. There is also a new ferment about public welfare. Since some, if not all, of the original factors that led to the spread of public welfare in the 1930's have changed, what is and what should be the role of this sprawling bureaucracy? The answers to these questions vary between the various social classes and the attitudes of their members. Possibly a clear policy decision will result from the compromising and bargaining among major economic and social groups.

IS WELFARE A RIGHT OF CITIZENSHIP?

In the preface to his provocative work on administrative responsiveness in public assistance, Alan Keith Lucas effectively drew the battle line in the contemporary class conflict over public welfare principles and administration. He states that:

> . . . persons who, in the absence of other means of support, must look to the government for enough money to maintain health and decency (and do so by meeting eligibility requirements for aid established by Congress) are not thereby any the less free American citizens, with all the privileges and responsibilities that belong to citizenship. While some may be lazy or lacking in traditional qualities of rugged individualism, others are sick, old, handicapped, fatherless, or caught in the ineluctable workings of an economic system that no longer rewards only the industrious or punishes only the slack. To discriminate against relief clients as a class makes no more sense than to discriminate against Negroes as a racial group. The virtue or lack of worth lies in the individual, not in the group.[19]

Americans are split into a number of unequal groups with some maintaining that assistance to individuals and families is a right and a privilege of citizenship while others consider the concept opposed to the American ideology of work and enterprise. This discussion, no more than others which preceded it, will not resolve the issue. Unlike society's attitude toward access to health as a human right discussed in Chapter 5, no similar commitment has been made to assist the victim of economic deprivation derived from the recipient's human status. It is, rather, dispensed to those who are in need for specified reasons such as age, loss of parental care, or physical disability.

The monumental Universal Declaration of Human Rights, adopted in 1948 by the General Assembly of the United Nations, does set forth man's legal right to assistance rather than assistance granted as charity at the discretion of the giver. It states:

> Everyone has the right to a standard of living adequate for the health and well-being of himself and of his family including . . . the right to security in the event of unemployment, sickness, disability, widowhood, old age or other lack of livelihood in circumstances beyond his control.

In other words, when assistance is recognized as a legal right an applicant is judged eligible by objective requirements, such as a means test and the maintenance of communication on his economic circumstances, not on how he behaves himself in terms of middle class moral or social values. As A. Delafield Smith maintains:

> Law never seeks to buy behavior. It seeks to give reign to moral law. It seeks to allow the individual to benefit or suffer from his choices and sacrifices as freely as possible. This is quite inconsistent with the idea that the free exercise of rights is essential to democratic equality.[20]

In a society that has long since relinquished man's dependence on his physical environment and substituted man's dependence on other men for most of his needs, we have failed to come to grips with our inability to distribute economic goods and services equally. The widespread acceptance of the Protestant ethic has allowed us to assume that these inequities could be eliminated if (a) the poor were willing to work, (b) they could be trained or retrained for work, and (c) jobs were made available. Improving the lot of the poor will take careful refining of these assumptions. Five million poor are persons over age 65, plus millions who are physically unemployable. Both of these groups are unable to work. Many of the poor are children, most of whom are not encouraged or even allowed to work. Of 69 million children in the United States in 1963, some 15.6 million were poor.[21] Yet our present policies punish these helpless, unfortunate children for what society terms the shiftlessness of their parents. As for the remainder of the poor, continuous programs of training and retraining for technological changes in an industrial society must be maintained if that society is to develop its economic potential. Even if mass training of the unemployed and underemployed poor were to occur, it would require over 3 million jobs to absorb only the unemployed poor into the work force. Essentially, what is being suggested is the economic achievement of full employment which would move many unemployed poor into the labor force and raise their income. It is questionable whether the United States will be able to achieve full employment in this decade—or in any future decade.

Encouraging, prodding, or putting people to work, to fulfill the middle class concept of a meaningful life, appears to be a utopian dream at this point in our economic development. The goal of substantially reducing poverty in our society—if it is to be reduced—is dependent, therefore, upon other types of assistance programs which challenge the dominant values of this society. Either they reflect on the middle class ethics regarding work, charity, and morality, or, by attempting to regulate the personal lives of recipients, they deprive the latter of his right to self determination.

Thus, American society faces the complex dilemma of eliminating poverty. Society has defined poverty as a social problem which affects large numbers of people and believes that something remedial is possible. Private agencies and government have pasted and clipped programs together into a relatively ineffective patchwork quilt of assistance and services. To each they have attached eligibility stipulations which deprive the recipient of pride, privacy, dignity and fulfillment in his own and more specifically in the eyes of the "big middle-class brother" watching over him. On the whole, while middle class Americans recognize that some people—the blind and the sick for example—must be helped financially, they tend to feel that the majority of poor who apply for public assistance are the dregs of society, and are shiftless, lazy, and could support themselves if they wanted to. Even the aged may be included in the criticism: if they had planned better, saved more, or hadn't squandered their resources when they were younger, they wouldn't need help. Basic are the prevailing attitudes that no one is owed a living, that assistance is not a right, and that man controls his own destiny. And these are the values taught children in the financially stable American home and in the majority of middle-class-oriented schools.

Society has changed considerably. Man no longer works out his destiny alone, for better or worse, within his natural environment. Social institutions define a man's status and his chances of success in terms of social class factors such as education, race, work motivation and behavior. He does not control his destiny. Once trapped in poverty, he finds it almost impossible to escape.

The dilemma, then, is one in which affluent society does not recognize man's right to assistance. On the other hand, an assistance program which could foster man's mobility out of poverty through the development of his independence, pride, and commitment to new sets of values, cannot be developed until assistance is recognized as a right. Attaching stigmas, furtively looking for immorality and denying assistance to the violators create barriers between the poor and the remainder of society. It is difficult to explain why assistance for the basics of shelter and food should be related to morality or why the poor should be expected to exhibit greater morality than is observed among the rich. A resolution of the dilemma must be related to a careful analysis of the relation of contemporary values to public welfare in the United States in terms of developing programs which can effectively and successfully move the remedial poor into the mainstream of contributing citizenship. Denying men the right to privacy, pride, or to be good or bad within the legal structure of society obviously has not been the answer.

DIFFERING CLASS VIEWS ABOUT PUBLIC WELFARE AND POVERTY

The upper class in America tends to be so removed from the direct impact of poverty on its own members that, paradoxically enough, it furnishes some of the outstanding thinkers and doers in the struggle against poverty. To name only a few examples of members of established upper-class families, men such as Franklin D. Roosevelt, Nelson A. Rockefeller, Averell Harriman, and Henry Ford III, have taken leading roles of one kind or another in efforts aimed at preventing or controlling poverty. Generally, however, distance from day-to-day contact with poverty and the poor, and a desire to control the economy and society has resulted in an adherence to the classical economic position that the free market economy holds the best answers to unemployment and poverty.[22] Various studies have noted the concentration of economic wealth and power in the upper class.[23] Increase in production, as related to economic growth, seems in this classical view, the soundest course to follow.

The upper class seems increasingly willing to view poverty as a phenomenon produced and fostered by our industrial and urban way of life, which must be dealt with as promptly and effectively as possible in order to make sure that all citizens can participate in and contribute to our booming economy. If the "poor" can become the "not so poor," they will not only be happier, but they will be more apt to buy automobiles, television sets and refrigerators. They read the same newspaper ads and billboards and can be expected to have the same aspirations and expectations. The upper class is perhaps more prone to launch new programs to reduce poverty than it is to take any direct interest in the poor as distinct individuals. Social action and social change are vehicles of paramount interest and concern. Bergel notes that the upper class is not adverse to new trends and innovations, even if controversial.[24] These views have led to upper class leadership, sponsorship or acquiescence in the passage of the Social Security Act, the spread of public welfare, the development of stock options for all employees, the creation of employee-ownership and employee-participation systems in industry and business, and a host of programs and services in public health, mental health, vocational rehabilitation, education, recreation, and other fields. Warner and Lunt note the upper class comprises a significantly high proportion of the membership in associations organized for charity.[25]

The upper class is pragmatic enough to want programs that will do the job they're supposed to do. Public welfare is currently under upper class surveillance as a system which may not be as effective as other approaches to the solution of the poverty problem. But what are the alternatives? And what would be done with public welfare employees if their positions were abolished? Any strong, well-led and articulate movement with sound views on these matters will probably get the attention and perhaps the support of the American upper class.

The middle class in the United States has a more direct experience with poverty and to some extent, public welfare. Some middle class members today were poverty-stricken in the 1930's, irrespective of class affiliation at that time. Many have employees who are, or have been, in the poverty group defined as having $3,000 annual income for a family or $1,500 for an individual, or as defined under other criteria. Most have had contact with friends, relatives or acquaintances who were temporarily in circumstances of poverty.

Since poverty in an affluent and money-oriented society is stigmatized, many of the middle class may reject the conditions and condemn those afflicted by the condition.[26] There is evidence that persons in higher occupational groups are more conservative than those in lower ones.[27] The middle class, by and large, views poverty as preventable and controllable by the actions of the individual himself, although sometimes grudgingly, exceptions are made for children, the ill, the disabled and the aged persons. Even these groups are somewhat suspect, since supposedly the parents of the children could and should have looked and planned ahead and the ill, disabled, or aged should have foreseen these conditions and prepared for them through savings or insurance according to some in the middle class. Yet, many in the middle class do recall the "terrible days" of the 1930's when even the well-educated, responsible and competent individual could not find work no matter how hard he tried.[28] There is a certain ambivalence of feelings, therefore, in many of the middle class leaders.

Public welfare was tolerated, even urged and applauded, as long as it seemed to be a necessary safeguard against depression and particularly when it primarily served the "worthy" poor—the widows, the industrially displaced, the ill, the disabled, and the aged. But these are the groups that are now being increasingly handled under the Social Security Act. The public welfare clients tend now to be a new and different breed— more permanently a part of poverty. Now that public welfare is not essential for its original purposes, its usefulness has declined in the eyes of many of the middle class. Moreover, as other economic brakes against depressions and recessions have been devised, and as the rate of withholding under the Social Security Act increases, some middle class members have become somewhat lukewarm about Social Security. It is not unlikely that some of the hostility toward public welfare, specifically toward the Aid to Dependent Children program, may be hostility displaced from Social Security which is politically better protected and entrenched, as well as hostility displaced from the minority-group poor people who make up the AFDC population.[29]

A word may be in order about the important occupational groups which usually are included within the middle class. This is especially pertinent since the United States is predominantly a middle class oriented society. Public policy decisions, including those about public welfare, tend to favor the interests of middle class occupational groups.

Business can be broken down for our purposes into people with an attachment to the ideology of classical economics, and people like the managerial businessmen who roughly follow Keynesian thinking.[30] The former group sees public welfare as a very questionable enterprise, believing that government should stay out of such affairs and leave issues of employment, unemployment, and economic growth to the operation of the free market, and to individual and church-centered philanthropy. The latter applaud governmental activity in public welfare as it relates to hedges against depressions and recessions and as it minimizes protest movements among the underprivileged.[31]

Labor, the intellectuals, the black middle class and similar groups support any governmental services, including public welfare, which tend to elevate the individual economic, educational and social status of all members of society and create a floor below which no person is allowed to fall. The ideological basis for the position is both economic, in terms of redistribution of wealth to all citizens, and humanitarian. The early leadership of the Congress of Racial Equality and the National Urban

League worked toward a coalition strategy that would weld middle class groups such as Negroes, laborers, intellectuals and religious groups into a political majority that would effect changes in social legislation and public welfare. The National Association for the Advancement of Colored People has made its major contribution in the courts and legislatures by attacking the legal bases for segregation.

There seem to be at least three real reasons why middle class support still has strength sufficient to defeat any efforts to dismantle public welfare. First, public welfare is the only system of social service available to people in most of our more than 3,000 counties in the United States. Second, both for humanitarian as well as economic reasons, there is substantial agreement that some kind of financial help must be available for assistance to the aged, to children, and to those disabled not yet protected by the Social Security program.[32] Social services other than financial aid are needed, in the view of most middle class members, to guard against widespread social discontent and economic recessions as well as for the humanitarian reason of providing help to all citizens in solving personal and social problems.

A third reason for maintaining public welfare is that it provides jobs for a substantial number of middle class citizens. It is commonplace throughout the nation for youths of both sexes who have graduated from college without a clear-cut career objective to be recommended to public welfare departments for a year or so of experience "while they decide what to do with themselves." Such recommendations are made not only by parents and relatives directly, but by friends and acquaintances of parents who happen to be politicians, judges, business leaders, or community leaders.

It may very well be that the latter reason is far stronger than most analysts and writers realize. As we have seen, almost 200,000 jobs are involved with the number increasing steadily.[33] This number exceeds that of local fire protection personnel in the nation, and is half the size of the nation's police personnel. The total welfare payroll in October 1966 almost equalled the payroll for local fire protection.[34] Moreover, there has been a very definite pattern of control of employment at the local level in most states. There is a body of evidence that indicates a strong continuing resistance toward increasing the qualifications—education as well as experience—for these positions even though there is a very large staff turnover. Although kept low, salaries are high enough to satisfy a young person who is just starting out after his college education. There are probably several hundreds of thousands of people in the country who have a year or so of public welfare experience before going on to careers in teaching, civil service, business or industry. In addition, many middle class citizens remain in public welfare jobs in spite of the fairly low salaries and other negative conditions for a variety of reasons. Some men and women enjoy work where the needs and problems are highly visible. Others may have less admirable motives, since there is a lack of pressure and competition in the public welfare bureaucracy for a high degree of skill, proficiency or measurable results, and since there are opportunities to exploit and abuse the public welfare clients. The types of workers mentioned above are not always the best groups of people to aid the poor, the disabled and the disadvantaged to become happier and more productive citizens. The public welfare system is a job market and must be seen in this light if any viable solution to the public welfare problem is to be offered.

The middle class tends to distinguish clearly between the public welfare workers and the clients. The former are also the people being helped, sometimes even more visibly than the latter. The middle class is pragmatic, fairly open-minded, action-oriented and policy-focused about the workers. But in reference to the clients—the poor—the middle class is more apt to be dogmatic, slow to action or change, research-oriented and disposed toward a case-by-case rather than a community-wide or society-wide approach to prevention or treatment. The middle class is more apt than the upper class or lower class to state that the poor are no doubt lazy, incompetent, disabled, or in some other way individually unable or unwilling to work to support themselves. In their opinion an appropriate approach to prevention or treatment of this problem is to examine each individual and design some appropriate means to get him back on his feet and into the job market.[35] Frequently, also, the middle class stresses the cost of public welfare with the belief that welfare breeds illegitimacy, improvidence, and the danger of cheating in terms of eligibility. Frequently middle class people have made references to the public welfare recipient driving up in a Cadillac to collect his check. Although investigations very seldom bear out statements of this sort, it does not seem to have much effect in curtailing the rumors.

The lower class is too close to the poor, measured by any standards, to be as detached as the upper class or as condemning as the middle class. Even those upper lower class members, who are not on public welfare caseloads, often have friends or relatives who are or have been. Many of them have had direct experience of some kind with both poverty and public welfare. They recall the Great Depression or have had it pictured vividly to them if they are too young to recall it. Yet the lower class has had almost as full an exposure to the advantages of an affluent society as either of the other classes. They read many of the same books, newspapers, magazines and billboards. They watch the same movies, television programs, plays and sports events. The working class aspirations include several automobiles, boats, travel and many of the same goals of middle class individuals. Therefore, their attitudes and feelings toward poverty and the poor are a blend of sympathy and contempt. Most of the class express a dislike of relief and share the middle class values of self-help and independence.[36] The lower class child is apt to be taught that he must get ahead if he possibly can. He is told that he must not end up like Uncle Bill. Adherence to moral principles while getting ahead is not quite as important as success, although, if possible, it's a good idea to be ethical.

The lower class in the United States is not politically impotent, although segments have been. The rise of labor to important policy-making power, particularly with the executive branch of the Federal Government, has meant that some of the lower class goals have had a chance to be translated into reality. However, they are funneled through the middle class labor leadership and molded in the crucible of compromise and adjustment with intellectuals and other middle class groups before being finally attained so that many alterations occur. Certain needs such as the extension of minimum wage coverage that will benefit the lower class, are more apt to be stressed by labor than by the extension of public assistance and welfare provisions to the poor described by Harrington as "beneath the welfare state."[37]

In the following statement by Stokely Carmichael, a leading black power advocate, the dilemma and a possible solution is seen through the eyes of a man identified with the black lower class.

> . . . We should begin with the basic fact that black Americans have two problems: they are poor and they are black. All other problems arise from this two-sided reality: lack of education, the so-called apathy of black men. Any program to end racism must address itself to that double reality.
>
> Almost from its beginning, SNCC sought to address itself to both conditions with a program aimed at winning political power for impoverished Southern blacks. We had to begin with politics because black Americans are a propertyless people in a country where property is valued above all. We had to work for power, because this country does not function by morality, love, and nonviolence, but by power. Thus we determined to win political power, with the idea of moving on from there into activity that would have economic effects. With power, the masses could *make or participate in making* the decisions which govern their destinies, and thus create basic change in their day-to-day lives.[38]

Similarly, Saul Alinsky's work in Chicago and the approach of the VISTA workers have been predicated on the assumption that, if individuals in the culture of poverty could confront their environment through collective efforts, the frustration, apathy, alienation, pessimism, fatalism and despair of the permanent poor could be overcome.[39]

Lower class views of poverty and public welfare are largely personalized, colored by fears and hopes, and generally are not well-crystallized into ideologies or social policies. However, the lower class sees the poor as being the people who are left out of modern social and economic progress for a variety of reasons: technological, educational, social, psychological, and political. The lower class often states that conditions would be better if the economy were owned and controlled by the government.[40] The poor are not necessarily any less deserving, but are more accurately described as unluckier. The public welfare system is unsympathetic, rigid and responsive to middle class ideology. Harrington pictures the feeling of the poor that their fate depends on the "stranger from welfare." Overworked caseworkers confront the poor with bureaucratic routines and probing, impersonal and even hostile procedures. The poor often see the public welfare system as another manifestation of authority. Walter B. Miller has noted the ambivalence in the lower class reaction to authority, "the pose of tough rebellious independence . . . frequently concealing powerful dependency cravings."[41] The best approaches to prevention and control of poverty in their eyes might include more widespread and adequate education, including vocational education, the eradication of slums, higher minimum wage laws, increased aid to the disadvantaged through some system not concerned so much with eligibility checks although some initial appraisal may be justified, and governmental responsibility for providing jobs when industry cannot or will not.

The lower class would probably vote to alter drastically the present public welfare system and substitute some means for providing a minimum income to all individuals and families, such as the negative income tax, the guaranteed annual income or the family allowance system handled centrally at the national level through Social Security or a new program. The present public welfare departments could continue to provide social services without the stigma and ferment involved in the provision of tax funds to the disadvantaged.

THE RATIONING OF WELFARE SERVICES

Any society is faced with potentially infinite human needs and limited economic needs by using price as the regulative mechanism to keep resources with which to work.[42] Although the free market copes with demands and resources in balance, social services differ in two essential characteristics. Social services meet needs which the society and individual regard as basic but expensive. Also, social services do not use the price mechanism as the device for distribution and allocation.

Historically, the problem was handled by assuming that social needs did not exist, or if they were recognized they were judged to be a private responsibility. Rising expectations on the part of the public, the growth of public welfare as a primary concern of government, the pressures of urbanization, the organization of labor, the economic depression, and the civil rights revolution have forced a reappraisal of the method of rationing social services. Accordingly, covert controls appear to have emerged which serve to keep needs and resources in balance without the painful necessity of too openly discussing and enacting restrictive public policies. These controls include deterrence, eligibility, delay, misunderstanding and dilution. Each is briefly sketched below.

Deterrence

A variety of policies have evolved which deter individuals and families from applying for assistance. Policies have been developed which deliberately set up inadequate public welfare grants in which the standards are below a subsistence level or in which the policies or rules serve to exclude many persons. An illustration of how this process works can be seen from the Southern Regional Council's study of public assistance grants in the 100 poorest counties in the nation, 97 of which are located in the southern states.[43] With median family incomes ranging from $1,260 to $1,956, these counties need public assistance desperately. In addition, the gap between need and resources is most acute since the counties are rural and have little industry and high unemployment. In their poorest counties, the grants for Old-Age Assistance ranged from a median of $47.19 in North Carolina to $73.39 in Virginia in 1965. Frequently, the state sets a need standard which it is unable to meet. For example, in 1965 Alabama set an ADC standard in its poorest counties of $177 for a mother and three children and only reached a maximum of $81. The actual median ADC grant in Alabama that year was $51.84. The standards of living used by the states are also inadequate. Those for an aged adult living alone range from South Carolina's $77.55 to Alabama's $124.85 and ADC standards for a woman with three young children range from Arkansas' $124 to Tennessee's $198.

Many ADC eligibility rules exclude families which have husbands or other men in the home or where more than a certain number of illegitimate children have been born. In regard to repeated illegitimacies, Mississippi requires a fine or imprisonment of up to 90 days for the parent of a second illegitimate child, and a subsequent conviction can go to $500 and six months in jail. Louisiana's law for this crime sets the fine at up to $1,000 and the imprisonment up to a year. One of the effects of these laws is to force the mother to tell the truth about the father or face criminal action, lie, attempt an abortion, or seek financial help elsewhere.[44] Several southern states have considered the enactment of compulsory sterilization laws for AFDC mothers with repeated illegitimate children, which would serve several simultaneous latent functions: 1. to limit the birth rate of lower-class black children, and 2. to save welfare funds through deterrence of applications.

Another deterrent which is often effective are the laws or regulations governing recoveries, liens, and assignment limitations. Tennessee requires that payments made to an abandoned or deserted wife or child are recoverable by the state from the husband or parent. North Carolina provides for recovery of all OAA assistance through a lien on real property. Other states have various means for regaining some or all the monies expended on various types of grants.[45] The income from other sources of real or personal property may not exceed a relatively small amount. In regard to income, none of the poorer states allow the highest possible exemption from personal income established in the Social Security Act Amendments of 1965.[46] Many allow only slightly more than the mandatory floor. Six of the Southern states disregard no income for OAA recipients, 11 disregard no income for APTD* recipients, and only a few states disregard any income in AFDC.[47] Similarly, recipients in all states are strictly limited in terms of the amount of property, real and personal, they may own to qualify for assistance.[48] Virginia adds restrictions to make certain that no sale or transfer has occurred within five years of application.[49] North Carolina limits cash, savings, bonds, insurance and other property to $500.[50] Alabama makes an applicant ineligible for a year if he has disposed of a homestead in order to become eligible for welfare unless he is destitute and a community problem.[51] In Arkansas ownership of an automobile valued at over $1,000 disqualifies the applicant.[52]

Furthermore, the manner and attitude with which applicants are received and dealt with can be strong deterrents. An air of suspicion, condescension, censor, an assortment of official forms to be filled out, and a large cadre of impersonal and businesslike officials all become effective deterrents. Past experiences or reports from friends and relatives can create fearful expectations that may serve a deterrent function, as may the thought of stigma, failure, inadequacy, or charity. For example,

* Aid to the Permanently and Totally Disabled.

critical articles on public welfare in popular magazines such as *Reader's Digest* may have deterred tens of thousands of people from applying for needed assistance.

Eligibility

Whereas deterrents may effect individuals, eligibility restrictions may exclude entire groups of the population. From the outset, public welfare programs have tended to be established on the basis of certain categories. These categories, by their very nature, lay the groundwork for exclusion because general assistance for instance was never mandatory and some states have not established that category.

Adherence to established standards of moral conduct is a frequently-used eligibility device as is willingness to yield certain personal liberties.[53] Some states make particular use of age limitations to deny aid to the needy, often under the pretext of avoiding an overlap of welfare programs. For example, states generally require a minimum age of 65 years to qualify for old age assistance, although ample evidence exists to indicate that some people become senile and incapable of work before this age. Recipients of Aid to the Permanently and Totally Disabled have an age span of 18-65, although one could visualize its need for many 16 and 17 year olds. Mississippi requires that recipients of Aid to the Blind, if under 18, be in attendance at a school for the blind or some analogous institution. Texas limits its aid to the blind to 21 and over. AFDC age restrictions vary from 16 to 18 in many states with a built-in discouragement for many children to complete high school.

Another eligibility mechanism of growing importance is the requirement that forces parents or relatives responsible for a child on ADC to work if jobs can be found. Over the objections of social welfare leaders, the 90th Congress included this provision in the Social Security Act Amendments of 1967, although provisions were made for expansion of day care facilities to care for the children of working mothers. The Chamber of Commerce of the United States supported this policy by stating unequivocally that "there is a job available for every person in this country who is willing and able to work."[54]

There is an implicit assumption, that among other requirements:

A really needy person will not be a newcomer, will not sin, will have nothing to hide and therefore will submit to whatever searches of his physical premises are asked of him, and will accept intrusion into his emotional privacy by the welfare agency that dispenses services along with money.[55]

But one of the most extensive uses of eligibility as a rationing mechanism is in administrative boundaries, specifically in geographic residence. The states and federal government alike have resisted the welfare proponents' pressure to drop all residence requirements, because these requirements obviously appear to have the latent function of serving as an effective rationing device. The Southern Regional Council refers to residence as the most severe restriction of all.[56] The maximum allowable residence requirements were originally established at five years in the Social Security Act of 1935, and a half dozen states have consistently adhered to the maximum although about half of the states in the U.S. have dropped to a year.[57] Only a few states have dropped the residence requirement, insisting only on presence and intent. A variation of the state residence requirement is that of citizenship limitation. In the Southern Regional Council's study, referred to above, five of the 44 programs in the eleven states studied were found to require a welfare recipient to be a United States citizen.[58] The southern areas of Texas, for example, use substantial numbers of seasonal migrant laborers, chiefly of Mexican citizenship. By excluding them from public assistance eligibility, the state attains the three-fold result of getting cheap labor, incurring no welfare expenses from those who become incapacitated or otherwise in need, and establishing the example of ignoring all related social-cultural-economic problems that these laborers may tend to present. Professionals argue that need, not residence, should be the sole criterion, but policy-makers have seldom been impressed with this position. Even professional welfare officials at times have disagreed on this issue in fear of the consequences to their bureaucratic machinery if this rationing mechanism were removed. Empirical data are scare on the costs of a change in residence requirements. Steiner doubts that sweeping policy changes will occur until such data are available.[59] However, some courts are challenging the constitutionality of residency laws. The District Court in Hartford, Connecticut recently struck down that state's one year requirement, noting that "the right of interstate travel also encompasses the right to be free of discouragement of interstate movement." *The New York Times* applauded the court's action with the statement that the facts show that needy persons do not pick up and move around to find a state with a particularly favorable welfare grant.[60] *The Wall Street Journal* contended that a significant number of people shop around for the best benefits. Therefore, eliminating residency laws will *hurt* the poor, since states will want to stay solvent by not paying more than nearby states.[61]

Delay

Delay is a tool which may be planned or unplanned but which usually takes the form of long waiting lines, assignment of future appointments and the like. Parker repeats a tragic-comic story from a novel of a social worker who describes the spontaneous remission of problems which occur as the result of long waiting lists, concluding that by the time they are seen at the clinic, nearly 90 percent are cured.[62] In terms of public welfare, the long waiting period serves to encourage the applicant to seek alternative sources of help, to move, to find employment far below his skills, to take children out of school to work, or even to steal.

Misunderstanding

Misunderstanding of the existence or function of a service is a commonplace rationing instrument. Public welfare departments seldom advertise their policies, addresses or procedures. Information about how much income one may have, the operation of lien laws, and residence requirement is not widely distributed. It is quite likely that many needy people simply do not understand the availability of the program or their own eligibility.

Dilution

Dilution involves the lowering of service and funds by spreading the resources thinly. In this alternative, an increased demand is not deflected, turned away, discouraged, ignored, or kept waiting. Instead the amount of time and other resources allocated to each recipient is simply reduced on the basis that the available resources must be divided among a larger number of the needy. In effect, this was a latent function of the decision of the Ways and Means Committee in the House of Representatives in the 90th Congress, 1967, to freeze the number of AFDC recipients at the total for a specified date. Such a freeze means ultimately a dilution of the monetary and other services.

The obvious need is for public discussion and debate on the entire issue of rationing services and a facing up to the alternatives and consequences. This seems to be happening more frequently at the federal level. Whereas traditionally public welfare policy-making has been largely automated, with programming confined to fixed categories and standards, the 90th Congress addressed itself much more thoughtfully to at least a few of the policy issues. Also, there has been a lack of presidential leadership, with one or two exceptions. President Lyndon B. Johnson stated, in signing the Social Security Amendments of 1967:

> The welfare system in America is outmoded and in need of a major change. I am announcing today the appointment of a Commission on Income Maintenance Programs to look into all aspects of existing welfare and related programs and to make just and equitable recommendations for constructive improvements, wherever needed and indicated. We must examine any and every plan, however unconventional, which could promise a constructive advance in meeting the income needs of all the American people.[63]

MANAGEMENT OF PUBLIC WELFARE

Former President Johnson's statement raises, beyond the level of theory, the possibility of approaching the diminution of poverty through such automated substitutes for public assistance as the guaranteed annual income, the negative income tax, or a system of family allowances. It also throws wide the doors to new organizational procedures such as the involvement of the poor. Several of the long and/or short term approaches to the complex and highly controversial management of public welfare in our society have substantial advantages and disadvantages. Some would require major philosophical changes for large numbers of Americans. A number of these proposals are discussed below.

Alternative Income Support Programs

The inadequacies of the principal vehicle for aiding the poor in the United States, the public assistance program, have been reviewed. It should be obvious that the level of income provided cannot meet the basic needs of its recipients. Perhaps the major criticism is that the majority of America's poor do not receive any assistance. Moreover, most of the public assistance programs are not applicable to the working poor. As a result, over two million heads of families who work full-time annually never receive sufficient earnings to raise the families above the poverty level. While there is no real consensus about the actual income needs of families, in the national attempt to attack poverty in the United

States a number of proposals offer additional income to the poor. At least one of the plans, family allowances, has a long history here and abroad.[64]

FAMILY ALLOWANCES.   Our society philosophically backs to the hilt the policy that equal pay for equal work without discrimination is the most desirable economic form. While such a policy is supportive of those high priority policies of equality of opportunity, it is oblivious to the basic needs of large families and results in major deprivation. The problem of providing large families with adequate income is and has been a provocative problem for industrial societies. Consequently, the first experiments to develop a system of supplementing the income of low-wage earners and families without wage earners were attempted almost two centuries ago in Great Britain.

The two major justifications for family allowances are: (1) the needs of children should be of paramount concern to a society, and (2) wage systems in most countries are not an adequate base for income distribution. In one form or other, most of the world's industrial countries maintain some form of program to meet minimum family needs. They range from the French program which is financed by employers and may represent an addition of two-thirds to the income of a family with five or more children, to that of the government sponsored Canadian program which supplies so little per child that allowances are an insignificant proportion of total family income. Generally the trend in other countries has been to raise the percentage of national income allocated to family allowances.

The United States has never adopted a major program to adjust the wage system to the diverse needs of families. There are some slight adjustments to family size made in the income tax regulations and AFDC does offer a variety of family allowances.

No serious consideration has ever been given to a family allowance plan in the United States, and a proposal for Senate study died without a hearing in 1956. Other proposals appear to be in the forefront of serious discussion; these are the negative income tax and a guaranteed income. *NEGATIVE INCOME TAX-GUARANTEED INCOME.*   There are a number of types of negative income tax proposals. Each attempts to use the income tax machinery as a mechanism to supply income to the poor. The simplest form is that which would permit nontaxable individuals and families to claim the unused portion of their current exemptions. This is a limited plan which would not greatly expand the income of the poor, but nevertheless would cost several billion dollars. At the other end of the continuum of proposals are those aimed at completely closing the poverty income gap by overhauling the present tax system to more adequately pay the poor enough to meet basic needs. Such a proposal, which would eliminate poverty, would cost well over $12 billion annually. A compromise plan between the above two proposals would guarantee an annual income which would cover 50 percent of the poverty gap—a halfway plan! The cost of such a plan would range approximately half way between the former two.

Critics of these plans are principally concerned with the probability that large numbers of Americans would be robbed of the incentive to work since the guaranteed income would be as much as or more than their earned income. In order to provide continued incentive to work, most plans permit the low-wage earner to keep a portion or all of his earned income. Dr. Robert J. Lampman, who has made the most exhaustive cost estimates of the different types of negative income tax proposals, maintains that by encouraging work incentive in this manner, the conservative cost of a program would be double the present poverty income gap. There is little question that the national goal of eliminating poverty involves conflicting mores and substantial financial resources.

Guaranteed income programs are not a panacea for poverty in the United States—only one suggested form of management. Whether based on a negative income tax or other financial arrangements, there are technical, financial, and ideological problems. Many of the technical and ideological problems center on rights and eligibility. The technical will be solved long before the ideological. The cost is certainly one of the severest limiting factors. Many contend that the federal budget cannot supply the billions necessary without considerable tax reform.[65] Nevertheless, neither the negative income tax, nor the guaranteed annual income, nor family allowance system has been proven ideal. We have already seen that the provision of funds alone does not necessarily bring a person out of a life of actual poverty. How a person or family spends the income or grant may be of critical importance. Caplovitz has recently documented the fact that "a combination of faulty laws, unscrupulous merchants and an unawareness of their legal rights frequently forces many low income families further and further into debt."[66]

THE INVOLVEMENT OF THE POOR

It has been suggested that policy-making in a democracy works most effectively when powerful groups espouse different stands on a given issue. In the give and take of debate, the search for substantiating evidence and data, the marshalling of support, and the clarification of goals and aims, there is a strong likelihood that a viable public policy will emerge. Until very recently, few attempts were made to encourage the poor to speak for themselves. Representation has been left to such organizations as the American Public Welfare Association, the National Association of Social Workers, and the National Social Welfare Assembly. Generally, these groups have been more interested in the social insurances, child welfare, mental health, enrichment of family life, and other programs implicitly directed more toward the middle or lower class than toward the poor. At best they have stood for a minimum floor under which income ought not to go, and at worst they stood for entrenchment of bureaucratic traditions, practices and ideologies unrelated to a new role for the poor. Steiner notes that few members of the National Association of Social Workers are employed in public assistance and most would not be affected by public assistance policy changes.[67]

Moreover, the low public image of welfare and welfare recipients and the bureaucratic structure and operation of welfare programs have reinforced feelings of helplessness and submissiveness on the part of recipients. In a study of the recipients' views of the public welfare system, Scott Briar found that they tended to dissociate themselves from the image they had of other recipients, tended to see themselves as suppliants asking for help rather than for their rights, expected to have little control over agency decision-making and perceived the agency as having considerable legitimate authority over recipients.[68] He concluded that few recipients have been exposed to organizations stressing their rights and agency obligations; that the elaborate procedures and relatively invisible decision-making apparatus of the welfare agencies serve to reinforce and perpetuate the recipients' perceptions of themselves as suppliants; and, indeed, that a social worker stance of kindness and understanding may accentuate the recipients' feelings of obligation and passivity. He suggests that agencies need to be consciously organized and operated to avoid the reinforcement of recipient attitudes of suppliance and submissiveness. In other words, public welfare agencies need to become "positive instruments for the inculcation in recipients of a conception of themselves as rights-bearing citizens, with all of the benefits this may have for increasing self-confidence and hope among these people."[69] There are a number of obvious ways this may be done. Specifically, we may:

1. simplify the eligibility and budgeting processes so that they will be intelligible to recipients with little education;
2. develop high visibility in the agency decision-making process;
3. enable high visibility of and accessibility to appeal procedures; and

4. redefine the social worker's role from that of an agent of the departments' rules and policies to that of an advocate to help the applicant secure his maximum benefits.

In a real sense, the proposals would enable welfare workers to represent the interests of the poor rather than the interests of the agency.

Briar's findings are documented in other sources. Herbert Krosney notes that public welfare's "clumsy forays into the morality of individual citizens violate the dignity of welfare recipients and reduce them to pawns of the bureaucratic state."[70] He suggests that the answer is to consider public assistance as a right rather than a privilege and applauds the development of increased advocacy for the rights of the poor through extended legal services, legal representation, legal counseling and preventive counseling.

Some changes in the involvement of the poor have occurred in the last two decades. In the 1950's the Public Affairs Program of the Ford Foundation initiated projects that emerged eventually as the Grey Area Projects in a number of cities, initially related to public schools and later to new interagency planning and coordinating groups. In the early 1960's the President's Committee on Juvenile Delinquency and Youth Crime undertook comparable demonstration projects. Both the Grey Area Projects and the President's Committee stressed environmental change, specifically vocational and educational opportunities, rather than individual change. Each attempted to secure local constituency for the program from recognized community leadership and from the segments of the population to be helped.[71]

By the late 1960's, greater emphasis was placed on the involvement of low income groups in programs financed by the federal government. An apparent growth was evident in the numbers of organized groups among the poor including the formation of welfare recipient rights groups in a number of states. The Technical Assistance Project of the American Public Welfare Association specifically encourages the formation of organizations of recipients strong enough to represent themselves, to hold meetings, and to share in policy-making and administrative decision-making.[72] Unaware, purposely or otherwise, of the traditional ways by which organizations encourage change, the organized poor have conceived of action approaches which are more militant. In 1968 *The Washington Post* carried an article indicating that the National Welfare Rights Organization was planning a "wholesale dumping of relief-supported children on the doorsteps of the nation's public officials July 1 . . . by their mothers to dramatize the brutality of new federal welfare laws."[73] The demonstration was planned to protest provisions included in the Social Security Amendments of 1967 compelling mothers to leave their children at day care centers and go to work.

In New York City, which contains 10 percent of the nation's 7 million welfare clients, one of the strongest pressures for welfare reforms acting upon the city welfare department has been a group of welfare clients' unions that have sprung up in the city and have spread to other parts of the country.[74] Originally intended to inform welfare clients of their rights under the laws and guide them in obtaining available funds, some of the unions are now determined to change drastically or destroy the system.

Involvement of the poor in policy-making, however, is far from an easy problem. Charles E. Silberman has noted that "the basic dilemma of the government's attempt to involve the poor . . . is that it is obliged, to some extent, to be manipulatory and paternalistic; and manipulation and paternalism are precisely what the poor don't need."[75] Marris and Rein observe that actual attempts to involve the poor in program-planning and policy-making in anti-poverty campaigns of the midsixties have faltered.[76] They conclude that the poor must be seen as an interest group competing for attention like any other interest group. Their success will be determined by their ability to organize and to assert their potential influence. Consumer boycotts and rent strikes have demonstrated that the economic power of the poor is collectively considerable, despite their poverty. Essentially, we might be forced to conclude that their appeal to the middle class conscience and the general fear of rioting and other forms of open conflict in the cities increases the poor's political power beyond their voting strength.[77]

In sum, it is questionable at this point in history whether government, social workers or other professions or groups will continue to speak for the poor or whether, ultimately, they will learn to speak and act for themselves.

A potentially significant development has been the discovery of new jobs for the poor in various fields of social service including the fields of anti-poverty and public welfare. Early enthusiasts such as Pearl and Riessman recognized that the Economic Opportunity Act of 1964 provided an opportunity for the employment of the poor in programs for the poor.[78] By obtaining service from the poor in place of providing service to the poor, a new strategy was developed for alleviating poverty. Proposals were presented for providing continuing education for the new jobs to provide opportunities for career development and advancement. Specific areas for the use of nonprofessionals included jobs as aides, assistants and associates in schools and community mental health programs, and as neighborhood workers and homemakers. Proponents did recognize a number of potential dangers or pitfalls in the utilization of nonprofessionals, including antiprofessionalism, deadend jobs, rejection of the poor by the indigenous nonprofessional, out-professionalizing the professional, etc.

In the long run, as with policy-making, the most viable course of action will be for whoever represents the poor to demand the educational, training, and vocational opportunities necessary for increased employment. Although governmental, professional, and various other interest groups can pave the way and make initial attacks on the inadequacies of the present structures, there will inevitably be differences in goals, objectives and means. There can be no substitute for a strong, militant pressure group or groups interested solely or primarily in jobs and education for the poor.

BRINGING ABOUT CHANGE IN THE INSTITUTIONALIZED MECHANISM

Public welfare is a bureaucracy, a system of providing financial assistance, a delivery system for social services, a safeguard against economic depression, a mechanism for recirculating money through the society, a market for jobs, and a communication channel between the middle class and the poor. To produce changes in it, one must first determine—and get substantial concurrence from major power groups— what it is one wishes to change and the direction of change. For example, to reduce the number of impersonal, routine-focused bureaucratic characteristics of public welfare, Harrington has proposed providing more adequate funding so that caseloads can be reduced and workers can have time to work more intensively toward retraining and rehabilitation.[79] Even this may be far from enough to change the objectionable features of bureaucracy. Research has indicated that lowering caseloads may result in investment of more time in recording and case conferences. It may be necessary to change organizational goals, norms, values and structure, *i.e.,* to redefine public welfare as a helping service rather than a financial service, before the bureaucracy can change. Obviously, it may also be necessary to employ more highly skilled workers, and to build in a system of rewards for competence in compassionate treatment of clients as opposed to parsimonious and efficient handling of public funds. In short, the demands of the American middle class have made public welfare into a bureaucracy and it is perhaps quite accurate to say that middle class values must undergo some shift before the system can undergo change.

Suggestions could also be formulated about change in the public welfare system if the goals of change were to make the delivery of financial assistance more efficient, or more economical, or more expeditious. Such suggestions might include automation of eligibility determinations, reevaluations, payment of funds and so forth.

Improvement of the public welfare system as a job market might include the development of new positions with specific functions for people with less than a college education such as friendly visiting with the aged and determining eligibility through contacts with relatives, friends, and financial establishments. Obviously, this goal would work in an opposite direction from the goal of economy or the allied goal of efficiency. Here we might prefer the possibility of inefficient procedures in order to create more jobs.

SUMMARY ON CONDITIONS OF CHANGE. We must stress the key role in any action of the commitment of major power groups. The adoption of resolutions at conferences of social workers or public welfare personnel, no matter how eloquent or timely, are apt to bring about little change in public welfare as a system, unless such power groups as labor, industry, minorities, parallelism, or intellectuals are mobilized to support vigorously an agreed upon course of action. The more a course of action appeals to a number of these groups, the greater change will be effected. The more systematic and objective attention is given to the values and perceptions of these groups, the more likely the course of action will be developed in such a way as to mobilize their support in limiting the gaps between our understanding of the causes of poverty and the means for eradicating it.

Selected Readings

American Public Welfare Association, *Challenge to Validity: Public Welfare Goals, Commitments, Barriers, Propositions* (July 1967).

"Should the Federal Government Guarantee Minimum Annual Income to All Citizens: Pros and Cons," *Congressional Digest* (October 1967).

Michael Harrington, *The Other America: Poverty in the United States* (Baltimore: Penguin Books, 1963).

Herbert Krosney, *Beyond Welfare: Poverty in the Supercity* (New York: Holt, Rinehart, and Winston, 1966).

Peter Marris and Martin Rein, *Dilemmas of Social Reform: Poverty and Community Action in the United States* (New York: The Atherton Press, 1967).

Edgar May, *The Wasted Americans* (New York: Harper and Row, 1964).

Robert M. O'Neil, "Unconstitutional Conditions: Welfare Benefits with Strings Attached," in Jacobus ten Brock, ed., *The Law of the Poor* (San Francisco: Chandler Publishing Co., 1966).

Arthur Pearl and Frank Riessman, *New Careers for the Poor: The Nonprofessional in Human Service* (New York: The Free Press, 1965).

Charles A. Reich, "Individual Rights and Social Welfare: The Emerging Legal Issues," *The Yale Law Journal*, 74 (1965).

Gilbert Y. Steiner, *Social Insecurity: The Politics of Welfare* (Chicago: Rand, McNally and Co., 1966).

Notes to Chapter 4

[1] U.S. Bureau of the Census, *Pocket Data Book, U.S.A. 1969* (Washington, D.C.: U.S. Government Printing Office, 1969), p. 201. A family is defined as a "group of two or more persons related by blood, marriage, or adoption, and residing together."

[2] *Report of the National Advisory Commission on Civil Disorders* (Washington: U.S. Government Printing Office, 1968), p. 253.

[3] *Ibid.*, p. 252.

[4] *Ibid.*

[5] *Statistical Abstract of the United States, 1968* (Washington, D.C.: U.S. Government Printing Office, 1968), p. 300.

[6] *Ibid.*, p. 301.

[7] *Ibid.*

[8] *Report of the National Advisory Commission on Civil Disorders, op. cit.,* p. 252.

[9] *Ibid.*

[10] *Statistical Abstract of the United States, 1957, op. cit.,* p. 442.

[11] *Statistical Abstract of the United States, 1968, op. cit.,* pp. 431-2.

[12] A classic review of early approaches can be found in Karl De Schweinitz, *England's Road to Social Security* (Philadelphia: University of Pennsylvania Press, 1943), pp. 1-29.

[13] Philip Ashworth, "New Policies for Pensions," in Bow Group, ed., *The Conservative Opportunity* (London: B. T. Batsford Ltd., 1965), p. 28.

[14] British Information Services, *Social Services in Britain* (1966), p. 5.

[15] Margaret S. Gordon, *The Economics of Welfare Policies* (New York: Columbia University Press, 1963), p. 2.

[16] Michael Harrington, *The Other America: Poverty in the United States* (Baltimore: Penguin Books, 1963), pp. 15-24.

[17] Oscar Ornati, *Poverty Amid Affluence: A Report on a Research Project* (New York: The New School for Social Research, The Twentieth Century Fund, 1966), and Lowell E. Galloway, "Book Review on Ornati's Book," *The Journal of Human Resources*, Vol. II, No. 4 (Fall 1967), pp. 541-3.

[18] For a discussion of the establishing of the constitutional principle that the government should guarantee economic security to all members of society, see Edward S. Corwin, "The Passing of Dual Federalism," Robert G. McCloskey, ed., *Essays in Constitutional Law* (New York: Ventage Books, 1957), p. 186.

[19] Alan Keith-Lucas, *Decisions About People in Need* (Chapel Hill: The University of North Carolina Press, 1957), pp. vii-viii.

[20] A. Delafield Smith, "Community Prerogative and the Legal Rights and Freedom of the Individual," *Social Security Bulletin*, IX, No. 8 (August 1946), p. 8.

[21] Alvin L. Schorr, *Poor Kids* (New York: Basic Books, Inc., 1966), p. 11.

[22] See, for example, August B. Hollingshead, *Elmtown's Youth* (New York: John Wiley and Sons, Inc., 1949), p. 452.

[23] *Ibid.*, p. 362.

[24] Egon Ernest Bergel, *Social Stratification* (New York: McGraw-Hill Book Company, Inc., 1962), p. 407.

[25] W. Lloyd Warner and Paul S. Lunt, *The Social Life of a Modern Community* (New Haven: Yale University Press, 1941), p. 426.

[26] For example, C. Wright Mills notes the basic insecurity and fear in the small business stratum of the middle class that results in a stress on individual virtue, hard work, self-idealization, and criticism of the failure. "The Middle Classes in Middle-Sized Cities," in Reinhard Bendix and Seymour Martin Lipset, *eds., Class, Status and Power*, 2nd Ed. (New York: The Free Press, 1966), pp. 278-79.

[27] John F. Cuber and William F. Kenkel, *Social Stratification in the United States* (New York: Appleton-Century Crofts, 1954), p. 232. Cuber and Kenkel refer to data collected by Richards Centers, *The Psychology of Social Classes* (Princeton: Princeton University Press, 1949), p. 57.

[28] Robert S. Lynd and Helen Merrell Lynd, *Middletown In Transition* (New York: Harcourt, Brace and Company, 1937), p. 415. They point out that the indignation of businessmen who protest most loudly against public assistance derives in part from the knowledge that they have a deep, kindly attitude toward anyone in dire need.

[29] For a statement of the entrenchment of Social Security, see Cuber and Kenkel, *op. cit.,* p. 341.

[30] R. Joseph Monsen and Mark W. Cannon, *The Makers of Public Policy* (New York: McGraw-Hill, 1965), pp. 26-43, 46-56.

[31] Lynd and Lynd, *op. cit.,* pp. 473-4.

[32] Cuber and Kenkel, *op. cit.,* p. 220, cite a study by Alfred W. Jones to show that the United States has a "central morality" which is humanitarian and approves of acts in the interest of human welfare and the alleviation of suffering. Alfred W. Jones, *Life, Liberty, and Property* (Philadelphia: J. B. Lippincott Co., 1941).

[33] Edgar May, *The Wasted Americans* (New York: Harper and Row, 1964), p. 104, estimates almost 35,000 public welfare caseworkers alone, as of 1963. In addition to steady growth in caseworkers, there are also a sizable number of administrators, consultants, specialists and supervisors. The *Statistical Abstract of the United States, 1967* (Washington: U.S. Government Printing Office, 1967) indicates 182,450 public welfare employees as of October 1966. This number includes clerks, typists, stenographers, receptionists, bookkeepers and other personnel. It represents an annual increase of 12,628 since October 1965.

[34] *Statistical Abstract of the United States, 1967, op. cit.,* p. 442.

[35] Lynd and Lynd, *op. cit.,* p. 494.

[36] *Ibid.*, p. 127.

[37] See, for example, the greater stress on programs to lift wages in AFL-CIO Executive Council Statement, "Waging War on Poverty," Louis A. Ferman *et. al., eds., Poverty in America: A Book of Readings* (Ann Arbor: University of Michigan Press, 1965).

[38] Stokely Carmichael, "Power and Racism," *Revolutions: Emphasis 67* (Tuscaloosa: University of Alabama Student Government Association, 1967), p. 12.

[39] See Elinor Graham, "Poverty and the Legislative Process," Ben B. Seligman, *ed., Poverty as a Public Issue* (New York: The Free Press, 1965), p. 266.

[40] Cuber and Kenkel, *op. cit.,* p. 248.

41 Walter B. Miller, "Focal Concerns of Lower-Class Culture," *Poverty in America: A Book of Readings, op. cit.,* p. 269.

42 Some of the material from this section is adapted from R. A. Parker, "Social Administration and Scarcity: The Problem of Ration," *Social Work,* Vol. 24, No. 2 (England: April 1967), pp. 9-14.

43 See Southern Regional Council, *Public Assistance: To What End?* (Atlanta, Ga.: November 1967), pp. 11-20.

44 *Ibid.,* p. 37.

45 *Ibid.,* pp. 37-39.

46 *Ibid.,* pp. 29-30.

47 *Ibid.*

48 *Ibid.,* pp. 26-29.

49 *Ibid.,* p. 28.

50 *Ibid.*

51 *Ibid.,* p. 36.

52 *Ibid.,* pp. 36-37.

53 See Gilbert Y. Steiner, *Social Insecurity: The Politics of Welfare* (Chicago: Rand McNally and Company, 1966), p. 108.

54 "We Can Get Anybody a Job," *Nation's Business* (January 1967), p. 35.

55 Steiner, *op. cit.,* p. 108.

56 See Southern Regional Council, *op. cit.,* pp. 21-22.

57 *Ibid.,* p. 133.

58 Southern Regional Council, *op. cit.,* pp. 22-23.

59 Steiner, *op. cit.,* pp. 138-9.

60 *The New York Times* (June 23, 1967).

61 *The Wall Street Journal* (June 28, 1967).

62 Parker, *op. cit.,* p. 11.

63 *The New York Times* (January 4, 1968), p. 17.

64 Paul H. Douglas, *Wages and the Family* (Chicago: University of Chicago Press, 1925).

65 George H. Hildebrand, "Second Thoughts on the Negative Income Tax," in House of Representatives Document No. 172, *Resolved: That the Federal Government Should Guarantee A Minimum Annual Cash Income to All Citizens* (Washington, D.C.: U.S. Government Printing Office, 1967), p. 154.

66 David Caplovitz, "The Other Side of the Poverty Problem," *Social Service Outlook,* Vol. 2, No. 4 (April 1967), p. 7.

67 Steiner, *op. cit.,* p. 241.

68 Scott Briar, "Welfare From Below: Recipients' Views of the Public Welfare System," in Jacobus ten Broek, *ed., The Law of the Poor* (San Francisco: Chandler Publishing Co., 1966), pp. 46-61.

69 *Ibid.,* p. 60.

70 Herbert Krosney, *Beyond Welfare: Poverty in the Supercity* (New York: Holt, Rinehart, and Winston, 1966), p. 141.

71 Peter Marris and Martin Rein, *Dilemmas of Social Reform: Poverty and Community Action in the United States* (New York: Atherton Press, 1967), p. 24.

72 *Public Welfare: Challenge to Validity: Goals, Commitments, Barriers, Propositions,* Technical Assistance Project (American Public Welfare Association, July 1967), p. 17.

73 "Moms to Dump Children in Welfare Laws Protest," *The Washington Post* (February 8, 1968).

74 Mary D. Nichols, "Nobody Loves Welfare," *Wall Street Journal* (August 8, 1967).

75 Charles E. Silberman, *The Myths of Automation* (New York: Harper and Row, 1966), p. 83.

76 Marris and Rein, *op. cit.,* p. 185.

77 *Ibid.*

78 Arthur Pearl and Frank Riessman, *New Careers for the Poor: The Nonprofessional in Human Service* (New York: The Free Press, 1965), p. ix.

79 See Elinor Graham, "The Politics of Poverty," Ben B. Seligman, *ed., Poverty as a Public Issue* (New York: The Free Press, 1965), p. 117.

CHAPTER FIVE

PERSPECTIVES ON AMERICAN HEALTH PROBLEMS

As a nation, Americans are continually searching for good health. They diet, exercise, sunbathe, vaccinate, immunize, disinfect, deodorize, sanitize, use tons of detergent, swallow thousands of pills, and demand varieties of medical and dental specialists and larger, more complex hospital and treatment units. Billions of private and public dollars are spent annually in the race for life. As a result, the medical successes which have been made are a matter of historical record. Typhoid and other water-born infectious diseases have been controlled through nationwide programs of water and sewage treatment. A startling increase in the life expectancy of Americans has occurred in the last six decades as a result of the control of communicable disease through public health sanitation. From a life expectancy at birth of 54.1 years in 1920, Americans in the nineteen-sixties could expect to live over twenty years longer.[1]

Polio, measles and mumps along with smallpox, whooping cough and diphtheria are becoming rare. The introduction of antibiotics has further decreased the level of illness, especially among children. A consequence of the increase in life expectancy has been an increase in the incident of chronic diseases, arthritis, cancer and cardiovascular disorders. Reflecting on the change, Stanley King states that,

> . . . This can be seen most strikingly in comparing the leading causes of death over the years, where influenza and pneumonia have dropped from first to seventh place, and tuberculosis from second to eleventh, to be replaced by diseases of the heart and cancer in the number one and two positions. Chronic, noncommunicable diseases, including mental disorders, have become the main health problem of the present age.[2]

Even in these areas, substantial gains are being made. Radical surgical techniques in orthopedics, heart, eye, kidney and liver diseases are altering substantially society's definitions of "invalid" and "infirmed."

DEFINITIONS OF HEALTH

Although there has been a legion of change, the major dilemma is both theoretical and practical: how does our society define health and how does it attempt to implement the definition? Medical care throughout history has reflected the particular definition of health which a society has embraced, restricting and limiting alternative patterns of care and organization of services. The nature of the changes in the leading causes of death in the United States reflect the emergence of a new concept of health and sickness from one of concentration on avoidance of disease

135

and injury to one of attempted prevention through health planning. In combination with continuous programs of immunization, there has been added an emphasis on annual physical examinations which include extensive laboratory tests geared to the age group of the patient in terms of statistical health problem areas by age. There are concerns for diet and the elimination of problem foods, for cigarette smokers, for the development of recreation and recreation programs for patients under heavy psychological pressures. New concepts in dental care such as the emphases on daily sanitary cleansing of the entire mouth combined with the consumption of floridated water and annual floride treatment of the teeth could eliminate the major problems of tooth decay in the United States.[3]

These changes in the nature of treatment combined with cultural and attitudinal changes in American society have resulted in the development of several new definitions of health which are considerably broader than the traditional concepts. Three definitions attracting numbers of vocal followers whose general acceptance and implementation could appreciably alter man's attitudes toward and his effectiveness in fighting disease are *comprehensive medicine, social medicine,* and *positive health.* The traditional concepts limited health to the avoidance of disease; treatment for sickness and injury reflected and differed in terms of the socioeconomic level of the affected family. The major difference between the old and the new concepts is that the latter include all men regardless of social class and it relates health to all aspects of man's environment. For example, the concept of comprehensive medicine commands the resources of society in addition to those of the physician and auxiliary health workers in the treatment and prevention of illness. Comprehensive medicine would treat the whole patient and study man in his environment.[4] The philosophical concept of social medicine reflects that the health professions can be effective only if they encompass the total picture of man and environment, not man as distinct from environment but environment with man in it. The philosophy of social medicine differs from comprehensive medicine, which starts with the patient and his ills, by focusing on society and its ills and the way these affect the health of the individual.[5] The third conception, positive health, has gained world acceptance. Health has traditionally been defined in negative terms—as the absence of disease. The new concept of positive health regards it as the releasing of potential. This definition, which has increased in popularity as a result of its embodiment in the constitution of the World Health Organization, asserts that "Health is a state of complete physical, mental and social well-being and not merely the absence of disease or infirmity."[6]

Underlying each of these definitions is the supposition that all people, regardless of race, religion, nationality, place of residence, social class, and income level are entitled to health. If we were to take a poll, most of us would agree that the World Health Organization's definition of health should be applicable to all people everywhere, in front of and behind the iron and bamboo curtains, in the ghettos of the metropolitan inner city and "across the tracks" in the American small town. While we may wish for a variety of ills to befall an enemy, competitor or one we dislike, we would not wish him to have a heart attack, to develop cancer or to be stricken with plague. For several very simple and at the same time highly complex reasons, agreement would end at that point.

The definitions of health cited above are based on the development of a high level of scientific knowledge and complex systems of organization. In an insightful article in *Fortune*, editor Walter Guzzardi, Jr. pinpointed one of the major threats to the management of American health problems:

> . . . Today, because medical knowledge is racing ahead a thousand times faster than it was. . . , the problem of how to apply the knowledge to the patient is multiplied. But it is still basically a problem of organization—the dovetailing of discoveries, techniques, training, and the diverse skills of the specialists into one economical and efficacious product—that confronts modern medicine.[7]

Definition vs Application

The belief that all Americans, regardless of social status and earning capacity, are entitled to the best medical care that is available has spread and substantially crystallized. However, advocates of the broadened definitions of health have found that these are not easily applied. It is a fact that many members of our society do not receive adequate medical or dental care. What Guzzardi and others have indicated is that science has infinitely more to give than people actually receive.[8] In a decade when substantial gains have been made to offer us more years of life, at least statistically, thousands still die prematurely who could have lived if the right health workers had been able to intervene at the appropriate time.[9] Because of economic, social and religious factors, huge reservoirs of medical knowledge are accumulating that we cannot fully apply. The more knowledge we compile the more we realize that while this is essential it is not "all." Knowledge is wasted unless it can be applied. Most of the difficulties we encounter in the application of medical knowledge to all Americans are caused by nonmedical factors which determine our success or our failure. "Whether," as Sigerist puts it, "a given society is willing and able to accept the advice of its physicians (and other health scientists) depends to a very large extent on its religious and philosophic views, on its social and economic conditions."[10] Succinctly, the way large numbers of people and influential groups are beginning to define health and medical care is creating new problems and changing or illuminating old problems of applying medical knowledge. While morally men may accept health care as a "right" of all people, much of our culture, our folkways, our personal desires for status differentiation, and the ever increasing demand on our pocketbooks reject its practicality. The application of medical knowledge is affected:

1. by religious/philosophical views held by societal members and groups,
2. by the folkways and mores which have suggested the way knowledge should and ought not to be applied,
3. by the availability of services, and
4. by the economic ability of the individual to pay for them.

The remainder of this chapter focuses on the relation of each of these agents to contemporary health problems of American society and to those additional problems which may evolve with efforts to extend health care to all Americans. Such an extension of services creates major difficulties for contemporary patterns of organization, to folkways and mores, and to the economy, and require extensive adaptation.

RELIGIOUS/PHILOSOPHICAL ATTITUDES AND THE PROVISION OF HEALTH CARE

From the very beginning of time, man has been in a life and death struggle with the environmental forces which surround him. His early struggles to understand, interpret and control nature led him from an interpretation of stones and trees as objects embodying supernatural powers to the direction of the same physical and chemical forces as healing and beneficial powers. Down through the centuries man has progressed in his overall public view of the sick. In his tribal days, a man suffering from a serious illness was feared and often abandoned by his fellows. He was considered dead socially before he was dead physically. Sickness was either the result of witchcraft or the wrath of the Gods.[11]

With the centuries new attitudes developed. In Semitic civilizations, sickness as well as other forms of individual and societal adversity were viewed as punishment for man's sins. Once this commitment to reason had been made, it proceeded down the centuries. In the Middle Ages, plagues and epidemics which took thousands of lives were considered to be the will of God—God's inflicted punishment upon man for his sinfulness. Which of us in twentieth century America, wallowing in scientific progress and discovery, has not silently wailed during the discomfort of flu or the pain of a broken bone: "What have I ever done to deserve this!" Not many! As Sigerist reflects, "the days are not far remote when people believed that mental diseases were the result of a disordinate life, or that venereal diseases were the logical punishment for sexual promiscuity."[12] Perhaps it is not even as remote as Sigerist's selected use of the term "days" indicates!

The attitude in the ancient Greek city state represented another extreme position toward the sick. It placed a high status on health, both of body and mind. Care of the sick who could never expect a complete recovery was considered unethical. All defective children were destroyed.[13]

From the Greek attitude toward the sick, the pendulum swung hard in the opposite direction as Christianity emerged. Christ's concern for the sick, the poor, the sinner, His healings and promises of redemption, placed the sick in a new societal position. At least in God's eyes and in the eyes of the devout, the sick man was no longer considered inferior or sinful; he was suffering with Christ and would be rewarded. Christianity enjoined the believer to care for the sick. This new position of the sick, within economic and scientific limits, continued and flourished down through the centuries side by side with rudimentary threads of tribal, semitic and Greek belief.

While contemporary society differs from that of our ancestors, while our attitudes toward the sick and sickness have changed over the centuries, while we provide funds for research in mental health, drug and alcohol addiction, and venereal disease, our attitudes have not kept pace with advances in scientific knowledge. In a class experiment, nine out of ten senior university students in a Medical Sociology class stated that if there were a choice, they would prefer to have heart disease, kidney/liver disorder, tuberculosis, a venereal disease and mental illness, in that order, stating that there was "less stigma attached," it was "nicer" or "more acceptable" to have the first two than the last two. Even the well-trained and professionally committed among us are susceptible to these concepts of "right" and "wrong," or "good" and "bad." A professor of public health with both a medical and a Ph.D. degree and years of professional experience admitted that the conclusions of a graduate student in a paper on the control of venereal diseases in American society upset him. The paper maintained that the abolition of "red light districts" in major American cities during the latter part of the 19th Century was disfunctional to the treatment of venereal diseases because it geographically scattered prostitutes. The author further concluded that the interest and control of prostitution by organized crime syndicates employing physicians to control venereal disease was functional to health care.

The addictive disorders of alcoholism and drug addiction and mental illness provide additional examples of the attitudes toward sickness and on the management of a health problem. Addictive disorders and mental disease are classified as social problems because each has become interwoven in the value systems of community and society. Moralistic attitudes relating these with unacceptable behavior patterns interfere with the scientific diagnosis and treatment of a disorder as health problems.

A conflict has developed between medical, lay and legal forces. Lay views of mental illness affect treatment in several ways. They may determine whether or not the patient and his family will allow an illness to be diagnosed professionally, what arrangements will be made for medical care and patient acceptance of treatment. Even though statistics reveal that there are hundreds of thousands of patients in mental hospitals in the United States [14]—indicating that some diagnosis has been made—stigmatization of mental illness has existed for centuries. While most Americans with some college education would deny negative feelings toward the mentally ill, they would hasten to attribute these feelings to others who are less informed. For most of us, mental illness represents a behavior deviance which is fraught with apprehension and desire for avoidance. Public response to mental illness, in many instances, is isolation and denial.[15] Just as in the tribal days of old, much of society would prefer to deny that the mentally ill exist.

Social Class and Societal Attitudes

Negative attitudes toward the sick and sickness are not restricted to one social class or another. The classes vary in terms of understanding and ability to secure, utilize and pay for professional assistance and facilities. The rich—with the exception of the public family, *e.g.,* the ruler or the king whose eccentricities become public record—have usually been able to purchase the best medical care available and to maintain it within the shroud of secrecy. Addictive disorders and mental illness may be diagnosed and the patient cared for at home, in a private office or sanitorium, far from the public eye. The upper, more affluent, classes can afford and therefore have available a wider choice of practitioners and treatment centers. However, the upper or middle class family has been no more willing than a lower class family to admit that a family member is afflicted with a mental illness, alcoholism, drug addiction, or a venereal disease.

Perhaps one of the reasons that general, overall attitudes toward the problem illnesses in American society seem to differ so little is the fact that all classes are affected by these diseases. While some studies indicate variation in the type of mental illness which occurs in the various social classes, mental disorders are found in all classes.[16]

Management of Religious/Philosophical Attitudes

Some difficult areas of problem management involve a change of attitudes. Some forms of overt behavior may be changed more easily than their underlying attitudes. Over the last two thousand years, the expulsion of diseased persons from the community, as in the case of those suffering from leprosy, has been discontinued. Eliminating this level of anti-social behavior was one thing, but eliminating the negative attitude and substituting a more socially acceptable one based on medical knowledge is another.

The history of the development of several of the religious/philosophical attitudes toward sickness and health indicate a long history rooted in folkways and mores, and deeply embedded in the cultural development of man's relationship with his God/Gods and his fellow men. In twentieth century America these views are still relevant for most of us, although pitted against the legion of scientific discoveries which should change them. The problem of altering these views has been the function of a number of professional and lay organizations and government.

On the highest level, the World Health Organization has attempted to define health in a more functional manner and has widely publicized the definition and its interpretation. It has further supported the intent of the latter by developing programs dispersing and implementing scientific findings all over the world. WHO has explored and carefully defined a range of health problems. For example, in the controversial area of drug addiction where some authorities feel that control could best be maintained through drug doses under medical supervision,[17] the World Health Organization argues that "the maintenance of drug addiction is not treatment."[18]

On the national level, the U.S. Public Health Service supports services in major health areas ranging from communicable diseases to mental health. It maintains centers and hospitals in which research is combined with the most advanced scientific knowledge and treatment. The U.S. Public Health Service Hospitals at Lexington, Kentucky and Fort Worth, Texas, which treat drug addicts, have international reputations for excellence. Programs of Public Health education which inform the American people of what their "proper" contemporary attitude toward a variety of diseases ought to be also are supported.

Related to the role of government in attitude change is the enactment of legislation nationally and locally. This is a major management arena, albeit a controversial one. Most of us would respond positively to the National Mental Health Act of 1946 which established the National Institute of Mental Health within the U.S. Public Health Service, or to the continued research on venereal disease! The laws or statutes classifying alcoholism and drug addiction as criminal rather than health problems have become extremely controversial. The fact that members of all social classes are involved has forced redefinitions within the framework of health and treatment. Traditionally, law represented the major management force in the control of communicable disease ranging from required immunization of school children to treatment of water and sewerage. Man's religio-philosophical view that God would protect him from contagion did not offer adequate societal insurance against plagues and epidemics. Even with the fantastic record of achievement in disease control through law, each new discovery and protection plan is fought until it is legally settled. The foes of immunization against diptheria and typhoid—on the grounds of "unnaturalness"—sprang up anew in the fight during the fifties and sixties against fluoridation of water.

Professional groups such as the American Medical Association, American Bar Association, American Red Cross, American Public Health Association and the National Association of Social Workers conduct educational programs, hold workshops, review, initiate, support and oppose legislation which defines health differently from their norms. These groups make powerful friends and "death-blow" enemies. Several of these organizations spend considerable sums of money annually to influence attitudes. Changing attitudes however is a tricky, complex business and one is never quite sure that the converts weren't in the pews all along.

Involved in some phase of health problem management are special interest groups such as Alcoholics Anonymous, Tuberculosis Association, National Foundation, Heart Association, Arthritis Foundation, and Planned Parenthood, which through citizen contributions focus attention on one health problem, attempt to educate the public in terms of the latest scientific evaluation of the illness, and often allocate research funds to further understanding.

On the other hand, there are forces operative in American society which support and maintain the old folkways and mores, which look on disease and illness as punishment for evil, and which see immunization and other forms of treatment as unnatural and wrong. The fragmentation of the church into a number of commitments—conservative and fundamental as well as social gospel—has resulted in the continuation and maintenance of the view that illness is God's punishment. In many fundamental "store-front" churches and religious groupings, this theme is still preached and believed. Some religious groups condemn either overtly or covertly various medical practices such as blood transfusion and surgical procedures. In Christian Science, for example, the practitioner must not assume that disease is real in any sense. In Mary Baker Eddy's guide *Science and Health*,[19] Snowden estimated that sickness and suffering as well as sin and death are denied at least three thousand times.[20]

In addition to religious beliefs there are autonomous groups which spring up to fight new programs and new treatments when the proposal is put to a popular vote. Groups opposed to the treatment of water with chlorine or fluoride have waged active political campaigns, because contrary to scientific fact, they believe that their introduction to the water supply is "unnatural" and physically harmful.

THE HEALTH PROFESSIONAL: A DILEMMA OF NUMBERS AND ORGANIZATION

Health care in any society depends not only upon scientific discovery but also on manpower trained to apply their knowledge to practice and organized to accelerate the process of application. With the change of public attitude in the fifties and sixties toward access to medical care as a right rather than a privilege, the development of numbers of effective personnel efficiently organized to readily apply scientific knowledge has gained increased recognition. For example, in the fall of 1967 an announcement of major medical import was made indicating "mounting evidence that a technique may have been found to prevent Rh disease from developing."[21] Rh disease affects tens of thousands of families annually. Babies suffering from this illness are the result of mothers who have Rh negative and have become immunized against Rh positive blood. The new research which prevents Rh negative mothers from developing antibodies against Rh positive blood, was based on the work of a medical scientist, Theobald Smith, whose research was completed in 1909. A *New York Times* editorial comment on the discovery was illustrative of many of the "new" attitudes: "Once again the value of basic research has been dramatically proved. But laymen must wonder why a half century had to pass before Smith's work could begin to be applied to help save lives."[22]

Another side of the dilemma is the availability of health personnel. For decades there have been frequent reports about the shortage of doctors, nurses, dentists and auxiliary health personnel. Often these were qualified by further statements relegating the problem to inadequate distribution of available professionals. Cities had an overabundance of practitioners. Responsively, many states offered stipends or preceptorships to medical students promising to practice for a year or more in a rural community.

Whether there would have been enough personnel, if distributed differently, to serve the families who could afford to pay for services is a moot question at this point in history. When Congress enacted Medicare and Medicaid programs after years of effort rooted in pioneering movements for health insurance in the thirties and forties, the picture was inexorably altered. Large groups of Americans could demand medical services for the first time without the concern of robbing the family budget or of placing the need for medical care in competition with other family demands. The new programs were the first concrete steps taken by Federal and state governments toward underwriting some of the nation's health care. The negative relationship of economic disadvantages to the alleviation of illness was eased through these programs. Although disillusioning, no matter how altruistic and self sacrificing an image we may conjure for the health professionals, no indication from as early as the nineteen twenties has failed to relate the supply of health personnel with a community or area's purchasing power.[23]

The Doctor Shortage

The physician is the key member of the medical service team. Where the number of physicians are adequate, the environment seems to attract other health personnel such as the dentist and nurse. When the environment appears unfavorable to physicians the supply of auxiliary medical personnel declines and a more detrimental situation develops in which lone physicians may be left with no assistance from other professionals in carrying the work load. The physician is the magnet whose decisions attract or repel, create or prevent the placement of other health personnel and facilities. A shortage of physicians in one state or area will seriously affect the latter's access to all other health personnel and services. The shortage of doctors described by government officials and major health organizations in the late sixties is the result of many factors, at least four of which are major:

1. distribution of personnel,
2. increase in the demand for service because more people are covered by health programs including Medicare and Medicaid,
3. increase in the number of medical specialists including researchers and medical school faculty, and
4. the slow percentage increase in the number of medical students.

DISTRIBUTION.   In late 1967, a number of newspapers alarmingly stated that there was a mounting shortage of doctors throughout the United States.[24] The old problem of distribution has been further aggravated by new methods of financing. For decades it has been difficult to arrive at an acceptable definition of the line between shortage and sufficient personnel. An optimum standard has been defined as one physician for every 742 persons,[25] or a more practical standard of one physician per 1,000 persons.[26]

Interpretation of a physician to patient ratio must take into account several factors: the average incidence of all types of illnesses including pregnancy; consideration of the professional time required for proper diagnosis, treatment, and preventive services; the organization of medical services; and other unique features of the specific social and geographical area. In addition, the type of physician classified in the ratio must be defined. Most figures include all types of locally available physicians such as teachers, researchers, public health men, and industrial physicians. Tabulation of all of these specialists overstates the supply of physicians actually engaged in clinical practice. For example, in 1964 the ratio of doctors to patients in the U.S. was one to every 662 patients when all physician groups were counted together and one for every 1,030 patients when only physicians in private practice were considered. Wider discrepancies existed between states even when the data for physicians were unrefined. New York boasted a ratio of 1 to 473 while Mississippi had a ratio of 1 to 1,351, and Alabama, South Carolina and South Dakota had ratios of approximately 1 to 1,250 patients.[27] Dentists in private practice and nurses follow a similar pattern. The national average ratio for dentists is 1 per 2,222 persons, while New York has a 1 to 1,492 ratio and South Carolina has one dentist for every 5,263 persons.[28] The national ratio distribution of professional nurses is 1 per 336 persons; Massachusetts has one nurse for every 199 and Arkansas only one for every 833 persons.[29]

The most striking examples of poor manpower distribution are in rural areas and in the central cities, or urban core. A trade publication, *New Medical Material,* conducted studies in 1959 and 1962 to determine the location of doctorless towns. The magazine found 1,079 of these communities in 1959 and an additional 373 three years later. Some figures estimate that there were as many as 5,000 doctorless communities in 1967 with that number increasing rapidly.[30] "The situation in rural areas is getting worse," stated Norman Davis, director of medical programs for the Sears Roebuck Foundation which has helped over 100 towns find doctors in the last decade. Davis maintained that only general practitioners can offer services to rural areas and that the supply of G.P.'s does not meet the demand.[31]

Rural communities generally do not possess either the cultural facilities which appeal to professional people or the medical resources required by doctors. If rural communities or small towns could be made culturally interesting for the doctor and his family, available personnel could better be distributed. The professional family often feels that most rural residents are their social and intellectual inferiors and that the rural community lacks cultural outlets. There is no theatre, no "good" music, often no golf or other recreation they are accustomed to, no lectures and no art. A study made by the New York State Medical Society indicated that the major causes of physician dissatisfaction in rural areas were long, unrelieved working hours, inadequate time to study, inadequate time to spend at medical meetings, and lack of the educational stimuli generally found around hospitals, medical centers and clinics.[32] Whatever the reasons, they were further complicated when the federal government extended financial Medicare and Medicaid assistance to many American families. Since 30 percent of all Americans live in rural communities and hamlets, many Medicare and Medicaid recipients are now able to pay for services which are not available.

With changes in national affluence and urban ecology, the urban core and slum have been added to the areas lacking services. An excellent example of the urban problem is found in the Watts area of Los Angeles County, California, the center of racial rioting in the summer of 1965. Milton I. Roemer found, in a study of the southeastern and southern districts involved in the riots, that the ratios of physicians per 100,000 population was 38 in the southeastern section and 45 in the southern as compared to the 127 in the rest of the nation. The two districts had approximately 15 dentists per 100,000 as compared to a state ratio of 67. Out of eight hospitals in the districts, only two were accredited by the Joint Commission. The areas had only one public health nurse for each 5,230 people although the standard ratio for this type of area is one for each 2,000 persons.[33]

The decaying surroundings and limited opportunity for financial rewards provides little inducement for a physician to practice in the inner city slum. A study by St. Luke's Hospital in the Columbia University area of New York City sought to determine the number of general practitioners in the area. The section has families of high and low incomes and a corresponding diversity of housing. Very few G.P.'s under the age of 30 had set up practice in the community. Unlike the pattern of the past, few recent medical school graduates had chosen to open offices in the area.[34] The slum would not get its share of physicians even if the total U.S. complement miraculously tripled overnight.

With several additions the slum approximates many of the negative aspects of the rural community. The middle or upper class physician's family does not wish to live in a poor housing area with inadequate schools and limited opportunities for cultural activities. Excluding family living, the physician cannot afford, in terms of his social class expectations, to establish an office in a neighborhood where treatment must be limited to the financial ability of the patient and where he and his property may be in constant physical danger. Another important factor is that most physicians are white and whites do not wish to live in a predominantly Negro slum area. Just as in the rural area, only men with special humanitarian commitments select this type of practice when more (socially and economically) lucrative practices are available in better business or residential areas. Since most urban Negroes live in slums, they are seriously affected by this change in practice. The gulf which has existed for generations between the health level of whites and nonwhites has widened.[35]

SPECIALIZATION.   Dr. William H. Stewart, while Surgeon General of the United States Public Health Service, stated in 1966 that "Specialization has completely altered the meaning of the physician-population ratio by which manpower needs have been measured for many years."[36] This trend has been the result of the ever increasing complexity of medicine in terms of basic research, sophisticated equipment, and a legion of drug developments and discoveries. It has also been the result of the recognition that the G.P. is one of the few workers in American society expected to labor 24 hours a day. Such a work schedule restricts family social life and interpersonal relationships to the extent that a G.P. may feel he has little or no personal life.

Two alternatives which are often interrelated are to go "academic" or "research." The number of full-time medical school faculty increased from 4,000 in 1952 to 18,000 in 1967; an increase of 350 percent. This increase was not reflected in the number of medical students which increased by only 35 percent. Faculty may elect to carry on research on a part-time or a full-time basis. There have been tremendous increases in the private and public funds available to medical schools for this function. In a little over one generation, research support from the Federal Government has risen from almost nothing to approximately $500 million a year in 1968.

All three alternatives to general practice—specialization, teaching and research—offer much higher status and easier access to other symbols embraced in the American stratification system. In communities where stratification is more rigid, regardless of income level, the G.P. may be relegated to a middle class position while the specialist will be classified as upper class.

The Medical School

With shortages of medical personnel increasing annually, attention has focused on medical student recruitment, cost of medical education, training programs, and medical school dropouts. Primarily responsibility in these and most areas regulating physician supply and adequacy must be assumed by the nation's medical schools. As a branch of higher education which has maintained high admissions levels and low student/faculty ratios, medical schools have been subject to self-study and public criticism. Some critics have argued that the number of medical students could be increased if faculties devoted less time to research and more to teaching. Other analysts contend that most medical schools train too many specialists and too few of the "good old garden variety" general practitioner.

By the late sixties, unable to meet the major societal demands of supply and demand, medical schools were forced to contend with serious internal problems. The most pressing problem has been financial. Consistently, faculty research involvement and failure to expand admissions policies have been attributed to the latter. According to a 1967 report by the Association of American Medical Colleges, every academic medical center in the United States was in trouble financially and some were in desperate straits.[37] Ten institutions were heading toward and two more were on the verge of bankruptcy unless substantial financial gains were made.[38] Marquette's medical school's deficit in the 1965-1966 and 1966-1967 years was $800,000 with a deficit of approximately $3 million in the last decade. New York Medical College lost $1 million between 1964 and 1967.

As a result of the rapid increase in Federal and private research funds, most of the medical schools in the country appeared to have had phenomenal budget increases during the last twenty or thirty years. In comparison, other sources of revenue to cover day-to-day expenses and capitalization costs for plant and equipment remained stable. Major schools such as Yale University School of Medicine, the University of Rochester School of Medicine and Dentistry, Duke University School of Medicine, and Columbia College of Physicians and Surgeons faced serious budgeting problems.[39]

COSTS OF MEDICAL EDUCATION.   Financial crisis forced substantial increases in medical school tuition. While doing little to eliminate the overall financial problem of the medical school, tuition hikes add to the problems of student recruitment. Including charges other than training, plus the costs of room and board, incidentals run close to $4,000 a year in at least 13 private medical schools. Even though loans are available and fees are less in the state-supported schools, costs remain prohibitive to many. In 1967 more than half of the medical students in the United States came from the 34.7 percent of American families boasting incomes over $10,000 a year.[40] While it has always been difficult for students from low-income families to attend medical school, the struggle has intensified. For example, during a decade in which only 3 percent of the nation's doctors are Negro and the problem of Negro health in the United States is crucial, Dr. Robert C. Berson of the Association of American Medical Colleges reflected that Negroes would be favored for admission to most medical schools but relatively few apply.[41]

STUDENT RECRUITMENT.   Each year only half of the approximately 18,000 college students who apply for admission to medical schools are accepted. While there has been some increase in the number of students enrolled in medical schools in the last decade, twenty-five schools, including the prestigious Harvard and Johns Hopkins, have had little numerical change for a quarter of a century.

Since 1940 the number of college degrees granted by American colleges has more than tripled while the number of applicants to medical schools has decreased.[42] The cost of a medical education has been one deterrent and the intellectual and status attraction of other disciplines has been another. Exciting careers in nuclear physics, space engineering, and mathematics have held major attractions for undergraduates and graduate students which may have lured the better students away from medicine. Stereotypes of the medical applicant as intellectually superior to other professional groups faded as studies revealed he fell below applicants in the natural and physical sciences and engineering with physicists and mathematicians at the highest end of the scale.[43]

There has been little doubt concerning the high regard in which all income, age, and educational groups in the United States held the physician. The study of prestige of occupations conducted by Cecil C. North and Paul K. Hatt and the research of others indicated that the physician was ranked on the highest level of all professionals. Respondents had a more accurate concept of the role of the physician than of the physicist.[44] The view of the physician as a humanitarian with a high income, living in the best section of town, driving good cars, wearing good clothes, with country club membership was a major assist in recruitment of students. With changes in the ordering of professions, medicine must compete with new and vital fields of work.

DROPOUTS.   It is often assumed that once an applicant for medical school has survived the intense competition for admission, he will successfully complete the educational program and enter the professional ranks. This has not been the case. An increasing number of first year medical students do not graduate. The dropout rate for entering students by late 1967 exceeded the 10 percent level and was rising rapidly; 500 to 600 first year students drop out annually.[45] The cost in dollars and cents is estimated in the hundreds of millions of dollars. In one ten year period, the total number of dropouts, approximately 6,556, equalled the total combined annual graduating classes of all U.S. Medical schools.

Considering the need to increase the number of physicians and the low medical school admission rates, medical schools might well revise admission policies to decrease the effect of dropouts. Revisions would be based on a more careful assessment of those socioeconomic and cultural factors of applicants which may be related to school and practice success. It would not be a lowering of academic levels for admission. An alternative should be developed which would either lower dropout rates through changes in admission qualifications or would increase first year admissions to offset the effect of dropouts.

Manpower Management

As the definition of health as a "right" of all men is expanded and accepted, the problems of its application in terms of the shortage and inequitable distribution of trained professionals becomes more acute. One program or approach cannot resolve the multiproblem complex of providing medical education and adequate personnel to care for millions of Americans. Additional sources of financing educational programs and of reorganizing services and work loads are prerequisite.

With the recognition that most of our medical schools, public and private, face crippling financial problems has come the realization that the federal government holds the key to the problems of medical education. No other institution in our society possesses comparable financial resources. Federal programs have supplied funds for the construction of new medical, dental and nursing school buildings. Loans and scholarships have been made available to students in the health care professions. Funds are often provided for staffing and equipping community health clinics, for scientific research, and for the expansion of regional medical centers.[46] In addition, other programs have been suggested. It is felt that a huge Federal program is needed to assist medical schools so that the number of doctors graduated annually could reach 15,000 by the end of the nineteen-seventies. More monies must be found to meet the day-to-day operating expenses of medical schools.

Even with an increase in the supply of doctors, there is no assurance that places would be filled in the understaffed areas or that the supply could ever keep up with new concepts and research in health care. The most effective efforts of management must be directed toward better utilization of those highly trained men and women who are available. Horse and buggy practice and organization of medical care must be publicly reevaluated. Americans must recognize that a warm, friendly, first name relationship with a family physician may be socially and psychologically satisfying but not necessarily medically efficient. Just because a doctor likes a patient, is concerned about him, lets him know he cares, doesn't mean he is equipped to diagnose, cure or care for him. The linking of "good" health care with primary physician-patient relationships does not seem to be functional to the implementation of the WHO definition of health. More rational, more systematic, and more imaginative approaches must be developed and adopted.

Several directions may prove effective. One concerns the training and utilization of new personnel or the redefinition of functions of existing personnel to assist physicians and dentists. A board-certified pediatrician, orthopedist, internist, and a general practitioner need not give an injection or take a blood sample. Personnel for performing these routine, time-consuming tasks could be trained quickly. The space age has opened new doors. Electronic and mechanical equipment, which has been developed to monitor the physiological functioning of orbiting astronauts could be utilized on earth. Most of this equipment would prove more accurate and time saving than that which has been used. Masses of written systematic records would be made available for diagnosis.

Giving the doctor additional hands through time saving personnel and devices does not suffice. A second "direction" must be the reorganization of American medical practice. Beginnings have already been made to develop group practice of medicine as a more efficient organizational arrangement. The "solo" practice which has been the "sacred cow"[47] of the medical profession has become vulnerable in terms of rising office and equipment costs, improbability of a lone physician having time to pursue further study, and the dependence of modern medicine on a variety of colleague specialists. Group practice is defined as a "formal association of three or more physicians providing services in more than one medical field or specialty, with income from medical practice pooled and redistributed to the members according to some prearranged plan."[48] It allows for sharing of expenses for facilities such as offices, equipment and assisting personnel, and allows for more systematic and complete records which should provide a higher quality of care. The cultivation of a system of medical records requires a variety of supervision which is usually not highly developed by the solo doctor. Well-kept records, although time consuming to maintain, may be examined and a physician's work checked. In general, formal and cooperative practice arrangements between physician's can provide better medical care than informal, solo arrangements.[49]

In an attempt to prevent the exodus of doctors from the city core and to attract the medical school graduate, child care and other types of medical clinics have been organized in slum areas. The Office of Economic Opportunity in 1966 and 1967 constructed clinics in such metropolitan trouble spots as Watts in Los Angeles, Columbia Point in Boston, North Lawndale in Chicago and in the south Bronx, New York. Some clinic experiments are being attempted in rural areas in which medical, dental and social services are dispersed. The slum clinic provides a higher quality of medical care where adequate facilities and equipment have been in short supply. They relieve pressures on municipal hospitals which have born the brunt of medical service as doctors moved out of the city neighborhoods.

Another view toward reorganization are plans to develop links between doctors, clinics, hospitals and medical centers creating interdependent, interrelated and interservice units which could ultimately increase the numbers of families receiving adequate health care. Dr. Martin Cherkasky, a leading hospital administrator, has suggested that with the assistance of federal funds, we could construct "pyramids of regional health care topped by 'nuclear hospitals' and their medical schools" to which district hospitals, clinics and practicing physicians would be related.[50]

A noteworthy example of a national effort to attack heart disease, cancer, and stroke through the development of regional programs began in 1966 with a federal appropriation of $2,066,000 for regional planning and a first stage implementation budget of $80 million in 1968.[51] The program waged against the diseases that cause 71 out of every 100 American deaths consists of individual, regional programs drafted by the regions themselves to meet their own needs and circumstances. The programs will attempt to educate the public so that lay leaders will be able to share the responsibility for effective planning. An emphasis is placed on continuing education in advanced medical techniques, and on better communication and increased cooperation between doctors, medical schools, and communities. Hopefully, regional plans for the entire nation will be approved in 1970. As new forms of organization evolve, they are tested, and their effectiveness gauged, and innovative approaches to health problems should emerge.

A more controversial management plan than those mentioned recommends the utilization of doctors from other programs of health education, *e.g.,* osteopaths, and chiropractors. Although there is considerable antagonism between the medical doctor and the osteopathic and chiropractic doctor, thousands of people in the United States utilize the services of nonmedical practitioners. Often hospital staff positions and other work situations are denied these nonmedical practitioners. The inability of the medical profession to solve the problems of supply and distribution of practitioners will facilitate the extensive utilization of practitioners from health occupations that do not possess professional status comparable to that of medicine.

FINANCING HEALTH CARE

"If money were no object, I'd get the best medical and dental care and I'd eat and live in such a way that I'd be in great shape," "Even with our health insurance, we can't afford optimum health care." These and a legion of additional comments combined with government releases and newspaper stories indicate that the cost of health services is high and increases annually. In addition, many laymen and professionals equate the use of services with the ability of the patient to pay.

The more medical science has learned about the treatment and control of disease, the more complex its application in terms of hospitalization, equipment, and skilled personnel and the greater the expense. Between

1950 and 1967, private consumer expenditures for medical care rose from a total of $8.5 billion to $30.4 billion.[52] Estimates suggest that by 1975, private medical care costs will reach $46.6 billion.[53]

If one uses a broad definition of health, the provision of health care is extremely complex. As we have suggested, a consensus might be developed on who is entitled to health in our society, but thereafter the methods of organizing health services and the methods of financing them are extremely controversial. The major battles on health organization since the thirties have been heatedly waged in terms of the methods for financing health care. The dispute focussed on two dimensions of financing. First, how shall the physician be paid for services rendered and second, how shall the family or individual pay for needed services. While both are interrelated, the latter has been more overtly controversial than the former.

Methods of Paying Physicians

The three principal methods for paying physicians for services are (1) fee for service, (2) salary, and (3) capitation. When the first method is utilized, the physician receives a fee for each service performed, such as an office call, a phone call, a hospital visit, a surgical operation, an x-ray, a urinalysis. The cost of each item is determined and varied only by the doctor in terms of such factors as difficulty of the case or affluence of the patient. Fee for service is usually related to solo practice.

The salary method is that used in most forms of employment such as teaching, industrial management, government employment or office work. The doctor is paid for his time, weekly, monthly, annually, without regarding the number of services he has rendered or the number of patients he has seen. The amount of the salary may vary with the training, experience, specialties, and responsibilities of the physician. Salary is usually related to an organized practice rather than an individual office.

Capitation is a payment method in which the unit of remuneration is the person served. The doctor agrees to take care of a person or family for a specific period of time for a given sum of money. The physician is paid regardless of whether the person is sick or well. This method has been used for large groups represented by an agency or organization which pays so much per month for all services needed.

All three methods have been utilized in the past. The Greek city-states paid salaries to physicians for the care of the free poor. During the feudal periods, physicians attached to manors were paid salaries to care for the lord's family. Medieval guilds paid physicians by a capitation system of so much per year for each member to be attended if he became sick.[54]

With the growth of both industrialization and urbanization, physicians broke group attachments and became private entrepreneurs. Services were offered to all on a fee basis. As a result, although both salary and capitation had long and honorable histories,[55] the fee for service method of payment became entrenched in western civilization. So firmly had it become the accepted pattern in the United States that, unlike the European system, it permeated the hospital where fees were charged for services. Even when private insurance programs were developed to pay for hospital care, the fee system was so established that it was the method utilized for disbursing funds.

Without regard to the advantages and disadvantages accruing from each method, the value of each method changes with the passage of time. The fee method has been advocated as the personification of freedom, quality, and "true" attitudes of physician concern for his patient. Arguments equating better organization of available personnel and lower cost with other payment methods have been inundated with cries of sloppy, impersonal, controlled services.

Essentially the fee for service method provides greater freedom for the doctor. It encourages the provision of many services since payment is made for each service. On occasion, this has been considered a serious problem. Milton I. Roemer reported that a "medical care program for prisoners was showing an inordinately high rate of appendectomies and elective orthopedic surgery, . . . When the payment system was changed from fee-for-service to part-time salary, the rate of surgical operations . . . abruptly fell."[56] The fee system also involves cumbersome accounting methods. For years the medical profession used their interest in maintaining a fee system of payment as an argument against governmental or private insurance programs, thereby relating the payment plan with personal versus impersonal care. Only a few daring souls challenged "the establishment" on the issue. This raises several questions.

Forms of capitation have been discussed for years. Practically it has only been utilized by doctors operating under a health insurance plan such as the Health Insurance Plan of Greater New York. There, physicians are in medical groups or clinics and therein practice independently in separate offices. To be successful, any insurance plan must have a large subscription group to offset the statistical chance of bankruptcy. It has been suggested that a form of capitation could offer better preventive health care. Since a fee has been paid to cover a period of time, the physician would be free to contact patients to come to the office for

new treatments, immunization and examinations. Under the fee-for-service system, a physician hesitates to directly inform patients that they
ought to have flu shots, measles or mumps vaccines, or other newly developed preventive programs. There is little question that the salary
method is the most economical for the patient. Although it is questioned,
criticized, fought and seldom included in legislative proposals for health
insurance, the long-term trend in the United States is toward greater use
of the salaried medical man. Myrdal suggests it is the world trend.[57]

The solution or management of the problem of payment, whether it is
a selection of one or a combination of the three, must consider and
satisfy both the needs of the patient and the physician. A system which
allows for the identification of superior performance by professional
peers has been built in more often in some form of group salaried practice. If the health professions are to recruit, to fill their positions in our
system of division of labor, acceptable rewards must be developed. The
academic fields attracting young men and women away from the health
fields are salaried, peer-prestige positions. Second and equally important,
the payment system must allow patients to meet their needs.

Meeting Patient Needs: Insurance

As the cost of medical care has risen, Americans have turned to
insurance as a method of coping with expense. Medical insurance plans
had been successfully utilized in Europe decades before they were
initiated in the 1930's in the United States. While the earliest health insurance plans were developed by employers or consumers, phenomenal
growth did not take place until hospitals and physicians initiated the
Blue Cross and Blue Shield plans. From a humble beginning with less
than 5 percent of the population covered by all available types of health
insurance, coverage rose until by 1967, 83 percent had hospital, 76
percent surgical, and 62 percent had medical insurance.[58] Obviously,
coverage is extensively limited to hospital bills and physicians in-hospital
care. It has been estimated that even with the extensive growth in coverage, insurance pays only 24 percent of the total costs of the medical
care burden.[59] The growth of Blue Cross-Blue Shield proved the actu-
arial feasibility for the extension by commercial insurance carriers into
the health field, particularly as labor and salaried professional groups
demanded insurance programs as part of their fringe employment benefits.

Lest there be a misunderstanding, the health professions did not
develop an insurance plan out of the recognition of a felt need for which

others would or could not respond. They developed a program as a counterattack to governmental plans in the thirties and later threats of national health insurance proposals in a number of federal bills during the forties and fifties. The road to the first federal program of Medicare and Medicaid was a hell-hole of bitter, ugly battle. The fact that coverage is limited, that insurance costs have increased, and that substantial sectors of health care are unprotected by voluntary insurance programs indicates problems and areas for change. Class factors are particularly meaningful as an evaluatory measure. Whereas 88 percent of families with incomes over $7,000 are covered by hospital insurance, only 34 percent of families with incomes under $2,000 and 52 percent of families with incomes between $2,000 and $3,999 are insured.[60] Another glaring gap which acted as the spur in enacting the Medicare legislation on health insurance of the aged in 1965 was the inadequate coverage for this group. This is the population segment with the greatest medical needs, growing larger, with limited financial assets.

If world history has meaning, we may expect major expansions by the United States government in the health insurance field. Medicare was merely the foot in the door. The ambitious insurance proposals of the forties for a program covering all Americans proved too ambitious; a piecemeal approach directed to the same end, one by one covering the problem groups, such as the aged, the totally disabled and children, seemed to be more politically palatable. The history of voluntary insurance in other countries has shown that the successes in terms of economic and administrative feasibility and the failures in terms of insufficient coverage for many people lead to an enlarged mandatory program of social insurance. It no longer suffices to provide care for the indigent and the affluent. Assistance must be provided for the *medically indigent,* the individual or family able to provide the necessities and some of the luxuries, who needs little or no assistance in the business of life unless a major illness for which he has not adequately saved or for which he is not adequately insured wipes him out.

There have been at least two major concerns of opponents to the extension of insurance programs. First, it has been suggested that if all members of a society were to be covered financially for health care, the demands for service would be so huge they could not be met by existing practitioners. This criticism is a damning one. It indicates what insurance proponents have claimed for decades: that millions of Americans are deprived of adequate medical care because of their economic position in society. It is basically the same argument as that used in population control—a "good" war, plague, flood, assists and is functional in limiting population! Instead of determining the alternatives to limited services or population growth, the device which requires the least amount of planning or change is given high value. There can be little doubt that the increased demand would necessitate major reorganization of services and substantial increases of both major and auxiliary medical personnel.

Second, opponents have adamantly maintained that mandatory government health insurance would not be, as proponents suggest, only a financial or payment device. They argue that it would affect the pattern of medical care. This, in fact, is true. The longer a mandatory program operated, the more control the public, through elected officials and technical agencies, would have over the quality and economy of health services. There is no question that a broad insurance program for all Americans would alter the operational patterns of hospital and medical care.

Medical Care: Hospital Costs[61]

Americans, privately and publicly, spend over 30 billion dollars annually for personal health care.[62] There is no indication that the cost of medical care will decrease in the years ahead. In fact, future price increases are inevitable. The concern is not with whether prices will rise, but with how rapidly they will rise. In addition to the increased public belief that medical care should be available to all Americans, there are other factors which are pushing up the demand for services. Among the most important of these are the increasing numbers of people covered by health insurance, the population explosion, and rising income levels.

A major area of family health expenditure in which there has been a significant upward shift in the national proportion of expenditures is for hospital care. While a variety of other types of medical care prices including physicians' fees have also increased, hospital expenditures will be utilized as examples.

Hospital services are the most expensive form of medical care in the United States. An increased share of the consumer's health dollar is being spent for hospitalization. While in 1950, 24 percent of private medical expenditures were spent for the latter, by 1965 it had risen to 30 percent, and by 1969 it was 38 percent.[63]

The increases are the result of a combination of factors. The number of services hospitals perform for patients has grown. These include the basics of room, board and laundry, laboratory tests, pharmaceuticals, highly complex and specialized equipment and facilities, and utilization of a large storehouse of personnel ranging from the skilled professional to the unskilled laborer.

A second factor is the increased use of hospitals. In order to protect themselves from hospital charges, more and more Americans have purchased hospitalization insurance. First coverage and then more extensive coverage has been the cry of organized labor until one would be hard pressed to locate a full-time job today that does not include a hospital insurance policy as part of the employment benefits. The very fact of insurance has increased the willingness of patients to be hospitalized and the willingness of physicians to recommend hospitalization. In fact, since less expensive medical care services which might represent a better care alternative, such as nursing homes, outpatient care and convalescent hospitals, are not covered by most insurance programs, the physician is more apt to recommend hospitalization since payment is secure.

A third dimension in price increase is the rising wage of employees in a tight labor market. Because the income of hospital employees has been lower relative to other sectors of the economy, they have risen more rapidly with increases in the minimum wage laws which covered hospital employees for the first time in 1967. A second element in the rise in overall wage cost is the increase in the number of employees needed to care for each patient per day. While more sophisticated treatment equipment has been introduced, few ways have been found to combine their use with the substitution of automation for manpower. Rather, more semi-skilled employees have been replacing unskilled workers as levels of care have risen.[64] Added to wage costs are all those non-wage costs which have been steadily increasing: food, heat, light, building costs, air-conditioning, etc. An important area of price increases, both in and out of the hospital, is the cost of drugs. The price of drugs has not increased significantly compared to other medical costs. It is the increasing use of drugs reflecting the development and success of new drug products and the increase in quantities used that has made many families cognizant of the increased burden of drug expenditures. In addition, there has been an increase in the use of prescription drugs rather than over-the-counter items. In 1959 the number of prescription drugs purchased per family annually was 11 at a cost of $33 as compared to 14 at a cost of $46 annually in 1965. While the price of individual products has not increased markedly, drug products are higher than they would be if there was considerable competition by wholesale or retail establishments. The pharmaceutical industry is highly concentrated with large sums spent for intensive advertising campaigns to differentiate brand names from the generic names of drugs. It has been estimated that the drug industry spends approximately $3,000 per doctor per year for advertising to the medical profession.[65] As a result the physician may be unaware that a less expensive drug exists.

The effectiveness of certain drugs to control syphillis and tuberculosis and the increased use of sedatives and tranquilizers, among many others, indicate the rising importance of drugs. Only through sustained competition and documented proof of the therapeutic equality of brand-name drugs with their generic counterpart will cost be controlled.

ACCOUNTABILITY.   The dilemma the facts above present is one of rising costs and increased use of hospitals because of the wide-spread insurance coverage of Americans. Hospital staffs and administrators have few incentives to attempt cost-reducing innovations when bills are predominantly paid by a third party—insurance companies or government. Some systems of cost reduction are beyond the resources of the smaller hospital. The 1967 report to the President of the United States on Medical Care Prices by the Department of Health, Education, and Welfare[66] recommended that the National Center for Health Services Research and Development support research aimed at more effective organization, the implementation of cost-reducing innovations, and the development of demonstration projects in government hospitals. It also suggested that HEW review the formulas for reimbursement used in Medicare and Medicaid to develop "practical ways of increasing the incentives for hospitals and other health facilities to operate efficiently."[67]

Since the increased insurance coverage of Americans is partly responsible for the increased utilization of hospitals, public and private health insurance plans should be broadened to cover less expensive medical care services such as nursing homes, home services, outpatient care, and physicians' office visits.[68] As long as Americans are concerned about their health and recognize the value of hospital care, demand for services will increase.

Patterns of Management

Public and private efforts to improve the quality and availability of health care have not been markedly successful. A number of programs have been provided by local, state, and federal governments such as hospital and health facility construction through matching local and federal funds under the Hill-Burton Act, care for military veterans and their families through a separate medical care system, Public Health Service medical care programs, crippled children's services, maternal and child health services, Medicaid and Medicare. Medicare is the first major step toward developing governmental health insurance. The program came into effect on July 1, 1966 as partial insurance for almost all persons 65 years of age and over to cover most costs of hospitalization and, under an additional plan, part of reasonable doctor bills and certain other health service costs. During the first year of operation, 10 million Americans over the age of 65 enrolled in the program. A total of $3.2 billion covering 10 million doctor's bills and 5 million hospital charges was expended.[69] The insurance for hospital care or Plan A is financed by Social Security taxes on workers and employers. Plan B for doctor bills is paid by a levy of $3 a month from each insured person matched by the federal government from general tax funds.

Medical Assistance or Medicaid is a voluntary federal-state program which was developed in 1965 to provide medical care for the medically indigent of all ages. Eligibility is determined by each participating state. As a consequence, rules on eligibility and benefits vary from state to state. Medicaid is administered by the state and is financed by both state and federal government or state, local and federal government. The percentage of federal contributions depends upon the average per capita income for a given state.[70]

In addition, numbers of other state and local services have been provided such as maternal and infant care projects, comprehensive services for children in low-income areas, migrant health services, and neighborhood health centers. While all these programs have assisted, they have not solved or even managed the problems of America's health. Many of these programs have been bitterly fought over the years and challenged as being the first steps toward "socialized medicine"—a term almost as emotionally charged as "Communist!" While a number of organized groups representing various interests within the health field have acted and reacted over the decades, the efforts of the American Medical Association have been outstanding.

AMERICAN MEDICAL ASSOCIATION.   From its national headquarters in Chicago, the hundred year old American Medical Association has spoken powerfully for its over two hundred thousand members on every aspect of health affairs. On most occasions, it has spoken as the medical physician's only voice. It has extended its concerns to many areas: raising the quality of medical care, setting conditions for practice and for payment, and attempting to prevent governmental intervention into segments of national health care. In most states, the A.M.A.'s voice has set standards for education and training, controlled state regulatory bodies and supervised its own standards without further political control or supervision from government. In many states, political power in these areas has been delegated to organized medicine.[71]

The A.M.A. has contributed to many health activities. It has played, for example, a major part in promoting high standards for drugs and medical products. Measures, however, which sought to provide more adequate health care in areas of broad national concern through extension of governmental services have been bitterly opposed for decades. In the twenties, although pediatricians were in favor, the A.M.A. opposed the government sponsored child health legislation, the Shepherd-Towner Act. As a result, pediatricians recognized a need for an organization which might, on occasion, represent their interests independent from the A.M.A. and formed the American Academy of Pediatrics.[72] The A.M.A. opposed the development of many public health activities such as immunization and venereal disease programs. When a public health physician instituted new programs which were disapproved by private practice colleagues, he sometimes had to resign from local medical societies.[73]

However, the dominant area of A.M.A. concern has been with governmental efforts to develop a system or systems of health insurance. Every attempt possible was made to block these proposals, particularly Medicare. The A.M.A. position on whether health care for the senior citizen and the indigent should be tax supported was extremely vocal, aggressive and, not surprisingly, unchallenged by any segment of the medical profession. After the passage of Medicare, several A.M.A. presidents asked the membership to cooperate with the "law of the land." The membership generally assumed that although the campaign against Medicare had been lost in 1966, the A.M.A. would fight to prevent further government intervention. In a return to stronger positions, the 1968 A.M.A. president challenged the concept discussed earlier of health care as a right of all people rather than a privilege. He called for physicians to take a stronger position in opposition to government participation in health area planning. The president characterized as unnecessary and "wasteful" the United States Office of Economic Opportunity program of slum health centers.[74]

Three medical organizations representing 10,000 doctors took exception to A.M.A. positions which appeared out of touch with social change and social issues. The Medical Committee for Human Rights issued a statement in 1967, endorsed by the National Medical Association and the Physicians Forum, denouncing the election of Dr. Milford O. Rouse of Dallas, Texas, the 1967-68 president, as "yet another step backward" by the A.M.A. "reaffirming its conservative and obstructionist policy" toward Medicare and other Federal health programs." The statement concluded:

It is time for those whose conscience is horrified by such A.M.A. policies in the field of social medicine to reaffirm that health care is a right which ought to be guaranteed to all by our society, and not a privilege obtainable only through personal affluence.[75]

Since membership in the A.M.A. is still the professional union card, it is unlikely that these organizations will gain strength or that A.M.A. policy will change considerably. On the other hand, it is just as unlikely that governmental incursions into health care will stop. Sigerist has hypothesized the future in terms of the past:

> There is one lesson that can be derived from history. It is this: that the physician's position in society is never determined by the physician himself but by the society he is serving. *We can oppose the development, we can retard it, but we will be unable to stop it.*[76]

CONCLUSION

There are no overnight solutions to the problems of health care in the United States. A critical point is the lag between the public and political definition of medical care as a right and the historical definition of it as a privilege. The new pledge cannot be redeemed until there is further recognition by the health professions that health and sickness can no longer be an individual matter and will never again be an individual matter as long as the world's population continues to increase. The amassing of peoples in the decades to come within multihousing units and urban complexes so staggering that they defy our limited concept of urban living will create a degree of proximity between men which will necessitate the rapid development of new programs of health care. Man's very survival will depend upon the development of controls which assure him clean air to breathe, clean water to drink, protection from epidemic and crippling conditions of disease and environment, and medical care when needed. With increased pressures for food, housing, water, air, and employment in the twenty-first century, inadequate provision for health care could develop intolerable policies toward the sick.

In most areas of health service, adjustments and management of perceived needs should be developed through social organization. It would be of infinite value if the health professions could assist and/or lead in the selection of alternatives between the diverse and intensely competitive forms of organization possible to provide health care for all people. Medical leadership must, as Sigerist suggests, recognize that:

> The society in which we live is different from that of our ancestors. The physician is no longer a medicine man nor a craftsman nor a priest. He has new tasks, new functions, and new weapons. A new medical science serving a new type of society necessarily requires new forms of medical service.[77]

Selected Readings

Evany, Karl, *Health Service, Society and Medicine* (London: Oxford University Press, 1960).

Freeman, Howard, *et. al., eds., Handbook of Medical Sociology* (Englewood Cliffs, N.J.: Prentice-Hall, Inc., 1963).

Galdston, Iago, *The Meaning of Social Medicine* (Cambridge, Mass.: Harvard University Press, 1954).

Halsey, Hunt G. and Marcus S. Goldstein, *Medical Group Practice in the United States,* Public Health Service Publication No. 17 (Washington, D.C.: U.S. Government Printing Office, 1951).

Hollingshead, August B. and Frederick C. Redlich, *Social Class and Mental Illness* (New York: John Wiley & Sons, Inc., 1958).

Jaco, E. Gartly, *ed., Patients, Physicians and Illness* (Glencoe, Ill.: The Free Press, 1958).

Marti-Ibanez, Felix, *ed., Henry E. Sigerist on the History of Medicine* (New York: M.D. Publications, Inc., 1960).

Myrdal, Gunnar, *Beyond the Welfare State* (New Haven: Yale University Press, 1960).

Paul, Benjamin D., *Health, Culture and Community* (New York: Russell Sage Foundation, 1955).

Roemer, Milton I., *ed., Henry E. Sigerist on the Sociology of Medicine* (New York: M.D. Publications, Inc., 1960).

Scott, W. Richard and Edmund H. Volkart, *eds., Medical Care* (New York: John Wiley & Sons, Inc., 1966).

Notes to Chapter 5

[1] Stanley H. King, *Perceptions of Illness and Medical Practice* (New York: Russell Sage Foundation, 1962), p. 19; and U.S. Bureau of the Census, *Pocket Data Book, USA 1969* (Washington, D.C.: U.S. Government Printing Office, 1969), p. 63.

[2] *Ibid.*

[3] James F. Hughey, "Tuscaloosa Community Dental Program," mimeographed (1967), pp. 1-3.

[4] Joseph Matarazza, "Comprehensive Medicine: A New Era in Medical Education," *Human Organization,* 14 (Spring 1955), pp. 4-9.

[5] Iago Galdston, *The Meaning of Social Medicine* (Cambridge, Mass.: Harvard University Press, 1954).

[6] "Constitution of the World Health Organization," *Chronical of the World Health Organization,* Vol. 1 (Geneva, Switzerland: Interim Commission, 1947).

[7] Walter Guzzardi, Jr., "What the Doctor Can't Order—but You Can," *Fortune* (August 1961), pp. 96-105.

[8] *Ibid.*

[9] Milton I. Roemer, ed., *Henry E. Sigerist on the Sociology of Medicine* (New York: M.D. Publications, Inc., 1960).

[10] *Ibid.*, p. 56.

[11] Felix Marti-Ibanez, ed., *Henry E. Sigerist on the History of Medicine* (New York: M.D. Publications, Inc., 1960).

[12] *Ibid.*, pp. 26-27.

[13] *Ibid.*

[14] *Patients in Mental Hospitals, 1957* (Washington D.C.: U.S. Government Printing Office, 1960).

[15] Elaine and John Cumming, *Closed Ranks* (Cambridge: Harvard University Press, 1957).

[16] August B. Hollingshead and Frederick C. Redlich, *Social Class and Mental Illness* (New York: John Wiley and Sons, Inc., 1958).

[17] Lawrence Kolb, "Narcotic Addiction—An Interview," *Spectrum 5* (March, 1957), p. 136.

[18] *Chronicle of the World Health Organization,* "Drug Addiction or Drug Habituation," 11 (May, 1957), p. 165.

[19] Mary Baker Eddy, *Science and Health with Key to the Scriptures,* definitive eds. (Boston: Christian Science Publishing Society, 1934).

[20] J. H. Snowden, *The Truth About Christian Science; the Founder and the Faith* (New York: Westminister Press, 1920), p. 150 ff.

[21] *The New York Times* (November 29, 1967).

[22] *Ibid.*

[23] W. A. Posey, "Medical Education and Medical Service" *Journal of the American Medical Association,* 84, 86 (January 24, February 7, 14, 21, 1925; May, 15, 1926), 84: 281-85, 365-69, 437, 441, 513-15, 592-95; 86: 1501-08.

[24] *The New York Times* (September 28, 1967).

[25] R. I. Lee and L. W. Jones, *The Fundamentals of Good Medical Care* (Chicago: University of Chicago Press, 1933).

[26] U.S. Public Health Service, Division of Public Health Methods, *Standards of Adequacy in the Supply of Medical and Public Health Personnel and Facilities* (Washington, D.C.: February, 1942, Processed).

[27] U.S. Bureau of the Census, *Pocket Data Book, U.S.A. 1967* (Washington, D.C.: U.S. Government Printing Office, 1967), pp. 139-140.

[28] *Ibid.*, p. 140.

[29] *Ibid.*

[30] *The New York Times* (September 28, 1967).

[31] *Ibid.*

[32] *Ibid.*

[33] Milton I. Roemer, "Health Resources and Services in the Watts Area of Los Angeles," *California's Health* (February–March, 1966), p. 123-143.

[34] *The New York Times* (September 28, 1967).

[35] See Rashi Fein, "An Economic and Social Profile of the Negro American," *Daedalus* (Fall, 1965); and Jean Mayer, "The Nutritional Status of American Negroes," *Nutrition Review,* Vol. 23, No. 6 (June 1965), p. 161.

[36] *The New York Times* (September 28, 1967).

[37] *Ibid.*, (September 30, 1967).

[38] *Ibid.*

[39] *Ibid.*

[40] U.S. Bureau of the Census, *Pocket Data Book, U.S.A. 1969 op. cit.*, p. 198.

[41] *The New York Times* (September 30, 1967).

[42] U.S. Bureau of the Census, *Pocket Data Book, U.S.A. 1969 op. cit.*, p. 166.

[43] *The New York Times* (October 30, 1967).

166   *Perspectives on American Health Problems*

[44] See Albert J. Reiss, Jr., *et al., Occupations and Social Status* (New York: The Free Press of Glencoe, 1961).

[45] *The New York Times* (September 30, 1967).

[46] Office of Economic Opportunity, *Catalog of Federal Assistance Programs,* (Washington, D.C.: U.S. Government Printing Office, June 1967), pp. 20-25, 58-62.

[47] Karl Evany, *Health Service, Society and Medicine* (London: Oxford University Press, 1960).

[48] G. Halsey Hunt and Marcus S. Goldstein, *Medical Group Practice in the United States,* Public Health Service Publication No. 17 (Washington, D.C.: U.S. Government Printing Office, 1951).

[49] Elliot Freidson, "The Organization of Medical Practice," in Howard Freeman, *et. al., eds., Handbook of Medical Sociology* (Englewood Cliffs, N.J.: Prentice-Hall, Inc. 1963), p. 312.

[50] *The New York Times* (September 30, 1967).

[51] *Ibid.* (April 15, 1967).

[52] U.S. Bureau of the Census, *Pocket Data Books, U.S.A. 1969 op. cit.,* p. 141.

[53] Philip R. Lee, "Health and Well-Being," *The Annals,* Vol. 373 (September 1967), p. 206.

[54] Felix Marti-Ibanez, *op. cit.*

[55] *Ibid.*

[56] Milton I. Roemer, "Paying the Doctor, Implications of Different Methods," in W. Richard Scott and Edmund H. Volkart, *eds., Medical Care* (New York: John Wiley & Sons, Inc., 1966), p. 137.

[57] Gunnar Myrdal, *Beyond the Welfare State* (New Haven: Yale University Press, 1960).

[58] U.S. Bureau of the Census, *Pocket Data Book, U.S.A. 1969 op. cit.,* p. 322.

[59] Milton I. Roemer, "The Future of Social Medicine in the United States." Unpublished paper presented at the Annual Meeting of the Medical Sociology Section of the American Sociological Association, Miami Beach, Florida (August 30, 1966), p. 5.

[60] U.S. Bureau of the Census, *Pocket Data Book, U.S.A. 1967 op. cit.,* p. 143.

[61] Much of the following discussion is based on: Department of Health, Education, and Welfare, *A Report to the President on Medical Care Prices* (Washington, D.C.: U.S. Government Printing Office, 1967).

[62] Louis S. Reed and Ruth S. Hanft, "National Health Expenditures, 1950–1964," *Social Security Bulletin,* 29 (Washington, D.C.: U.S. Printing Office, January, 1966), p. 13.

[63] Department of Health, Education, and Welfare, *A Report to the President on Medical Care Prices, ibid.,* p. 27; Edmund K. Faltermayer, "Better Care At Less Cost Without Miracles," *Fortune,* LXXXI, No. 1 (January 1970), pp. 79-83.

[64] *Ibid.,* pp. 28-29.

[65] *Ibid.,* p. 37.

[66] *Ibid.,* p. 8.

[67] *Ibid.*

[68] *Ibid.,* pp. 3-5. See also Ronald Anderson and Odin W. Anderson, *A Decade of Health Services: Social Survey Trends in Use and Expenditure* (Chicago: The University of Chicago Press, 1967).

[69] *The New York Times* (October 25, 1967).

[70] *Questions and Answers: Medical Assistance "Medicaid"* (Washington, D.C.: U.S. Government Printing Office, 1967).

[71] W. Richard Scott and Edmund H. Volkart, *eds., Medical Care* (New York: John Wiley & Sons, Inc. 1966), p. 177.

[72] Rue Bucher and Anselm Strauss, "Professions in Process," *The American Journal of Sociology,* 66 (January, 1961), pp. 325-34.

[73] James H. Rorty, *American Medicine Mobilizes* (New York: W. W. Norton and Co., Inc., 1939), pp. 254-55.

[74] *The New York Times* (July 2, 1967).
[75] *Ibid.*
[76] Felix Marti-Ibanez, *op. cit.* Authors' italics.
[77] Henry E. Sigerist "The Social History of Medicine," *Western Journal of Surgery Obstetrics and Gynecology*, 48 (December, 1940), pp. 721-72.

CHAPTER SIX

CRIME IN THE UNITED STATES

INTRODUCTION

In the past decade crime has climbed spectacularly to the pinnacle of American social problems. Politicians, social scientists, journalists and citizens have found crime a fascinating, bewildering, and complex subject for study and speculation. The Congress, the political groups and the public media have presented questions about crime in the United States and suggested possible management policies for the problem.

The problem of crime highlights many contradictions and dilemmas in American society. Crime can be a form of rejection of social ties and obligations, a protest against injustice, a quick avenue to material wealth in a nation that values wealth regardless of its origin, a symptom of individual maladjustment or maladaptation to society, a sign of inadequacies in the societal institutions, and a normal pattern of the life and times of the businessman. Crime can be any of these phenomena and probably is a product of all of them.

For example, in the past few years, we have seen deliberately planned civil disobedience by persons protesting the involvement of the United States in Vietnam, protesting the injustices in treatment of minority groups, the refusal of university administrations to allow students to participate fully in decision-making affecting curriculum and other aspects of university life, and the conditions in prisons and other correctional facilities. These people sometimes have considerable public support and sympathy. These groups and individuals are seldom incarcerated, even though they are often arrested. Incarceration, if it does occur, is apt to be a token affair of a week or so.

We have also had widespread lawbreaking by individual businessmen and corporations, such as illegal restraint of trade, violations of pure food and drug laws, illegal pollution of water and air, illegal manipulation of funds, and violation of income tax laws. Often these offenses go unreported and unpunished. Businessmen are apt to ignore them under the slogan "business is business," and to insist that only murder, rape, robbery and burglary are really crimes. They do not see themselves as offenders, nor does the American public always see them as offenders, even though their aberrations may cost lives or millions of dollars, impair health, or weaken social institutions. These "white collar criminals" are themselves the same social class as judges and jurymen and can employ skilled attorneys even if they are apprehended and charged. They are seldom imprisoned and are not included in criminal statistics to a degree consonant with the damage their behavior does to the nation.

On the other hand, we have had groups organized as criminal syndicates with no pretense of righting injustices. Rather, theirs is an interest in making money quickly by delivering illegal goods and services to a large American market. Gambling, prostitution, abortions, narcotics, and

169

quick loans without normal collateral are among the goods and services that are being supplied by professional criminals for a price. These criminals carefully plan their activities to the point of having attorneys ready to apply for writs of habeas corpus if they are apprehended and to the level of having fixed or bribed the police, the prosecution staffs, the courts or the press.

In between the extremes of professional criminals, professional businessmen and professional crusaders are the amateurs and the would-be professionals, drawn largely from the lower class, who commit offenses from such motivations as impulse, anger, hopelessness, self-pity, and lust. These offenders account for most of the criminal statistics since they seldom have planned their crimes thoroughly and are more apt to be caught. They usually have inadequate legal counsel and have not bribed or fixed police or prosecution officials. Sometimes they really want to be caught or at least do not do everything possible to avoid capture. Studies of prison inmates ordinarily focus on this group, inasmuch as they are the people who populate the jails, reformatories, prisons and correctional institutions throughout the nation. The hopeless, angry, frustrated or confused individual cannot handle himself in jail or court in the sophisticated and competent fashion of either the professional criminal or the professional crusader. The poor judgment that led him to commit an ill-planned act of robbery, murder, arson, theft, rape, or assault becomes the poor judgment that leads him to be sentenced to prison.

Crime illuminates clearly the interaction between the individual and society. As the society's institutions become archaic, dysfunctional, or unresponsive to emerging needs, crime is among the first social problems to become aggravated. If a large group of individuals, for example, are exposed to information about high standards of living, but are denied access to employment and education as avenues to achievement, some of them will turn to crime. These individuals are apt to be ambivalent and confused about the criminal behavior and will usually get caught. If enough people are involved in this condition, the behavior may take the form of rioting, looting or insurrection. If the laws of the society prevent use of goods or services which are widely desired, a band of efficient professional criminals will spring up and few of them will get caught. If the policies of the nation are intolerable or repulsive to a minority group, they are apt to become civilly disobedient as a form of protest. If the nation's financial structure rewards enterprise and initiative, regardless of the directions taken, white collar crime is apt to mushroom.

This chapter will examine each of these categories of crime with the hope of getting a clearer picture of the interplay of society and individual, of the role of social class in crime, and of the directions and conflicts in crime management. First, however, it is necessary to review the definitions of crime and to examine the extent of crime.

WHAT IS CRIME?

There are two broad definitions of crime, each having a number of variations as developed by different criminologists, students of criminal justice, and sociologists. The first of these is the *legalistic* definition which stresses that no offense or infraction of the mores or item of destructive behavior can be termed "crime" unless it is committed in violation of a specific statute.[1] Usually the legalistic definition goes on to indicate that a punishment or sanction must also be provided in the statute. Frequently, there is the requirement that the offense must be proven in court by established procedures and with adequate safeguards against arbitrariness or self-incrimination.

There are several inherent assumptions in this legalistic definition of crime. One is that the society is advanced enough in its technology, communication skills and approach to justice to have set down written statutes governing the behavior of citizens. Moreover, it must have fashioned processes of arrest, trial, defense and conviction or absolution. Another assumption is that the acts defined as criminal by statute are injurious to society.[2] In practical terms, this means that the social class or other groups which get the laws enacted will determine what acts are injurious or are no longer injurious. A third assumption for the democratic society is that the statutes will be enforced equally and fairly for all citizens. This assumption insures that the administration of justice will be a predictable, reliable means of making certain that crime is recognized and dealt with in the best interests of the society.

The second definition of crime has emerged largely as the result of the failure of modern societies to meet the test of the second and third assumptions previously listed. Modern societies have enacted into criminal statutes, for one reason or another, an enormous number of acts which are clearly not injurious to the values, social institutions, lives or property of the society. In newspapers throughout the United States, a compendium of absurd ordinances and laws ran for years as a syndicated column, with cartoons, ridiculing such criminal statutes still on the books as failure to attend church and leaving an unattended horse outside certain establishments. Blue laws include Mississippi's ban against grocery stores being open for business on Sunday and Massachusetts' proscription of changing the oil or greasing an automobile on Sunday. Attempted suicide is a crime in some states. During the time of Henry VIII in England, it was a crime to predict the death of the king and driving with reins was once a crime in Russia.[3] Moreover, other offenses proscribed by statutes, such as homosexuality and abortion, are offenses against rather diffuse and not universally accepted values.[4] The lack of victims to initiate the enforcement process results in extremely few convictions, and many professional and related groups are pushing for the substitution of alternative policies for handling the behavior. On the other hand, many offenses considered by criminologists and sociologists to be very harmful to social values and institutions, such as some of the "white collar crimes," are not in the criminal statutes, and when there specifically, they are seldom enforced. White collar offenses not usually in the criminal statutes include most instances of misleading or false labeling of merchandise, certain forms of misuse of funds, many practices in restraint of free trade or enterprise and shady practices by public officials including nepotism and diversion of contributions to personal use. Many criminologists believe that such acts weaken political and economic institutions, destroy confidence in the society, promote an attitude of corruption and apathy, and generally undermine societal values.

Most significantly, acts may be perpetrated by one social class and labeled crime because the agents of law enforcement and criminal justice are oriented to deal with the members of that class as potential criminals. Yet, the same behavior may sometimes be shrugged off as "sowing of wild oats" or "business is business" if committed by members of another social class.

In order, then, to derive a more objective framework for understanding crime, a *sociological* definition has been offered by various students of the subject.[5] This definition usually includes acts in violation of the criminal law whether or not the offender is caught, arrested, prosecuted or convicted. It may also include acts injurious to the society whether or not such acts have been incorporated into the criminal statutes.

Many sociologists can agree that crime is crime whether or not the offender is caught or convicted; the fact that he did commit an act in violation of a criminal code is enough to establish that a crime was sociologically, as compared with legally, committed. This information may be extremely valuable for research purposes without necessarily doing violence to the reputation or self-concept of the perpetrator. The more legally minded criminologists differ with such a viewpoint, however, claiming that it is unsound and unwise to term any act a crime unless the sanctions have been imposed.[6]

The concept that behavior may be criminal even though no criminal law has been violated is held by a comparatively small number of sociologists, some of whom have modified their own positions at various times.[7] Yet, if crime is defined broadly as behavior in violation of any code, whether written or verbal, or whether criminal, civil, or administrative, much white collar crime would be included. The argument of the proponents of such a definition is that there is value in going beyond the existing criminal code to see what behavior ought to be proscribed by criminal statutes. Sociologists, in this view, should accept responsibility for trying to assess the effect on social values and institutions of behavior prohibited by administrative and civil codes and for considering whether it should be dealt with as in fact criminal behavior.[8] (A presumption here may be that it has been handled by administrative codes or civil law rather than criminal codes simply because of the high social status of the usual perpetrators of the acts.) Although a large element of social action, as well as normative judgment, may enter into the use of such a broad definition, for some specific purposes it may be defensible and even desirable.[9]

A further step not yet clearly taken by any criminologist or sociologist, would be to define behavior injurious to societal values or institutions as crime, whether or not any code at all is violated. Such a definition would clearly place the criminologist in a position of deciding what behavior ought to be legally proscribed and punished because of the potential damage it might do. As sociology becomes a much more precise science, it is not inconceivable that prediction would become accurate enough to make such a definition possible. However, it should be noted that other professions and disciplines could legitimately lay claim to a share of authority and responsibility in deciding what behavior should be proscribed—the legal profession, anthropologists, historians, economists, political scientists, clergymen and physicians. It is likely that when knowledge is rich enough to permit more complete assessment and prediction, society will establish some appropriate machinery for the practical application of this knowledge.

TRENDS IN INCIDENCE AND DISTRIBUTION OF CRIME

There are several aspects to an assessment of the magnitude and direction of the crime problem. We may explore the total amount of crime at a given time. We may examine trends. Or we may ask whether people are actually more prone to commit offenses today than they were in the past. These are really three separate, although related, questions.

National statistics regarding crimes known to the police, collected and published annually by the Federal Bureau of Investigation in *The Uniform Crime Reports*, are considered to be a more reliable index than arrest statistics, court or prison statistics.[10] This is true because many crimes are cleared or adjusted between recording and arrest, or between arrest and prosecution and conviction.

Yet even the number of crimes known to the police and contained in *The Uniform Crime Reports* is a poor index of crime. A great many crimes are not reported to the police or never get into the statistical records. For 1967, *The Uniform Crime Reports* indicated a total of more than 3.8 million serious crimes reported, a 16 percent rise over 1966.[11] The President's Commission on Law Enforcement and Administration of Justice recently initiated the first survey of actual crimes committed, arranging for the National Opinion Research Center of the University of Chicago to survey 10,000 households to find out if any member of the family had been a victim of crime in the past year. This survey was followed up by indepth studies in the cities of Washington, Chicago and Boston. These surveys revealed that the actual amount of crime is several times greater than that reported in *The Uniform Crime Reports*.[12] The Commission expressed the judgment that even these new rates understate the actual amounts of crime, since the person interviewed in the household knew more about offenses against him than he did about offenses against other family members. The Washington survey was even more dramatic, indicating actual crime to be between three and ten times more than that reported.[13] Most interviewees stated that they did not report the offense because they felt the police could not do anything. The second most frequent reason was that the offense was a private matter or that the victim did not want to hurt the offender. In any case, it is clear that our crime statistics do not presently reflect the actual extent of crime.

Biderman and Reiss have noted recently that the answer to the question of how much crime there is depends on whether one takes a "realist" position or an "institutionalist" position.[14] The former uses as indicators the number of criminals and their acts of crime. The "institutionalist" position uses as indicators the prevalence of criminals and their acts that receive *institutional validation*. Institutional validation refers to arrests, court appearances, sentences, commitments to institutions and so forth.

Our statistics do not help us a great deal in assessing the trends of crime incidence. The United States has maintained national crime statistics only since 1930.[15] Changes made in the reporting system since then make many comparisons unreliable.

Crimes of violence in the United States have increased markedly from 1933 to 1965.[16] *The Uniform Crime Reports—1967* indicates that violent crimes rose 16 percent from 1966 to 1967, with murder up 11 percent, forcible rape 7 percent, robbery 28 percent and aggravated assault 9 percent.[17] Crime rates, which take account of population increase, are increasing almost as sharply. The murder rate went up 9 percent over 1966, the aggravated assault rate 8 percent, forcible rape 6 percent, and robbery 27 percent.[18]

Property crime rates have risen even more sharply during the period from 1933-65.[19] From 1966-67 alone, the increase in burglary was 16 percent, the rate being 15 percent.[20] Larceny-theft increased 17 percent from 1966 to 1967, the rate being 16 percent.[21] Auto theft increased 18 percent over 1966, with a rate of 16 percent and with population growth allowed for.[22]

Over the 1960-67 period, the rate for aggravated assault climbed 51 percent, forcible rape 46 percent, robbery 70 percent, burglary 62 percent, larceny-theft 87 percent, and auto theft 82 percent.[23]

Criminologists, including the staff of the President's Commission on Law Enforcement and Administration of Justice, have been cautious in accepting the data of *The Uniform Crime Reports* at face value for a variety of reasons: (1) Due to the substantial amount of unreported crime, even small changes in reporting, recording or classifying procedures can have significant effects on published crime trends. (2) Changes in expectations of the poor and minority groups have resulted in crime in districts where offenses were formerly unknown or ignored being reported and handled. (3) The increasing professionalization of the police has led to improved detection, reporting and recording practices. (4) The substantial increase in insurance coverage against theft has induced more people to report offenses, particularly auto theft. (5) As a result of the post-war birth explosion, the percentage of youths in the teens and early twenties has been increasing much faster than other age groups. If one sets the fifth fact alongside the enormous increase in youth crimes, it is clear that the volume of crime and the crime rate alike are closely related to the population explosion in the earlier age groups. *The Uniform Crime Reports—1967* notes that the "arrests of juveniles for serious crimes increased 59 percent from 1960 to 1967, while number of persons in the young age group, 10-17, increased 22 percent."[24] It may be of further interest that 62 percent of the auto thefts, 55 percent of the larceny-theft, 54 percent of the burglaries, and 65 percent of arson cases were committed by the 10-17 age group in 1967.[25] Arrests on the other hand for persons 18 and over increased only .8 percent from 1960 to 1967.[26] The President's Commission on Law Enforcement and Administration of Justice comments that the rate of offense per individual in the 10-17 age group is many times that in older groups, so the arrest statistics must be understood to refer to a relatively smaller number of youths who are repeatedly apprehended.[27] It may also be very possible that older individuals are more successful at evading arrest.[28] They are also less apt to "ask for" apprehension because of guilt feelings. (6) The crime rates are far higher in urban areas than in rural areas, reflecting the larger number of offenses and police and the greater public concern about crime, as well as the larger number of opportunities available and the greater likelihood of association with criminals.

Other authorities differ with the conclusion of *The Uniform Crime Reports* that crime is continuing to climb steadily in volume and rate. The more guarded conclusion of the President's Crime Commission is that the number of offenses has been increasing due in large part to population growth, that most forms of crime are increasing faster than population and that it is likely that each year police agencies are dipping deeper and deeper into the reservoir of unreported crime. After a close analysis, Daniel Bell concludes that there is probably less crime today than a hundred or fifty or even twenty-five years ago. He points out the lack of uniform definitions of crime, the lack of uniform standards of reporting, the actual decline of murders and homicides, the decreases in crime in certain cities, and the key role of youths and minority groups in the crime picture.[28]

Perhaps the most rational conclusion is that the greatest part of the crime increase reflected in *The Uniform Crime Reports* can be attributed to the factors outlined above; that there is no convincing evidence that we are in the throes of a staggering crime wave, but that some modest increases in crime may be underway. For one reason, there are more laws to be broken in an urbanized, industrialized nation. A simple cataloging of a few crimes unheard of a few decades ago can illustrate the point. Such practices as fraudulent stock issues and monopolistic practices are among many new offenses related to economic changes. A host of new laws have grown out of industrialization: child labor legislation, interstate commerce regulations, and minimum wage laws. New laws have developed from urbanization: disturbing the peace, discharging of firearms, and traffic laws. Mobility of people has brought about school attendance laws, registration of vehicles, and tax assessments. Automation has produced laws to protect employee rights, patent rights, etc. The expansion of civil rights has brought a wave of new legislation. Although all of these examples do not necessarily result in criminal prosecution, in many instances criminal prosecution is initiated. Roscoe Pound once remarked that "of one hundred thousand persons arrested in Chicago in 1912, more than one half were held for violation of legal precepts which did not exist twenty-five years before."[29] Allen has added that the tendency certainly has not slackened since 1912.[30] Sutherland and Cressey comment that at least a half million new laws have been enacted in the past fifty years.[31]

Another reason for modest increases is that the rise in aspirations and expectations of all groups and classes has gradually brought about a complex situation in which every citizen wants his own rights and opportunities protected, and yet every citizen also expects a safe and stable community more commonly found in tightly organized and structured societies with advantages going largely to the elite.

It is perhaps remarkable in the light of all these complexities and stresses that our crime is as low as it is and is increasing so modestly.

It may also be noted that there is no evidence to support the contention that individual Americans are any more criminal, or less law-abiding, than their counterparts a decade, fifty years or a hundred years ago.[32] The riots of 1863 in New York City were no less violent than those of Watts in 1966 or Detroit in 1967. There were some 4,500 persons lynched in the United States between 1882 and 1930, and very few since 1930.[33]

Variations by Age

While youths have higher arrest rates, as we have discussed earlier, these rates reflect largely such offenses as car thefts and larceny from cars. This kind of crime has been increasing and will probably continue to increase.

Nationally, youths under 15 years of age comprised 10 percent of the total police arrests for the year 1967.[34] Youths under 18 accounted for 24 percent of all arrests, and youths under 21 accounted for 37 percent of all arrests. These percentages were even higher in suburban areas, the under 15 group accounting for 13 percent of arrests, the under 18 group, 34 percent, and the under 21 group, 48 percent.

The trends are significant. For the period 1960-1967, police arrests for all offenses, except traffic offenses, rose 11 percent. During that same period, police arrests of persons under 18 rose 169 percent, while the number of persons in that age range in the population only increased 22 percent. *The Uniform Crime Reports* notes that involvement of youth, as measured by police arrests, continues at a pace more than three times their percentage increase in the total population.[35]

Variations by Residence in Rural or Urban Areas

Some offenses are largely characteristic of metropolitan areas of the nation. In 1967, for example, an estimated total of 592,660 auto thefts were committed in the standard metropolitan statistical areas, as compared with an estimated 23,557 auto thefts in rural areas.[36] Since the total number of auto thefts in 1967 was 654,924, it can be seen that this is predominantly an offense of metropolitan America. The rural population in 1967 was roughly 19 percent of the total population, and the metropolitan population roughly 68 percent, yet the rural areas accounted for only 3.6 percent of auto thefts and metropolitan areas 90 percent.

Similar variations occur for larceny, burglary, aggravated assault and robbery, the rural areas accounting for only 7, 8, 12, and 2 percent, respectively. The total volume of crime is indicated by *The Uniform Crime Reports* to be increasing less in rural areas than in large cities—12 percent in rural areas and 17 percent in cities.[37] Although it has been in suburban areas that the sharpest upswing of crime has occurred in recent years, a 16 percent rise took place in 1967, less than that in large cities.

Regional Differences

There is abundant evidence that crimes of violence are much more frequent in the Southern states than elsewhere in the nation. In 1967, the East South Central states had 1,196 murders and nonnegligent manslaughters, with a total population of 12,970,000.[38] The New England states had 275 murders and nonnegligent manslaughters, with a total population of 11,321,000. With only a slightly larger population, the South Atlantic states had over five times the number of murders. These same states had about twice as many instances of forcible rape as New England and almost three times as many cases of aggravated assault. The East South Central states had almost as much murder as the East North Central states, although the latter states have over three times as many people.

Glaser stresses that the higher rates of violence exist in the South although there is less urbanization and less police coverage of assaults and similar crimes. He considers the South to have a cultural tradition supporting violence, which goes far to account for the high rates of

Negro crimes of violence.[39] Sutherland and Cressey cite studies to show that Negroes are more likely, in any event, to be arrested, indicted, and convicted than whites committing identical offenses, although the difference varies with the offense, the region, the sex, the area of residence, and the educational status.[40] It would therefore appear that the concentration of Negroes in the South accounts for much of the regional difference in amount of crime reported.

Who Are The Victims?

In crimes of violence, the offenders and victims are commonly from the same social class and live in relatively close proximity.[41] Crimes of violence are committed against persons with whom the offenders have personal dealings and close contact. For example, 31 percent of all murders in 1965 were within the family, 21 percent involved triangles or lovers' quarrels, and 27 percent resulted from altercations among acquaintances.[42] Only 16 percent resulted from robberies, gangland slayings, and sex offenses. (In the other 5 percent, the reasons for the killings were unknown.) Victim-offender relationships in rape and aggravated assault are similar.

In crimes of violence, therefore, Negroes generally murder or assault other Negroes, and Puerto Ricans living in New York City murder or assault other Puerto Ricans. It is Negroes, in fact, who are most likely to be victimized in crimes against the person. A Negro man in Chicago is six times as likely to be victimized as a white man.[43]

Crimes against property, on the other hand, are generally committed against strangers.[44] There is an atmosphere of impersonality and lack of personal antagonism in crimes against property. Several sociologists have noted that there are always vulnerable groups to property crimes in each society, *e.g.,* Sutherland and Cressey state that the profession of theft exists in modern society because victims are more interested in getting their money back than in abstract justice.[45] Victims who are trying to get something for nothing make circus grifting possible, as well as other forms of confidence games. It is fair to conclude that the attitudes of victims are extremely important to the continuation of crimes against property, including organized crime.

SOCIAL CLASS AND CRIME

The predominant values protected by criminal statutes are middle class values—statutes prohibiting theft, burglary, rape, robbery, arson, murder, kidnapping, auto theft.[46] These values are those affecting chiefly property rights and the dignity of the person.[47] Middle class American society cherishes the protection of the right to have and keep property legally obtained and the right of the individual to enjoy his property in safety and decorum.

Lower class values are not as well protected by the criminal statutes. For example, the right to physically punish someone for an offensive remark, a slight or an aggressive action, is not protected in our middle class statutes, being limited to defense against another's violent assault. Yet lower class people often value fighting prowess as highly as middle class people value property rights.[48] Similarly, freedom to wander about without funds, freedom to criticize authority, and freedom to gamble are not always well protected although these are more or less commonly held lower class values.

The middle class also controls the administrative machinery of criminal justice which interprets and even at times effectively "makes" the criminal law.[49] Thus, police are expected to uphold middle class values and institutions even though policemen as individuals are often drawn from the lower class.[50] Probation officers, judges, prosecutors, defense attorneys, parole boards, prison wardens, and newspaper editors are middle class people concerned with safeguarding middle class interests. Seldom does a lower class person become a judge, a warden, or a chief probation officer. When he does, he is apt to assume middle class values and to become a functioning member of the middle class.

The law makers are also middle class, with legislators at the local, state and national levels being primarily interested in creating a stable environment for the middle class. With lawmaking, law interpretation, and the administration of justice clearly oriented toward middle class interests, it is to be expected that a majority of the offenders who are apprehended, arrested, tried and convicted are members of the lower class.[51] At each stage of this process, a number of middle class individuals are screened out.[52] Middle class people are unlikely to report criminal acts of their neighbors and friends. Even when reports are made of middle class people being involved in criminal acts, the police are slow to apprehend and slower still to arrest.[53] Of the middle class people arrested, only a handful accused of very serious acts are remanded to court. A recent study by the Stanford Research Institute revealed that 90 percent of offenders placed on probation had incomes of less than $5,000.[54] An analysis of prisoner backgrounds indicated that 23.9 percent were laborers, as compared with 5.1 percent in the total population, whereas only 5.8 percent of the offender population were in high status jobs compared with 20.6 percent in the general population.[55] Execution of middle class persons for first degree murder is rare in most jurisdictions.[56] It is an oversimplification to attribute this partiality of the criminal justice process to the ability to afford competent legal counsel. Of course, this is a strong factor.[57] It is more accurate to emphasize that the entire system is stacked in favor of the middle-class: we have a middle class criminal process established and operated, as a practical matter, to prevent lower class attacks on the middle class value system.

Most institutionalized offenders are lower class and thus the studies made of institutionalized offenders are often studies of lower class people. Few serious criminologists rely any more on such studies, pointing out that a true sample of offenders must include a fair representation of middle class people whose offenses are less often dealt with by the police, courts, and prisons.

As American society has moved in the last several decades toward recognition of the need to have a greater element of fairness, objectivity, and equality in our system of justice, it has become increasingly obvious that an overhaul of our entire approach may be in order.[58] Laws may need to be reviewed and revised to provide for equality of handling, and the machinery of justice revamped and protections extended to the lower class. The possible directions would seem to include:

1. a system of increased repression of lower class, minority group people,
2. a watering down of the middle class values so that the gap between middle class and lower class values is narrowed,
3. an elevation of the lower class to a middle class posture, or
4. an insurrection or revolution.

It seems likely that all four of these directions, and others as well, may be simultaneously underway in contemporary American society.

In a sense, the gap between middle class and lower class values is already narrowing. Daniel Bell is among those who point out the recent blurring of class lines and the middle class acceptance of lower class values such as violence as a way of handling problems.[59]

ORGANIZED CRIME

A great deal of attention in recent decades has been devoted to the threat of organized crime in America. This attention has taken such forms as Congressional investigations, sustained efforts to break up organized crime by the Federal Bureau of Investigation and by other units of the U.S. Department of Justice and other federal agencies. There has also been an outpouring of articles in the press and magazines such as a two-article series in *Life Magazine* in September, 1967, stressing more intensified activities of state and local law enforcement groups, an awakened interest in research, and the organization of public and private crime commissions.

Organized crime has been defined as "criminal syndicates or rings whose members engage in criminal activities as a source of livelihood."[60] It is a rational organization like a business except that the services provided are largely illicit services. It should be noted that organized crime as such is not against the law—having a secret organization in existence for the purpose of amassing huge profits from legal and illegal activities. What is illegal is the usury, gambling, dealing in narcotics, extortion and many other activities carried on by organized crime.[61] The characteristics of organized crime—corruption of officials, use of strongarm techniques, contempt for law, infringement of individual rights—make it a particularly complex threat to a democratic society.

What makes organized crime significant as a particular category of criminal behavior is that it is in the process of being defined by the American public as a social problem. Its services meet a demand and its members are not defined as criminal in many instances. Organized crime goes about its work on a rational systematic basis, usually in secrecy so that hard data are not easy to obtain and only the most knowledgeable criminologists and law enforcement officials are in a position to understand fully its threat to American society.[62]

Perhaps the earliest, widespread public knowledge of organized crime dates from the work of the Kefauver Committee in the United States Senate. In 1951 it uncovered the existence of a nationwide crime syndicate known as the Mafia which controlled most of the rackets in the large cities.[63] As early as 1929, however, the Wickersham Commission had stimulated the interest of the executive and legislative branches of the federal government in the problem.[64] More recently, the Federal Bureau of Investigation has confirmed the operations of the group, which has changed its name to La Cosa Nostra, in these words:

> La Cosa Nostra is the largest organization of the criminal underworld in this country, very closely organized and strictly disciplined. They have committed almost every crime under the sun. . . .[65]

Life Magazine adds the alternative titles: the Outfit, the Syndicate and the Mob, preferring to use the latter.[66] Cressey prefers "confederation."[67] In recent years, even a significant percentage of the public is convinced that an organized crime syndicate exists in the major cities. A

Harris Poll in 1966 found that about a third of the people polled in a number of large cities believed the syndicate was operating in their city.[68]

Although most responsible agencies and authorities concede the existence of La Cosa Nostra, with some exceptions, there are still disagreements and unanswered questions about its structure and operations. For example, the President's Commission on Law Enforcement and the Administration of Justice states that the core of organized crime consists of twenty-four groups or families.[69] Former assistant attorney general Fred Vinson, Jr. considers this number misleading, terming some of them subgroups, and suggests that a more accurate figure is ten to sixteen.[70]

There is consensus that La Cosa Nostra is exclusively Italian and chiefly Sicilian in its membership, although at least one nonmember, Meyer Lansky, is the syndicate's chief financial counselor and architect of the "skimming" system whereby tax-free cash is surreptitiously taken from gambling profits in Nevada and other sources.[71] Yet the point is made by some authorities that La Cosa Nostra itself does not represent the whole of organized crime in the United States. However, little is known about the other organizations.[72]

The syndicate appears to date from the time of Prohibition, but currently receives its earnings chiefly from such sources as gambling, including illegal sports betting. The illegal wagering in the nation is conservatively estimated at $20 billion per year.[73] La Cosa Nostra's take of this is judged to be at least $6 billion.[74] The gambling operations range from lotteries, including the numbers racket, to off-track horse betting, bets on sporting events, dice games and illegally-operated casinos. In the large cities, very few gambling operations are independent of the organization. Gambling has become the principal support of La Cosa Nostra primarily because the public is apathetic regarding the prosecution of gambling.

Other illegal activities include loan sharking or shylocking, which is considered to be the second largest source of revenue for organized crime.[75] Loans are provided to gamblers, narcotics users, small businessmen who are unable to borrow money through legitimate channels, and employees of mass industries who need cash to pay off gambling debts or meet other expenses. The interest rates for these loans vary from 1 to 150 percent a week according to the circumstances. The usual interest is about 20 percent a week, with a rise in rates if prompt payment is not made. With such enormous profits from interest, the lender is more concerned with perpetuating interest payments than in collecting the principal. It appears that loan sharking is a multibillion dollar business.

The procurement, distribution and sale of narcotics is the third of the core operations that support organized crime. This enterprise is operated like any importing-wholesaling-retailing business.[76] At the top level are importers of multi-kilogram shipments. "Kilo-men" purchase from an importer-supplier at the rate of a kilogram at a time. They dilute the heroin by adding about 3 kilograms of milk sugar for each kilo of heroin. The heroin then goes through the hands of "quarter-kilo men," "ounce men" and "deck men," more adulteration occurring at each level. Street peddlers do the retailing in 5-grain bags or packs, the cost to the consumer having multiplied to 300 times the original cost.[77]

Prostitution and bootlegging are declining sources of illegal revenue, perhaps in response to changing needs and interests on the part of the public as well as in response to the "coming of age" of organized crime itself with the resulting desire of leaders to be more respectable. Other illegal activities include juggling stock shares and selling munitions to foreign governments.

In the past several decades, organized crime has gained power and respectability by moving into control of legitimate businesses, including food products, realty, restaurants, garbage disposal, produce, garment manufacturing, bars and taverns, securities, labor unions, vending machines, supplying of linen to night clubs and supplying of some forms of labor. Superficially, one might consider this trend a socially desirable one. Yet studies and investigations have shown that a lawful business does not remain legitimate once organized crime takes it over.[78] The effort is usually made to use strongarm methods to gain monopolistic control over the field of business.[79] At the very least, organized crime uses legitimate business as a vehicle for "skimming" off tax-free cash. They select legitimate businesses in which there is a heavy cash flow and a relatively unstructured handling of funds.

But the present trend has much more serious implications. Cressey notes that real trouble starts when criminal syndicates "undermine basic economic and political traditions and institutions," and he considers real trouble to have already started in the United States.[80]

A recent *Life* editorial sounds the same warning, pointing out that the sophisticated adaptation of "the modern tools of economics and technology to the task of taking over great chunks of the economy" can lead to the even greater damage of chewing holes "in the fabric of our political system."[81]

Documentation of the mechanics of protection and corruption as essential ingredients in organized crime can be found in various recent sources. Gardiner details the politics of vice and corruption in one U.S. city during the 1940's, 1950's, and 1960's. Although most of the public officials were honest, 10 out of 155 members of the police force, including the police chief, were on the payroll of the syndicate, as were the mayor, the city treasurer, several state legislators, and several city councilmen.[82] The *Life* series gives the account of a February, 1963 meeting in Mountainside, New Jersey at which several members of the Vito Genovese "family" discussed the greed of a top-level officer in the New Jersey State Police. This officer was being reported to have received a total of $7,250 a month for ignoring gambling in four parts of New Jersey but was demanding a double payoff for each of the summer months.[83] In different places and at different times, organized crime has corrupted prosecutors, judges, and regulatory agency officials, as well as the officials previously listed.[84] Corruption, including the coverup as well as the fix, has even extended, in the opinion of *Life Magazine's* Sandy Smith, to the censoring of the official report on organized crime of the President's own Crime Commission.

> As an apparent result of political pressure, specific findings relating to official corruption were watered down or omitted. . . . One commission investigator thinks . . . the report was emasculated by [Executive Director James] Vorenberg because we didn't dampen this and dampen that. There were protests from officeholders in Chicago and enormous pressure on us *not* to be specific.[85]

Organized crime operates in all sections of the nation, and a survey of police departments indicate that 80 percent of the cities over a million population report the existence of organized criminal groups, as well as 20 percent of the cities between 250,000 and a million, and over 50 percent of the cities between 100,000 and 250,000 population.[86] Many smaller cities of less than 100,000 population pay tribute to nearby larger cities. About 80 percent of the Cosa Nostra, however, is based in New York City, Chicago, and northern New Jersey.[87]

The hierarchical structure of each of the families includes a boss who has absolute authority subject to the possibility of being overruled by the commission which is the highest ruling body in the United States.[88] The primary functions of the commission, which comprises the bosses of the nine most powerful families, are judicial. It is the ultimate authority on organizational disputes. Below each boss is an underboss who assists the boss in his primary functions of maintaining order and maximizing profits. He also acts as the primary channel for orders and information. On the same level as the underboss, there is a position of counselor or advisor who is a staff officer providing advice on a range of matters. He is usually an elder member who did not quite make the grade as a boss. Also on this level is a "buffer" who serves as a go-between and a spy upon lower-echelon personnel, without however having the authority of the underboss.

The next level of rank is the lieutenant who serves as the chief of an operating unit. He may also have messengers and buffers who lack administrative power. In the larger families, there are one or more section chiefs under each lieutenant. About five soldiers, "buttons" or members report to each section chief. Some families may have as many as 250 members, others as few as 20. All told, there are estimated to be between 2,000 and 4,000 members of the confederation or La Cosa Nostra. Large numbers of employees, not necessarily of Italian-Sicilian descent, serve beneath the members as street workers who take bets, sell narcotics, drive trucks, make deliveries, and carry the main burden of the direct contact with customers. They have little or no insulation from the police. Other less formal positions in the organization include the roles of "corrupter," "enforcer," "executioner," and "money mover," any of which may be assumed by a person also holding a formal position.

The structure outlined above serves to insulate the leaders from direct participation in any illegal activities, while at the same time insuring that decision making is concentrated at the top. The boss actually is a despot with life-and-death power over the lesser levels in his family. This power is insured not only by the hierarchical structure but by the operation of a code of honor which requires members to be loyal and to maintain secrecy, to be rational and "cool," to be respectful to superiors in the organization, to be manly and courageous, and to be sharp and knowledgeable.

As the organization shifts toward becoming more of a business than a despotic government, however, some parallels emerge to any social unit's change from feudalism to a modern economic system. The need for security and secrecy has begun to decrease and the need for expertise has increased. The authority of rank is being gradually replaced by the authority of the expert. Recruitment for organized crime nowadays is more a matter of seeking the skills of purchasing agent, lawyer, accountant or executive than of a "gorilla" or "tough guy." Most recruits have college degrees and are prepared to use a variety of new skills and abilities.

At least one writer predicts that these developments will mean that underlings will, in the next decade, begin demanding their rights and opportunities to achieve and share more fully in the good things of organized crime. He predicts rebellions comparable to those of the Negro if these rights are not forthcoming.[89]

Management of the Problem

Law enforcement agencies are hampered by a lack of enthusiasm for control of organized crime on the part of the government and public which support them, by the lack of coordinated intelligence, by defects in the evidence-gathered process, by the commitment to due process of law, and by the lack of adequate resources: a sufficient number of trained personnel, adequate equipment and an ample budget.

The first of these handicaps stems ultimately from the fact that organized crime is not clearly defined and perceived as crime. The American demand for illicit goods and services, which has provided the opportunity for organized crime to flourish, also operates to blur the issue. Whereas the ordinary criminal is obviously predatory, the person participating in crime as a rational systematic activity is offering a tangible service to society in the way of illicit gambling, drugs, labor or other services or goods.[90]

Any permanent management program therefore would seem to require that the public be convinced of the danger that organized crime presents, so that a rational choice can be made between giving up the illegal services and goods one way or another or deciding to continue to live with the threat that organized crime presents. A widespread campaign of public education already underway will enable the nation, for example, to decide whether it might be best to legitimize gambling and narcotics under governmental control and supervision.[91] There is considerable support in the United States today, in any event, for handling narcotics as a medical rather than a law enforcement problem. If public opinion crystalizes in this direction, organized crime may lose one of its more lucrative activities.

When the choices are crystal clear, it may be conceivable, although hardly likely, that a significant fraction of the public may be induced to give up gambling rather than to risk the growing damage to the economic and political institutions. It is more conceivable that the American public may be willing to legalize gambling and thereby reduce the financial base of organized crime.[92] At the least, an aware public will be able to assess the merits of supporting various measures. To better inform the public and to overcome the apathy, the President's Crime Commission has recommended the establishment of state and local crime commissions under both governmental and citizen sponsorship.[93] Mass media are also urged to become more concerned about organized crime, with each newspaper in metropolitan areas designating a full-time reporter to the investigation of organized crime.[94]

The lack of coordinated intelligence stems from the extremely fragmented condition of law enforcement. Former assistant attorney general Vinson estimated that there are over 40,000 law enforcement agencies in the country.[95] It is almost impossible to establish and maintain well coordinated programs of intelligence, planning and action with this number of agencies. A corollary problem is that this huge number of agencies cannot recruit and retain competent personnel. The average patrolman has a starting salary of $5,300 a year, and little incentive to remain in a law enforcement career. Most agencies are too small to be able to develop adequate training and retirement programs.[96] It seems clear that educational requirements and salaries need to be raised substantially, and that arrangements be made, perhaps at the state level, for the coordination or pooling of such services as standard-setting, recruitment, and training. The President's Crime Commission recommends a special intelligence unit in each major city with intelligence-gathering and intelligence-sharing conducted also at state and federal levels.[97]

In order to strengthen the evidence-gathering process, the President's Crime Commission suggests the impaneling of at least one investigative grand jury annually in each major city or jurisdiction, with the right of appeal to replace local prosecutors or investigators with special personnel.[98] A general immunity statute is proposed as a way of overcoming the reluctance of members to testify against their leaders, as well as special residential facilities for the protection of witnesses.

Many authorities favor the legalized use of wiretapping and eavesdropping as a necessary step in the evidence-gathering process. The arguments on both sides of this specific issue highlight some of the basic issues and problems encountered in the management of organized crime as a problem.

Lawrence Speiser, Director, Washington Office, American Civil Liberties Union, testified against the Proposed Federal Wire Interception Act on July 12, 1967 on the basis that the act would violate the 4th Amendment's prohibition against unreasonable searches and seizures. He specifically noted that wiretapping is "inherently uncontrollable and usually uncontrolled," and that such legislation would court "abuse on a wholesale basis."[99] Attorney General Ramsey Clark agreed, stating that wiretapping should be allowed only in matters of national security.

> A tap cannot be selective and must record all that goes over the wire. . . . The needs of law enforcement can be met without reliance on such large-scale intrusions on personal privacy.[100]

On the other hand, New York County District Attorney Frank S. Hogan, whose office convicted a number of organized criminals, has stated unequivocally that:

> "telephonic interception, pursuant to court order and under proper safeguards, is the single most valuable and effective weapon in the

arsenal of law enforcement, particularly in the battle against organized crime."[101]

Later, he notes, "there must be some invasion of our liberties if we are to offer any protection to members of society."[102]

In the case of *Berger v. New York*, the U.S. Supreme Court, in 1967, held that a New York statute authorizing electronic eavesdropping was "too broad in its sweep resulting in a trespassory intrusion into a constitutionally protected area."[103] The President's Crime Commission split on the desirability of legislation granting carefully circumscribed authority for electronic surveillance to law enforcement officers, the majority favoring such legislation and a minority questioning its desirability.

The probability is that viable alternative means will be sought and found for securing evidence against organized criminals. Yet, if the threat of organized crime continues to grow, it is not impossible that some reconciliation will be achieved between the demands for personal privacy and for control of organized crime so that some form of electronic surveillance could be utilized. The U.S. Supreme Court decision in *United States v. Katz*, in December 1967, confirms that carefully planned and controlled wiretapping with judicial consent secured in advance upon the basis of already secured evidence and with protections against obtaining other information not essential to the case is constitutional. However, not all authorities agree on the usefulness of such techniques. For example, although the 90th Congress in its second session in 1968 incorporated provisions for wiretapping under controlled circumstances, in the Safe Streets and Crime Control Act of 1968, Attorney General Ramsey Clark made no use of the provision during 1968. Fred M. Vinson, Jr. has stated that the Supreme Court decisions affecting evidence gathering have had little or no effect on the fight against organized crime, since the Cosa Nostra has a large staff of bondsmen and lawyers and since Cosa Nostra members do not generally make willing witnesses.[104] Not all authorities even agree that organized crime is growing. Vinson states that it is not increasing in size but, rather, that the pressure of prosecution and investigation is driving it into legitimate business.[105]

A growing effort is already being made against organized crime. From 1961-66 alone, a total of 185 Cosa Nostra personnel were indicted, of which number 102 were convicted.[106] In the fiscal year 1967, the U.S. Government deployed a total of 1,378 men at a cost of $22,355,000 in the fight against organized crime.[107]

If organized crime is to be controlled or eliminated, it will be necessary above all to block out avenues for curtailing the corruption essential to the operations of organized crime. Methods will need to be found for creating incorrupt climates in public and business organizations, even if this requires some abridgement of the "business is business" and "you scratch my back and I'll scratch yours" philosophies. There is more than a little evidence that it is the American value systems of success, material comfort, and economic rationality that contribute heavily to the perpetuation of organized crime.

One last observation is significant. Daniel Bell stresses that organized crime has a functional role in our society, providing a "queer ladder" up into the middle class for successive waves of immigrants, minority group members, and the disadvantaged.[108] As an addition to the measures already discussed it may help for alternative ladders into the middle class to be provided for the benefit of persons now recruited into the lower levels of organized crime. If it did nothing more, this measure would decrease the supply of runners and lower level workers, which would aid in forcing the leaders into the open.

The Positive Role of Organized Crime

Organized crime has been an integral part of American society for some time and offers a number of positive contributions. It tries increasingly to avoid public displays of violence and appears to strive for some kind of peaceful organization and division of profits. The customers do not often complain, because they are receiving a wanted service. Organized crime provides a channel of upward mobility, particularly valuable for immigrants and minority-group members. Organized crime provides support to political parties, business, labor and community welfare organizations. Although it may be suggested that these same contributions could, and should, be made through a more legal channel, it still must be recognized that organized crime is not completely without its services and advantages to certain segments of society.

WHITE COLLAR CRIME

Criminologists have recognized, at least since 1941, that offenses committed by businessmen as a consequence of business activities and practice were not handled similarly to such offenses as burglary or rape, either by the statutes or by the processes of criminal justice.[109] The statutes have tended to handle business violations as infractions of administrative codes, as offenses against the civil code or, at most, as minor infractions of the criminal code. The system of criminal and civil justice has dealt in a generally restrained fashion with these offenses, prosecution and conviction rates being very low. Sutherland, for example, found that seventy large corporations, in 980 violations of laws against restraint of trade, misrepresentation, infringement and unfair labor practices, were in criminal proceedings in only 16 percent of the cases, the other 84 percent being handled in civil and equity courts and by administrative commissions.[110]

There is growing evidence that white collar crimes are costly to society from a number of standpoints, although the public has been largely concerned with the common crimes of violence and theft that are more easily understood and feared. Physical injury or death may result from tainted foods or harmful drugs manufactured and sold in violation of the Pure Food and Drug Act or of local health laws. Financial losses may be sustained by such actions as the marketing of worthless or injurious products in violation of Post Office Department regulations, by frauds in violation of the controls of the Securities and Exchange Commission, or by the sale of goods falsely represented in advertising. Above all, there may be damage to the social, economic and political institutions of the nation.[111] This last type of cost involves erosion of morals, loss of confidence in the free enterprise system, spread of bitterness against middle class businessmen, and promotion of distrust of laws and courts.

One essential difference between white collar crime and robbery or burglary is that white collar crime is characteristically concerned with violation of trust.[112] By virtue of his office or position, the white collar criminal is expected to perform in certain ways to safeguard the interests of his employer, public, clients or other individuals. A partial listing of white collar crimes would therefore include embezzlement, theft of company secrets, fraud to maintain job or status, sabotage, padding of expense accounts, falsification of records, manipulating of inventories, use of defective material by builders, fixing of prices, peddling of influence and vote by a legislator, illegal activities of reorganization committes in receiverships and bankruptcies, restraint of trade, infringement of patents and copyrights, misrepresentation in advertising, unfair labor practices, financial manipulations, and wartime crimes such as black-marketeering.[113] Professionals are occasionally guilty of white collar criminality since they are in positions of trust. Physicians, for example, may give illegal prescriptions for narcotics, perform illegal abortions, make fraudulent reports, give false testimony in court, and split fees.[114] Attorneys sometimes misappropriate funds in receiverships, secure perjured testimony from witnesses, or initiate fraudulent damage claims. Politicians and governmental employees are often in a position to pad payrolls, misappropriate public funds, sell influence or decision-making power, obtain kickbacks from employees, divert campaign funds to personal use, or put relatives illegally on the payrolls. Business concerns are guilty of a wide range of offenses, from illegal restraint of trade to bribery and misleading advertising.

The violation of trust perpetuated by white collar criminals occurs only when the trusted person views this position in keeping with "culturally provided knowledge about and rationalizations for using the entrusted funds for solving a non-shareable problem," according to research by Cressey.[115] Violation of trust is then both a cultural and a psychological phenomenon. The rationalization usually takes the form of the temporary borrowing of funds. The clear conception of a financial problem as nonshareable does not always result in trust violation, but it opens the door to it if the other conditions are present. Cressey's theory then has the three elements of an unusual economic need which the trust violator is ashamed to share, the opportunity and knowledge to commit the fraud or violation, and the rationalizing to quiet the violator's conscience.

A second major difference between white collar crimes and other forms of crimes lies in the offender's conception of himself.[116] He is likely to perceive himself as a law-abiding citizen rather than as a criminal. At most, he sees himself as a transitory lawbreaker as in the case of a person violating a traffic law. He may continue to perform a number of other roles such as citizen, Sunday School teacher or club member. Because of his high social status, the public is unlikely to classify him as a "real criminal," since he has not committed the stereotyped crimes of murder, arson, or burglary. This public attitude reinforces his own conception of himself as does the shared attitudes of business or professional colleagues regarding certain forms of illegal behavior which are considered inevitable, forgiveable, or even right and necessary.

White collar crime may be highly organized. Fee-splitting among physicians, political corruption, corporation criminality, and labor union criminality all require a considerable degree of organization. An outstanding recent example of organization was the price-rigging violations of the antitrust laws by many of the largest electrical equipment companies.[117] Twenty-nine leading companies were convicted in 1960 of illegalities amounting to almost two billion dollars a year. The organization included secret meetings, concealed bidding, a special jargon, and special procedures.

There is evidence that white collar criminality is learned behavior and that the rationalizations may be widespread. A study of World War II black-market dealings by businessmen revealed a general agreement as to the inevitability and even the desirability of illegal practices.[118] Rationalizations, information about techniques, and knowledge about opportunities were all shared.

A third major difference between white collar crime and other forms of crime is that the societal reaction is diffuse, variable and confused. White collar criminality is new, stemming from relatively recent industrial, urban conditions, and societal attitudes are not yet crystallized. There has been relatively slow public awareness of the dangers of white collar crime and laws have been enacted very gradually for this reason. White collar crimes are less visible than murder, rape, or burglary and their impact is more intangible. White collar crimes are committed by persons generally held in high esteem, and it is not easy for the public to evaluate these offenses objectively. American society is marked by a heavy stress on economic success with some diminution of emphasis on achievement, personal excellence and hard work.[119] Such amoral success-striving, divorced from ultimate values, leads to corrosion of norms and a general disregard of laws which are not in keeping with business and professional practices.

For several reasons, white collar crimes are reported to police far less frequently than such crimes as auto theft, robbery, and murder. White collar crimes are often not discovered promptly and sometimes not at all. And, when they are discovered, the perpetrator often cannot be readily identified.[120] Also, the victim is apt to be a corporation, a government agency, or the public rather than an individual who will complain and see that action is taken. And, finally, victims are apt to be more tolerant of these offenses and to include them as part of normal expenses.

Management of the Problem

There have been several suggestions made for the management of white collar crime. Bonding of employees would cut down the embezzlement, inventory losses and record juggling estimated to cost American business over four million dollars a day.[121] Better employment practices, control procedures, bookkeeping systems and administrative methods have also been suggested. Enforcement of laws related to business activities should be more vigorous. At present, only about one out of ten offenders is brought into court and many of them are treated casually.

The public will need to be better informed about the costs and dangers of white collar crime and better research data obtained regarding incidence, affected areas of the national economy, and trends. Professionals may need closer public controls such as those rendered by licensing, malpractice suits, and disbarment proceedings.

CRITICISMS.   There have been many criticisms of the concept of white collar crime. Perhaps the most common objection has centered on the vagueness and lack of clarity of the concept. Some criminologists and sociologists have considered white collar crime an unserviceable formulation on this ground alone.[122] Others have suggested ways of making the concept more rigorous. For example, it has been proposed that categories of white collar crime be distinguished, perhaps along the lines of offenses by individual professionals or entrepreneurs, offenses of policy-making officials for corporations, and offenses by employees against corporations.[123] It has also been proposed to clarify the behaviors that constitute white collar crime since, at present, the activity of a farmer in watering milk for public consumption and the making of unnecessary repairs by a television repairman could be termed white collar crime, although both are in nonwhite collar occupations.[124] One solution offered has been to include all violations that occur in the course of occupational activity and then to change the term to "occupational crime."[125] This solution has been accepted by at least one prominent criminologist in his latest text revision.[126] If adopted, it would tend to eliminate from the formulation non-occupational offenses such as income tax evasion and violation of rent control laws.

It has been further suggested that ambiguities in the concept could be controlled if only behavior punishable by law is included in the formulation.[127] This proposal would eliminate sharp business practices, unethical behavior, contract violations, and similar behavior not punishable by law. The term "occupational deviation" might be employed for non-criminal behavior violating institutionalized expectations of an occupation.

A suggestion incorporating several of these ideas has been made to not only limit the concept to violations of criminal statutes but also to restrict its use to corporate violations of a fairly homogeneous nature.[128]

Not all criminologists are so enthusiastic about restricting the use of the concept. One British writer prefers to see white collar crime remain as a comprehensive sociological concept dealing with a large number of clearly delineated subtypes.[129]

The Positive Role of White Collar Crime

A particularly thorny question concerns the distinction between law-breaking on the one hand and criminal status on the other. Almost all criminologists concur that the white collar criminal is not defined by himself or others as a genuine criminal or deviant. Group affiliations are very important in this distinction and it is sometimes very difficult to get at these affiliations and identifications. Nor is it easy to study the attitudes and decision making of lawmakers, judges, and lawyers. For these reasons, one writer has noted that white collar crime tends to bring into focus the neglected relationships between criminal behavior, criminal law, administration of justice and social structure.[130] Another text proposes that a systematic analysis of the policies and decision making of governmental agencies is needed.[131]

In addition to offering an advantageous springboard for studying the effect of societal reaction on the behavior and concept of offenders, white collar crime plays several other "positive" roles in an urban, industrial society oriented to money-making as an especially valuable goal. White collar crime allows businessmen, professionals and corporations to maximize profits and thus raise the gross national product without being overly concerned about the niceties of law and the constraints of social justice. It protects the money economy, helps to allow a minority of the society to exert a key control over policy-making, and keeps middle class values dominant by offering a way to reconcile sharp and even illegal business practices with middle class morality.

Although these are not seen as positive contributions by some criminologists or by persons concerned about social justice, it can fairly be said that white collar crime has been functional to certain segments of American Society.

RIOTS AND CIVIL DISOBEDIENCE

The pressure for equality of opportunity, for equality in the process of justice, and for the right for all individuals and groups to share in public policy has grown in American society. The 1960's has not been a decade of passive acceptance of injustice, discrimination, poverty and other inequities in the human condition. A number of reactions against injustice and inequality have arisen and in a sense they form a continuum.

Almost all Americans agree that *legal protest* against injustices or social problems is the most democratic and desirable way of influencing changes in public policy. Few would question the value of responsible minority action to bring about change: attempts to have social legislation enacted, campaigns to alter public opinion, efforts to get more socially-minded court decisions in test cases, pressure to bring about administrative reforms and improvements. Most Americans would agree that such legal and responsible protests actually serve to prevent or mitigate the potential tyranny of majority rule, and may call attention to possible threats to the social order, social values, or social institutions.

Far fewer Americans ascribe as meaningful and responsible a role to *civil disobedience* as a means of pressing for social action and social change, although there is some evidence that its acceptance as a strategy is increasing. Civil disobedience is clearly much further along the continuum toward crime as compared with legal protest.

It may be noted that there are several forms of law violation which are not usually, but could conceivably be considered civil disobedience [132] These include inadvertent violations, individual or widespread evasions such as the evasion of the Fugutive Slave Act during the Civil War, or open flouting of an unpopular law such as the Eighteenth Amendment. Civil disobedience, however, has been defined as

> any act or process of public defiance of a law or policy enforced by established governmental authorities, insofar as the act is premeditated, understood by the actor(s) to be illegal or of contested legality, carried out and persisted in for limited public ends and by way of carefully chosen and limited means.[133]

The usual distinction from crime, however, hinges on the open, frank willingness to be arrested for deliberate violation of a law considered to be unjust, unfair, discriminatory, protective of undesirable subcultural values or destructive to overall societal interests. A second allied form of civil disobedience is the breaking of an admittedly just law in order to protest another injustice. Frequently the point is made that it is not really civil disobedience at all when the "offender" tries to avoid arrest or to dispute the facts of the case. Civil disobedience is thus an open challenge to the merits of a particular law, process or procedure, and involves the willingness of an individual or group to go to jail in order to call public attention to the inequity of the situation. Perhaps the best known early instance of civil disobedience in the United States was Thoreau's refusal to pay income taxes which he stated would be used to support the war against Mexico.

Civil disobedience is a fairly complex strategy not easily understood by the American public, and although its use is growing, it is not always possible to keep its use within the appropriate and planned limits. In some instances, marches, sit-ins, or protest movements, planned as deliberate civil disobedience to laws against loitering, disturbing the peace, unapproved public meetings, and even more comprehensive targets, have turned into riots. Perhaps the most effective approach to civil disobedience involves only one dedicated individual or a small group with strong convictions and sound understanding of the issues. The attempt to involve large numbers of people in civil disobedience may backfire because of the problems in insuring that the entire group is fully aware of the purposes, limits and grounds rules. Moreover, it is generally agreed that civil disobedience is most defensible after repeated and unsuccessful legal protests. How long the wait should be and how many unsuccessful legal protests should be made are not easy questions to answer. Nor is it easy to cope with the ethical dilemmas posed by the confrontation of a powerful, determined minority and an equally determined majority with its greater strength and power. At what point is it necessary that the minority terminate its efforts in order to insure the continuity of the society itself? On the other hand, should a society be preserved in its present form if a strong minority considers the majority position to be untenable?

Pemberton suggests the following requirements for sound exercise of civil disobedience:

1. willingness to exhaust reasonable alternatives.
2. openness and selflessness, including willingness to accept the penalties imposed by law.
3. readiness to accept responsibility for the consequences of its behavior.[134]

Three principal factors suggest an expanding role for civil disobedience: our increasing knowledge of political behavior and institutions in democracies; the impact of the Nuremberg verdicts and the Eichmann trial on modern thinking about the individual's political responsibilities; and the influence of Camus and other writers who relate the growth of man with a maturing and independent social conscience.[135]

Riots may well grow out of the attempt to answer the questions noted above. If a minority is sufficiently convinced of the validity of its claims against the intolerance or injustice of the majority, and if legal protest and civil disobedience have produced insufficient change, a minority may move toward spontaneous riots or toward planned insurrection, rebellion or revolution.

A riot is defined as

. . . an outbreak of temporary but violent mass disorder. It may be directed against a particular private individual as well as against public authorities, but it involves no intention to overthrow the government itself. In this respect, riot stops short of insurrection or rebellion, although it may often be only a preliminary to the latter.[136]

Riots are an indication of social unrest, and the occurrence of riots preceded the American, French and Russian revolutions. Riots have had religious, political, economic and racial underpinnings. The United States suffered riots in 1812, the 1830's, 1844 and the 1850's, with the abolitionist riots preceding the Civil War, the railroad strikes of the 1870's, the Chicago riot of 1886, the race riots of 1917-19, 1922, the 1930's, and the recent riots of the 1960's.

Spontaneous riots characteristically have some emotional spark to set off the combustion, as well as the underlying discontent about unfair conditions. No planning is involved although leaders may form at some stage or persons with specific objectives may enter to try to direct or control the rioters toward their established ends.

Insurrection, on the other hand, may be perceived as a planned attempt to influence public policy further along the continuum from legal protest and civil disobedience. It is widespread civil disobedience aimed at rejecting, at least temporarily, the entire system of law and order. It is obviously a serious threat to the fabric of the society. Rebellion technically is aimed at the breaking off of a part of the territory and population of a given nation, and revolution is aimed at overthrowing the government. This discussion will not be concerned with rebellion or revolution which are not seriously considered to be imminent in the United States today although the present riots may foreshadow more serious future efforts at rebellion or revolution. Lieberson and Silverman distinguish riots from lynching in that riots "involve an assault on persons and property simply because they are part of a given subgroup of a community."[137] Lynchings are directed toward a given individual such as a collective response for some particular act he has committed. They studied the 72 race riots listed in the *New York Times Index* for the period 1913-1963 and found that precipitating incidents often involved highly charged offenses committed by one group against the other, such as attacks on women, murder, or police brutality.[138] Riots are more likely to occur when social institutions function poorly or when grievances cannot be resolved. Populations are predisposed to riots by such conditions as lack of close contact with government, lack of representation on police force, and a close correspondence in employment and income patterns of white and black workers.

Oberschall has developed a sociological analysis of riots in which he finds a number of determinants of social action that must all be present for a riot to occur.[139] These include such socioeconomic factors as high unemployment, low income, racial cleavages, inaccessible and unsympathetic authorities, and a generalized belief or state of mind pinpointing a specific target for blame. When these factors are all present, any incident such as a police arrest or shooting can trigger a riot. Oberschall determined that the major source of black frustrations prior to the Los Angeles riot of 1965 was the state of police-black relations, and there was a generalized belief among the black population in Los Angeles that police were discourteous, uncivil, unfair and brutal to Negroes.

Waskow has also found that in almost all riots, the behavior of the local police was a factor in the beginning of the riot.[140] Police partiality results in whites feeling the normal protections afforded by the law to Negroes should be suspended and in Negroes feeling that the law is no longer a resource to them with their only protection residing in their own strength of arms. Police refusal to tolerate nonviolent forms of creative disorder results in the feeling that only violence is left as the last resort.

Management

The traditional American policy for coping with riots and insurrection has been the use of armed force. This policy was employed in a number of riots in the 19th and 20th Centuries with considerable success and widespread public support. The riots in a large number of American prisons in the 1950's and 1960's were largely put down by force and the threat of force. Yet this policy is being modified in the late 1960's under the impact of strong minority pressures for equality, justice and fairness, coupled with the increasing public concern about conditions of discrimination and inequity. Perhaps it is fair to say that force has never been an exclusive policy in the 20th Century: for example, in the prison riots, after the disturbance was quelled, attention has frequently been given to a certain amount of improvement of underlying conditions of idleness, corruption, unfairness and squalor. Often the attention to these underlying problems, however, has been perfunctory and less than adequate.

Today the pressures are increasing for more comprehensive and effective attention to the underlying causes of riots. The recommendations of the American Correctional Association and other bodies for riot prevention in prisons detail a variety of recreational, vocational training, educational, religious counseling, and treatment programs. The recommendations of the President's Advisory Commission on Civil Disorders encompass improvements in jobs, education, housing, police practices, and welfare programs as steps to curtail urban rioting.

For example, the Commission recommended the creation of two million new jobs, elimination of racial barriers to employment and promotion, and the provision of incentives for the employment of the hard-core unemployed.[141] The logic of these recommendations is as follows. Although black incomes have risen rapidly in the past two decades, they still remain far below those of whites. The median family income for Negroes was only 58 percent of that for whites in 1966, and the gap between the two has grown between 1947 and 1966 (from a median difference of $2,174 to a median difference of $3,036).[142] The middle and higher income groups in the black population have gained considerably since 1947, but about two-thirds of the lowest income group (about 20 percent of black families) has made no significant gain.[143] Unemployment rates among blacks are double those for whites. Black workers are still concentrated in the lowest skilled and lowest paying occupations, and discrimination in salaries and promotions is still evident.[144] It would appear that the increases in actual earning power among Negroes is overbalanced by the greater awareness of discrepancies and discrimination as Negroes share in the rising expectations of Americans without sharing equally in the gains.

Although it may take many years for the recommendations of the President's Advisory Commission to be enacted into law, action on some of them will be taken in the next few years. The trend is clear for the underlying causes of urban discontent and disorder to be understood and for programs of prevention to be launched.

Nevertheless, some troublesome and complex questions will need to be faced before some of the recommendations or variations of them can be followed. Organized efforts to eliminate the basic causes of urban discord will encounter a number of complex issues. The agents of change will determine the role for federal agencies and for private industry in a variety of areas such as increasing employment opportunities for the poor and the untrained, providing housing for low income families, improving slum schools, and expanding educational opportunities at both ends of the school population continuum—for those of college age and for three and four year olds. New and better methods for financing these programs will be required since the property tax soon will be confiscatory in many cities. Existing agencies and programs which have not proven effective will require reorganization such as the nation's welfare system. In this instance greater effectiveness may be achieved by improving the provision of family planning services, which have been hampered in the past by religious and moral objections. Finally, in each of these areas the rights of individuals and the needs of society for stability and effectiveness will require delicate balancing. It is in the context of such issues that solutions to urban disorder must be sought and there are apt to be no easy answers.

Controlled creative disorder—allied to civil disobedience—including such activities as sit-ins, marches, boycotts, freedom rides and rent strikes may serve as an alternative to riots. Yet it seems that riots have to be experienced before these alternatives are seriously considered.[145] If the police try to smash nonviolent creative disorder, they risk the outbreak of a real riot. If they step back and allow these disorders to be worked out in a way comparable to labor strikes and lockouts, it is unlikely that riots will develop. But this requires a neutral stance on the part of police, a preference for the higher forms of law as opposed to order, and a degree of sophistication about the reciprocal effects of violence and counter-violence. It would require a particularly high degree of skill and sophistication to be able to de-escalate a near riot into controlled creative disorder.

Waskow points to the difficulty of inventing appropriate forms of nonviolent disorder in the North where there are more adolescents and young men without jobs or education.[146] He also stresses that some form of federal police force must be created to prevent violence from being used by either side in a racial conflict.[147]

Harvey Wheeler recently agreed that moral alternatives to riots need to include a new constitutional right to civil disobedience.[148] He has stressed the almost insurmountable difficulties people in the present culture of poverty encounter in trying to pull their way up into middle class society and a public acknowledgement of the right to civil disobedience offers some additional help to them.

The Positive Role of Civil Disobedience and Riots

Civil disobedience and riots may serve as indicators of serious dysfunctions in the entire social structure, in one or more social institutions, in societal values or in some other area. From the standpoint of any given society, the occurrence of sporadic riots and civil disobedience should serve to alert the leadership and citizens alike to review and analyze the basic problems and strains responsible for the incidents. Corrective and preventative measures are then possible. In a real sense, riots and civil disobedience may be extremely beneficial in staving off possible fracturing disintegration or collapse of the society itself.

To see how this process has worked in actual practice, one can turn to the widespread prison riots of the past several decades. Prison riots have pointed up the gross neglect and mismanagement in our penal institutions, due to overcrowded conditions, substandard personnel, enforced idleness, unwise sentencing and parole practices, lack of professional leadership and professional programs, political domination, and inadequate financial support.[149] Without the riots, the long-term results may have been even more serious. An oppressed minority might have begun to define itself as unable to achieve any advantages from society and could have resorted to rebellion or revolution, perhaps in league with other groups having comparable perceptions and feelings of hopelessness.

Managing Crime and Individual Rights

The policies selected for controlling crime should be consistent with the norms governing individual rights or they will be dysfunctional to the structure of our society. Another way of saying this is that we need law as well as order, and a major part of the law protects individual rights.[150] Perhaps the most pernicious effect of white collar crime, organized crime and riots is that they infringe individual rights in one way or another. In a sense, the real problem of crime control in 20th Century America is that of insuring individual rights to all citizens. Our national bias for viewing crime as an individual matter denoting individual incapacity or weakness has precluded our approaching crime as an organizational matter.[151] When we know better how to set up a social system with real social justice and protection of individual rights, we may find crime to be a less urgent problem. Crime may be analogous to a headache in calling attention to more serious underlying crises in the social structure.

The classical position in the United States has been that persons are believed to be innocent of any offense unless proven guilty in a court of law with adequate protections to the accused. Yet these protections were not always available to the accused who were unable or unwilling to insist upon them. For example, the accused person who was too poor to afford legal counsel has not always been assured of free counsel from a court-appointed attorney, and even if such an attorney were available, he was often inexperienced and was not always given time or opportunity to prepare an adequate defense. In 1948 a student of constitutional law asked: "Does not indeed liberty require that the state do as much to defend the accused who is helpless to defend himself, as it does to prosecute him?"[152] In short, many of the legal protections required financial resources, knowledge about good attorneys and enough knowledge of the law to insist on the legal protections. As might be expected, it has been the professional criminal, the white collar offender, and the middle class occasional offender who have assured themselves of the full benefit of these legal protections. The poor, the lower class individual, the minority group member, the immigrant, the migrant worker, the child, and the mentally disturbed or retarded person have been among those who have not always known about, been able to afford, or had enough determination to insist upon their legal rights and protections.

Perhaps these changes are a part of a broader shift toward the guarantee of equality of opportunity to Negroes and other minority group members in the nation. Perhaps, also, these changes reflect to a degree the high position of the basic American value of efficiency and practicality. Can a system of criminal justice work and survive in a democratic society if it treats individuals unequally or unfairly? Even more to the point of efficiency, can the society allow a considerable part of the population, in an economy geared to mass production and high purchasing power, to remain outside the "normal" pattern? So the values of humanitarianism, equality of opportunity, freedom, rationality, and individualism have all operated together to force attention to the rights of offenders and accused persons.

A listing of decisions of the U.S. Supreme Court affecting the rights of offenders and accused persons included the following:[153]

1957: A confession is inadmissable in federal courts unless suspect is taken before a magistrate without unnecessary delay and advised of his constitutional rights.

1961: Evidence obtained by illegal search or seizure cannot be used in state prosecutions, even if it is reliable.

1963: States must furnish lawyers for indigent defendants in felony prosecutions.

1964: The Fifth Amendment's protection against self-incrimination applies in state as well as federal courts.

1966: Before questioning a suspect in custody, police must advise him of his right to remain silent, to have a lawyer, to be provided a lawyer if he is indigent, and to be questioned only after the lawyer is present.

1967: Juvenile delinquents must be given the same protections that adults receive.[154]

1967: Electronic eavesdropping is unconstitutional if not conducted in such a way as to protect individual rights.

Although it is now clear that the right to legal counsel, the right to appeal, the protection against self-incrimination, and the right to a speedy hearing before a magistrate are to be guaranteed to all citizens, the door has been opened to consideration of a great many other issues. Among them can be listed the following:

1. *The right to adequate treatment for the social, psychological, emotional, biological, cultural or other condition which caused or influenced the commission of the offense.* The Kent and Gault decisions of the U.S. Supreme Court clearly implied that the original intent of the juvenile court to provide individual treatment had never been achieved due to lack of adequate treatment resources. The abridgement of due process of law, ostensibly to provide for a relaxed rehabilitation-focused atmosphere, has really led to a kind of kangaroo court in which few protections were available, no treatment resources were utilized and a punitive atmosphere often prevailed. The sex offender laws in Wisconsin, New Jersey and other states have also encountered problems from lack of adequate treatment resources. It can be anticipated that the next decade will see appeals to state supreme courts and the U.S. Supreme Court relative to the failure to provide adequate treatment and rehabilitative services to adjudicated offenders. For example, in city after city and county after county, drunks have been sentenced repeatedly to 30 to 90 days in jail for public drunkenness or disturbing the peace. No treatment has been provided to these misdemeanants to cure the alcoholism with which they are afflicted. The President's Commission on Law Enforcement and Administration of Justice noted that the criminal justice system seems ineffective to deter drunkenness or to treat the alcoholic offender. The Commission suggested instead the establishment of detoxification units, diagnostic units, supportive residential housing, coordinated social service programs, and aftercare programs as aspects of a comprehensive treatment program.[155] We will, no doubt, see suits brought by, or on behalf of, these individuals to push their claim to adequate rehabilitative services. Perhaps in anticipation of such suits, some jurisdictions are beginning to repeal such laws or to prosecute only when drunkenness is an accompaniment to other offenses. Boston and New York City operate referral and treatment centers for alcoholic offenders.

Boys and girls sent to training schools for delinquents are customarily told by juvenile judges that they are being committed in order to receive treatment, reeducation or training. But usually they go to overcrowded and understaffed facilities with no treatment services worthy of the name. It may not be long before suits are brought to insist upon adequate rehabilitative programs, or to insist alternatively upon discharge.

Home conditions may often be a factor in the commitment of boys and girls to state training schools for delinquents. In fact, there is a considerable body of evidence that shows that poor home conditions are a primary reason for the commitment, *regardless of whether the home conditions were clearly a factor in the commission of the offense.* This situation has led to the ironical dilemma that two boys apprehended for car theft are handled differently—the boy from the "good" home going back to his parents who are assumed to be able to discipline him properly, while the boy from the "bad" home goes to the training school. Studies of high school and college youths show that they have committed as many and as serious delinquencies as youths known to courts and training schools.[156] Even though such studies should be examined with some caution, in view of the tendency of some middle class youths to exaggerate and dramatize relatively minor escapades, there is still a clear indication of differential handling. It is likely that suits will eventually be brought to enforce fairness of handling as well as the provision of appropriate services and facilities.

Parents are seldom provided with appropriate counseling, guidance, and rehabilitative services. Perhaps this is because they can vote and no judge dares to establish services expressly for parents. It is likely that suits will sooner or later be brought to force treatment services for parents whose children are apprehended.

As we look into the more remote future, it may be conceivable that an offender will someday bring a suit alleging that community conditions caused or heavily influenced his criminal acts and insist on appropriate changes in community structures, relationships, attitudes or services.

2. *The right of redress against incompetent, brutal, ignorant, unfair, prejudiced, hostile or unskilled law enforcement, judicial or correctional personnel.* Just as the law now guarantees to every citizen the right of redress for injury to name or reputation, property rights, or health, it is likely that the courts will be asked to rule that alleged or adjudicated offenders have a right to redress for incompetent, brutal, unfair, prejudiced or hostile treatment by a law enforcement, judicial or correctional official. In other words, it can be logically claimed that every man or woman has a right to decent, fair, skilled, and competent service from the officials who deal with him in the process of arrest, detention, trial and disposition. This right will no doubt ultimately be insisted upon through due process of law.

The fact that such court rulings have not already been sought is perhaps a function of the lower class membership of most offenders, who are largely poor, uneducated and apathetic. But the universal provision of legal counsel, already a fact, will change these circumstances in many ways. Young attorneys may see the possibilities in making a name for themselves by bringing suits in behalf of mistreated and abused clients.

Another factor inhibiting such court rulings in the past has been the public inclination to favor public rights and needs over those of the lower class, dirty, and often dangerous offender. But the civil rights revolution in the 1950's and 1960's has brought about some willingness to seek a better balance between individual rights and social control.

Already the more farsighted and knowledgeable law enforcement officials are supporting a changed role and stance for the police. One recent statement may serve to document the trend:

> . . . I believed when I was Police Commissioner in New York City and I believe it today—that it is essential that our law-enforcement effort be oriented toward respect for individual rights.[157]

Yet a changed role for the police will not be quickly affected. Skolnick has discussed, in a penetrating analysis, five features of the policeman's occupational environment which weaken the conception of the rule of law as the chief aim of police conduct. These include the social psychology of police work, the policeman's stake in maintaining his position of authority, police socialization as it affects administrative bias, the pressure on police to be efficient and to produce, and the covert character of much of his conduct.[158] Nor will professionalization of police work facilitate a quick reconciliation of law and order as conflicting goals, for the police are "increasingly articulating a conception of professionalism based on narrow view of managerial efficiency and organizational interest."[159] It is not easy for the police to adjust themselves to the idea that the main purpose of law, the protection of individual liberties, makes their task more difficult. On the other hand, it has not been easy for the community to provide police with the understanding, cooperation, support, training, and status to do their job properly. At times the individual police officer finds himself representing society by arresting an offender in the face of danger to the police officer himself. At other times, he may be required to use a degree of knowledge of the law that has not been provided to him. At still other times he may find himself in the middle of a cycle of attack and counterattack with minority groups without any training in the sociology or social psychology of minority group behavior. It has been perhaps less than fair to expect him to always use the same degree of expertise, detachment and objectivity that society expects of the judge or the attorney.

Already the door to reform or correctional treatment has been pushed slightly open. For the first time in American history, a three-judge panel ruled that a U.S. District Court should have heard the case of an inmate at Clinton State Prison at Dannemore, New York, who claimed that he was put in solitary confinement in a dirty "strip cell" without heat for 33 days in 1965 and 21 days in 1966.[160] He was unable to keep himself clean as he was denied the use of soap, towel and other conveniences; the toilet and sink were encrusted with slime and human excremental residue. He was required under threat of being beaten to jump to attention when a guard appeared. He was not allowed to sleep for some days and at night the window was open to subfreezing temperatures. He had no bed or coverings and tried to sleep on the floor. The complaint had been dismissed by the U.S. District Court in keeping with the tradition that courts have never interfered with the management of jails and prisons. The underlying rationale has been that prison officials needed a free hand to maintain discipline. This handsoff attitude has generally served to protect and perpetuate the monotony, abuse, and neglect characteristic of many American prisons. The U.S. Court of Appeals, Second Circuit, decided that if Lawrence Wright's complaint was true, it constituted cruel and unusual punishment in violation of the Eighth Amendment and ruled that the federal courts should extend to state prisoners the right to seek injunctions against cruel and inhuman punishment. In commenting on the issue of federal interference in the operation of a state prison, circuit Court Judge Irving Kaufman concluded that New York did not offer Wright any adequate avenue to an injunction barring a repetition of the punishment.

Although this decision may evoke a storm of controversy in which prison officials charge the courts are instigating discontent and moving into the operation of units of the state governments, it seems likely that the U.S. Supreme Court will uphold such a decision and that the majority of the public will support the courts.

CONCLUSION

Crime as a social problem has been traditionally understood as an individual phenomenon—people-committed acts repugnant to the society and injurious to the interests of society.

It is more often recognized today that this has been an oversimplification that has not aided the nation to shape a sensible social policy to prevent or control crime and has not aided social scientists to understand crime as a social phenomenon.

Social problems are created when a sizeable part of the population redefines troubles or situations as social problems. They can also be redefined in terms of the way they are understood and handled by the society.

208 *Crime in the United States*

Crime seems to be in the process of redefinition in the United States. We are in the early stages of laying aside the former preoccupation with individual offenses and substituting a concern with widespread conditions characteristic of an advanced industrial society at a level of affluence, automation, and urbanization.

This discussion has thus focused primarily on such offenses as organized crime, white collar crime, and riots, which indicate *social* dysfunctions rather than *individual* dysfunctions. These are offenses requiring a relatively high degree of organization, planning and leadership. They are also offenses which serve social purposes as well as doing social damage. They require attention to the social structure itself, its institutions, values, or relationships, for sound programs of change.

Selected Readings

Clinard, Marshall B. *Sociology of Deviant Behavior,* Third Edition (New York: Holt, Rinehart and Winston, Inc., 1968).

Cressey, Donald R. *Theft of the Nation* (New York: Harper and Row, 1969).

"Combating Crime," *The Annals of the American Academy of Political and Social Science,* Vol. 374 (November, 1967).

Glaser, Daniel. "National Goals and Indicators for the Reduction of Crime and Delinquency," *The Annals of the American Academy of Political and Social Science,* Vol. 371 (May, 1967).

Lieberson, Stanley and Arnold R. Silverman. "The Precipitants and Underlying Conditions of Race Riots," *American Sociological Review,* Vol. 30, No. 6 (December, 1965).

Mannheim, Hermann. *Comparative Criminology* (Boston: Houghton-Mifflin Company, 1965).

Oberschall, Anthony. "The Los Angeles Riot of August 1965," *Social Problems,* Vol. 15, No. 3 (Winter, 1968), pp. 322-41.

The President's Commission on Law Enforcement and Administration of Justice, *The Challenge of Crime in a Free Society* (Washington, D.C.: U.S. Government Printing Office, 1967).

Report of the National Advisory Commission on Civil Disorders (Washington, D.C.: U.S. Government Printing Office, 1968).

Schur, Edwin M. *Crimes Without Victims: Deviant Behavior and Public Policy* (Englewood Cliffs, N.J.: Prentice Hall, Inc., 1965).

Skolnick, Jerome H. *Justice Without Trial: Law Enforcement in Democratic Society* (New York: John Wiley and Sons, Inc., 1966).

Waskow, Arthur I. *From Race Riot to Sit-In, 1919 and the 1960's* (Garden City, N.Y.: Doubleday and Company, Inc., 1966).

Notes to Chapter 6

[1] See, for example, Paul W. Tappan, *Crime, Justice and Correction* (New York: McGraw-Hill Book Company, Inc., 1960), p. 10; Robert G. Caldwell, *Criminology*, 2nd Edition (New York: The Ronald Press Company, 1965), p. 29; Edwin H. Sutherland and Donald R. Cressey, *Principles of Criminology*, 7th Edition (Philadelphia: J. B. Lippincott, 1966), p. 4.

[2] In using the term "injurious" in this context, a number of indicators may be relevant: (1) A substantial number of people adversely affected. (2) Loss of efficiency sustained by the society or some important segment of it. (3) Significant interests adversely affected, such as the overall economy, the business community, the political structure. (4) Damage to important national values, such as the free enterprise system or equality of opportunity.

[3] Herbert A. Bloch and Gilbert Geis, *Man, Crime and Society* (New York: Random House, 1962), p. 67.

[4] See Edwin M. Schur, *Crimes Without Victims: Deviant Behavior and Public Policy* (Englewood Cliffs, N.J.: Prentice-Hall, Inc., 1965), pp. 5-8. Also see Sanford H. Kadish, "The Crisis of Overcriminalization," *The Annals of the Academy of Political and Social Science* (November, 1967), p. 158.

[5] An outstanding reference is Marshall B. Clinard, *Sociology of Deviant Behavior*, 3rd Edition (New York: Holt, Rinehart and Winston, Inc., 1968), p. 213.

[6] Tappan, *op. cit.*, pp. 17ff.

[7] Edwin H. Sutherland originally held a fairly strict view of crime as violation of criminal statutes. See Edwin H. Sutherland "Crime and Business," *The Annals*, Vol. 217 (1941), p. 112. Later, he broadened his definition: "Is 'White-Collar Crime' Crime?," *American Sociological Review*, Vol. 10 (1945), pp. 132-39. See Daniel Glasser, "National Goals and Indicators For the Reduction of Crime and Delinquency," *The Annals of the Academy of Political and Social Science* (May, 1967), p. 105, for a clarification of the term "criminal law."

[8] Schur notes that sociologists may have a legitimate direct interest in contributing to the formulation of criminal law, *op. cit.*, pp. 9-10.

[9] *Ibid.*

[10] Edwin H. Sutherland and Donald R. Cressey, *op. cit.*, p. 28.

[11] Federal Bureau of Investigation, *Crime in the United States: The Uniform Crime Reports—1967* (Washington: U.S. Supt. of Documents, 1968), p. 4.

[12] The President's Commission on Law Enforcement and Administration of Justice, *The Challenge of Crime in a Free Society* (Washington: U.S. Supt. of Documents, 1967), p. 21. Also see Albert D. Biderman, "Surveys of Population Samples for Estimating Crime Incidence," *The Annals of the Academy of Political and Social Science* (November, 1967), p. 17.

[13] *Ibid.*

[14] Albert D. Biderman and Albert J. Reiss, Jr., "On Exploring the 'Dark Figure' of Crime," *The Annals of the American Academy of Political and Social Science* (November, 1967), p. 9.

[15] The President's Commission, *The Challenge of Crime, op. cit.*, p. 23.

[16] *Ibid.*

[17] *The Uniform Crime Reports—1967, op. cit.,* p. 4.

[18] *Ibid.,* pp. 7-15.

[19] The President's Commission, *The Challenge of Crime, op. cit.,* p. 23.

[20] *The Uniform Crime Reports—1967, op. cit.,* p. 17.

[21] *Ibid.,* pp. 23-24.

[22] *Ibid.,* pp. 26-28.

[23] *Ibid.,* pp. 9-28.

[24] *Ibid.,* p. 1.

[25] *Ibid.,* p. 121.

[26] *Ibid.,* p. 118.

[27] The President's Commission, *The Challenge of Crime, op. cit.,* p. 28.

[28] Daniel Bell, *The End of Ideology* (New York: The Free Press, paperback edition, 1965), p. 151 ff.

[29] Roscoe Pound, *Criminal Justice in America* (New York: Holt, 1930), p. 23.

[30] Francis A. Allen, *The Borderland of Criminal Justice* (Chicago: The University of Chicago Press, 1964), p. 3.

[31] *Ibid.,* p. 11.

[32] The President's Commission, *The Challenge of Crime, op. cit.,* p. 31.

[33] *Ibid.,* p. 23.

[34] See *The Uniform Crime Reports—1967,* p. 32 and p. 121. Other data provided here are from these pages.

[35] *Ibid.,* p. 32.

[36] *Ibid.,* p. 60.

[37] *Ibid.,* p. 4.

[38] *Ibid.,* p. 64.

[39] Glaser, *op. cit.,* pp. 109-111.

[40] Sutherland and Cressey, *op. cit.,* pp. 146-50.

[41] *Ibid.,* p. 23, and The President's Commission, *op. cit.,* pp. 39-40.

[42] The President's Commission, *The Challenge of Crime, op. cit.,* p. 39.

[43] *Ibid.,* p. 40.

[44] Sutherland and Cressey, *op. cit.,* p. 23.

[45] *Ibid.,* p. 293.

[46] Hermann Mannheim, for example, notes that our whole approach to crime may be colored by unconscious distinctions related to class. Hermann Mannheim, *Comparative Criminology* (Boston: Houghton Mifflin Company, 1965), p. 461.

[47] It can be seen that the self-fulfilling prophecy is at work here. (See Robert K. Merton, *Social Theory and Social Structure,* Revised and Enlarged Edition, New York: The Free Press, 1957, Chapter XI). As Schur implies, *op. cit.,* p. 3, defining certain acts as criminal and the violators as criminals shapes the behavior of both the underclass and the society-at-large.

[48] Glaser notes that the tendency to settle differences by violences varies inversely with social status. Glaser, *op. cit.,* p. 109.

[49] A study of various publications will verify this point, *e.g.,* The President's Commission on Law Enforcement and Administration of Justice, *Task Force Reports: The Courts* (Washington, D.C.: U.S. Government Printing Office, 1967), p. 4 ff.

[50] See, for example, Biderman and Reiss, Jr., *op. cit.,* p. 7.

[51] Terence Morris, *The Criminal Area,* London, 1957, concludes that *"legally defined* delinquency is a social characteristic of the working classes in general and the family of the unskilled worker in particular." Quoted in Mannheim, *op. cit.,* p. 462. Also see W. Lloyd Warner, *Yankee City* (New Haven: Yale University Press, 1963), pp. 203-6, 246-7. He finds the lower classes to account for 90% of arrests although there is little difference between actual rates of commission of offenses between the upper and lower classes. ". . . The social controls of the class

system operate in such a way as to hide successfully all [upper class offenses] from the authorities." (p. 247).

[52] Biderman and Reiss, *op. cit.*, p. 6. Also, The President's Commission, *Task Force Report: The Courts, op. cit.*, p. 6.

[53] One of the early studies on social class found that middle-class Negroes in a southern town took pride in the fact "that no one has been in jail or arrested." John Dollard, *Caste and Class in a Southern Town* (New Haven: Yale University Press, 1937), p. 89.

[54] The President's Commission, *The Challenge of Crime, op. cit.*, p. 45.

[55] *Ibid.*

[56] Clinard notes that a disproportionate number of persons executed are Negroes, young people and the poor. Marshall Clinard, *op. cit.*, p. 212.

[57] The recent polls and surveys conducted for the President's Commission on Law Enforcement and Administration of Justice found that half the persons interviewed agreed that people who have money to employ lawyers do not have to worry about the police. See Jennie McIntyre, "Public Attitudes Toward Crime and Law Enforcement," *The Annals of the American Academy of Political and Social Science* (November, 1967), p. 44.

[58] See, for example, Gunnar Myrdal, *Challenge to Affluence* (New York: Pantheon Books, 1962), p. 50 ff.

[59] Daniel Bell, *The End of Ideology* (Glencoe, Ill.: The Free Press, 1960), p. 157.

[60] Clinard, *op. cit.*, p. 282.

[61] See Donald R. Cressey, "Methodological Problems in the Study of Organized Crime as a Social Problem," *The Annals of the Academy of Political and Social Science* (November, 1967), p. 108.

[62] *Ibid.*, pp. 106-9.

[63] *Report of the Special Senate Committee to Investigate Organized Crime in Interstate Commerce*, 3rd Interim Rep., Senate Rep. No. 307, 82nd Congress, 1st Session, 1951, p. 150.

[64] Testimony of former assistant attorney general Fred M. Vinson, Jr., "The Federal Effort Against Organized Crime," *Hearings Before a Subcommittee of the Committee on Government Operations, (Department of Justice)*, U.S. House of Representatives, Part I, April 5, 13 and May 16, 1967, p. 5.

[65] Testimony of J. Edgar Hoover, *Hearings Before the Subcommittee on Departments of State, Justice, and Commerce, the Judiciary, and Related Agencies Appropriations of the House Committee on Appropriations, (Department of Justice)*, 89th Congress, 2nd Session, 1966, p. 272.

[66] "The Mob," *Life Magazine*, Part I (September 1, 1967), p. 15.

[67] Donald R. Cressey, "The Functions and Structure of Criminal Syndicates," President's Commission, *Task Force Report: Organized Crime* (Washington: U.S. Government Printing Office, 1967), p. 28. In his recent book, however, he expresses himself as satisfied with the term Cosa Nostra. Donald R. Cressey, *Theft of the Nation* (New York: Harper and Row, 1969), p. 20.

[68] *Hearings Before the Subcommittee on Criminal Laws and Procedures of the Committee on the Judiciary*, United States Senate, 90th Congress, 1st Session, 1967, p. 966.

[69] The President's Commission, *Task Force Report: Organized Crime, op. cit.*, p. 6. Also see Donald R. Cressey, *Theft of the Nation, op. cit.*, X.

[70] Testimony of former assistant attorney general Fred M. Vinson, Jr., *op. cit.*, pp. 24 and 48.

[71] *Life, op. cit.*, p. 43.

[72] Cressey, "The Functions and Structure of Criminal Syndicates," *op. cit.*, p. 28.

[73] Vinson, *op. cit.*, p. 38.

[74] *Ibid.* Also see Cressey, *Theft of the Nation, op. cit.*, p. 75.

[75] The President's Commission, *Task Force Report: Organized Crime, op. cit.,* p. 3.

[76] Cressey, "The Functions and Structure of Criminal Syndicates," *op. cit.,* p. 35.

[77] *Ibid.*

[78] Cf. "The Mob," *Life,* Part II, (September 8, 1967), p. 98.

[79] Bloch and Geis, *op. cit.,* p. 245.

[80] Cressey, "The Functions and Structure of Criminal Syndicates," *op. cit.,* p. 25. Also see Cressey, *Theft of the Nation, op. cit.,* p. 1.

[81] Editorial, "We Can Break the Grip of the Mob," *Life Magazine* (September 8, 1967), p. 4.

[82] John A. Gardiner, "Wincanton: The Politics of Corruption," The President's Commission, *Task Force Report: Organized Crime, op. cit.,* pp. 64-70.

[83] "The Mob," *Life,* Part I, *op. cit.,* pp. 44-45.

[84] The President's Commission, *Task Force Report: Organized Crime, op. cit.,* p. 6.

[85] "The Mob," *Life,* Part II, p. 103.

[86] The President's Commission, *Task Force Report: Organized Crime, op. cit.,* p. 5.

[87] Vinson, *op. cit.,* p. 48.

[88] The following paragraphs on structure are summarized from Cressey, "The Functions and Structure of Criminal Syndicates," *op. cit.,* pp. 33-36.

[89] *Ibid.,* p. 56.

[90] *Ibid.,* p. 29.

[91] Former assistant attorney general Fred F. Vinson, Jr. cites the experience in England to point out that legalizing gambling may well increase the amount of illegal gambling, *op. cit.,* p. 54.

[92] See Cressey, *Theft of the Nation, op. cit.,* pp. 290-97.

[93] The President's Commission, *Task Force Report: Organized Crime, op. cit.,* p. 23.

[94] *Ibid.,* pp. 23-24.

[95] Vinson, *op. cit.,* p. 43.

[96] *Ibid.,* p. 43.

[97] The President's Commission, *Task Force Report: Organized Crime, op. cit.,* p. 20. Cressey also proposes training of police for organized crime work. Cressey, *Theft of the Nation, op. cit.,* p. 297.

[98] *Ibid.,* p. 16.

[99] Hearings Before the Subcommittee on Criminal Laws and Procedures of the Committee on the Judiciary, United States Senate, 90th Congress, 1st Session, pp. 1179-81.

[100] *Ibid.,* p. 358.

[101] *Ibid.,* p. 1093.

[102] *Ibid.,* p. 1094.

[103] U.S. Supreme Court, No. 615, April 6, 1967.

[104] Vinson, *op. cit.,* p. 26.

[105] *Ibid.,* p. 56.

[106] *Ibid.,* p. 19.

[107] *Ibid.,* p. 20.

[108] Daniel Bell, *op. cit.,* pp. 116-7.

[109] See Edwin H. Sutherland, "Crime and Business," *op. cit.,* p. 112.

[110] Edwin H. Sutherland, *White Collar Crime* (New York: Holt, Rinehart and Winston, 1967, paperback), pp. 23-25.

[111] The President's Commission, *The Challenge of Crime, op. cit.,* p. 48.

[112] See Norman Jaspan with Hillel Black, *The Thief in the White Collar* (Philadelphia: J. B. Lippincott Company, 1960), p. 9.

[113] *Ibid.* Also see The President's Commission, *The Challenge of Crime, op. cit.,* p. 47, and Clinard, *op. cit.,* pp. 270-2.

[114] Clinard, *op. cit.,* p. 271.

115 Donald R. Cressey, *Other People's Money* (Glencoe, Illinois: The Free Press, 1953), p. 139.

116 See Clinard, *op. cit.*, p. 272.

117 See John Herling, *The Great Price Conspiracy: The Story of the Antitrust Violations in the Electrical Industry* (Washington: Robert B. Luce, Inc., 1962); and Richard A. Smith, "The Incredible Electrical Conspiracy: I," *Fortune, 63* (1961), pp. 139-51.

118 Marshall B. Clinard, *The Black Market* (New York: Holt, Rinehart and Winston, Inc., 1952), p. 338.

119 Robin M. Williams, Jr., *American Society: A Sociological Interpretation,* 2nd Ed. (New York: Alfred A. Knopf, 1960), pp. 417-21.

120 See Glaser, *op. cit.*, p. 114.

121 Jaspan, *op. cit.*, p. 234.

122 See, for example, Tappan, *op. cit.*, pp. 8-10 and Bell, *op. cit.*, p. 382.

123 Bloch and Geis, *op. cit.*, p. 402.

124 Donald J. Newman, "White Collar Crime," *Law and Contemporary Problems,* Vol. 23 (1958), p. 737.

125 Earl R. Quinney, "The Study of White Collar Crime: Toward a Reorientation in Theory and Research," *The Journal of Criminal Law, Criminology and Police Science,* Vol. 55 (1964), p. 210.

126 Marshall B. Clinard, *Sociology of Deviant Behavior, op. cit.,* p. 269.

127 Quinney, *op. cit.*, p. 210.

128 Gilbert Geis, "Toward a Delineation of White-Collar Offenses," *Sociological Inquiry* (Spring, 1962), p. 171.

129 Hermann Mannheim, *op. cit.,* pp. 474, 481.

130 Vilhelm Rubert, "White-Collar Crime and Social Structure," *The American Journal of Sociology,* Vol. LVIII (November, 1952), p. 264.

131 Donald R. Taft and Ralph W. England, Jr., *Criminology,* Fourth Edition (New York: The Macmillan Company, 1964), p. 204.

132 John de J. Pemberton, Jr., "Is There A Moral Right to Violate the Law?" *The Social Welfare Forum, 1965* (New York: Columbia University Press, 1965), p. 184.

133 Christian Bay, "Civil Disobedience," in the *International Encyclopedia of the Social Sciences* (New York: The Macmillan Co., 1968), p. 473.

134 *Ibid.,* pp. 191-93.

135 *Ibid.,* p. 483.

136 K. Smellie, "Riot," in *Encyclopedia of the Social Sciences* (New York: The Macmillan Company, 1934), p. 386.

137 Stanley Lieberson and Arnold R. Silverman, "The Precipitants and Underlying Conditions of Race Riots," *American Sociological Review,* Vol. 30, No. 6 (December, 1965), p. 887.

138 *Ibid.,* p. 896.

139 Anthony Oberschall, "The Los Angeles Riot of August 1965," *Social Problems,* Volume 15, No. 3 (Winter, 1968), pp. 322-41. Oberschall draws his analytic framework from Neil J. Smelser, *Theory of Collective Behavior* (New York: Free Press, 1962), Chapter 8.

140 Arthur I. Waskow, *From Race Riot to Sit-in, 1919 and the 1960's* (Garden City, N.Y.: Doubleday and Company, Inc., 1966), p. 209.

141 *Report of the National Advisory Commission on Civil Disorders* (Washington, D.C.: U.S. Government Printing Office, March 1, 1968), pp. 231-6.

142 *Ibid.,* p. 123.

143 *Ibid.*

144 *Ibid.,* pp. 124-26.

145 Waskow, *op. cit.,* p. 302.

146 *Ibid.,* p. 285.

147 *Ibid.,* p. 287.

148 Harvey Wheeler, "A Moral Equivalent for Riots," *Saturday Review* (May 11, 1968), p. 51.

149 See Peg and Walter McGraw, *Assignment: Prison Riots* (New York: Henry Holt and Company, 1954), p. 217.

150 For an analysis of the distinction between law and order, see Jerome H. Skolnick, *Justice Without Trial: Law Enforcement in Democratic Society* (New York: John Wiley and Sons, Inc., 1966), especially pp. 1-12.

151 See Donald R. Cressey, "Methodological Problems in the Study of Organized Crime as a Social Problem," *op. cit.*, p. 105.

152 John Raeburn Green, "The Bill of Rights, The Fourteenth Amendment and the Supreme Court," reprinted in Robert G. McClosky, *ed., Essays in Constitutional Law* (New York: Vintage Books, 1957).

153 Adapted from *U.S. News and World Report* (December 18, 1967), p. 37.

154 On January 5, 1968, *Time Magazine* carried an item indicating that, in the light of the U.S. Supreme Court's *Gault* decision, the Illinois Supreme Court has ruled that a juvenile must be proved guilty beyond a reasonable doubt, like anybody else. Traditionally, the "preponderance of evidence" has suffered in juvenile courts.

155 The President's Commission, *The Challenge of Crime, op. cit.*, pp. 233-37.

156 See, for example, Austin L. Porterfield, *Youth in Trouble* (Austin, Texas: Leo Potishman Foundation, 1946), p. 41; James F. Short, Jr., and F. Ivan Nye, "Extent of Unrecorded Juvenile Delinquency: Tentative Conclusions," *Journal of Criminal Law, Criminology, and Police Science*, Vol. 29, No. 4 (November-December, 1958), pp. 296-302.

157 Testimony of Former Police Commissioner Vincent L. Broderick, *Hearings Before the Subcommittee on Criminal Laws and Procedures of the Committee on the Judiciary*, U.S. Senate, 90th Congress, 1st Session, p. 1168.

158 Skolnick, *op. cit.*, p. 231.

159 *Ibid.*, p. 238.

160 *Time Magazine* (January 5, 1968), pp. 46-47.

CHAPTER SEVEN

CONFLICT AND CONFORMITY: THE CHURCH AND SOCIAL PROBLEMS

Religion means different things to different people depending upon their cultural orientation and social characteristics. Religion may be a personal creed, a way of life, a set of moral imperatives, or a group of shared meanings which people hold in common with others. In the name of religion, people have gone to war, arbitrated for peace, crusaded for justice, tried "witches," imprisoned men and exiled nonbelievers. While some attributes of religion may be described as sacred, religion is a social phenomenon despite diverse ways in which men define and implement religious beliefs. Like other social institutions, religion reflects man's continuing search for relevant responses to his social environment.

Religion in America serves a dual function. It operates as a religious institution supporting the "sacred" needs of people and serves as a social institution appealing to homogeneous groups. Although people are united through the commonality of religious values, they are also separated by diverse religious groups to which they belong. Not only are the institutionalized functions of religion two-fold and potentially conflictive, but religious groups per se may be socially divisive. Having little political and legal power, religious groups rely heavily upon moral and ethical appeals to conscience. Despite diverse social norms, variable role ascription and limited power, historians tend to credit religion with motivating man to improve his lot in life.[1]

Freedom of religion is basic to the American value system and is guaranteed through the First Amendment to the Constitution. Closely allied with this concept is the assumption that a pluralistic society like ours strengthens commitment to democratic principles by allowing diverse groups to maintain distinctive belief systems. The practice of religion under these circumstances should pose few problems. Nevertheless, the same attributes of religious pluralism which enhance religious freedom and support democratic cohesion, also intensify competition and conflict between diverse religious groups. Some groups resisting change try to maintain traditional beliefs and rituals, whereas other groups, wishing to adapt to change, introduce new values. Regardless of orientation, the competitive nature of religious groups forces them to cope with both internal and external problems if they are to survive.

The typologies of church and sect differentiate two general categories of religious groups which respond to life's challenges in different ways. This chapter examines the role of church and sect in contemporary society while focusing major attention on problems of organized churches.

SOCIAL CHANGE

In 1790 fewer than 10 percent of the American population belonged to organized church groups.[2] Those who were church members were

217

politically powerful upper class Protestants whose religious affiliations were traditional and inherited. Religious interest spread to a larger segment of the population following the massive Protestant revivals of the 19th Century which induced persons, irrespective of social class, to join organized churches and religious sects. The influx of poor European immigrants to the United States after the Civil War changed the nation from a homogeneous society of white, Anglo-Saxon Protestants to a pluralistic society of Protestants, Catholics and Jews.

Jewish and Catholic minorities generally settled in cities whereas Protestant strongholds were dominantly rural and middle class. Some of the established Protestant denominations, cognizant of socioeconomic needs of immigrant groups, turned from religious evangelism to social welfare programs for the poor. These churches were known as Social Gospel churches, and represented the first major break with traditional American individualism.[3] Social Gospel advocates argued that good and evil are collective attributes which require collective social concern, and that religion's chief focus should be the improvement of the collective social order. Although the "Social Creed of the Churches," framed in 1912 by liberal churchmen, did not reflect majority lay opinion, it nevertheless provided a Protestant approach to social and political issues.[4]

Christian fundamentalism, emphasizing personal salvation, appealed to persons antagonistic toward social gospel concepts. At the same time that the Social Gospel grew in prestige, fundamentalism grew in strength. Social Gospel concepts flourished until after World War I, when industrial and economic prowess became increasingly dominant. "Big business" controls extended into religious organizations, and persons who supported Social Gospel concepts were often squeezed out of churches in favor of social conservatives.[5] Liberal clergy who favored the social gospel and criticized denominations which perpetuated social class differences were often replaced by conservative clergy whose salaries were dependent upon influential businessmen. Shifts away from the philosophy of the social gospel and a return to individualism at the expense of the social ethic tended to make churches generally more conservative than formerly. A study of 387 church boards of major Protestant denominations in 1932 showed that control of the churches at that time rested heavily upon the professionally elite middle and upper classes, especially bankers and managerial personnel.[6]

Despite the declining popularity of social gospel churches, social gospel ideology influenced the church's future role in a changing society. Perhaps for the first time, the American church had been challenged to take a significant moral stand on human social conditions. The depression years brought a revival of the Social Gospel, but most social justice was achieved through political parties, governmental agencies and labor unions. Ecumenical movements of the 1930's reflected social gospel ideals, and some politically conservative churchmen strongly supported ecumenical liberalism. Ecumenicists worked toward the ideal of a unified church based on the Christian concepts of the brotherhood of man, rather than toward a church dominated by theological consensus.[7] They defined their own socioreligious-political boundaries and pushed for interchurch cooperation to achieve their goals. They also supported their demands for a unified church by asserting that other social institutions lacked the ability to cope with problems, whereas a united church could readily effect social action and social reform.

Modern ecumenical movements challenge contemporary churches to religious unity and communal social involvement in contemporary issues. Support for ecumenicism varies. Some religious groups perceive it as a threat to local autonomy, some consider it an added religious dimension, whereas others equate it with secular dominance over the sacred aspects of religion.

Within the past one hundred years, our population has expanded, our social institutions have redefined their functions, and urbanization and industrialization have increased dramatically. Despite the expansion of scientific knowledge and technological skills, human disorganization persists and the lower classes have fallen behind the norms of an affluent society. Although science cannot assure improved social conditions, it has influenced the alleged scope of religion. Some of the traditional "sacred" concepts of man's relationship to his physical and social environment have been redefined in the light of scientific knowledge and secular values. Since secularism shifts social responsibility from religious to worldly authority, secular societies evolve systems of social ethics and de-emphasize religious dogma.[8] The absolutism of "sacred societies" is questioned in a world dominated by scientific data, and absolute truths become increasingly unique when scientific knowledge expands. In turn, the church is challenged to make new responses to changing norms, expanding knowledge, and social innovation. There are religious groups which emerge as antagonists to social change, rejecting secularism and social ethic concepts, and opposing religious adaptation to change.

SOCIAL CLASS

When Yinger defines religion as a "system of beliefs and practices by which a group struggles with the ultimate problems of life,"[9] he is generalizing about the scope and function of religion. Implicit in his definition are assumptions that there are relevant, religiously oriented concepts which are intimately associated with human aspirations and expectations. However, he says little about men's problems, or about the ways in which they struggle to meet them. For the poor the ultimate problem may be survival, whereas for more advantaged groups, problems may relate to security and stability. Problem definition and problem solution are influenced in part by man's social environment, and by values which he attaches to his environment. Every community has some system of stratification linking its social organizations to its social system. Like other groups, religious associations are closely linked with stratification patterns. Educational level, occupation, income, residential choices and social preferences influence the kind of religious group one selects, the kinds of programs one supports.

Unlike cultures which have a single religion or church, America's religious interest reflects pluralistic, democratic concepts of differences. Membership in religious groups and related religious experiences are interpreted through value systems closely intertwined with America's social class system.

In the United States, religion's appeal to the majority of the population and the inference that religious affiliation reinforces respectability tends to make religious affiliation socially desirable, if not prestigeful. Religious affiliation does not guarantee high social status, but in a society which is socially supportive of religion, nonconforming or nonreligious behavior tends to make individuals morally suspect. Various surveys show that as many as 90 percent of all Americans identify with religion, that 60 percent consider themselves members of a church,[10] and that 43 percent attend church weekly.[11]

Gordon asserts that in the United States there are actually two distinct sets of stratification structures which crisscross.[12] One set is based on social status, economic power and political power differences, regardless of ethnic background. The other set comprises status and power relationships based on racial, nationality background and religious categories. Gordon coins the term *ethclass* to describe a subsociety which emerges from the crisscrossing of ethnic strata and social class.[13] A person's ethclass might be lower middle class white Protestant, upper middle class white Irish Catholic, upper lower class Negro Protestant, etc. In other studies, Gordon shows that intellectuals interact outside their religious groups more often than the general population despite ethnic and religious differences.[14]

Some studies of eminent scientists show that religion plays little part in their lives and that few scientists are actively associated with formalized religious groups.[15] Other studies show that scientists and intellectuals appear to be more indifferent to religion than most middle class Americans.[16] Wilensky and Ladinsky report that among professionals, lawyers and engineers tend to have stronger religious identification than professors.[17] Thus, some of the variables which correlate significantly with social class position vary within the different strata of the same social class.

Based on church attendance, fewer persons with elementary school education attend church than those with a college education—41 percent and 47 percent respectively.[18] Fewer families with less than $3,000 annual income attend church than families with incomes of $7,000 and over—40 percent and 45 percent respectively.[19] Despite America's strong identity with religion, major support for organized religion comes from the better educated and more affluent segments of society. In turn, the better educated and more affluent persons control, in large measure, the goals and dominant values of major religious groups. Alienation of the lower classes from the religious middle classes reflects, in part, the unwillingness of socially diverse groups to accommodate to each other, and the inability of the middle class church to compensate for lower class socioeconomic deprivation. Many lower class persons turn to informally organized religious sects or to other social institutions rather than participate in middle class organized religious groups. Many studies variously relate religious affiliation with social class differences. Moberg uses a composite of several studies based on social class position to rank major, dominantly white Protestant denominations in the United States.[20] Despite this generalized ranking system which is based on income and social prestige, there are rank variations within the various denominations. Moberg's ranking in descending order places the Episcopal Church at the top, followed by the Unitarian, Congregational, Presbyterian, Christian Science, Friends, Methodist, Disciples of Christ, Lutheran, Baptist, Mormon, Eastern Orthodox, Assemblies of God, Pentecostal, Holiness and Jehovah's Witnesses Churches. Even though social class differences are significantly reinforced by church-class variables, they may not be as significant as formerly. Mobility, broad and extensive communication with other segments of society, coupled with rapid and continuous social change, tend to weaken the discrete significance of social class and church affiliation. Nevertheless, the concepts of social class delineate diverse value systems which cluster around religious interest and significantly influence the kind of religious organization which develops.

Residential choice and the kind of church to which one belongs reflect social class position.[21] In turn, the social status of the community determines, in part, the kind of people and the type of church bodies it attracts. Church size is significantly correlated with size of community and socioeconomic status of the community. In general, the greater the proportion of religious people in the higher socioeconomic levels, the larger the church; the greater the proportion of people within lower socioeconomic levels, the smaller the church.[22] People may select a particular religious group such as Catholic, Protestant, Jewish, because it has a body of religious beliefs or because a particular church is liberal or fundamentalistic in its teachings. They also select religious groups which most closely resemble their socioeconomic positions and social aspirations. Religious affiliation tends to reinforce social and personal homogamy, and religious groups tend to perpetuate social class identities and differences.

Protestants, Catholics and Jews

In the United States today, roughly two-thirds of those who claim religious identity are Protestant, one-fourth are Catholic and about 3 percent are Jewish.[23] It is difficult to generalize about these broad religious categories because traditional Old World concepts of religion and 19th Century immigration patterns have been influenced by American social norms and rapid social change. During the 1880's in the United States, there was considerable Protestant opposition to Catholic immigrants because Catholics were socially undesirable to the Protestant culture—they were very often poor, uneducated, unskilled. At that time, Protestants dominated the rural areas, whereas Catholic immigrants settled in the least desirable sections of the cities. The dichotomy between new Catholic immigrants and early Protestant settlers assumed socioeconomic, regional and religious overtones.[24] Despite their generally improved socioeconomic positions, remnants of the old stereotype of Catholic inferiority still persist.

Jewish immigration to the United States started about 1815 and continued until passage of the Immigration Acts in the 1920's. In general, Protestants discriminated less against poor urban Jews than against poor urban Catholics, but Catholics discriminated significantly against the Jews.[25] Some of the Catholic discrimination against Jews was prefaced by the Christian-nonChristian dichotomy, partly on minority competition between the groups. As a gesture of ecumenical unity, the Pope, in the late sixties, absolved the Jews of collective guilt for Christ's death. Compared with other minority groups, Jews have achieved considerable success in business, education and science. Anti-Semitic attitudes may be less related to Jews as a religious group than to Jews as symbols of economic success. Their respect for education and strong family ties have reinforced their ethnic cohesion despite less cohesive religious beliefs than other religious groups.

Traditionally, each of the major religious groups has been stereotyped as being uniquely different from the others. In addition to broad cultural differences, there is also considerable diversity within each of the groups. Lenski's Detroit studies show that, in general, white Protestants have higher income and higher occupational status than white Catholics, but white Protestants and white Catholics have about the same percentage of members in the lower working classes, 25 percent and 27 percent respectively.[26] White Catholics compared with white Protestants had fewer in the upper middle class—12 percent and 19 percent respectively.[27] The relative social class position of Jews varies with city and region, but, in general, the majority of urban Jews are in the middle and upper classes. Lenski's studies show 73 percent of Jews in the middle classes and 26 percent in the working classes, as compared with 44 percent and 56 percent respectively for white Protestants, 39 percent and 60 percent respectively for white Catholics, and 12 percent and 88 percent respectively for Negro Protestants.[28]

Although significant numbers of Protestants are in the upper middle classes, and are inclined toward religious liberalism, some lean heavily toward religious fundamentalism. They measure the importance of religion and religious zeal in terms of personal salvation and dedication to that end. There is significant correlation between levels of education and liberal thought, but the Putney and Middleton studies of 1,126 Christian students in 13 colleges and universities show that despite college training, college students with fundamentalistic religious beliefs tend to be conservative in politics and economics, authoritarian in beliefs and discipline and greatly concerned with social class status.[29] Within the Protestant Church, a broad range of goals and beliefs separate fundamentalists from liberals, polarizing the scope and function of religion.

Catholics are part of an ecclesiastical hierarchy which is structured to exert control over Catholic religious doctrine and to provide "answers" for theological questions. Nevertheless, within the basic precepts of faith and morals, the Catholic community shows considerable variety in opinion and behavior.[30] The influx of rural Negroes into the urban Catholic Church tends to keep urban Catholicism strongly lower class, whereas traditionally Protestant suburbs are becoming a mix of Protestants, Catholics and Jews. If urban Catholic churches increasingly recruit lower class Negroes, the stereotype of Catholic poverty and social disadvantage will persist despite general upward mobility of major portions of the Catholic population. In Hirsch's studies of American scientists, he attributes the paucity of Catholic scientists to the traditionally low quality of Catholic parochial education which was initially contrived to meet the needs of unskilled Catholic immigrants, as well as to the lower class positions and ethnic backgrounds of most American Catholics.[31] He concludes that future generations of Catholics will benefit from generally improved educational facilities and thus be competitive with Jews and Protestants.

If quality education becomes generally accessible, religious nomenclature may be less discriminatory and less indicative of social class than presently. However, religious stereotypes persist, and members of religious groups become identified with these stereotypes. Currently, Protestants and Jews have greater access to better jobs, skills and professions than most Catholics, and as a consequence, have more favorable social class positions than most Catholics.

Despite Hollingshead's contention that next to race, religion is the most decisive factor in mate selection, interfaith marriages are increasing.[32] Thomas concludes that although religion is an important variable, it is only one of many factors which determine interfaith marriages.[33] Amount of education, degree of professionalization and level of income help define the desirability or acceptability of interfaith marriages. Among the three major religious bodies, marriages between Protestants and Catholics are most common. Thomas estimates interfaith marriages for Catholics at about 30 percent, for Jews about 7 percent and for Protestants about 10 percent.[34] Persons who are upwardly mobile or who rank a particular religious group as significantly more prestigious than another may aspire to marry into a prestige religious group. Formerly, ethnic background tended to check intermarriage across religious lines, but declines in immigration quotas, greater social tolerance, secularization and upward mobility syndromes tend to weaken religiousethnic controls.

The effects of interfaith marriages may be personally destructive— divorce rates are high for those who marry outside their faith—or personally satisfying for persons consciously looking for a broader relationship than one based solely on religious homogeneity. Interfaith marriages are potentially weakening to religious groups which intermarrieds reject and reinforcing to groups which they select. Interfaith marriages tend to increase competition between diverse religious groups as each tries to attract new and hold old members.

Numerically small religious groups are seriously threatened by marriage outside the group, whereas larger groups can more readily absorb losses. Of the three major religious groups, the Jews are numerically the smallest and the least likely, statistically, to marry outside the group.

Interfaith marriages could mean significant loss of personal and group values and threaten social and organizational stability. Conversely, interfaith marriages precipitate wider tolerance for other religious groups, reduce personal and cultural prejudices, and reinforce broad social cohesion. Some studies show that interfaith marriages tend to reduce size of the family, but that persons married to coreligionists tend to have larger families.[35]

Since religious affiliation is influenced by income, education and other aspects of social homogamy, one of the latent functions of endogamous religious affiliation is the reinforcement of social class differences. In addition, it preserves social norms and belief systems and insures generational continuity and continued membership in the group. Religious groups which lose their appeal are destined to be weak, insecure, and ineffective.

The Negro Church

In the United States, religious belief systems have been traditionally categorized as Protestant, Catholic and Jewish. Some scholars insist that the Negro Church is legitimately a fourth category since in at least one respect, it is significantly different from the other three.[36] Black religious activity focuses heavily on the lower classes, whereas among the whites, religious interest is dominated by the middle classes. About half of the Negroes in the United States claim some relationship with religion, and of these, about 90 percent are in the lower income groups.[37] The remaining 10 percent are considered middle class. The religious black in America is predominantly Protestant, affiliated with the Baptist denomination. Of the 10 million blacks claiming religious affiliation, 63.5 percent are Baptist, 23 percent Methodist, and 5.8 percent Catholic.[38] Recent surveys show that 44 percent of the nonwhite population in the United States attends church weekly, compared with 43 percent of the white population.[39] Unlike white middle class church members who have a variety of social interests, lower class Negroes rely heavily upon the church for religious experiences and social activity.

Drake and Cayton's early studies of Bronzeville describe "respectable lowers" as church people.[40] They found that in families where both spouses attended church, the family more closely resembled generalized concepts of middle class families, whereas in female headed families or in families in which only the adult female was active in church affairs, the church merely focused on middle class values without helping internalize the values.[41] McLoughlin's studies show that, in general, younger Negroes are less interested in religion per se than the older generation, and that among the young there is more concern with social action than with social respectability.[42] Instead of being pushed into the ministry because there is nothing else available, young black men now choose the ministry because it is a springboard to civil rights activity.[43]

The evolution of the Negro church in America reflects the dominant and changing cultural patterns of the nation. Black slaves who were brought to America were not Christian. In 1667 the Virginia assembly made it legal for slaves to be baptized as Christians, and so, historically, Christianity became the first legitimate and socially sanctioned activity in which the American Negro slave was allowed to participate.[44] The plantation slave preacher interpreted Christianity to the slave, and through the Christian religion *explained* the Negro's servitude. The plantation preacher was the bridging leader between the slave and white society. Sometimes he interceded for the slave, sometimes he acted for the master. The black preacher helped the slave survive, and at the same time gained prestige and power for himself. When white supremacy was reestablished late in the 19th Century, black efforts to bring about social change were suppressed and the black preacher lost prestige in both white and black communities.[45] At various times in history, Negro churches have actually helped perpetuate the racial system. The Negro's intense belief in a better life after death sustained him, and in some ways, made him feel superior to his white "oppressors." Accommodation, one characteristic of the black church in the late 19th Century, inhibited social change and delayed the emergence of aggressive leadership.

Migrations of Southern Negroes to the North following World War I helped broaden black horizons, exposing them to evidence of social change and arousing them from their accommodative lethargy. Northern black ministers of that period were known as "race men," and it became generally assumed that black ministers would take an interest in social problems.[46] After World War II, some Negro clergymen interested in achieving political and civil rights became "protest" leaders.[47] Initially, at the grass roots level, civil rights was in the hands of the Negro minister. Today, "everyman is now in search of his own dignity, and he expects his minister to lead him in finding it. Those unprepared to lead are on their way out."[48]

Made in the 1940's, Loescher's studies of interracial practices in local Protestant congregations show that at that time, less than one-tenth of 1 percent of black Protestants attended desegregated churches.[49] He noted that in the North in particular, where residential patterns were well defined, no white churches were integrated, and that neighborhoods undergoing racial change did not attempt to desegregate churches.[50] In the decade of the 60's, roughly 10 percent of the black population attended desegregated churches.[51]

Racial desegregation has been more pronounced among middle and upper class white churches than among lower class white churches or among Negro churches.[52] In general, desegregation implies permitting Negroes to attend services but not urging them to become participant members. The void between black and white Protestant churches is based partly on socioeconomic and cultural differences, and partly upon member reluctance to initiate change. Protestant churches are individualistic and autonomous, and support for social change or reform falls heavily upon individuals and local congregations. Campbell and Pettigrew's study of Protestant reaction to desegregation in Little Rock[53] shows that the churches responded to desegregation in much the same way as other social groups did during the crisis.[54] Instead of assuming moral responsibility, they acceded to existing norms and values.[55]

Church and Sect

Organized churches tend to serve the conventionally established social classes, whereas sects appeal to persons who are not integrated into the norms of the dominant social system. Criteria used by Niebuhr,[56] Pope,[57] Wilson[58] and others help differentiate between the typologies of church and sect. In general, the church accepts and adjusts to secular values, responds to worldly success as a social norm, and draws its members from those who are socially compatible with its goals. It delegates authority and responsibility to professionals and does not demand total commitment to all of its goals. In contrast, the sect rejects worldly values, isolates itself from society, does not adapt to social change, and requires total commitment to its goals. The dichotomy between church and sect places these groups in opposing positions which are mutually exclusive.

Rapidly changing societies create social unrest and frustration which demand new and immediate responses. Sects, unhampered by complex social organization and large membership rolls, respond quickly to new needs, whereas organized churches must, of necessity, respond more slowly. As protest groups, sects renounce worldly values, formal organization and stereotyped ritual. They have special appeal for the socioeconomically, politically and psychologically insecure, and thus, become havens for those who struggle against organized power. Sects defend the interests of persons marginal to prevailing norms, who feel threatened by social change or who are socially disoriented.[59] Although some sects appeal to higher status persons, sect membership is heavily concentrated among low income groups, rural migrants, new urbanites and the constantly mobile. The life span of any given sect is relatively short since some of the same conditions which give rise to sect formation precipitate their demise. Few sects survive over long periods of time—they either become church-like or they disappear. Sects are spawned by organizational dissension, whereas dissension seriously impairs organized church bodies.

The current trend toward rapid proliferation of sects among dissident middle class Protestants and Catholics reflects, in part, incompatability between church policy and social action, and critical concern for the theological relevancy to secular needs. Glock and Stark consider the trend toward increased sect formation among the middle classes a major problem which organized churches must face if they are to survive.[60]

Organized churches function most effectively when they sustain individual and group satisfaction and keep peace among the members. Social homogamy and religious endogamy contribute to socioreligious satisfaction and church stability. Nevertheless, despite these strong social supports, most congregations face problems which threaten congregational unity and social cohesion. It is at this juncture that traditional mechanisms which normally reinforce cohesion may be seriously strained.

RELIGIOUS LEADERS

Although many Americans show an interest in religion, few contemporary churchgoers want or expect the church and clergy to impose authoritarian and stringent controls upon them. Responsibility for church activities is usually delegated to professionals but, in general, congregations exercise considerable control over programs, policies and clergy. The professional minister, as coordinator between sacred and secular matters, must sometimes choose between congregational peace and his own moral commitment to issues.[61] As a professional, he is an agent— an employee of the church with significant obligations to his church. His role is institutionalized; its focus is to build up the church and to recruit members. Some church problems emerge because the minister and congregation do not achieve a consensus on the church's role in the community or the minister's role in the church. If these issues are not resolved, minister and members become opponents rather than proponents; instead of sharing in decision making, each tries to coerce the other. The minister's role of preserving the church thus becomes untenable unless he capitulates to congregational demands or changes their unfavorable attitudes in his favor.

Traditionally, the religious leader's role has been that of preacher, priest, and teacher.[62] Contemporary society places high priority on administrative and organizational roles for the clergy. As administrator, the minister manages church affairs. As an organizer, he involves the church in community and civic affairs and, in general, relates the church to the larger society.

In questioning 690 rural and urban Protestant clergymen, Blizzard found that respondents felt most effective, in rank order, as preachers, pastors, teachers, priests, administrators and organizers.[63] They enjoyed most their roles of pastor and preacher. Traditional ministerial roles made them feel most adequate, while the roles of organizer and administrator, for which they were poorly trained, were most difficult to assume. Blizzard concluded that despite increasing secular demands, seminaries and other professional training centers are not adequately preparing personnel for administrative and organizational roles.[64] Thus, one of the problems of helping the minister relate to his church stems from his inability to cope with the diverse problems confronting modern churches. Campbell and Pettigrew conclude that ministers facing church issues must decide initially whether or not the problems are religious, then decide what action is required within the context of religious ethics.[65] If ministers are inadequately trained or lack perception, they tend to confuse the religious issues with other issues and unnecessarily disrupt the church.

In contrast to the individualistic and autonomous nature of Protestant churches, the Catholic Church imposes role relationships which are defined by the Catholic hierarchy and implemented by bishops and parish priests. Within the parish, priests are the designated officials who provide spiritual guidance and maintain the social structure. Since the parish is a territorial assignment as well as a communally structured group, the priest is the leader.[66] Under few circumstances does the laity run the church. When disputes arise within the Catholic Church, the Pope has the final word. Traditionally, the Pope and bishops are the teachers and the priests carry out their teachings. Recent rebellion against the hierarchy by some parish priests reflects conflict between the church's ecclesiastical rigidity and the secular nature of social change. By a proclamation of the Pope in 1964, the bishops were to share power with the Pope and priests were to be consulted on church matters. Nevertheless, priests were to remain subordinate to bishops. Dissident priests pressing for reforms, oppose hierarchal authority and propose action independent of the bishops. They demand major roles in decision making, especially on issues relevant to justice, housing, unemployment and civil rights. Rebelling Catholic theologians contest the relationships

between Catholic authority, the infallibility of the Pope, academic freedom, and individual conscience.[67] Historically, the Catholic church has
concurrently supported both conservative doctrine and social liberalism.
Modern dissidents defining the dichotomy as unrealistic and untenable
rebel against discontinuities of church doctrine and social organization.
Compared with the Catholics, most Protestant denominations are orga-
nizationally and theologically freer to adapt to change, but few are
inclined toward major social reform or revolutionary change.

Campbell and Pettigrew's study of Protestant ministerial responses to
desegregation in Little Rock shows that the ministers did not succeed in
their desegregation attempts.[68] They failed as innovators because they
were young, new to their churches and inexperienced in dealing with the
older and more influential clergy. Being enthusiastic social activists,
they over-generalized and misinterpreted the intensity of American
commitment to democratic concepts.[69] As a consequence, they were
unable to establish rapport with their congregations and their initial
desegregation attempts failed.

In general, young militant religious leaders contrast significantly with
older stereotypes of socially passive, poorly trained ministers. As social
militants, one of their objectives is to bring social and political power to
the poor.[70] They insist that the church must openly support and induce
social change and that the church must be committed to social action.
Their emergence as an action group is linked with the special status
which Christian theology variously attributes to the poor, and to the
value which Americans place on equality. Historically, the poor have
been both holy and inferior. At various times in history, the church has
made each of these statuses "sacred."[71] Cox says this new breed of
militant churchman ". . . stands in the succession of Roger Williams
and William Penn."[72] Militant religious witnessing is reminiscent of
Free-Soiler, Abolitionist, Feminist and Social Gospel activists, and is
considered by some as authentically American. In assessing the impact
which these militants may have upon America's religious patterns, Cox
says that whatever their success, it will be due to their ability to stir the
church out of its rural nostalgia and push it into an urban future.[73]

Sects, inherently informal, do not require special training for their
religious leaders. Some are merely self-appointed "preachers" who lead
the services, since all sect members are free to participate in religious
affairs.

The majority of Negro churches are small, financially insecure, and
sect-like, and many black preachers have little formal training. As a
response to the broad problems of the black community, professionally
educated clergy, in cooperation with national funding organizations,

now train Negro preachers to manage social problems in their local congregations.[74] Instead of stressing theology and ecclesiastical dictums, they learn to cope with family problems, poverty, unemployment, and poor housing. This type of program reinforces the religious militant's assumption that alleviating poverty and social disadvantage is the major concern of the church. Differences in training, life style, social class and moral imperatives affect significantly the minister's role in any given church. In turn, his effectiveness as a minister is determined by his ability to meet the needs of his people.

RECRUITMENT OF MEMBERS AND CLERGY

The peak year for church attendance in the United States was 1958, when 49 percent of the adult population attended church, as compared with 43 percent in 1968.[75] Recent declines in church attendance are variously attributed to the dominance of secular values, the revolution in American values, the polarization of science and theology, and the numerical increases in both the young and aged in our population. Whatever the rationale, declining church support poses serious problems for organized churches.

Religious interest cannot be measured solely by church attendance, monetary contributions or membership rolls, but there is significant correlation between these variables and the status of any given church. In general, adults in the 30-49 age group attend church more often than those in the 21-29 age group or the over 50 age group—46 percent, 34 percent and 44 percent respectively.[76] The 30-49 age group is in the prime of life. They are professionally mature and socially active. Their child bearing responsibilities are resolved and they are not plagued with declining health and dwindling income. The church benefits directly and perhaps more significantly from their support than from any other single age group. Support by the "over 30" group becomes a dominant force in defining and implementing church policy, whereas the younger and older groups are often peripheral to decision making.

Membership recruitment problems reflect, in part, the inevitable lag between generations, conflicts between dominant and minority groups within the church, and the inability of various groups to reach a consensus on social and religious values. The socially concerned younger generation tends to stereotype the parental generation as materialistically conformist, morally apathetic, and socially irrelevant.[77] Their rejection of organized religion is especially strong when the rigid influence of family and religion thwart youthful idealism. In a scientifically advanced and rapidly changing society, young, highly educated activists emerge when the older generation has a disproportionate amount of socioeconomic and political power and higher social status.[78] In earlier decades, most young idealists were not overtly avowed radicals. Today, young American activists are visible and vocal, demanding to be recognized as agents of change. They criticize the church's unwillingness or inability to move from a socially passive to an active social role, and by-pass the church in favor of other social action groups. Although only a relatively small segment of youthful idealists is totally committed to social action, they challenge the church to choose between social action and social inaction.

In 1958, the peak year for church attendance, American churches were overcrowded and understaffed. In 1968, churches were less crowded and still understaffed. Most denominations report difficulty in attracting sufficient numbers of ministerial students and keeping the younger men in the ministry. Professions outside the church have generally greater appeal and are less personally restrictive. Social actionists and young theologians increasingly turn from ministerial opportunities to social work, teaching and psychiatry—fields which they consider more relevant to human needs.[79]

Liberal Protestant denominations emphasize social relevancy more than theology, whereas the Catholic Church traditionally emphasizes both theology and social reform. Young Catholics entering religious orders insist on quality education and an end to long and tedious theological training. They also want some of the same freedoms which the Protestant clergy has traditionally enjoyed—freedom to marry and autonomy within their congregations.[80] The Catholic Church, to protect itself, now requires novices entering religious orders to remain on probation for at least two years, to alternate worldly training with theological training and to undergo psychiatric tests as aids in evaluating their potential to withstand the rigors of religious life. By contrast, Protestant churches facing recruitment problems offer academic and social inducements which may have far reaching effects. For instance, some seminaries offering seminary training to husband-wife teams assume that if both are trained as a team, they will make significant contributions to the total church and community.

It is difficult to accurately assess the amount of conflict between personal belief systems and organizational authority, but conflict becomes increasingly visible when dissenters openly demonstrate against the Establishment. In 1968, for instance, only 3 percent of the Catholic clergy and laity openly dissented against Church policy, but their dissent was sufficiently troublesome to alert nondissenting Catholics and non-

Catholics to a variety of church problems.[81] In part, the foment revolved around differences in interpretation of the church's legitimate power and insistence by some clerics and laymen that individuals must have the right to make decisions of conscience which may be counter to church policy. In a broader context, problems revolved around issues of democratic organization and sex. As a substitute for participant democracy, the Catholic Church offers collegiality for the Pope and bishops, but the Church offers no accommodation on issues of celibacy and artificial birth control. Catholic dissidents insist that they wish to reform the Church, not destroy it, but the hierarchy insists that to reform basic tenets will destroy the Church.

RELEVANCY AND SURVIVAL

"The very moment that clerics become worldly, the world goes to hell faster."[82] This statement was not made by an earthshaking revivalist but by a liberal activist who, in assessing the current state of religion, decried the church's nervous scurrying for relevance. Hertzberg, contending that religion should satisfy metaphysical hunger instead of trying to be socially relevant, says liberal religion is out of date. In his estimation, America is moving beyond social questions and becoming concerned with ultimate human values.[83]

A growing number of sects voice similar concern with the role which organized religion currently plays. Middle class citizens question the church's apathy toward individual values, and criticize its businesslike approach to religious problems. Compared to earlier decades when few middle class persons belonged to them, sects are increasingly reflecting the middle class concern with problems of the secular society. It is possible that middle class sectarian groups may effect some change in prevailing norms, and that, like most protest groups, they will become a source of new social values. The impact of the middle class sect on dominant middle class values depends, in part, upon society's receptiveness to new values as well as its desire to redefine social and religious goals.

Underground cells and protest groups like CLEO (Christian Layman's Experimental Organization), protesting against meaningless dogma and stifling ritual, hope to make religion socially relevant and personally satisfying.[84] CLEO and similar groups identified with underground or resistance movements want to reform and not destroy the church. They supplement formalized aspects of ritual, liturgy and theology by personally administering sacraments, chanting litanies, and praying together.

To them, intimacy in religion transcends secular materialism and structured bureaucracies.

Whereas Gordon considers the sect another facet of social pluralism,[85] Glock and Stark regard sects as threats to organized religion.[86] Since religion functions at both personal and social levels, sects promote gemeinschaft-like or cohesive qualities which tend to limit communication with other groups. Lack of communication in turn creates hostility, misunderstanding and/or conflict. If under these conditions religion assumes the attributes of a private sector rather than of social experience, organized religion could lose its social effectiveness, becoming structurally and functionally decentralized.

Berger believes that by the 21st Century, under pressure from a massively bureaucratic society, religious persons will withdraw from organized religious groups and turn to sects instead.[87] Instead of voluntarily joining organized religious groups, they will huddle together in small groups to resist the massive secular society. When custom and habit are the basis for social organization, religion can be an important source of control, but it is not the only source of control. If organized religious groups lose their ability to respond to social need, other institutions will absorb this into their social functions.

CONCLUSION

Within a given society, social change and reform do not necessarily occur simultaneously or with equal intensity. Each depends upon existing sets of conditions which may be manipulated to induce or inhibit change. Since the institution of religion in America is separated from governmental functions, religion serves a supporting, not a controlling, role. Nevertheless, the secular world increasingly demands that religion justify its existence, that religious groups clarify their role in a technologically advanced society.

In assessing religion's role in contemporary society, it is evident that many issues which plagued religious groups one hundred years ago still persist. Religious and social separatism, chaos, apathy, organizational weaknesses—each has been a major issue at some prior time; each may become a major issue again. To remain viable, religious groups must find some value system which attracts social support, some kind of integrating force which commands social allegiance. Unless such conditions are likely, individualism and personal need take precedence over organizational needs.

The future of the church rests heavily upon its ability to objectively define its goals, evaluate its failures, and plan for its successes. Science, a willing but often rejected ally of religion, can provide significant insight into the origin and control of persistent church problems. Science can help the church perpetuate its influence by making its goals compatible with social need. Like other groups weakly committed to science, churches are unsure about science's role in religion, fearful that it may expose structural weaknesses which the church has traditionally tried to hide. Until the church is willing to use science as an ally, church problems are likely to reoccur with increasing intensity.

The aim of science is not to impose dogmatic controls on social groups but to provide significant data with which to evaluate persistent problems. To this end, science is willing to help in the search for ultimate meanings of man's moral, political, scientific and aesthetic existence. The social significance of church membership diminishes when the church constantly struggles with dissent, declining membership rolls and inadequate financial support. General humanistic concern for social justice and alleviation of poverty have been rallying cries for church unity, but despite surficial unity, churches experience deep and divisive problems of human relationships. In some instances, religious idealism is dedicated to the common good, but applies only to selected groups. If organized religion could realize its ideals, it could become a significant force in society rather than a handmaiden.

Selected Readings

Cutler, Donald R., ed. *The Religious Situation: 1969* (Boston: Beacon Press, 1969).

————, ed. *The Religious Situation: 1968* (Boston: Beacon Press, 1968).

Demerath, N. J. III. *Social Class in American Protestantism* (Chicago: Rand McNally, 1965).

Durkheim, Emile. *The Elementary Forms of the Religious Life* (London: George Allen and Unwin, Ltd., 1915).

Glock, Charles Y. and Rodney Stark. *Religion and Society in Tension* (Chicago: Rand McNally, 1965).

"Religion In America," *Daedalus*, 96 (Winter, 1967).

Troeltsch, Ernst. *The Social Teachings of the Christian Church*, Olive Wyon, trans. (New York: Macmillan, 1932).

Weber, Max. *The Protestant Ethic and the Spirit of Capitalism* (New York: Scribner, 1948).

Notes to Chapter 7

1 Paul A. Carter, *The Decline and Revival of the Social Gospel* (Ithaca, N.Y.: Cornell University Press, 1956), p. 3.

2 Liston Pope, "Religion and Class Structure," *The Annals of the American Academy of Political and Social Science,* Vol. 256 (March, 1948), pp. 84-91.

3 Carter, *op. cit.,* pp. 3-17.

4 *Ibid.,* p. 15.

5 Liston Pope, *Millhands and Preachers* (New Haven: Yale University Press, 1942).

6 Carter, *op. cit.,* pp. 64-65.

7 *Ibid.,* pp. 183-200.

8 W. Seward Salisbury, *Religion in American Culture* (Homewood, Ill.: Dorsey Press, 1964), p. 280.

9 Milton Yinger, *Religion, Society and the Individual* (New York: Macmillan, 1957), p. 9.

10 Salisbury, *op. cit.,* p. 90.

11 Gallup Poll, 1968, *The New York Times* (December 22, 1968).

12 Milton M. Gordon, "A System of Social Class Analysis," *Drew University Studies,* No. 2 (August, 1951), pp. 15-18.

13 *Ibid.,* p. 51.

14 Milton M. Gordon, *Assimilation in American Life,* (New York: Oxford Press, 1964), Chapter 3.

15 Wallace S. Sayre, "Scientists and American Science Policy," in Bernard Barber and Walter Hirsch, *eds., The Sociology of Science* (New York: Free Press, 1962), p. 600.

16 Harvey Brooks, "The Scientific Advisor," Robert Gilpin and Christopher Wright, eds., *Scientists and National Policy Making* (New York: Columbia University Press, 1964), p. 95.

17 Harold L. Wilensky and Jack Ladinsky, "From Religious Community to Occupational Group: Structural Assimilation Among Professors, Lawyers and Engineers," *American Sociological Review,* Vol. 32 (August, 1967), p. 548.

18 Gallup Poll, *op. cit.*

19 *Ibid.*

20 David O. Moberg, *The Church As a Social Institution* (Englewood Cliffs, N.J.: Prentice Hall, 1962), pp. 458-9.

21 Russell R. Dynes, "The Relation of Community Characteristics to Religious Organization and Behavior," Marvin Sussman, *ed., Community Structure and Analysis* (New York: Thomas Crowell, 1959).

22 *Ibid.*

23 Statistical Abstract of the United States, 1968, (Washington, D.C.: U.S. Government Printing Office, 1968), Table 49, "Religion Reported by the Population, By Color, Sex and Residence: 1957."

24 Claris E. Silcox and Galen M. Fisher, *Catholics, Jews and Protestants* (New York: Harper and Brothers, 1934), pp. 1-31.

25 *Ibid.*

26 Gerhard Lenski, *The Religious Factor* (Garden City, N.Y.: Doubleday, 1961), p. 73.

27 *Ibid.*

28 *Ibid.*

29 Snell Putney and Russell Middleton, "Dimensions and Correlates of Religious Ideologies," *Social Forces,* XXXIX, No. 4 (May, 1961), p. 289.

30 Joseph H. Fichter, *Social Relations in the Urban Parish* (Chicago: University of Chicago Press, 1954).

31 Walter Hirsch, *Scientists in American Society* (New York: Random House, 1968), p. 15.

32 August B. Hollingshead, "Cultural Factors in the Selection of Marriage Mates," *American Sociological Review*, 15 (1950), pp. 619-27.
33 John L. Thomas, "The Factor of Religion in the Selection of Marriage Mates," *American Sociological Review*, 16 (1951), pp. 487-91.
34 *Ibid.*
35 Bruce H. Mayhew, Jr., "Behavioral Observability and Compliance With Religious Proscriptions on Birth Control," *Social Forces*, Vol. 47 (September, 1968), pp. 60-70.
36 Lewis M. Killian, *The Impossible Revolution?* (New York: Random House, 1968).
37 Salisbury, *op. cit.*, p. 463.
38 Edwin S. Gaustad, "America's Institutions of Faith," Donald R. Cutler, *ed., The Religious Situation, 1968* (Boston: Beacon Press, 1968), p. 841.
39 Gallup Poll, 1968, *op. cit.*
40 St. Clair Drake and Horace R. Cayton, "The World of the Urban Lower Class Negro," *A Study of Negro Life in a Northern City* (New York: Harcourt, Brace and World, 1945).
41 *Ibid.*
42 William McLoughlin, "Is There a Third Force in Christendom?" *Daedalus* (Winter, 1967).
43 C. Eric Lincoln, *Sounds of the Struggle* (New York: William Morrow & Co., 1968), p. 132.
44 Leonard Broom and Norval Glenn, *Transformation of the Negro American* (New York: Harper and Row, 1965), p. 9.
45 *Ibid.*, pp. 9-15.
46 *Ibid.*, p. 14.
47 *Ibid.*, p. 13.
48 Lincoln, *op. cit.*
49 Frank Loescher, *The Protestant Church and the Negro* (New York: Association Press, 1948), pp. 77, 144-6.
50 *Ibid.*
51 David M. Reimers, *White Protestantism and the Negro* (New York: Oxford University Press, 1965), pp. 178-9.
52 Pope, *op. cit.*
53 Ernest Q. Campbell and Thomas Pettigrew, *Christians in Racial Crisis* (Washington, D.C.: Public Affairs Press, 1959).
54 *Ibid.*
55 *Ibid.*
56 H. Richard Niebuhr, *The Social Sources of Denominationalism* (New York: Holt, Rinehart and Winston, 1929).
57 Pope, *op. cit.*
58 Bryan R. Wilson, "An Analysis of Sect Development," *American Sociological Review* (February, 1959), pp. 3-15.
59 W. E. Mann, *Sect, Cult and Church in Alberta* (Toronto: University of Toronto Press, 1962), pp. 153-158.
60 Charles Y. Glock and Rodney Stark, *Religion and Society in Tension* (Chicago: Rand McNally, 1965).
61 Campbell and Pettigrew, *op. cit.*
62 Samuel W. Blizzard, "The Minister's Dilemma," *Christian Century*, 73 (1956), pp. 508-10.
63 *Ibid.*
64 *Ibid.*
65 Campbell and Pettigrew, *op. cit.*
66 Fichter, *op. cit.*
67 William A. Osborne, "Religion and Ecclesiastical Reform," *Journal For The Scientific Study Of Religion*, Vol. VII, No. 1 (Spring, 1968).
68 Campbell and Pettigrew, *op. cit.*

[69] *Ibid.*

[70] Harvey G. Cox, "The New Breed in American Churches: Sources of Social Activism in American Religion," *Daedalus* (Winter, 1967), pp. 135-50.

[71] *Ibid.*

[72] *Ibid.,* p. 148.

[73] *Ibid.,* p. 149.

[74] *Tuscaloosa News,* December 7, 1967.

[75] Gallup Poll, 1968, *op. cit.*

[76] *Ibid.*

[77] Lewis S. Feuer, "Conflict of Generations," *The Saturday Review* January 18, 1969.

[78] *Ibid.*

[79] "Rebellion in the Catholic Church," *Time,* November 22 1968.

[80] *Ibid.*

[81] *Ibid.*

[82] John Leo, "Rabbi Questions Clergy's Activism," *The New York Times* (March 10, 1968).

[83] *Ibid.*

[84] *The New York Times* March 29 1968.

[85] Gordon, *Assimilation in American Life, op. cit.*

[86] Glock and Stark, *op. cit.*

[87] Anthony Lewis, "A Bleak Outlook is Seen for Religion," *The New York Times* (February 25, 1968).

CHAPTER EIGHT

THE URBAN ENVIRONMENT: THE HOUSING CRISIS

The house encloses space in a manner which permits inhabitants to sustain a variety of interpersonal activities essential for the continuity of life. Since houses are built on foundations in America, they are tied to specific locations. The life expectancy of a house extends for many years; it may survive into an era when housing standards differ from those which governed the construction of the unit. Eventually homes become obsolete and need to be replaced. The adequacy of housing depends also on the materials employed, the manner and frequency of repair, the nature of heating, ventilation and plumbing facilities, the appliances in the home and the layout of the rooms.

In many ways, the effectiveness of the house depends on the characteristics of the neighborhood in which it is situated. Inhabitants cannot possibly include, within the walls of their dwelling unit, the varied services and facilities which the modern American family has come to regard as indispensable. While the dwelling unit is specialized to meet certain needs of families and of single individuals, the neighborhood is the locale for organizations and enterprises upon which the families depend, e.g., food, clothing, education, employment, worship, recreation, protection and other vital services. Residents of neighborhoods with inadequate services—sanitation or police protection—may be exceedingly discontented despite the soundness of dwelling units. Residences which are old and even overcrowded may not displease inhabitants if satisfaction with the neighborhood is great. For these reasons, one can see the validity of Spengler's view of the home as a "microhabitat within a macrohabitat."[1]

Housing and Health

The degree to which the dwelling unit provides adequate facilities and protection from inclement weather contributes to the physical and mental well-being of residents. These facilities reduce the probability of disease and accidents, and lessen concern over their occurrence.

Unfortunately the dimensions of health and housing are so varied and the difficulties of establishing and maintaining conditions of control so extensive that research on the subject does not offer conclusive evidence to those concerned with housing policy. While many studies indicate that poor housing is associated with certain health disorders, other studies provide ambiguous results. The great number of variables involved in unraveling relationships between housing and health leaves many questions unanswered. Although further inquiries are needed, a number of tentative conclusions can be drawn from the literature.

As preparation for their study, Daniel Wilner and his associates reviewed a number of studies on housing and health. Fifteen out of twenty-four studies reported a high correlation between housing and health, while the remainder yielded either uncertain or negative findings. Of sixteen studies concerned with housing and social adjustment, eleven reported a definite correlation while the remainder either were indefinite or negative. The majority of studies showed that good housing was associated with good health and social adjustment while poor housing correlated with higher rates of illness and lower adjustment levels.[2]

Wilner and his colleagues sought to measure the changes in health after low income Negro families in Baltimore moved from slum housing into a public housing project. Recognizing that improvement might not become immediately manifest, the researchers collected data on their subjects for three years, from 1955 to 1958, following the change in residential location. To ascertain the precise influence of housing variables, comparisons were made with a group of matched families that lived in poorer housing than the test group families.

Several dimensions of physical health were measured during the three year period. These included incidence of illness, accidents and disability. The types of illness studied included respiratory infections, childhood diseases, digestive disorders, tuberculosis and syphilis, among others.[3] The prediction that poor housing would produce higher rates of illness and disability among inhabitants and that good housing would produce lower rates was upheld for persons under thirty-five—particularly for children—but not for older persons.[4]

The researchers also examined a number of social factors, including self-concept, patterns of family interaction, satisfaction with housing, relations with neighbors, and attitudes toward the neighborhood. In several of these areas the differences between the rehoused and the slum families were considerable, while in others the magnitude of difference was less impressive. In general, respondents in the test group showed improvement in satisfaction with their housing accommodations, a notable increase in neighboring activities, and more pride in their neighborhoods. Much less difference between test and control families was reported for patterns of family interaction, aspirations for social and economic advancement, and manifestations of psychological irritations.[5]

One student of housing, Nathan Glazer, appears to have been unimpressed by Wilner's findings. He wrote:

> If we were dependent on Wilner's study alone to argue for the generally beneficial effects of better housing, our argument would not have much force. . . . We must also point out that Wilner studies the impact of housing *per se* in isolation from all other factors. . . . And . . . only a small improvement (in housing). . . .[6]

The impact of improved housing on physical and mental health and on patterns of social interaction might have been much greater if the change had been to an environment more favorable than that of a low income, segregated public housing project. The gains also might have been greater if the change in housing was accompanied by improvement in family income and family stability. To have the most beneficial results, housing policy should be coordinated with policy on employment, education, family and welfare.

Housing and the Family

Homes are centers for family activities and for the activities of each family member. Housing facilities affect the interaction of family members with each other, the adequacy of preparation for interacting outside the home, and the entertainment of non-family members within the home.

Two concepts which assist us in understanding these features of housing are suggested by Alvin Schorr in his scholarly evaluation of the housing literature. Schorr examines features of the dwelling unit which contribute to stress and situations which irritate and disturb the individual.[7] Facilities which prevent the family member from playing his domestic role or from preparing for role performance in the community intensify stress. A mother who does not have a stove in working order or an adequate refrigerator may find meal preparation a chronic source of anxiety. Similarly, teen-age children who battle one another for the use of the only bathroom or who lack privacy for studying may find living together a frustrating experience. Unpleasant housing conditions that inhabitants are incapable of changing can induce some members of the household, especially the younger ones, to spend little time at home and as much time as possible with their friends in the streets. This can weaken parental influence and, as we shall see below, increase the likelihood of community disorders.

Conversely, satisfaction with living conditions—facilities, furnishings, number and arrangement of rooms—creates an interpersonal atmosphere in which people enjoy living together and being in each other's company.[8] Parents derive greater satisfaction from playing with their offspring and from child-care when the dwelling unit facilitates such activities. Other factors being equal, family members tend to find joy in the home.

Overcrowding intensifies the stresses which may be generated by deficiencies in facilities or by interpersonal conflicts. The Bureau of the Census defines the term to mean more than one person per room in the dwelling unit. Serious overcrowding exists where there is more than 1.5

persons per room. Another view considers the total number of bed-
rooms and defines the dwelling unit as overcrowded when there is more
than one person per bedroom. A third view focuses on the use of rooms
for purposes other than those intended, *e.g.,* the living room serving as a
bedroom or the bathroom also being used by children as a place to
study. Another aspect of the dwelling unit concerns the layout of rooms,
especially of passageways. Crowding may occur even though none of the
conditions mentioned above exists, if hallways run through living areas
and movement from one part of the home to another requires passage
through living areas, reducing the privacy of household members.

In reviewing the literature on the effects of overcrowding, Schorr
mentions a number of consequences considered by students of housing.[9]
One researcher found that Negroes living in overcrowded conditions
suffered from lack of sleep, gaining only five hours a night due to a
shortage of beds. Another researcher concluded that overcrowding
generated a high level of irritation and excessive expenditure of energy.
Both conditions, the lack of sleep and wastage of energy, contribute to
indifferent role performance at work and in school, and possibly give
supervisors an erroneous impression of laziness or lack of interest.

Another condition thought to result from overcrowding concerned
overstimulation, especially sexual, resulting from the early initiation of
children into the nature and practice of sexual intercourse.[10] Occasions
when older children of one sex continue to sleep with a parent of the
opposite sex, due to the lack of beds, are not infrequent. The attachments
formed under these circumstances may seriously interfere with normal
sexual activity when the child becomes an adult.

When physical withdrawal to a separate room is not possible, efforts
to achieve psychological privacy may have serious consequences for the
child's perceptual processes. Silberman attributes the difficulties in hearing manifested by some lower class Negro children to the high noise
levels in their homes, where many people live in a few rooms. To gain
some privacy and quiet, the child ". . . is forced to learn how not to
listen; he develops the ability to wall himself off from his surroundings. . . ."[11] While this psychological substitute for physical privacy may
be functional in a crowded household, it creates difficulties for the child
in school. Since he has trained himself to screen out all noise, including
communication from others, the child tends to use these techniques in
the class room. By failing to differentiate between noise and the teacher's
instructions, the student renders himself incapable of performing his
lessons.[12] Teachers may be inclined to attribute slowness in learning to
mental inadequacies, and fail to recognize the intellectual capacities of
the child.

Housing and Self Concept

Schorr also stressed the degree to which the individual's assessment of self, of his capabilities, and of his worth and value depends on the physical environment in which he lives. The individual views ". . . house and place . . . as extensions of one's self . . ."[13] and he embraces the symbolic meanings of these physical elements of the habitat. Physical features of home and neighborhood also affect a person's estimate of the efficacy of purposive action for changing features of the social environment. Residents of areas regarded as inferior or marginal by the community often feel incapable of improving the environment. A defeatist attitude leads to apathy and passivity even though the person may live in circumstances which cry out for improvement. Schorr therefore asserts that the psychological influence of slum housing on inhabitants, especially poor persons, strengthens attitudes which keep them in impoverished circumstances. Since many low income persons are convinced that efforts to better economic circumstances will end only in failure, energies are allocated to other purposes. Submarginal housing contributes to a self-fulfilling prophecy[14]—a pessimistic appraisal of mobility chances which results in behavior that makes the expectation come true. Schorr considers the improvement in the housing environment of low income families essential for facilitating their climb out of poverty. Belief in the possibility of a marked improvement in living conditions appears to be a prerequisite for motivating the hard work and disciplined behavior which may bring occupational advancement. Change in housing by itself does not suffice, however. The opportunity for economic mobility also must be present.

HOUSING AND STRATIFICATION

Many of the features of housing which influence the individual's perception of self derive from the interdependence between the dwelling unit and the class system. The character of the neighborhood is a vital element in this equation. The "quality" of the house and of the neighborhood are interrelated; poor neighborhood facilities depreciate the market value of housing, and housing which imposes harsh living conditions on residents often leads to neighborhood activities which accelerate deterioration of the locality. Families are attracted to a neighborhood both by the character of its housing and by its shopping, educational, religious and recreational facilities. Families with very low incomes seldom have a choice in either housing or neighborhood, but are compelled to live in areas which more affluent families avoid.

Satisfaction or dissatisfaction with both the home and the neighborhood often depends on the symbolic meaning of each in relation to the family's prestige aspirations. The nature of housing and facilities in a neighborhood, the type of homes and their cost, the "character" of schools and churches and the standing of residents in the community's hierarchy of classes acquire a symbolic meaning which exercises a measure of independent influence on the allocation of home buyers to the respective neighborhoods in the community. Usually the older residential neighborhoods lie close to the central business district, have the highest proportion of dilapidated buildings and the lowest prestige rating. In some cases, however, such as the Beacon Hill section in Boston,[15] many *nouveau riche* families aspire to owning a town house in the area close to the dirty, noisy and congested sections of the city and in this way maintain the neighborhood's prestige. It can therefore be concluded that a neighborhood with a high prestige rating attracts potential residents, and the competition for residences in the area maintains property values. Neighborhoods with low prestige ratings attract only those who cannot afford to live elsewhere.

An insight into the forces relating housing to the class position of its inhabitants can be obtained from a study made early in the thirties by W. Lloyd Warner, an influential student of social stratification in America. At the end of the chapter on housing in Yankee City, a Massachusetts community of 17,000 residents, Warner wrote:

> Yankee City houses are thus symbols of status in the society. The cultural differences in the family life of the several classes are reflected in house type and symbolized by it. The house is, moreover, the *paramount* symbol of the *unequal distribution of the valued things of life* among the several classes.[16]

To many community members, the home stands for and represents the economic condition of the residents, the background and lineage of the family, and conformity to the rules concerning care and upkeep of property. Prestige ratings of dwelling units usually are transferred to the inhabitants. For this reason, in Yankee City and elsewhere, families which are rising in the class hierarchy make great efforts to obtain housing commensurate with the level to which they aspire. In communities like Yankee City, whose history extends back to a "golden era" of great families, the homes which these families inhabited possess a lineage and status which make them highly desired. These homes command a high price on the market although the design of the abode and the materials from which it is constructed may be "old-fashioned" by current standards. Middle class families aspiring to positions in the upper class often consider acquisition of a home that had belonged to a distinguished family as indispensable for completing the upward journey. These phenomena reflect the tendency for the prestige ratings of homes to be transferred to the residents, and that of the inhabitants to the abode. This factor helps us to understand Schorr's viewpoint, expressed previously, that housing influences self-perceptions and the prospects of low income families escaping from poverty.

Warner also analyzed the variations in the housing of the members of the six classes of Yankee City. Included in his findings were the following:

In brief, as one descends in the class order, the type of house becomes smaller and less preferable, and as one ascends, the house tends to become larger and better. The upper classes get the better home; the middle classes, the ordinary houses; and the lower classes, the poor ones.

The various types of houses are also unequally distributed among the ethnic groups of Yankee City, . . . The Yankees and Jews are the only ethnic groups that occupy large and good houses in significantly high numbers. The French, Poles, and Greeks, on the contrary, are significantly low in this respect.[17]

The value of a person's house (owned and lived in) declines as the rank of his class decreases. The only exception to this rule is that the lower-upper houses have a higher median value than the upper-upper houses.[18]

Warner also found correlations between type of housing and neighborhoods in the community, with high prestige neighborhoods possessing high income housing inhabited by upper class families. Conversely, low prestige neighborhoods had the poorest housing and were inhabited by families in the lowest class.[19]

Since housing and stratification are closely linked, features of the former have been used as indicators of the class position of inhabitants. Chapin's living room scale measured such features as furnishings, "taste" of the interior decoration, orderliness, cleanliness and state of repair of the living room and its appurtenances.[20] Warner and his associates included both house type and neighborhood as two of the factors in their four factor index of status characteristics.[21] Each was rated on a seven point scale. Sewell's scale of the socioeconomic status of farm families included such housing features as construction materials, lighting, plumbing, appliances, and the number of persons per room.[22]

The factors which produce a large measure of homogeneity in the housing possessed by members of a class and of heterogeneity in the housing of different classes have aided our understanding of the overall structure of the city and of the processes of change in the total design. Over forty years ago, Ernest W. Burgess of the University of Chicago offered a general sketch of the spatial structure of the large, commercial city—the *concentric zone theory*.[23] One feature of this theory concerned the spatial distribution of the several classes. It was assumed that a direct relation existed between class position of the family and distance from the central business district, with the wealthiest families living at a great distance from and the poorest closest to the center. Many subsequent studies showed variations in certain phenomena, especially pertaining to social breakdown—physical and mental illness, delinquency and crime, and suicide—which correlated with varying degrees of precision to this pattern of spatial distribution of the classes.[24] A related but more descriptive approach concentrated on the cultural and social organization of distinctive groups within each class inhabiting specific areas of the city. The working class, for example, was not treated as homogeneous, but was viewed as being composed of distinct minority groups, each tending to be found in a specific area. This approach led to intensive studies, among others, of the Jewish neighborhood,[25] the Negro community,[26] rooming house areas and luxury apartments houses,[27] skid row and its institutions.[28]

Knowledge of how the several classes utilized space in order to enhance their place in the social order also assisted the urban sociologist to understand certain processes of change. A few years after Burgess propounded the concentric zone theory, Homer Hoyt offered a modification in the form of the *sector theory*.[29] Hoyt demonstrated the influence of high prestige subdivisions upon patterns of residential growth. These subdivisions stimulated the growth in adjacent locations of subdivisions for upper income families. Families with high prestige aspirations preferred to be as spatially close as possible to elite families. Finally, the *theory of invasion and succession* was suggested as an explanation for the patterns of change in the area distribution of the population. The theory and the studies which it encouraged examined the factors inducing familes of one class to abandon or remain in their neighborhood when families of a lower class sought to move in. Such an invasion could terminate in one of several outcomes: a takeover by the newcomers and abandonment of the neighborhood by long-term residents, a defeat of the invasion or a type of integration between newcomers and long-term residents.[30]

The brief review of the spatial features of urban stratification suggests the pervasive and tight interlocking of class, housing and neighborhood. This constellation of forces has important implications for planning the eradication of slums and new housing areas. Past experience indicates that the residential integration of diverse ethnic, religious and racial groups may have the best prospect for success within a given class, but not across class boundaries. If true, this hypothesis may well influence the decision of planners and city officials on ᵗ site selection for low income housing projects and for efforts to overcome patterns of racial segregation in community housing. Before examining the matter further, some of the factors responsible for class segregation in residential areas must be considered.

With notable exceptions, position in the class system of American society is based largely on an individual's achievements in major institutions, especially economic, educational, and political. Successful competition for the most responsible and influential positions in the complex organizations which comprise each institution entitles the individual to receive a variety of valuable rewards. These benefits, both material and psychological, are distributed to office holders if duties are performed satisfactorily. In most cases, however, the individual does not have an inherent right to his office. Even for the most successful business and political leaders, holding on to one's social position involves some uncertainties. A sudden and unanticipated change in the economic and political weather can lead to a drastic decline in their standing within the bureaucratic hierarchy.[31]

This type of determination differs considerably from stratification systems which assign members position on the basis of inherited or ascribed qualities. Under the latter system, membership in the "right" family or in the nobility assures lifelong tenure in the elite. Whatever the consequences of this arrangement for the operation of social institutions, the individuals who rank at the top enjoy considerable security. Matters are more precarious for the middle and upper classes in a society with achieved patterns of stratification, such as America. Here, no set of titles, lineage or ancestry suffices to guarantee lifelong tenure in the higher levels of the stratification system. Other factors have greater importance as symbols of class position, since ascribed features are of relatively little significance. For example, the house is one of the paramount symbols of economic and social standing. Its value, however, is also a function of spatial proximity to houses of comparable quality. Since ascribed features carry relatively little weight in America, more emphasis is placed on organizing space to reduce the prospect of informal contacts between persons of widely different positions in the stratification hierarchy. One mechanism for accomplishing this end is homogeneity of prices for housing in a neighborhood. This device operates to exclude families with insufficient means and safeguards the status and self-concept of inhabitants.

It may seem that efforts to break down ghetto walls, especially those based on race, are doomed to failure in an achievement-oriented society. Matters seldom are so simple. Boundary lines dividing the classes are not distinct and clear-cut. Furthermore, the economic and social range within each class is extensive. Hence the segregation by income of families within neighborhoods may permit considerable heterogeneity of education, occupation, religion, ethnic and even of racial background. We do not know, at the present time, the degree of heterogeneity which can be planned into new housing projects and communities. The efforts in the decades ahead to deal with class and racial segregation will provide many of the answers to this question.

HOUSING THE MIDDLE CLASS

In this section, we will endeavor to gain some appreciation of the incidence of poor and adequate housing in the nation and of the housing policies which are responsible. This assessment will better help us to understand the severity of the housing problem in America.

In some respects, the housing policies of the nation have been very successful. Since the thirties, these policies have strengthened the economy by maintaining high rates of employment and capital expenditures. Forged in the thirties, the federal contributions to public housing, urban renewal and the home insurance program have helped control the "boom and bust" cycle which once plagued the national economy. From strictly a housing viewpoint, these policies have stimulated a considerable addition to the housing inventory, thereby overcoming a shortage of housing which developed during World War II. During the decade of the fifties, for example, almost thirteen and a half million housing units were added to the nation's housing inventory.[32] The vast number of new housing units directly benefitted most the families whose annual incomes exceeded the national median—families which were middle and upper class. Veterans' Administration and Federal Housing Administration assistance programs enabling families to obtain a thirty or forty year mortgage increased substantially the proportion of families owning homes, from about 40 percent in the forties to 63 percent in 1962.[33] This development laid the foundation for one of the major trends in America during the postwar era, the rapid growth of suburbs in metropolitan communities with an overwhelming predominance of white families in these areas. The government-supported mortgage programs enabled many white families to buy homes in the suburbs while Negro families were prevented from doing so, either by the lack of income or the refusal of lending agencies to provide mortgage money. The government's housing policies benefitted the white middle class by enabling many to become home owners and to escape the cities.

These have been popular policies. National surveys in the thirties and forties revealed that 70 percent of the families preferred to own their homes.[34] The ideal of living in a single family home has become almost universal in America in the postwar era. A survey completed in 1967 reported that 85 percent of the families polled favored this type of dwelling unit. Suburban living also was shown to be immensely popular; only 15 percent of the families indicated a preference for residing within fifteen miles of a metropolitan center. Four out of ten families preferred a home in the country to one in the suburbs.[35]

National policies which enabled vast numbers of middle income families to realize their housing dreams are not to be taken lightly. The change from apartment living to a detached home, from a crowded city neighborhood to a roomy suburban street, gave countless families greater freedom to manage their households and interpersonal relations. Nevertheless, these policies contributed to the prevalence of substandard housing among low income families. One student of housing defines the problem as follows:

> The issue with respect to new construction is whether and under what circumstances home building can induce a high level of abandonment among substandard units. . . .[36]

For Grigsby, the problem is one of moving low income families from substandard to standard dwelling units. Viewed from a larger persepective, the problem concerns the ability of the federal government and the private housing industry to provide adequate housing for families of all income levels and to break up the pattern of racial segregation which has come to dominate metropolitan areas.

Since the private housing industry produces few dwelling units for low and even moderate income families, the prospects of eliminating substandard housing by this mechanism alone are slim. In 1966, the median price of new one-family houses exceeded $21,000.[37] A house in this price range required a minimum income of more than $8,300. V.A. and F.H.A. financing brightens the picture somewhat: the median price of government-assisted housing ranged from $17,000 to $18,000, a level requiring a family income of roughly $7,000. The availability of new housing in this price range was limited since, in June, 1966, F.H.A. and V.A.-assisted housing comprised only 15 percent of all private non-farm housing starts,[38] and in 1964, only 11 percent of new, single family homes built for sale were priced below $12,500.[39] Since in 1965 more than half of the nation's families had annual incomes of less than $7,000,[40] very few could compete for new housing. These facts suggest the possibility that a substantial number of low income families will live indefinitely in inferior housing.

Housing Low Income Families

Many families whose incomes fall below the national median live in dwelling units that have been discarded by families who have purchased a more expensive abode. A majority of families residing in housing classified by the Bureau of the Census as substandard,* have poverty level incomes. In 1960, 63 percent of the families living in substandard housing had annual incomes of less than $3,000.[41]

Although between 1950 and 1966 the number of substandard dwelling units was substantially reduced from slightly less than 15[42] to about 5.7 million units,[43] the ratio of nonwhites living in this type of dwelling unit in 1966 was three times greater than that for whites, three out of ten nonwhite compared to one out of ten white households.[44] In absolute terms, however, the number of white households living in substandard dwelling units greatly exceeded that of nonwhites, 4 and 1.7 million respectively[45]—a total of close to 6 million households.

The proportion of nonwhite and white dwelling units classified as overcrowded, more than 1.01 persons per room, also suggests the divergence from the national average in the living conditions of Negro families. In 1960, a fourth of the dwelling units in urban areas occupied by nonwhite families were classified as overcrowded in contrast to 8 percent of white dwelling units.[46]

A closer look at the housing picture for low income families helps us to understand the nature of their hardships and the need for amelioration. These families pay a larger part of their budget for housing than families with a moderate budget. Families with incomes below $3,000,

---

* The Bureau of the Census defines substandard housing as units which are dilapidated and lacking one or more of the following plumbing facilities: hot running water in the structure, flush toilet and bathtub or shower for private use of household members. A dilapidated structure requires extensive repairs, rebuilding, razing or was of inadequate original construction. A deteriorated dwelling unit has one or more defects of an intermediate nature which require correction if the structure is to be safe and adequate.

both white and nonwhite, allocated roughly a fourth of the budget for housing while for families with higher income, the proportion was less than a fifth.[47] The need to allocate a larger than "normal" share of the family budget for housing may prevent a family from purchasing other necessities, such as clothing, and medical or dental care. Children in these families suffer from neglect since too little money is available for the necessities of life.

Although low income families are compelled to spend a higher fraction of their budget for housing, they receive less in the quality of accommodations than families with higher incomes. A survey made by the Bureau of Labor Statistics in six cities found that more than 60 percent of low income families and less than 30 percent of families with adequate incomes lived in areas rated undesirable. In Atlanta, Georgia, half of the low income families and about a fifth of the better income families lived in dwelling units lacking hot water.[48] To gain a more complete picture of the environment in which poor families reside for most of their lives, we must consider conditions in the ghetto.

THE NEGRO GHETTO

The isolation of the ghetto from the community at large, coupled with poverty, insecurity, and subordination of its inhabitants represent conditions of life to which members adapt in various ways. These responses include the specialization of services and activities of social institutions, especially the church and family life, and the structuring of informal social relations. In time these features of community structure acquire a distinctiveness often referred to as a "subculture," a design for living and social heritage which can be distinguished from that found in middle class neighborhoods. Slums, therefore, encompass more than dilapidated houses and dirty streets. The concept refers also to institutions, values and principal strategies for coping with the hardships and deprivations of everyday life. Improving the physical structure of the neighborhood may not suffice to better the life chances of inhabitants. The culture of slum life also must be changed.

Kenneth Clark, the psychologist, stresses some of the negative features of Harlem, America's most famous Negro ghetto. In addition to the "physical ugliness—the dirt, the filth, the neglect,"[49] Clark scores the institutional deficiencies of the area which impoverish the cultural life and increase the dependency of the ghetto and its residents on the larger, white community. Clark notes the absence of cultural and economic organizations which are common elsewhere in New York City. Harlem does not have a museum, an art gallery, or an art school and it has only a handful of libraries. Economically the community has few manufacturing or wholesaling establishments and very few office buildings. With two exceptions, its banks are branches of downtown, white-owned banking organizations. For the most part, Harlem's economy does not require a large proportion of white collar workers, persons who generally rank in the middle class. The numbers racket, which is a highly lucrative business, also is controlled by white outsiders. Hence, neither organized crime nor big business provides opportunities for economic advancement to Harlemites.[50]

On the other hand, Harlem has an abundance of bars, liquor stores, pawn shops, beauty parlors, fortune tellers and churches. The economic life of Harlem centers on the consumption rather than production of commodities, and on providing a variety of services for local residents but not manufacturing commodities for the metropolis or nation.[51] Harlem is a satellite of the larger city, unable to control its destiny and fulfilling functions of relatively little value to the total city.

Living conditions in Brownsville, a Negro ghetto in Brooklyn, are typical of many slums.[52] Brownsville had been a working class, Jewish neighborhood until the end of World War II when families began to leave the area. The section is inhabited by 125,000 persons, most of whom are Negro and Puerto Rican.

Virtually all buildings in the neighborhood are either dilapidated or lacking in one or more of the essential plumbing facilities. Only 4 percent of the structures meet basic standards. As one would expect, low income families predominate, with median family income below $3,500 per year, less than two-thirds of the 1966 annual median income for black families in the northeastern United States.[53] But the area has very high rates of juvenile delinquency, narcotics addiction, infant mortality, venereal disease and welfare cases.

Living in the tenements of Brownsville presents a number of hazards for inhabitants. Some families have survived the winter without heat or hot water. A gas stove which operates twenty-four hours a day provides heat for one family, whose youngest child has had pneumonia. In another apartment, the ceiling leaks over the baby's crib. Rats are another menace. One mother reported that she "found her daughter playing with a rat . . . that was so big the child was calling, 'Here, kitty, here, kitty.' "[54] Another mother, in describing the conditions which her children face daily, undoubtedly portrayed the style of life for most youngsters in the neighborhood. She said:

The kids are crowded in at night with the rats and the roaches, they get up in the freezing cold to get into the bathroom that usually doesn't work. . . .[55]

Despite these conditions, apartments in the area are not inexpensive. Rents vary from $60 to $80 per month although many of the buildings have been stripped by vandals. More than 500 have been completely deserted, and in some instances, whole blocks have been abandoned. The director of a mission church described life in Brownsville with this terse statement: "If there is a hell, many people in Brownsville will take it in stride."[56]

The conditions of Brownsville exist throughout New York City. Another journalist described housing for the poor in this metropolis in the following terms:

Housing for the poor in this city is halls reeking with urine and containing leaking pipes and falling plaster. It is small children crowded into tiny rooms with no heat, and the sharp winter wind cutting through cracked glass.

Most of all, housing is fear: fear of vandals and narcotics addicts, fear of thieves and muggers, fear of the landlord who will throw you out if you complain, fear of being old and helpless in a fivestory walk up, fear for your children in a hundred different ways. Poor housing is the symbol, and the cause, of hopelessness.[57]

Two conditions physically endanger the residents of the ghetto and play an important role in their demoralization. The first concerns the accumulation of garbage and debris in the streets of slum neighborhoods and the second concerns the exceedingly high crime rates. The first condition represents a serious health hazard, while the second endangers the physical well-being of inhabitants. Living in these circumstances intensifies the despair and hopelessness which pervade the ghetto.

Even in cities like New York and Chicago where garbage pickups in slum areas occur more often than in higher income neighborhoods, the accumulation of garbage in the streets far exceeds that which occurs elsewhere. One can imagine the conditions in cities where the frequency of pickups is the same as or less than those in the higher class neighborhoods. Garbage accumulates rapidly for a number of reasons: these include, among others, the very high population densities, the failure of many landlords to provide adequate garbage disposal facilities, a heavy volume of "bulk refuse" produced by the high moving rate of tenants and businesses, a large number of abandoned cars, and a great sensitivity to the garbage problem since the streets are used as "outdoor living rooms in summer" and as recreation areas.[58] These factors explain the comment by one observer that a New York slum neighborhood looked as if it had been abandoned by the Sanitation Department.[59] Few middle class persons can conceive of living on a street which appeared to have been "abandoned" by sanitation workers.

Traditionally, in the cities of America, the older residential areas which lie close to the business center have engendered high crime rates, regardless of the ethnic or racial composition of the area. The Negro ghetto likewise has high crime rates relative to that of middle income, white neighborhoods. Most of the crimes are committed by Negroes against Negroes: a study in Chicago found that in one seven month period, 85 percent of the crimes committed by Negroes "involved Negro victims."[60]

Negro residents of the city are exposed to much greater risks of being victimized and attacked by persons engaged in criminal activity.

. . . For nonwhites, the probability of suffering from any index* crime except larceny is 78 percent higher than for whites. The probability of being raped is 3.7 times higher among nonwhite women, and the probability of being robbed is 3.5 times higher for nonwhites in general.[61]

To the insecurities of slum residents engendered by unemployment and underemployment and by poor sanitary conditions must be added the serious danger of physical assault by criminals.

Residents of the Negro ghetto consider the area a dangerous place to live. In a study of a Negro area in Detroit in which a "large amount of rowdy, violent and delinquent behavior" was noted by participant observers, two-thirds of the respondents expressed concern over the lack of personal safety. This led many residents to hold the area in low esteem, and for two-thirds of the respondents to indicate a desire or intention to leave.[62] Such feelings do not manifest pride in one's neighborhood.

The forces which compel low income families to reside in these neighborhoods intensify the feeling of personal helplessness. Since residents would not choose this environment if better alternatives were available, and because escape for most families is exceedingly difficult, many feel overwhelmed and dominated by forces they consider beyond their control.

---

* The index refers to the FBI crime index, which includes homicide, forcible rape, aggravated assault, robbery, burglary, grand larceny, and auto theft.

Housing and Urban Riots

The housing inadequacies in the black ghettos of American cities contribute to the occurrence of riots and disorders. The stresses and frustrations engendered by the deficiencies of slum dwelling units generate a considerable amount of dissatisfaction. This discontent seems to be so widespread in some of the low income, Negro neighborhoods that it contributes noticeably to the grievances against the community felt by many inhabitants. A survey of Negro residents in twenty of the cities having major disturbances in 1967 found housing to be on the first level of intensity as a grievance, listed after police practices and unemployment, in that order.[63] Housing was a source of serious discontent in eighteen of the twenty cities in which the interviews were conducted.

> Grievances in the housing area were found in 18 cities and were ranked first in five cities, second in two cities, third in five cities, and fourth in two cities. . . .[64]

The conditions complained about most often concerned poor enforcement of the housing code—suggesting the prevalence of decay and deterioration—and overcrowding and discrimination in the sale and rental of dwelling units.[65]

Inadequacies of housing in the Negro ghetto not only heightened tensions, but played a part in the incidents which precipitated the riots. These events generally occurred at night, at the end of a long, hot day. "More than 60 percent of the 164 disorders occurred in July alone."[66] The final incident which led to the eruption of violence also occurred when many people, generally estimated at 50 or more persons, were on the street.[67] Living in overcrowded dwelling units with inadequate ventilation forced many of the residents into the streets. Enduring cramped quarters on a hot day may also have made many inhabitants irascible and excitable. Had the housing conditions been better, fewer persons would have been on the street late at night, and fewer would have been angry or tense. Under these circumstances, the event which led to the riot might have passed unnoticed.

An alternate explanation of the riots offered by sociologist Robert Blauner considers these events a reaction to the helplessness of ghetto inhabitants—a state comparable to the colonial status of some underdeveloped countries. The riots represent an effort by local residents to regain control of their neighborhood by expelling the white intruders.[68] For this reason, during many of the riots, the agents and symbols of the white community have been attacked, police- and firemen, businessmen and merchants. Whatever the causes of the riots, the facts and discussion make it abundantly clear that national housing policies must not be confined to the dwelling unit, but must include conditions in the neighborhood.

PROBLEM MANAGEMENT: TRADITIONAL APPROACHES

The executive and legislative branches of the federal government have been firmly committed over the years to two basic principles. The major responsibility for the provision of housing for all segments of the American population rests with the private sector of the economy, fiscal institutions, construction companies, real estate firms and building trades unions. Agencies of the federal government work through and with these organizations. They also must rely on the initiative and responsibility of officials of the local municipality. With leaders of these private organizations, these political leaders must work out the ways by which local needs can be met with the assistance and advice of federal agencies. The latter act as the coaching team, offering money and asistance, but execution is left to the players.

As demonstrated by the evidence on residential segregation presented in chapter 1, with each passing year, the nation's metropolises more closely resemble a solid black core surrounded by rings of white suburbs. Ironically, during an era of unprecedented economic growth and prosperity, the structure of accommodation between the races in America's cities continues and expands the forms of segregation developed and perpetuated by the rural South. Under these circumstances, patterns of urban *apartheid* symbolize the inadequacies of the objectives, programs and structural relationships between the several levels of government and of the private sector of the economy. Transformation of the cities into permanent black ghettos would destroy the promise of America as an equalitarian society in which all men, regardless of race, are thought to possess dignity and value. To understand the prospect for the future, we must consider the forces which have rendered so difficult the elimination of the Negro ghetto.

The Postwar Building Program in America

The federal government cooperated with the building industry in order to satisfy the desire of millions of families who wished to own a home in a suitable community. Federal Agencies made available an abundant supply of money for home mortgages and for mortgage insurance. The amount of equity initially required by the home buyer was reduced to a low level and the term required for paying the mortgage extended over a time period bringing the price of the dwelling within reach of families with annual incomes as low as six and seven thousand dollars.

Since low income families could not compete for the purchase of homes, the housing market could not adequately serve the needs of people in this stratum. While the public housing program was designed to provide decent housing for low income families, it never received the attention and priority that had become attached to the housing market for middle income families. This disparity of interest is evident from the fact that over ten million middle and upper-income units were constructed under the F.H.A. housing mortgage program and only eight hundred thousand units under the public housing program.[69] This total roughly equals the number of units authorized for the first three years of the public housing program.[70]

The single family, detached house has become the dominant housing type for residential use in America. Glazer reports that:

> In 1960, no less than 70 percent of all housing units in this country were one-family houses, detached; another 6 percent were one-family, attached . . . a mere 11 percent were in structures with more than five units.[71]

Even in metropolitan areas, 60 percent of all housing units were detached, single family buildings.[72]

The growth of suburbs since the end of World War II (in which the family-owned home constituted the dominant form of residence) had several important consequences. For many families, the transition from renter to owner symbolized economic and prestige advancement, and the realization of both a personal and of the American Dream, an experience which undoubtedly strengthened national loyalties and attachments. Many parents obtained security in the belief that raising children in surroundings free from the central city dirt, congestion and vehicles, and with better recreation facilities, represented a more "wholesome environment." The preference for owner residences in the suburbs also may be viewed as a continuation of the agrarian tradition in America, as expressed in personal efforts for home and therefore communal beautification.[73]

The federal policies which aided the white middle class to move to homes in the suburbs also confined black people and the poor to the central city. These policies laid the foundation for spatial segregation of the races in metropolitan areas. For approximately thirty years, various federal agencies, especially the Federal Housing Authority, either required or allowed private builders and lenders to exclude Negro families from their residential projects. From 1935 to 1950 the building manuals of the F.H.A. warned that neighborhoods occupied by members of different racial groups were likely to deteriorate rapidly and therefore were poor financial risks. The agency refused to provide mortgage insurance for these developments.[74] This ruling compelled builders and realtors to prohibit the sale or rental of units in white neighborhoods to Negro families. Hence the practice of writing racial covenants into agreements covering the sale of houses, and prohibiting the purchaser to resell to Negroes, had the approval of the federal housing agencies. The Supreme Court's ruling in 1948 that state courts could not enforce these restrictive covenants had little influence. Federal housing officials took no overt action to prevent builders and realtors from discriminating against Negro families in the sale of homes.[75]

The policies of federal agencies limited the housing opportunities of middle income Negro families. Hill cites one study of housing availability in 17 cities for white and Negro families with incomes between 7 and 10 thousand dollars. If the same proportion of Negro families had purchased homes as had whites, the expected number of Negro home owners would have been three times greater than the actual.[76]

In Detroit between 1940 and 1952, only 2 percent of the 87,000 new private housing units were built for Negro occupancy.[77] Five-sixths of the subdivisions in New York's suburbs were racially restricted.[78] In California between 1950 and 1958, less than 1.5 percent of the 200,000 new homes financed by the V.A. and F.H.A. were sold to nonwhites.[79] Since 1964, in the nation as a whole, only a minute fraction of the new housing financed by the F.H.A. has been available to Negro families.[80] Such findings led one housing expert to conclude:

> . . . The most subtle and most effective form of housing discrimination is therefore the failure of the federal government to provide a realistic program of subsidized housing in suburb as well as city at costs the Negro can afford. . . .[81]

If, over the years, federal legislation and housing policies strengthened urban apartheid, then modifications in these enactments could increase the dispersion of Negro families throughout the metropolis.

HOUSING OBJECTIVES

Housing programs serve many purposes. On the individual level, housing influences the satisfaction of residents, their habitat and level of living. Housing can promote or hinder equality of opportunity, raise or lower the level of living of inhabitants. Housing programs also affect the design and beauty of the city. For the nation, building programs affect economic stability and growth. In terms of stratification, housing policies can change rates of class mobility and the position of minority groups in the stratification hierarchy. Forging policies and programs which can simultaneously achieve many positive goals constitutes a task of great difficulty and importance. The previous discussion has shown that economic growth and pleasing both the middle class and the housing industry have dominated most housing programs. The problem for the future is to design and implement programs which also materially assist lower income families and disadvantaged groups.

Housing programs are a relatively recent development in America, beginning on a large scale in the late thirties. The public housing program, initiated in 1937, sought to provide decent housing for poor families. The urban renewal program was launched twelve years later to assist cities to halt the spread of physical decay. During this period, federal policies on home mortgages encouraged the growth of suburbs and home construction for the middle class. A number of programs were developed later to counteract the shortcomings of earlier programs. Improvements in public housing have been tested and a program enacted to help working class families purchase homes. The model cities program coordinates the efforts of a number of different agencies in the redevelopment of slums. Finally, to overcome racial segregation in cities, open housing has become the law of the land.

PUBLIC HOUSING

The difficulties of producing dwelling units at prices which low income families can afford has deterred many construction firms from seriously trying to meet the needs of this segment of the market. The "trickle down theory" is offered as the strategy for meeting the housing needs of low income families. Since housing will improve as these families acquire the residences abandoned by middle income families, the theory justifies production of housing for the middle class.

In practice, the theory has several flaws. The price of an apartment or house formerly occupied by a middle class family does not automatically fall to a level which is within the reach of low income families. The decline in rent usually takes some time before a low income family can compete for it. During the interval, taste and need for housing changes, and housing considered adequate by the standards of an earlier decade may not be acceptable by current standards. The dwelling units and buildings can be dilapidated or lacking in some essential facility.

The supply of decent housing for minority group members also is limited by discriminatory practices. Therefore, increasing the number of middle class dwelling units does not automatically expand the supply of good low income housing units.[82] Agencies of the federal and local government need to be involved in the low income housing field since the building industry over the years has shown little ability to cope with the problem.

The public housing program has operated since 1937, constructing approximately eight hundred thousand units. Although this level of production falls far below the current number of substandard dwelling units in the national housing inventory, it is doubtful if a greater output would have appreciably improved environmental conditions. Public housing has not been popular with the people whom it was intended to serve. Several factors explain this circumstance.

Several students of housing in America have stressed the wide divergence between the residential environment of public housing projects and that of middle class citizens. Public housing projects usually contain a cluster of high rise apartment buildings close to the center of the city with little open space for social activities. Often these projects are surrounded by dilapidated buildings in a section considered by most community residents to be a slum. Catherine Bauer Wurster defined the problem when she wrote:

> . . . Life in the usual public housing project just is not the way most American families want to live. Nor does it reflect our accepted values as to the way people should live.[83]

Nathan Glazer, who agrees with Wurster's conclusion, contends that any architectural design for low income families which differs greatly from that preferred by the middle classes will be avoided by all those with the means to make other arrangements. To prove his point, Glazer cites the reaction to the modern design of a public housing project in San Francisco:

. . . Deviant architecture, even when it is deviant in a progressive direction, is taken to symbolize the deviant social condition of the population, and becomes a target of their aggression.[84]

Factors other than the design of the buildings and their spatial arrangement render public housing unpopular with the public. The rules which limit eligibility in public housing projects to very low income families stigmatizes the project as intended primarily for society's failures. This conclusion has some basis in fact. In 1964, the median income of families residing in public housing projects across the nation was less than $2,500.[85] The tendency for many families in these projects to be black and women-headed further stigmatizes the public housing project.

Recent accounts of public housing projects in several cities describe some of the worst features of this type of urban habitat. The Pruitt-Igoe project of Saint Louis, built in 1954, consists of "33 eleven-story slab-shaped buildings. . ." inhabited by "10,000 Negroes in 2,000 households."[86] While the Igoe section of buildings was intended for occupancy by whites and Pruitt by Negroes, most white families left and have been replaced by black families. A high vacancy rate, between 20 and 25 percent, suggests that many low income Negro families do not prefer to live in the project if a suitable alternative can be found.

Many of the criticisms voiced by residents may be attributed directly or indirectly to the concentration in one relatively small area of a substantial proportion of disorganized families with large numbers of children. Over half of the families in the project had female heads and public assistance[87] was their major source of income. These factors combined with several serious errors in the design of the project[88] increased the hazards of living in this environment. Residents complained of vermin, dirt and trash inside and outside the buildings, people using the elevator as a bathroom, robbery and burglary, drunkenness and assorted acts of vandalism.[89]

Speaking of the Robert Taylor Project in Chicago as a typical example of public housing, Herbert Hill deplored the concentration of thousands of residents (28,000 in twenty-eight "huge, ugly high-rise buildings,") in a seventy million dollar ghetto which residents referred to as the "Congo Hilton."[90] In Chicago, and in the rest of the nation, the public housing program keeps the Negro in his place by concentrating black population in ghetto areas. The architecture fails to enhance the self-esteem of residents. On the contrary, the projects "serve as enclosures to pen in thousands of people whose personal identity is submerged in an anti-social architecture."[91]

The public housing program also has its defenders, of whom Roger Starr, executive director of the Citizen's Housing and Planning Council of New York, is one of the more persuasive. In New York City the program has not failed in Starr's opinion. Many low income families, when given a choice, prefer an apartment in a public housing project to one in a privately owned structure leased by the municipal housing authority.[92] Public housing units are superior in maintenance, in protection against fire, in light and air, and residents generally have more "community spirit."[93] According to Starr, the failure of public housing is not due to any weakness in the concept of a project designed for low income families. Deficiencies derive from the use of this program for other purposes, *e.g.,* removal of the families from an area to be converted to other uses, or to the cost limits per unit which often lead to unnecessarily harsh and uniform structures.[94]

In most cities, however, public housing has not satisfactorily met the needs of low income families. Rather, it has strengthened the boundary between this stratum and the rest of society, and increased the difficulties of upward mobility. This has been done in several ways. First, establishment of public housing authorities to develop and operate the projects rather than the private building industry, which serves the rest of the population, discredits the housing program. The efforts of the government thereby become identified with poor families.[95] Since the apparatus serving the needs of the two levels of society has been differentiated, the efforts of each have not been integrated into an overall, long-term housing program for the cities. In the future, one remedy would be to make greater use of private enterprise for housing the poor.

Other boundary defining aspects of public housing include concentration of projects in the core area of the city, near slum and blighted areas, rather than in the suburbs. Uniformity in the design of the buildings and massing many of these structures in a relatively small area imparts an "institutional character" to the project similar to that associated with municipal hospitals and mental institutions.

Current legislation for public housing provides for several innovations which should diminish its institutional character and increase its attractiveness as a housing environment. One set of changes, the "Turnkey" program, establishes a role for private firms. These firms may contract with local public housing agencies to build a project on privately-owned land. Once the project is completed, it may be managed either by the local agency or by a private firm. Although the program is relatively new, it has reduced by half the time needed for construction of public housing projects.[96] Acceptance of the program by both private developers and local housing agencies has been enthusiastic. This is reflected in an increase of 240 percent in the number of Turnkey units under construction in 1967.[97]

Major modifications of design may weaken the identification of public housing with a "captive" population of social *rejects*. Instead of constructing many high rise buildings within a relatively small area, as in the case of Pruitt-Igoe in St. Louis, much smaller buildings—mainly four stories—now are being built on small, scattered sites and even on a portion of a city block. The buildings are designed to encourage personal interaction, intimate social groupings and avoid the cold atmosphere of conventional projects. Arranging the buildings to enclose open spaces, in the form of plazas, parks or both (which are carefully landscaped) helps to create, in fact and in symbol, a more cohesive neighborhood environment and to increase the satisfaction of residents.[98]

Cognizant of the needs of public housing residents, many of whom are beset by a variety of complex problems, provisions have been proposed for counselling and social services. It has been suggested that federal funds be used for advising residents of public housing projects of the resources in the community for employment, education, health and welfare services. Organizations of residents can participate with management in the administration of the project.[99] Residents will have a better opportunity to communicate grievances and dissatisfactions to the managers. If this phase of the program succeeds, some of the local residents should acquire confidence in their ability to modify the social environment.

Although recent legislation places greater emphasis on the public housing program, doubts concerning the adequacy of the number of new units remain. The rate of past construction, roughly 25,000 units per year for 31 years, requires more than a generation to replace the present number of substandard dwelling units in the nation.[100] The number of units constructed under this program throughout its history merely equals the amount currently needed in New York City to eliminate 800,000 substandard housing units.[101] In New York and in many other cities, the rate by which standard units deteriorate is matched merely by the number of substandard units replaced by new residences. Hence the backlog of substandard units remains unchanged.

Current legislation calls for the construction of about the same number of public housing units in the next five years as have been constructed between 1937 and 1968, or 775,000 units, an annual rate of close to 160,000 units.[102] Assuming that this rate can be implemented, the success of the public housing program depends on the effectiveness of the "Turnkey" program and the degree to which the changes in design and location of the projects enable them to blend more readily into surrounding middle class neighborhoods.

Urban Renewal

Twelve years after the passage of The Housing Act of 1937, which established the public housing program, the attention of the Congress focused on the overall physical and economic needs of cities. Increased use of the automobile led to the rise of the suburban shopping center and the exodus of white, middle class families, leaving in their wake many deteriorating economic and residential areas. To prevent the spread of blight and to strengthen the central business district, Congress passed The Housing Act of 1949.

The act sought to change patterns of land use as an adaptation to the redistribution of population and economic activities, and to enable the city's economy to remain competitive in response to the growth of suburban shopping centers and industrial parks. It also encouraged a municipality to use powers of eminent domain to assemble large tracts of land. After the parcels had been acquired, the site was sold to developers at a cost considerably below that which had been paid by the municipality. The new owners cleared the area and then rebuilt it according to prearranged plans. A variety of projects could be built, including a shopping center, housing project, civic center or some other type of development, if agreeable to municipal and federal officials. The federal government financed the greatest portion of the monies involved, paying the difference between the cost of acquisition and clearance of the area and the price when sold by the municipality.[108] In this manner the federal government encouraged the efforts of local leaders and businessmen to improve the design and functioning of the city.

Although highly controversial and considered by some articulate critics as having failed to attain its principal objectives, the urban renewal program was essential for improving land use patterns. This could not be accomplished without use of eminent domain to assemble large tracts of land. The layman can hardly appreciate the complexity and difficulty of this task. Parcels of land and the structures which occupy them in one small neighborhood can be owned by dozens of people and institutions— banks, companies, etc.—many of whom reside in distant municipalities. The refusal of one or more owners to sell can kill a proposed project. At the very least, prolonged haggling over price can seriously delay and increase the cost of the program. Use of eminent domain greatly simplifies the task, for the right of an owner to retain his property or to bargain over price is not permitted to prevail over the interest of the municipality.[103]

The urban renewal program assisted construction of a wide variety of economic, residential, cultural and educational structures in the nation's cities. In New York City, the program contributed to the creation and completion of Lincoln Center, a complex of buildings devoted to the performing arts. These include an opera, a symphonic concert hall, a theater, a school of dance, a school of music, a library and a museum.[104] The Golden Gateway Project in downtown San Francisco provides for, among other things, a "twenty-block-long pedestrian mall with intersecting malls and plaza."[105] In Philadelphia, the urban renewal program played a significant role in the Society Hill project, the redevelopment of a very old residential area in the downtown section of the city. The project had several purposes—to restore the area's historic attractiveness as an eighteenth century neighborhood, and to induce tourists to visit the city and the area by preserving this residential component of the city's colonial heritage. Restoration included conversion of some dwelling into fashionable residences for prosperous families in an effort to persuade higher class families to return from the suburbs.[106]

Urban renewal programs brought 120 million dollars to New Haven in a little over a decade. This is the equivalent to 790 dollars per resident. The city also benefitted from private investment and a hundred million dollars in highway funds.[107] The program redeveloped the central business district by redesigning a ninety-three acre area in which were built a department store, hotel, bank building and parking areas.[108]

Urban renewal programs throughout the nation have rebuilt downtown areas, preserved buildings of historic value, constructed housing for middle and upper income families, assisted the expansion of universities and strengthened a variety of cultural functions. Much of the dissatisfaction with urban renewal derives from projects which destroyed viable neighborhoods, increased the degree of racial segregation and reduced the housing inventory for low income families. For example, urban renewal in Boston destroyed a cohesive and stable Italian neighborhood.[109] Renewal projects also have moved Negroes out of interracial neighborhoods and effectively resegregated them. The tendency for urban renewal to displace more Negro than white families increases segregation in public housing projects. The displaced Negro families raise the proportion of Negroes residing in these projects and this circumstance induces more white families to leave.[110]

Urban renewal plans often fail to coordinate projected slum clearance and redevelopment with the housing needs of the families to be displaced. Renewal projects often reduced the number of dwelling units available to the displaced families, thereby forcing these families to pay higher rents and to live in very cramped quarters. Scott Greer summarized this aspect of urban renewal programs when he wrote:

> At a cost of more than three billion dollars the Urban Renewal Agency (URA) has succeeded in materially reducing the supply of low-cost housing in American cities. . . .[111]

Urban renewal programs often failed to assist the displaced families and businesses to obtain adequate quarters at reasonable prices. This failure added greatly to the burden of breaking social ties with the neighborhood in which the family had resided for many years. Residents of the West End of Boston responded to plans for redeveloping the area and resettling of inhabitants with various forms of grief and psychological disturbance. One investigator of the neighborhood viewed relocation as a "crisis with potential danger to mental health. . . ."[112]

Model Cities Program

The model cities program was intended in part to overcome some of the weaknesses of the urban renewal program by providing incentives for local public agencies to coordinate redevelopment efforts within the framework of a comprehensive plan. The program strives to combine the features of urban renewal which strengthen the municipal economy and tax base with provisions to improve the housing and services available to low income families.

The Demonstration Cities Act, enacted by Congress in 1966, authorizes the federal government to pay cities a substantial cash bonus if the activities of local, state and federal agencies are coordinated and concentrated within designated areas of the city in a total effort to improve land use and services. The program requires additions to the supply of housing for low and moderate income families, involvement of residents in the planning and rebuilding of the area, employment of residents in building projects, a plan for the relocation and compensation of families and businesses to be displaced, and maximization of choice for housing by these families. The act endeavors to produce maximum gains for the city and all its inhabitants by integrating renewal with improvement in the housing, employment, political involvement and services available to families in the areas affected.[113]

Participating cities are required to select for development an area possessing a substantial amount of the community's substandard and deteriorating housing. The area could include much, if not all, of the area of a small city or a neighborhood in a large city. The act requires development of a comprehensive plan which sets forth the specific changes to be accomplished in the area. The plan must provide for effective relocation procedures, receive the endorsement of groups and leaders representing local residents, provide for the revision of outmoded building codes and other ordinances, and design buildings attractively, using the latest technology wherever feasible.[114]

The federal government rewards municipalities which accomplish these objectives with a substantial cash bonus. The total federal contribution to a municipality could equal 90 percent of the cost of redeveloping an entire area. The municipality may use the supplemental grant to upgrade a variety of services for area residents, *e.g.,* schools, library, recreation, sanitation, etc.

A number of other programs hold much promise for improving both housing and the environment for American urban residents. The Office of Urban Research and Technology of the Department of Housing and Urban Development devotes much of its resources for experimentation on the technology of home construction. Innovations which would reduce the cost of good housing and bring it within reach of working class families would simplify the tasks of H.U.D. Less money would be required for subsidizing housing, as the building industry could provide housing for families on all income levels.

Another plan for increasing the production of housing for less affluent families requires the participation of large industrial concerns. This could be accomplished by the establishment of housing partnerships in which private corporations invest and participate. Capital and technical experts would be used to assist local firms in planning and constructing housing projects. By making these assets from major corporations available to local firms, the latter would be encouraged to produce housing for less affluent families.[115]

H.U.D. also has financed efforts to design the city of the future. The long-run solution of urban problems may require an urban plan superior to those in which we presently live. The program assumes that decentralization of the urban population is imperative, that adding cities to metropolitan areas will be self-defeating. Spilhaus and his associates intend to house a quarter of a million people at a considerable distance from other cities.

Plans for the experimental city include elimination of pollution, underground systems of transportation, communication and service mains, underground storage of building materials and the dismantling of buildings when no longer usable, distribution of food pneumatically, a transportation system using pods which are controlled by computers and the control of all wastes by recycling and use of a dome over some sections of the city.[116] While some of these ideas may not prove practical, others may become as distinctive of the city of tomorrow as dirt, decay, pollution and segregation are of the city of today.

HOME OWNERSHIP FOR LOWER INCOME FAMILIES

Traditional federal housing policies aided either the middle class to buy homes in the suburbs or poor families to obtain public housing. The vast number of families between these two levels received little or no help. Several programs have been developed in the sixties to assist families with incomes between $3,000 and $8,000 to obtain decent housing. One program helps these families to become home owners, and thereby acquire an important symbol of middle class status. Other programs are designed for those families who, for one reason or another, prefer to rent a home or an apartment. In both instances the programs seek to increase the amount of housing available to these families by improving their ability to compete in the housing market. The programs provide a subsidy earmarked for housing which raises the annual income of these lower income families.

The cash subsidy strengthens housing demands in the private market sector for families who otherwise would be unable to compete against families with higher incomes. By enabling these families to bid for homes and apartments, their range of housing choice will be increased. Housing outside the ghetto, in the central city and in the suburbs, could be within the financial reach of many of these lower income families. The programs should encourage migration out of the ghetto and racial integration of the suburbs. Success of the programs depends in part on how families that do not need the subsidy treat those who do. If the latter are ridiculed or made to feel inferior, many families may hesitate to apply for the low interest or rent subsidy programs. Success depends also on the level of funding provided by the Congress.

The Housing and Urban Development Act of 1968 established a program of subsidized interest rates and rent payments to assist families with annual incomes between $3,000 and $7,000 to buy a home. Since the units to be purchased either will be new or older ones that have been substantially improved, the program will increase the supply of housing available for these families. A million families of low and moderate incomes, many of whom will have been displaced from urban renewal areas, can become homeowners over the five year period of the Act.[117] The monthly subsidy may vary from 38 to 50 dollars per family, or between 450 and 600 dollars per year.[118]

The subsidy provisions increase the annual incomes of recipient families by as much as six hundred dollars although the payments go not to the family but to the mortgagee. The government provides a housing allowance for selected low-income families. Whether or not the program improves the housing environment of lower income families depends on the ability of these families to meet the recurrent and nonrecurrent costs of home ownership. Unusually large maintenance expenses may prove to be beyond the means of some of these families.

A similar program helps families who are not ready for or do not desire to own a home, but prefer renting an apartment. This program was initiated by The Housing Act of 1961 and has operated on a limited scale between 1961 and 1967 at an annual rate of only 11,000 units. The program provides a subsidy for reducing interest rates to the 1 percent level, and holding the family rent at a level no greater than 25 percent of monthly income.[119] The program aids families with incomes from $4,000 to $8,000 to obtain good housing.

The 1968 Housing Act also continued and expanded the rent supplement program, initiated in 1966, which complements the reduced interest rate program for rental units. The program pays the difference between the actual rent and a figure representing 25 percent of the monthly income of low and moderate income families. The program avoids the practice in public housing projects of requiring families to move whose incomes increase beyond a stipulated level. Under the rent subsidy program, the amount paid by the federal government is reduced as family income increases.

OPEN HOUSING

Elimination of racial segregation in the nation's metropolitan communities requires the same freedom for a black family to acquire housing as white families presently enjoy. Exercise of this freedom on a large scale simplifies solution of many critical problems: desegregation of urban schools, reducing unemployment of black workers, reducing the rate of black families broken by divorce or separation, encouraging Negroes to develop pride in self and in race. Two developments in the late sixties provided the basis for achieving these ends, passage of an open housing law and a Supreme Court decision on housing discrimination.

An open housing provision of the Civil Rights Act of 1968 prohibited discrimination in the sale or rental of dwelling units in apartment buildings and other multifamily structures, and in real estate developments. Real estate brokers also were prohibited from discriminating in the sale of single family residences; however, the law did not prevent the owners from engaging in such acts. These provisions covered approximately 80 percent of the housing market, and opened the suburbs to black families with the requisite financial resources.[120]

The decision of the United States Supreme Court in *Jones* v. *Mayer* went beyond the law enacted by Congress. The Court prohibited racial discrimination in all sales and rental of property, regardless of whether the owner or a broker handled the transaction. The decision of the Court was based on the Civil Rights Act of 1866 which, in turn, had been passed to enforce the 13th amendment. This amendment declared that citizens of all races had the right to purchase, sell, lease and transfer real and personal property. In this connection the Supreme Court stated:

> At the very least, the freedom that Congress is empowered to secure under the Thirteenth Amendment includes the freedom to buy whatever a white man can buy, the right to live wherever a white man can live. If Congress cannot say that being a freeman means at least this much, then the Thirteenth Amendment made a promise the nation cannot keep.[121]

Since the 1968 law can open a large residential section to potential black homeowners, it may facilitate rapid desegregation of the suburbs. It permits the U.S. Attorney General to legally attack segregation in a neighborhood or development where existence of a pattern of discrimination can be demonstrated. Both the 1968 law and the ruling of the Supreme Court permits the prospective home buyer to sue the owner or the broker in cases where discrimination is thought to have foiled the transaction. The former may be more effective, for it provides stiffer penalties. The court may award damages of up to a thousand dollars to the plaintiff while the 1866 law provided merely for a court order against discrimination.

Progress toward breaking down patterns of segregation in residential areas will come more slowly through suits against individual owners and brokers. Here the battle is fought one house at a time, and many cases will have to be won before homeowners recognize the futility of discriminatory practices in the sale or rental of housing. Progress may not be rapid either in efforts to counteract discrimination in neighborhoods and residential developments. The number of suits initiated by the Attorney General and the skill of staff attorneys depends on the resources Congress allocates to this federal agency. Ramsey Clark, Attorney General in the Johnson administration, discussed the limited resources of his office in respect to the magnitude of the assignment:

. . . The Civil Rights Division—as devoted a group of people to the principles of this country as has ever been collected in one place, . . . —*is fewer than a hundred lawyers.* . . . Their burden is to enforce the Voting Rights Act, to litigate school desegregation in perhaps 30,000 school districts over the U.S., to bring Title II of the Act, promising open accommodations, to a reality; to enforce all of our Civil Rights Laws. *This small resource would be inadequate for one state. It would be inadequate for one single law throughout the United States.* . . .[122]

A Federal District Court provided additional assistance for efforts to overcome racial segregation in urban centers. The case may have far reaching consequences for it concerned practices on selecting sites and residents for public housing projects which have been used throughout the nation. The Court held invalid the system whereby projects for Negroes in white neighborhoods were vetoed consistently in Chicago since 1954 for racial reasons. The laws of the land required sites for public housing projects to be selected without regard for the racial composition of the surrounding neighborhood. The Court also invalidated the practice of restricting the number of Negro families in the housing projects situated in white neighborhoods.[123]

If this decision against locating public housing projects for Negroes in Negro neighborhoods is upheld, one of two alternatives will result. The public housing program no longer will be used to maintain patterns of racial segregation. New housing projects, initially at least, will promote desegregation. On the other hand, one should not underestimate resistance to this desegregation trend. Opposition from residents of white neighborhoods may be so great that city officials will make little or no effort to build new public housing projects. The decision of the court could mark the end of public housing in America. The efforts of municipalities to overcome discrimination in housing should not be overlooked. By the end of 1968, fair housing laws had been adopted in 243 municipalities,[124] and in at least 23 states.[125] These laws reinforce various national laws and court rulings. Cooperation between local, state and federal agencies will help end racial *apartheid* in America.

CONCLUSION

Our discussion of changes in major housing programs conceals the complexity of processes of evaluating results and developing new proposals. By linking recognized flaws in a housing program with a specific remedy, we may have exaggerated the rationality of adjustive processes. The impression that for each recognized weakness a legislative remedy has been found might seem valid. But such is not the case. This view fails to consider the length of time required both for recognizing the weaknesses in a housing program, for developing alternatives and for winning acceptance of a particular approach. In some instances, improvement is frustrated by failure to gain consensus on a new approach. Even if major governmental leaders agree on a specific program, the resources may be unavailable for implementation on a large scale. This seems to be the case for the rent supplement and low interest rate programs, discussed above. Finally, detection of the dysfunctions of a program may not occur until great harm has been done, as seems true of the contribution of government mortgage policies to racial segregation.

Selected Readings

Abrams, Charles. *Forbidden Neighbors* (New York: Harper & Brothers, 1955).

_____ *The City Is The Frontier* (New York: Harper & Row, Publishers, Colophon Books, 1965).

Fisher, Robert Moore. *20 Years of Public Housing* (New York: Harper & Brothers, 1959).

Greer, Scott. *Urban Renewal and American Cities* (Indianapolis: The Bobbs-Merrill Company, Inc., 1965).

Lowe, Jeanne R. *Cities In A Race With Time* (New York: Random House, 1967).

Report of the National Advisory Commission on Civil Disorders. (New York: Bantam Books, 1968).

Schorr, Alvin L. *Slums and Social Insecurity* (Washington, D.C.: U.S. Department of Health, Education, and Welfare, 1963).

Weaver, Robert C. *The Urban Complex* (Garden City, N.Y.: Doubleday & Co., 1964).

Wheaton, William L. C., *et al.*, eds. *Urban Housing* (New York: The Free Press, 1966).

Wilson, James Q., ed. *Urban Renewal: The Record and the Controversy* (Cambridge, Mass.: The M.I.T. Press, 1966).

Notes to Chapter 8

[1] Joseph J. Spengler, "Population Pressure, Housing, and Habitat," *Law and Contemporary Problems*, XXXII (Spring, 1967), p. 194.

[2] Daniel M. Wilner, *et al., The Housing Environment and Family Life* (Baltimore, Md.: The Johns Hopkins Press, 1962), pp. 4-5.

[3] *Ibid.,* p. 243.

[4] *Ibid.,* pp. 243-4.

[5] *Ibid.,* pp. 247-51.

[6] Nathan Glazer, "Housing Problems and Housing Policies," *The Public Interest,* 7 (Spring, 1967), p. 22.

[7] Alvin L. Schorr, *Slums and Social Insecurity* (Washington, D.C.: Social Security Administration, U.S. Government Printing Office, no date given), pp. 12-13.

[8] *Ibid.,* pp. 14-16.

[9] *Ibid.,* pp. 22-25.

[10] *Ibid.,* pp. 17-18.

[11] Charles E. Silberman, *Crisis In Black and White* (New York: Random House, 1964), p. 270.

[12] *Ibid.,* pp. 270-1.

[13] Schorr, *op. cit.,* pp. 9-10.

[14] Robert K. Merton, "The Self-Fulfilling Prophecy," in *Social Theory and Social Structure,* rev. and enlarged ed. (New York: The Free Press, 1957), pp. 421-36.

[15] Walter Firey, *Land Use In Central Boston* (Cambridge, Mass.: Harvard University Press, 1946).

[16] W. Lloyd Warner and Paul S. Lunt, *The Social Life of a Modern Community* (New Haven: Yale University Press, 1941), p. 251. Authors' italics.

[17] *Ibid.,* p. 246.

[18] *Ibid.,* pp. 283-4.

[19] *Ibid.,* pp. 227-38.

[20] F. Stuart Chapin, *Scale for Rating Living Room Equipment,* Institute of Child Welfare Circular No. 3 (Minneapolis: University of Minnesota, January, 1930).

[21] W. Lloyd Warner, Marcia Meeker, Kenneth Eells, *Social Class in America* (New York: Harper & Row, Publishers, Torchbook ed., 1960), pp. 143-54.

[22] William H. Sewell, "A Short Form of the Family Socioeconomic Status Scale," *Rural Sociology* 8 (June, 1943), pp. 161-169. See also Raymond W. Mack, "Housing as an Index of Social Class," *Social Forces,* 29 (May, 1951), pp. 391-6.

[23] Ernest W. Burgess, "The Growth of the City," in R. E. Park, *et al.,* eds., *The City* (Chicago: University of Chicago Press, 1925), pp. 51-53.

[24] Calvin Schmid, *Suicides in Seattle, 1914 to 1925* (Seattle: University of Washington Press, 1928). Calvin Schmid, *Social Saga of Two Cities* (Minneapolis: Council of Social Agencies, 1937). Robert E. L. Faris and Warren Dunham, *Mental Disorders in Urban Cities* (Chicago: University of Chicago Press, 1939). Clifford R. Shaw and Henry D. McKay, *Juvenile Delinquency and Urban Areas* (Chicago: University of Chicago Press, 1942).

[25] Louis Wirth, *The Ghetto* (Chicago: University of Chicago Press, 1929).

[26] Horace R. Cayton and St. Clair Drake, *Black Metropolis* (New York: Harcourt, Brace & Co., 1945).

[27] Harvey Zorbaugh, *The Gold Coast and the Slum* (Chicago: University of Chicago Press, 1929).

[28] Nels Anderson, *The Hobo* (Chicago: University of Chicago Press, 1923). Paul Cressey, *The Taxi-Dance Hall* (Chicago: University of Chicago Press, 1932).

[29] Homer Hoyt, *The Structure and Growth of Residential Neighborhoods in American Cities* (Washington, D.C.: Federal Housing Administration, 1939).

[30] Harold Gibbard, "The Status Factor in Residential Succession," *American Journal of Sociology,* 46 (May, 1941), pp. 835-42; Clifton R. Jones, "Invasion and Racial Attitudes," *Social Forces,* 27 (March, 1949), pp. 286-92; Christen T. Jonassen, "Cultural Variables in the Ecology of an Ethnic Group," *American Sociological Review,* 14 (February, 1949), pp. 32-41; Richard G. Ford, "Population Succession in Chicago," *American Journal of Sociology,* 56 (September, 1950), pp. 156-60.

[31] For a presentation and critical examination of the functional theory of social stratification, see Reinhard Bendix and Seymour M. Lipset, eds., *Class, Status and Power,* Rev. ed., (New York: The Free Press, 1966), pp. 47-62.

[32] Glazer, *op. cit.,* p. 28.

[33] *Ibid.,* p. 31.

[34] *Ibid.*

[35] "A Home Where The Buffalo Roam," *The Public Interest,* 11 (Spring, 1968), pp. 90-91.

[36] William C. Grigsby, *Housing Markets and Public Policy* (Philadelphia: University of Pennsylvania Press, 1963), p. 25.

[37] Dorothy K. Newman, "The Low-Cost Housing Market," in *Housing Legislation of 1967. Hearings Before The Subcommittee on Housing and Urban Affairs, U.S. Senate, Ninetieth Congress, First Session, Part 1* (Washington: U.S. Government Printing Office, 1967), p. 229.

[38] *Ibid.*

[39] National Commission on Technology, Automation, and Economic Progress, *Applying Technology to Unmet Needs,* Appendix Volume V (Washington, D.C.: U.S. Government Printing Office, 1966), pp. v-18.

[40] U.S. Bureau of the Census, *Current Population Reports,* Series P-60, No. 51, "Income In 1965 of Families and Persons in the United States" (Washington D.C.: U.S. Government Printing Office, 1967), p. 2.

[41] Newman, *op. cit.,* p. 231.

[42] *Ibid.*

[43] United States Department of Labor and Bureau of Labor Statistics, *Social and Economic Conditions of Negroes in the United States* (Washington, D.C.: U.S. Government Printing Office, 1967), p. 55.

[44] *Ibid.,* p. 53.

[45] *Ibid.,* p. 55.

[46] *Ibid.,* p. 57.

[47] *Ibid.,* p. 61.

[48] Phyllis Groom, "Prices in Poor Neighborhoods," *Monthly Labor Review,* 89 (October, 1966), pp. 1085-1090.

[49] Kenneth B. Clark, *Dark Ghetto* (New York: Harper & Row, Torchbook edition, 1967), p. 27.

[50] Lewis Yablonsky, *The Violent Gang* (Baltimore: Penguin Books, 1966), p. 176.

[51] Clark, *op. cit.,* pp. 27-28.

[52] *The New York Times* (March 7, 1968), p. 39, p. 53, col. 2.

[53] Bureau of Labor Statistics and Bureau of the Census, *Social and Economic Conditions of Negroes in the United States, op. cit.,* p. 16.

[54] *The New York Times* (March 7, 1968), p. 39.

[55] *Ibid.,* p. 53.

[56] *Ibid.,* p. 39.

[57] *The New York Times* (May 27, 1968).

[58] *Report of the National Advisory Commission on Civil Disorders,* (New York: Bantam Books, 1968), pp. 272-3.

[59] *The New York Times,* (May 27, 1968).

⁶⁰ *Report of the National Advisory Commission On Civil Disorders, op. cit.,* p. 268.

⁶¹ *Ibid.*

⁶² Eleanor P. Wolf and Charles N. Lebeaux, "On the Destruction of Poor Neighborhoods By Urban Renewal," *Social Problems,* 15 (Summer, 1967), pp. 4-7.

⁶³ *Report Of The National Advisory Commission On Civil Disorders, op. cit.,* pp. 143-4.

⁶⁴ *Ibid.,* f.n. 214, p. 196.

⁶⁵ *Ibid.,* p. 146.

⁶⁶ *Ibid.,* p. 122.

⁶⁷ *Ibid.,* p. 123.

⁶⁸ Robert Blauner, "The Dilemmas of the Black Urban Revolt," *Journal of Housing,* 24 (December, 1967), pp. 603-606.

⁶⁹ *Report of the National Advisory Commission on Civil Disorders, op. cit.,* pp. 473-474.

⁷⁰ Glazer, *op. cit.,* p. 30.

⁷¹ *Ibid.,* p. 31.

⁷² *Ibid.*

⁷³ Daniel J. Elazar, "Urbanization and Federalism in The United States," in Joint Economic Committee, *Urban America: Goals and Problems, Compendium* (Washington, D.C.: U.S. Government Printing Office, 1967), pp. 197-201.

⁷⁴ Charles Abrams, *The City is the Frontier* (New York: Harper & Row, Colophon Books, 1967), p. 61.

⁷⁵ Herbert Hill, "Demographic Change and Racial Ghettos: The Crisis of American Cities," in Joint Economic Committee, *Urban America: Goals and Problems, Hearings* (Washington, D.C.: U.S. Government Printing Office, 1967), p. 141, 143, 144.

⁷⁶ *Ibid.,* p. 140.

⁷⁷ *Ibid.*

⁷⁸ Abrams, *op. cit.,* p. 62.

⁷⁹ Hill, *op. cit.,* p. 142.

⁸⁰ *Ibid.*

⁸¹ Abrams, *op. cit.,* p. 67.

⁸² Robert C. Weaver discusses this trickle down theory in *The Urban Complex* (New York: Doubleday & Co., 1964), pp. 50-51.

⁸³ Catherine Bauer Wurster, "The Dreary Deadlock of Public Housing," in William C. Wheaton, *et al.,* eds., *Urban Housing* (New York: The Free Press, 1966), p. 247.

⁸⁴ Glazer, *op. cit.,* p. 37.

⁸⁵ *Ibid.,* p. 36.

⁸⁶ Lee Rainwater, "The Lessons of Pruitt-Igoe," *The Public Interest,* No. 8 (Summer, 1967), p. 116.

⁸⁷ Lee Rainwater, "Crucible of Identity: The Negro Lower-Class Family," *Daedalus,* 95 (Winter, 1966), p. 212. This analysis of the Negro lower class family is based on the author's study of the social environment of the Pruitt-Igoe public housing project.

⁸⁸ Ten years after the project was built, seven million dollars were spent to overcome the inadequacies of the buildings. Cf. Herbert Hill, *op. cit.,* p. 139.

⁸⁹Rainwater, "The Lessons of Pruitt-Igoe," *op. cit.,* pp. 118-119.

⁹⁰ Hill, *op. cit.,* p. 138.

⁹¹ *Ibid.,* p. 139.

⁹² Roger Starr, "Statement," *Urban America: Goals and Problems, Hearings, op. cit.,* pp. 41-3.

⁹³ *Ibid.*

⁹⁴ *Ibid.,* p. 50.

⁹⁵ Wurster, *op. cit.,* p. 249.

96 *Housing and Urban Development Legislation of 1968. Hearings Before The Subcommittee on Housing and Urban Affairs Of The Committee On Banking and Currency, United States Senate, Ninetieth Congress, Second Session on Proposed Housing Legislation For 1968,* (Washington, D. C.: U.S. Government Printing Office, 1968), p. 76.

97 *Ibid.*

98 *The New York Times,* (April 19, 1968), p. 43.

99 *Housing and Urban Development Legislation of 1968, op. cit.,* pp. 76-77.

100 Newman, *op. cit.,* p. 232.

101 *The New York Times,* (May 27, 1968).

102 *Housing and Urban Development Legislation of 1968, op. cit.,* p. 75.

103 Charles Abrams, a severe critic of the urban renewal program, regards the use of the municipality's right of eminent domain as a chief virtue of urban renewal. See Abrams, *op. cit.,* pp. 156-7.

104 For an account of the development of the Lincoln Center which also answers many frequently voiced criticisms of the project, see Percival Goodman, "Lincoln Center, Emporium Of The Arts," in Jewel Bellush and Murray Hausknecht, eds., *Urban Renewal: People, Politics, and Planning* (Garden City, N.Y.: Doubleday & Company, Inc., Anchor Books, 1967), pp. 406-12.

105 Abrams, *op. cit.,* p. 168.

106 Jeanne R. Lowe, *Cities in a Race with Time* (New York: Random House, 1967), pp. 347-51.

107 *Ibid.,* p. 406.

108 *Ibid.,* pp. 430-63.

109 Herbert J. Gans, *The Urban Villagers* (New York: The Free Press, 1962).

110 Weaver, *op. cit.,* pp. 53-56.

111 Scott Greer, *Urban Renewal and American Cities* (Indianapolis: The Bobbs-Merrill Company, 1965), p. 3.

112 Marc Fried, "Grieving for a Lost Home: Psychological Costs of Relocation," in James Q. Wilson, *ed., op. cit.,* pp. 359-79.

113 *Housing Legislation of 1966. Hearings Before a Subcommittee of the Committee on Banking and Currency, United States Senate, Eighty-Ninth Congress, Second Session On Proposed Housing Legislation For 1966, Part 1.* (Washington, D.C.: U.S. Government Printing Office, 1966), pp. 5-9.

114 *Ibid.,* pp. 72-75.

115 *Housing and Urban Development Legislation of 1968, op. cit.,* pp. 103-104, 263-71.

116 Athelstan Spilhaus, "The Experimental City," *Daedalus,* 96 (Fall, 1967), pp. 1129-41; and "The Experimental City," *Science,* 159 (February 16, 1968), pp. 710-15.

117 *Housing and Urban Development Legislation of 1968, op. cit.,* p. 7, 66-69.

118 *The Wall Street Journal,* (April 26, 1968).

119 *Housing and Urban Development Legislation of 1968, op. cit.,* pp. 8-9.

120 *The New York Times* (April 11, 1968).

121 *The New York Times* (June 18, 1968), p. 32.

122 Ramsey Clark, " 'Equal Justice To All of Its People.' " *Southwide Conference of Black Elected Officials, Dec. 11–14, 1968* (Atlanta: Southern Regional Council, Inc., 1969), p. 49. Authors' italics.

123 *Civil Liberties,* 261 (April, 1969), p. 8.

124 "Trends In Housing," XIII (January, 1969), p. 7.

125 "Trends In Housing," XII (May–July, 1968), p. 3.

CHAPTER NINE

GOVERNMENT
AND
SOCIAL PROBLEMS
IN AMERICA

The crucial role of political institutions for the management, and possibly the resolution of complex social problems has previously been considered. Legislation, the rulings of courts, and the policies of administrative agencies in implementing laws have been among the devices most frequently used by political bodies for influencing the activities of diverse social institutions. Legislation frequently authorized programs designed to assist certain social strata or economic groups, or to improve particular kinds of communal services such as sanitation, education, health, housing. In recent decades the United States Supreme Court invalidated practices by state and local governments deemed incompatible with the civil rights of citizens, especially those pertaining to the exercise of the franchise, equality of educational, economic opportunities, and protection from the arbitrary exercise of police power. The policies of various governmental agencies in implementing legislative acts and Supreme Court rulings influenced the speed with which nonconforming practices were eliminated and social change accomplished.

The activities of governmental bodies were felt by economic, familial, religious, and educational institutions and by all the social classes of American society. Governmental bureaucracies on the national and state level function with varying degrees of success to direct the activities of organizations in these institutional areas toward the closer approximation of basic goals and values. As a consequence, certain facets of political activity have increased in importance. These include political decision making, or the deliberate process of selecting both goals and means from among a number of alternatives. The final chapters will attempt to provide an understanding of some factors which have enlarged the role of the state in American society and of one type of resource, information, which has a strategic part to play in decision making.

FACTORS IN THE INCREASING IMPORTANCE OF POLITICAL INSTITUTIONS

The growth in functions, revenue and manpower of political institutions did not occur in accordance with any overall plan or from the machinations of any power group. On the contrary, this change in social structure and social relationships took place in a nation which long has believed that government performs best when restricted to housekeeping duties, *e.g.,* coinage of money, regulation of trade, defense and security, while private organizations fulfill the most important activities. The free enterprise system, free markets and corporations run by their owners with little interference from outside groups, long has been considered responsible for the achievements of America. These beliefs maintain that the competition of the marketplace, regulated only by prices and supply and demand, would tend, in the long run, to produce a level of technology and wealth beneficial to all people if government did not intrude into the economic sphere. The rapid growth of activities and the complexity of governmental organizations in a society whose dominant beliefs have been antithetical to such a development suggests that powerful social forces were responsible for the change. Among the more important are the following:

1. Rapid and far-reaching changes in science and technology necessitated federal and state regulation of improvements in transportation, communication and industrial processes. As an example, shortly after the effectiveness of the steamboat for transportation had been demonstrated, an effort was made to monopolize its use on a certain waterway.[1] Had this attempt established a precedent for the use of technology, a capitalistic economy would have been impossible. The economy would have been dominated by those few organizations which had acquired monopolistic rights to the use of these inventions. In the case mentioned above, the Supreme Court of the United States in 1824 invalidated the New York State law which granted a businessman exclusive right to use the steamboat on the Hudson River between New York City and several New Jersey cities. This ruling led to a widespread use of the steamboat and an increase in commercial activity.

With each new invention that gained widespread use, problems arose which required legislation or judicial rulings to protect the interests of various groups and of the society as a whole. The rise of the railroad, for example, led to many controversies concerning rates for freight and to charges against the railroads of discrimination against certain economic groups and regions of the nation. The magnitude of the problem led to the creation of a federal agency in 1887, the Interstate Commerce Commission, to deal with the situation. Within a few years the Commission gained the right to impose maximum rates on the railroads.

A similar process characterized the introduction of the radio in the present century. Unless some procedure was adopted for assigning broadcast frequencies to each station, radio could not be used for communication on a national scale. Congress responded initially by establishing a commission to license stations and assign broadcasting frequencies.[2]

These examples illustrate one of the processes by which growth in the complexity of the structure of government and in the number of its responsibilities and activities took place. As novel situations arose from changes in the activities of the various private organizations in society which had national ramifications, pressures built up for remedial action on the federal level in order to structure these practices within the framework of a democratic, capitalistic society. Usually, Congress acted by passing legislation establishing an agency to handle the problem or assigning a new responsibility to an existing agency. In many instances the constitutionality of the laws were tested in the courts over an extended period of time.

2. The increased use of technology by economic organizations, the merger of local into national markets as the nation expanded and the technology of transportation and communication improved, and the increasing cost of research and development were among the factors which led over the years to the rise of the corporation. The dominance of bureaucratic structures in the nation's economy also stimulated the increase in responsibilities and size of the federal government, if for no other reason than to establish conditions which protected the consumer and the smaller business organizations. Among the laws adopted by Congressional acts to preserve freedom of competition and of the market were the Sherman Anti-Trust and the Clayton Anti-Trust Acts.

3. A massive expansion of governmental responsibilities resulted from the efforts to prevent both extreme depressions and inflations, and to control the "boom and bust" cycle which plagued the capitalist economy throughout its history, culminating in the thirties in the Great Depression. During the New Deal era, legislation was enacted regulating more closely such strategic economic organizations as banks, brokerage and investment firms, and stock exchanges. The Securities Exchange Act of 1934 established a commission to regulate the securities market and hopefully to prevent the types of fraudulent transactions which led to the 1929 "Crash."[3]

To stimulate economic activity and to reduce unemployment to manageable proportions, a variety of new governmental agencies were created to perform many new functions. These included, among others, the short-lived National Industrial Recovery Administration; the Federal Housing Administration and Federal Deposit Insurance Corporation to aid housing construction and to safeguard savings deposits; the Federal Communications Commission; several agencies to assist the farmer and agriculture, namely the Federal Crop Insurance Corporation, the Rural Electrification Administration and T.V.A.; the National Relations Labor Board to adjudicate labor disputes and the Social Security Board to assist industrial workers.

This tendency to create governmental agencies to deal with novel and serious problems continued in the postwar era, with establishment of such bureaus as the Civil Rights Commission, Federal Aviation Agency, U.S. Information Agency and the National Aeronautics and Space Administration. Overall, the rapid proliferation of the agencies of the federal government can be seen from the following statistics: the number of separate departments and agencies more than doubled between 1900 and 1930, from seventeen to thirty-nine, and almost doubled again in the next three decades when the number reached a total of seventy.[4]

4. The redefinition of the concept of citizen, the broadening of the term to include civil, economic and social rights and the trends to include in this status groups previously excluded—children, the aged, the Negro and the American Indian—also increased the responsibilities of federal and state governments.[5] Government in America now has accepted the responsibility for creating and maintaining those conditions which will permit every citizen to achieve a dignified way of life and to possess relative freedom from economic insecurity and racial or religious discrimination. This principle represents the foundation of the Welfare State, a concept signifying particular kinds of responsibilities which the state owes to the citizenry. High on the list of responsibilities are those pertaining to employment and financial resources. As one author expressed it, in an affluent society with a productive economy:

> . . . An income large enough to provide the basic necessities of life in adequate measure is regarded as the right of every member of society. . . .[6]

The depression of the thirties led to the rapid growth of the Welfare State, a development which had been initiated in the early years of this century in England in the latter decades of the previous century in Germany. The growing concern of governmental leaders about the welfare of the citizenry also contributed to the proliferation of government agencies to administer the tasks assigned them by the Congress. The legislation which established the Welfare State in America were the following: Social Security Act of 1935, National Labor Relations Act of 1935, Fair Labor Standards Act of 1938, The Employment Act of 1946 and, in the sixties, the bill establishing the Medicare program and the several civil rights acts. The impact of these and related legislation on the structure of government can be seen from the fact that the cabinets created early in this century, Commerce and Labor, were concerned with economic activities. In contrast, the following three cabinet departments, created since 1953, were concerned with social welfare and communities. These included the Departments of (1) Health, Education and Welfare, (2) Housing and Urban Development and of (3) Transportation.

The great increase in number and diversity of governmental responsibilities in this century and especially since the thirties is reflected also in changes in the Executive Office of the President. Prior to 1939, this area of the federal government had no official status and consisted pri-

marily of the Chief Executive and his administrative staff. The Executive
Office received official recognition in 1939, and it has since grown from
no formal sections to eight departments. These include, among others,
the Bureau of the Budget, Council of Economic Advisors, Office of the
Science Advisor, National Aeronautics and Space Council, C.I.A., and
the National Security Council.[7]

5. The rise of America, in this century, to the position of a world
power and a major leader in international affairs also has been accompanied by a considerable expansion both of governmental responsibilities
and of commerce with foreign nations. The role of the United States in
World War II, in the establishment of NATO and the initiation of the
Marshall Plan and intervention in Korea and VietNam require no elabo-
ration. These activities have led to the allocation of more than half of the
federal budget for defense purposes. The rapidity and magnitude of the
expansion of defense activities can be seen from the fact that in 1930
defense received roughly 25 percent of the federal budget.[8]

The international activities of the nation, both militarily and economically, are reflected in a number of agencies and departments created
since the thirties. These include, among others, the Department of
Defense, created by the merger of the three military services, and the
establishment of the Joint Chiefs of Staff. In addition, the C.I.A.,
N.A.S.A. and the National Security Council are agencies within the
Executive Office of the President. Economic responsibilities in the international arena are reflected in the existence of the Agency for International Development, Export-Import Bank and the World Bank.

The growing complexity of government on the federal and state level
does not represent a unique phenomenon in American society. It is
consistent with a broader trend, that of bureaucratization or the rise of
an "administered society."[9] The bureaucratic form of organization pre-
vails on all levels of society, from the local to the international, and in
most institutions. Government, the corporation, the union and the university are among the more important bureaucracies in America. The
spread of bureaucracy has been referred to as the "managerial revolution"[10] and the "organizational revolution."[11] Regardless of terminology,
this trend has caused concern among social scientists for the future of
democracy and the integrity of the individual.[12]

THE CHANGING SCOPE OF GOVERNMENT
IN AMERICA

This section concentrates on changes in governmental functions
quantitatively, providing a statistical view of such changes in functions,

finances and employment.[13] The increased activity of government in America is suggested by various statistics. Between 1790 and 1960, a period extending from the founding of the nation to the nuclear age, the number of functions performed by the federal government, some of which also are carried out by state and municipal governments, increased 200 percent, from 37 to 112. While the percentage increase was greatest at the national level, the gain did not seem to be at the expense of lower levels of government, for the number of functions performed by these units likewise increased. In 1790, less than three-fourths of the 37 functions and in 1960, all of the 112 activities were enacted by the federal government. During the same period, the proportion of functions performed by the remaining two units of government increased from 30 to 84 percent.[14]

As the number of functions performed by the federal government increased, the size of its labor force also grew. In 1821 the federal government employed less than 7,000 civilians or 0.2 percent of the nation's work force.[15] In 1950, the number had grown to more than 2 million, or 3.2 percent of the civilian labor force,[16] and it went to 2,705,000 or 3.6 percent of the civilian labor force in 1967.[17]

The increase in the federal government's share of the nation's tax revenue kept pace with the growth of responsibilities and personnel. In 1902, the taxes collected by the federal government made up a little more than a third of the total, 37 percent, with local government receiving 52 percent. By 1957, the latter's share had declined drastically to 14 percent while that of the federal government had climbed to 71 percent. The share raised by state government remained fairly constant at about 15 percent.[18] The growth of federal revenue also is reflected in the increase in the proportion of the Gross National Product allocated to the federal government. During the ninety years from 1870 to 1960, federal expenditures (in actual dollars) increased from slightly less than 6 percent of the Gross National Product to more than 15 percent. The magnitude of this change can be seen from the fact that the Gross National Product rose from $6,710 million in 1870 to $504,400 million in 1960.[19]

The size of the federal debt also has grown rapidly in this century. In 1900 the federal debt was 1.263 billion dollars, or $17 per person. By 1967 the debt exceeded 326 billion dollars or $1,638 per person.[20]

The outlay of federal funds has increased in recent decades. Between 1940, the year before the United States entered World War II, and 1969, expenditures increased from slightly more than 9 billion to an estimated 147 billion dollars, a fifteen fold increase in less than thirty years.[21] America's growing involvement in international and military affairs accounts for a considerable share of this increase. Allocations for national security required roughly 16 percent of the federal budget in 1940 and more than 62 percent in 1957.[22] The federal outlay for national defense in 1969 was estimated at 43 percent of total expenditures, with an additional 14 percent allocated for the war in Viet Nam.[23]

Consideration of selected federal programs indicates some of the sectors of American society for which the national government has accepted a large share of responsibility. Maintaining and improving the health of all Americans have been the objectives of several measures. These involve payments to individuals for the purchase of health services and payments to health institutions such as hospitals and medical schools. Between 1965 and 1966, federal expenditures for health rose from $5.1 billion to 7.3 billion dollars, an increase of 43 percent, due to the introduction of the Medicare program.[24] The federal government's proportion of national health expenditures increased from 12 percent in 1960 to 16 percent in 1966.[25] Passage of the Medicare bill in 1965 accounts for much of this increase.[26]

The federal government also increased its assistance in recent years to educational institutions. The federal government currently finances a variety of educational programs. A partial list includes the following: school lunches; programs to improve the teaching of science, mathematics and foreign languages; loan funds for construction of school buildings and dormitories; a matching grant program for medical and dental school buildings; vocational rehabilitation; funds for library materials and for instructional equipment, including television; financial aid to public schools in impoverished communities and many others. Federal expenditures for education increased from less than 2.3 billion dollars in 1964 to about 4.5 billion in the 1968 fiscal year.[27] The federal government provided about one-fifth of all the funds spent for higher education in 1968 and the proportion may rise to one-third as early as 1970.[28]

Federal aid accomplishes more than maintaining and improving the effectiveness of educational institutions. Part of the effort seeks to raise schools with poor performance records to a level more comparable to a "national average or standard." In this way the right of all children to obtain a quality education will be realized. Desegregation of public schools throughout the nation, to the extent that it succeeds, should have a similar effect.

The various housing objectives and programs of the federal government have been discussed elsewhere. The federal government has spent less for housing than for health and education, although the increase in recent years has been considerable. In 1967, the federal government spent 577 million dollars for housing and community development, but the estimated outlay for 1969 is more than 1.4 billion dollars.[29]

The dependence of the economy, public schools and colleges, state and local public assistance programs, the housing industry and urban redevelopment programs on federal assistance suggest the extent to which legislation and judicial rulings have become agents of change in American society. How the leaders of the several branches of the federal government respond to the symptoms of social disorder has a large bearing on how severe the problems will become and the extent to which social structure will approximate America's ideals.

IDEOLOGY AND THE CHANGING FUNCTIONS OF GOVERNMENT

During much of the nineteenth and part of the twentieth centuries, an intense controversy on the respective roles of public and private organizations accompanied changes in the functions of political institutions. With the expansion of governmental responsibilities since the New Deal and the more recent efforts in behalf of minority groups, it might appear that the controversy on the role of government finally had ended. While only a few extremist groups currently oppose the right of political bodies to intervene in economic matters and to protect and aid disadvantaged groups, controversy has not abated. However, the major themes and issues have changed. This can be attributed, in part, to the accumulation of knowledge on the types of problems which have and which have not yielded to governmental action. These experiences have led even the most sincere advocates of an enlarged governmental role to re-examine their original positions.

Some of the major doctrines concerning the role of political organizations as instruments for social change and for achieving the dominant values of American society must be considered. The doctrines can be classified into two categories, those expressing a pessimistic view and those expressing an optimistic view of the ability of governmental agencies to fulfill these ends. One who holds the pessimistic view would generally favor:

1. Orthodox laissez faire ideas on government, economic organizations and social stratification. This doctrine views the free enterprise economy as the major institution of a capitalistic society.

2. A theory of the bureaucratization of society which pays little attention to the public—private dichotomy emphasized by laissez faire doctrine.
3. An elitist view of national leadership which contends that a cohesive group of powerful men operate economic and political organizations to advance their selfish interests.

In contrast, a person who holds the optimistic view would favor:

1. The pluralist explanation of national power and of governmental operations which considers political processes to be responsive to a wide variety of interest groups.
2. The theory of the rational control of social and political processes which regards information as the strategic factor in achieving a richer life for *all* members of society.

The second view will be considered more fully in chapter 10.

That these theories differ on a number of important matters can readily be seen. While the first strongly disapproves of the involvement of political institutions in the economic arena and the remainder do not, the second and third theories express grave doubts on the long-term consequences for society of the rise of complex organizations, but for different reasons. The final two theories adopt a more positive position in appraising the activities of bureaucracies due, in part, to the operation of factors which are thought capable of guiding the activities of this type of social structure. Each of the five viewpoints recognizes the growing influence of rationalism and science in the affairs of men and of their organizations.

The Doctrine of Laissez Faire and Its Opponents

The doctrines discussed in this section have profoundly influenced the decisions and actions of leaders in powerful organizations. These sets of beliefs exercised considerable influence on the management of social problems and on the role of various organizations in seeking to achieve and prevent certain kinds of social change. These doctrines interpret the social world, specify the principal goals to be achieved by social activity, and dictate the actions to be avoided and those which are permissible. They relate the history of the society to the present and to the future, and spell out man's role in making the history of his nation.

Decision makers, the men faced with the necessity of choosing the policies to be enacted by an organization, are guided in their deliberations by the beliefs to which they subscribe. Measures disapproved of by men advocating laissez faire may be embraced by those subscribing to the principles of the welfare state. Situations regarded as reprehensible in the light of one belief system may be extolled by another.

Our brief history of social thought in America suggests that laissez faire doctrine interfered with and prevented effective problem management in an industrial nation—the stabilizing of the economy, reduction of unemployment and poverty, and improvement of the health and welfare of the population. Advocates of laissez faire could not enact Social Security and Medicare, to cite but a few significant pieces of social welfare legislation. In a similar vein, current controversies over the proper activities of public and private organizations may lead to the development of doctrines which can facilitate the solution of such urgent difficulties as racial tensions and conflict, division between city and suburb, persistence of organized crime and the rising incidence of certain types of illness. The following review of several important schools of thought seeks to illuminate a vital dimension of problem management.[30]

The theory of laissez faire dominated social thought in America for fifty years, from the eighteen-eighties to 1929.[31] Herbert Spencer, an English social scientist, contributed several essential components of this theory, especially the transposition of the Darwinian theory of competition and natural selection to competition in society. Spencer's belief in progress and evolution was a logical outgrowth of the view that men competing freely in the marketplace for economic goals inevitably would enrich society and civilization. William Graham Sumner, sociologist, borrowed heavily from Spencer in developing and defending laissez faire doctrine in America.

Concerned largely with relationships between government and the economy, the doctrine of laissez faire held that the competition of business organizations, guided only by self-interest and the price system, would create conditions of benefit to all members of society, rich and poor, strong and weak. The initiative, energy and imagination of entrepreneurs, stimulated by the competition of the market place and the opportunity to amass great wealth, would yield an ever more productive economy and a higher level of living. The role of government in a free enterprise system was secondary to that of economic organizations—a few housekeeping duties and the control of criminals. Since the economy needed little or no direction from governmental leaders, involvement in economic affairs was thought to produce harmful results. Indeed, proponents of laissez faire viewed the growth of the welfare state as the result of "interference" and "meddling" by government bureaucrats in affairs that were not their concern and not sincere efforts to control the sources of economic instability.[32]

To advocates of laissez faire, the inequalities and deprivations resulting from competition in the market place resulted inevitably from differences in the innate abilities of people. Since economic and social success was attributed to superior abilities, any program to modify the usual activities of economic and political organizations were unnecessary. Such efforts would do irreparable harm to the system of free competition and private property. Attempts by government agencies to guide the processes of social change would disrupt if not wreck the institutions responsible for the prosperity and wealth of the nation. To Sumner, government did not even have the authority to provide such essential services as municipal sanitation and public education. It had no justification for regulating the employment of children in factories.[33] The rights of property and the freedom of competition in a market lacking laws protecting the weak and controlled by the strongest economic organizations were essential ingredients of the "good society." Sumner's views on the role of government in society were summarized when he wrote:

> . . . If we do not like the survival of the fittest we have only one possible alternative, and that is the survival of the unfittest. The former is the law of civilization; the latter is the law of anti-civilization.[34]

This position left no room for social planning, or for public agencies to use knowledge and information to guide the development of communities, institutions and society as a whole. By implication corporations were the major beneficiaries of science and technology.

In the eighteen-eighties, when Sumner and other advocates of laissez faire were dominant in America, another sociologist, Lester F. Ward, advocated a far less popular view, but one whose influence has grown with the passage of time. Ward recognized and attacked the weaknesses of Sumner's analysis of society. He recognized that man and his institutions were not passive products of competition but had transformed the conditions in which economic transactions took place. Sumner's distinction between regulated and unregulated economic activity had little basis in fact. If such inventions as the steam engine, telegraph, electricity could transform the economy, then surely knowledge of social processes could be deliberately and consciously used to alter social structures for the benefit of all citizens.[35]

Ward attacked laissez faire where it was most vulnerable by demonstrating that the theory did not accurately describe the structure of the American economy. Ward showed that free competition had been destroyed by the rise of such giant corporations as Standard Oil and United States Steel, which used monopolistic power to dominate competitors and eliminate business rivals. Ward also recognized that the conceptions of law concerning property, contract and due process which prevailed in his day facilitated the growth of monopoly and the elemination of free competition. These developments were not the result of an "unregulated" economy but of man-made laws and interpretations of laws.

Changes in legal concepts and improvements in theories of social institutions and of social change could provide the basis for improving the organization of American society. Ward advocated public education, believing children from the slums, given the opportunity, could develop their talents. He also advocated social planning and the use of knowledge for the benefit of all citizens. To accomplish these ends, Ward had no hesitancy in urging the exercise of governmental power through the medium of legislation. These views, according to Commager, made Ward:

> . . . the prophet of the New Freedom and the New Deal, of all those movements looking to that reconstruction of society and economy through government intervention which is the most striking development in the political history of the last half-century in America. . . .[36]

Additional intellectual underpinnings of the welfare state were initiated by the writings of Oliver Wendell Holmes on the law and of John Dewey on education. While Ward recognized the necessity and desirability of using law and legislation as instruments for influencing social activities and social relationships, it remained for Holmes, a justice of the nation's highest court for thirty years, to formulate the principles justifying this interpretation of legal institutions. Holmes accomplished this feat by departing from many of his colleagues in the legal profession in interpreting the common law, the role of the Supreme Court and the powers of the Congress.

Holmes rejected a view of law which confined present formulations to a legal framework established by tradition and orthodoxy. Holmes refused to allow contemporary laws to be confined by the straitjacket of legal categories which had been handed down from past generations. Consistency of a law with formal legal categories and respected precedents no longer was a suitable criterion of adequacy. To Holmes, laws were made by jurists confronted with specific social situations and problems. Laws were devised and revised to cope with these exigencies in order to produce certain results and not to produce consistency with abstract legal categories. Holmes believed that law was a response to "felt necessities," and the power of the state often had to be used in a pragmatic fashion to assist society in reducing tension and conflict, and to further the welfare of the people. In the final analysis, Holmes recognized that combatting the many problems spawned by industrialization and urbanization demanded innovation and experimentation in legislation. These problems could not be met by adherence to views of the legal process which were prevalent when America and England were agrarian societies.[37]

Holmes adopted a similar position on the issue of judicial review of the constitutionality of legislation. It was grossly inadequate and inappropriate to judge the constitutionality of a law by the criterion of consistency of the latter with the former. On this subject he wrote:

> . . . the provisions of the Constitution are not mathematical formulas having their essence in their form; they are organic living institutions transplanted from English soil. Their significance is vital not formal; it is to be gathered not simply by taking the words and a dictionary, but by considering their origin and the line of their growth.[38]

The circumstances attending the writing of a law or provision of the Constitution and the manner of its development over a period of time, as well as its influence on various organizations and segments of the population, had to be included in evaluating its merits and demerits. For these reasons, Holmes frequently disagreed with those colleagues on the Court who refused to recognize the right of Congress to regulate the employment of children, to permit workingmen to join unions, and to enact laws on workmen compensation, among others. Holmes considered the Constitution an instrument for ordering society, resolving conflicts of interests and for achieving social progress. Interference with such efforts for reasons of formal legalism were misguided.[39]

John Dewey devoted considerable energy to a matter which concerned Lester Ward, the use of science and knowledge in social affairs. For Dewey, education was the central process. Through the proper activities of the schools, persons received the knowledge and training required for guiding social processes. He rejected the idea accepted by many adherents of laissez faire ideology that education should assist individuals to adapt to their surroundings. Dewey saw education as an instrument for assisting men to change the social order, to improve society and to enrich human capacities. Social problems were not regarded as insoluble, but remedial through systematic analysis and determined attempts at reform. In this manner a variety of social injustices and war as an instrument of international relations could be controlled.[40]

While laissez faire dominated the thinking of American leaders, it was impossible for government agencies to respond constructively to the many instabilities produced by an economy dominated by corporate giants that were a law unto themselves. Even minimal restrictions on the activities of business firms were attacked as an infringement on the rights of property owners, destined to destroy the free enterprise system. The rise of the welfare state, however, did not establish utopia. Expanding the power of political institutions to check the power of corporations generated some new and unforeseen difficulties. These pertained in part to the prevalence of bureaucracy in society.

Bureaucracy and Social Change

Ward, Holmes, Dewey and other scholars who believed in the benefits which society and mankind could obtain from the rational and intelligent use of knowledge generally expressed their viewpoint in a tone of optimism and faith in the future. Their theories on law, education and planning, along with the belief in Keynesian economic theory, provided the basis for much of the legislation enacted during the New Deal and the Fair Deal. These acts started the welfare state in America and controlled the previously uncontrollable economic cycle of "boom and bust." This achievement alone might appear to justify a faith in the continued "progress" and "advancement" of western civilization. However, these opponents of laissez faire paid relatively little attention to one of the revolutionary changes in industrial societies, the rise of the bureaucratic organization. Two German scholars, Max Weber and Robert Michels, who were active during the first decades of this century, recognized the close connection between the rise of bureaucracy and the growing influence of rationality and science in social affairs. Unlike their American colleagues, these social scientists were led by their investigations to adopt a pessimistic view of the future of democracy and of mankind. This conclusion derived not from doubts concerning the value of science, but from the changes in the distribution of power resulting from the growth of large and complex forms of social organization in many areas of society. It was feared that managers of bureaucracies would use science and other valued resources to attain ends which, while personally advantageous, might be detrimental to many other groups and organizations. Weber and Michels feared that the administrators of bureaucracies would not be sensitive to and in agreement with constituents seeking to "improve" some aspect of society. They raised the crucial question of how bureaucracies could be made responsive to diverse interest groups and not become the tools of any particular elite.[41]

Robert Michels argued that complex organizations have strong conservative tendencies which take hold even in groups dedicated to far reaching changes in society such as the units he studied—socialist political parties.[42] With the passage of time, these organizations undergo a transformation of objectives, from changing society to self-maintenance. This modification of goals is associated with another trend, the growing insensitivity of the organization's leaders to both the original ideals of the party and the interests of the rank-and-file. The organization comes to serve the interests of the officers in solidifying the economic and power gains which occupancy of executive positions conferred on them. Control of the bureaucracy enabled many party leaders to move from a lower to a higher class. Michels discusses in detail the various factors which enable the organization's leaders to ignore the desires and wishes of the membership. Superior know-how in managing the affairs of a complex organization, the dependency of members on the expertise of the officers, the skill of the latter in controlling communication channels and the information distributed to the membership, in buying off the leaders of opposition groups, contribute to the permanent entrenchment of *officialdom*. These factors also heighten the insensitivity of the officers to the original ideals and purposes of the organization. Michels, however, did not despair completely. Through education, members can acquire the skills and know-how needed to circumvent the inertia of the leadership and reconvert the organization into an instrument of social change.

An Elitist View of Politics

In the fifties, when the existence in America of a welfare state was assured, a sociologist, C. Wright Mills, put forth a pessimistic assessment of political happenings.[43] While Mills' theory on national power resembled those of Weber and Michels, it also differed from their views in certain important respects. For the latter, the power of top bureaucratic officials derived primarily from the positions which they occupied and from the character of the organization, especially those features which enabled officials to impose their goals on the organization. For Mills, who recognized and examined the influence of these top offices which he termed the "command posts," a major source of strength derived from membership of officials in a particular social class, an elite stratum. Membership in this class and participation in its organizations provided the basis for consensus on goals and similarity in outlook of those who held the strategic positions in bureaucracies. For Mills, complex organizations were made to serve the goals of this elite class, while for Weber and Michels the organizations functioned to benefit the top ranks of officialdom. For both schools of thought, a relatively small number of persons exercised very great power in society, ignoring the needs and desires of the masses and subverting democratic institutions.

Mills contended that the American government was controlled by a coalition of elites who had become increasingly insensitive to the needs and interests of groups other than those of their colleagues and associates. These men and women, according to C. Wright Mills, shared common social origins in the upper class, attended similar schools and universities, and occupied key positions in corporations, in top law firms, in the armed forces and in the national government. Members of these elite groups lived in the major metropolitan centers, were connected to one another by intermarriage, service on the boards of major corporations, membership in exclusive social clubs, and by vacationing at selected resort areas around the world. Sharing similar class origins, educational backgrounds and involvement in tight-knit circles of informal relations generated consensus on basic issues. Leaders of those elite groups translated viewpoints into policies and into specific actions to be carried out by various branches of the federal government.

According to Mills, the responsiveness of the national government to diverse interest groups and classes which was manifested in New Deal legislation came to an end when World War II began. Elite groups in the upper class came to dominate government in Washington while other groups and organizations lost influence. These included municipal leaders and the leadership of the national political parties, Congress, and thousands of voluntary associations. The rise of the power elite to national ascendancy undermined democratic institutions and transformed America into a mass society.[44]

Mills did not test his theoretical framework by analyzing specific governmental decisions or particular legislation to determine if "the power elite" had prevailed over the leaders and representatives of diverse interest groups. Mills' view of the power elite, which remains to be verified, contradicts the basic trends in problem management previously outlined.

Neither school of thought, concerned with bureaucracy and the elitist viewpoint, emphasized the distinction between the public and private spheres. For one school, the managers of bureaucracies dominated both political and economic affairs, while for Mills, the elites who ran government also established policies for economic affairs and other important activities. To these scholars, the faith of Ward, Holmes, and Dewey in the benefits which would accrue from social planning on a broad scale had little justification. Intellectuals and experts had been subordinated by the power group, elitist or bureaucratic, and were compelled to serve its ends.

The Pluralist View of National Power

Some scholars take issue with advocates of the elitist viewpoint, whether of governmental or bureaucratic elites. These scholars maintain that power and government in America remains pluralistic, or diffused among many different groups and organizations, with no single or coalition of elite groups capable of dominating all or most areas of social activity.[45]

Pluralistic features of the structure of national power exercise considerable influence on the distribution of wealth, privilege and prestige in a society's stratification system. This position has been expounded by Gerhard Lenski in a theoretical and empirical examination of the distribution system of many societies, ranging from those with a primitive to those with a highly industrialized economy.[46] Lenski's inquiry starts with the proposition that the degree of inequality in a society varies directly with the amount of goods and commodities available in excess of the survival needs of members. Lenski soon discovers that this proposition does not reflect the situation in industrialized societies. The latter tend to have less inequality than agricultural societies which generally have a far smaller surplus.

Lenski's explanation of the lesser degree of inequality in industrial than agrarian societies emphasizes institutional features which increase the political power of the lower classes. These are "constitutionalism" and citizenship. The first refers to the legitimacy of procedures permitting all adult members of society to participate in political affairs—the franchise, joining political parties and interest groups, the right to demonstrate and to lobby for specific legislation. These resources permit the many citizens in the lower classes to outvote the wealthy few and to concentrate a great amount of political influence on decision makers.[47]

Pluralistic features of democratic government include the rights of private associations and their access to major centers of power, along with the rights of citizen participation in politcal affairs. Private associations refer to organizations with limited purposes, whose membership is voluntary, and who regulate their internal affairs and lay down criteria of membership. They include such disparate organizations as trade associations, labor unions, service clubs, churches, philanthropies, historical and conservation groups.[48] Apart from pursuing their primary aims, private associations perform at least two important political functions. First, these groups protect members from arbitrary governmental actions, *e.g.*, efforts by government to limit the right to join associations or to deny a professional group the right to establish certification procedures. Associations, therefore, serve to contain the power of government and to protect the rights of members. Second, these groups represent members on political matters affecting their interests. Association leaders endeavor to influence governmental decisions by presenting the group's viewpoint and lobbying in various ways. Hence pluralist theory argues that such groups have direct access to the major centers of governmental power. Furthermore, the process of political decision making requires processes of bargaining and negotiation to arrive at an agreement which all concerned groups can accept.[49] Decisions reached in this manner are thought to more closely approximate the public interest than those made by a few elites.

From the standpoint of leadership, the pluralist view contends that no one or a few elite groups decide all or even most basic issues. The leaders represent a variety of classes and interest groups, and the composition of leaders engaged in decision making is not stable for all issues but varies from one to the other. Leadership on the national and even on the community level is specialized by area or type of problem. Groups which may be powerful in affecting economic policy may have little influence on matters concerning health, housing, welfare or national security. Within each area, leaders can also be differentiated by the amount of influence exercised at particular times. A leader may have greater weight on some issues in an area than on others. These variations in background of leaders, the institutional areas within which influence is exercised and in degree of influence help to increase the sensitivity of government to voters and to all organized groups which seek objectives in the political arena.[50]

LEADERSHIP THEORIES AND PROBLEM MANAGEMENT

The frequency, extensiveness and manner by which social change occurs differs for the theory of the ruling elite and that of pluralism. Innovations in government programs and improvements in the condition of various social classes occur when the dominant elites approve of the change. These groups have power sufficient to prevent either enactment or effective implementation of any program which they oppose. Adoption of programs beneficial to the lower classes generally occur when elite groups recognize such changes as favorable to their interests. In other instances, the ruling elites may derive the major benefits from these programs while other segments of the citizenry receive a few sops. By implication, the theory maintains that legitimate instruments for accomplishing social change, the entire governmental apparatus, are controlled by the ruling groups. The lower classes are compelled to go outside the system to accomplish their ends. Needless to say, the elite groups can ignore, where they so desire, the major tools of social reform espoused by Ward, Dewey, Holmes and others. Planners and social and natural scientists also are subordinated to the ruling groups.

The pluralist view contends that centers of power are highly sensitive to pressures emanating from organized groups. The type and amount of benefits which government distributes to these groups depends on the degree of political strength each has demonstrated relative to rival groups. Benefits of governmental action tend to be more widely distributed when a diversity of groups endeavor to influence the decision-making process. Each participating group is likely to receive some benefits. Groups which consistently do not or are unable to participate in the struggle over the allocation of services often will pay a disproportionately large share of the taxes for the few benefits received. A weak group or social class can be as miserable in a society with a pluralist as in one with an elitist power structure. However, the pluralist view offers the lower classes an obvious strategy for accomplishing change. Progress can be made through organizing groups to present the views of the class or minority group to decision makers, and to reward officials who help and to sanction those who do not.

From the standpoint of implementing long-range plans for social change, even those developed by social scientists, the elitist structure may offer more hope where these plans are thought to produce ends consistent with the material interests of the leaders. Elite groups often can overcome opposition through coercive means. Examples can be cited of programs of radical social change enacted in totalitarian countries, such as the collectivization of agriculture in the Soviet Union in the thirties, which could not be adopted in a pluralist system. Opposition groups would have to be assuaged through concessions of considerable magnitude. To obtain a workable program, officials may have to settle for a level of services which falls short of the models developed by planners. This strategy of compromise and arbitration should benefit a broader segment of the population than that possible through an elitist structure. However, resistance of groups to legislative programs retards the rate of change, which is more likely to be slow or incremental, and progress resulting from the legislation may be offset by changes produced by other parts of society. In Chapter 2 an example was considered in the argument that improving the economic condition of the ghetto would encourage in-migration of the poor, and thereby intensify problems of poverty.

Both the strengths and weaknesses of pluralist political structure for managing social problems are evident in social legislation which has tended to benefit the majority of citizens. On this point, a former planner and political scientist, presently a college president, said:

> . . . I believe the tendency to favor the center majorities is inherent in the political power structure of contemporary United States and in our definitions of the national interest. . . .[51]

The superior resources and votes of "center groups" are reflected in many of the housing programs discussed in the previous chapter, especially those favoring home ownership for families with modest incomes. Mortgage regulations, particularly those providing for lower down payments on new than on older dwelling units, contributed substantially to the rapid growth of suburbs in the postwar era.[52] Transportation policies hastened the development of the suburbs by providing residents with easy and relatively inexpensive access to places of employment in the central business district. The federal highway program subsidized construction of freeways while rapid transit facilities for lower income workers were neglected. Some of the consequences of this imbalance in transportation policies are presented in a recent study of transportation in New York City. In some boroughs, trips from the ghetto to industrial areas are often more time consuming and expensive than trips to outlying residential neighborhoods. For example:

> From the poverty areas of central Brooklyn, it is easier and faster to get to parts of the Bronx (15 miles away) than to nearby industrial areas only four miles away. . . .[53]

The public housing program provided new dwelling units far below the amount needed, and of a style which few people preferred. The public assistance program reached only a minority of the families in financial need and the benefits generally have not sufficed to lift the recipients out of poverty.

A number of other government programs provide support for the elitist theory of power in America. On occasion, powerful groups have been able to modify programs and influence the activities of government agencies to better serve their narrow interests. In some instances, however, the groups which succeeded in these endeavors were not those specified by Mills or by Michels—the top leaders of corporate, military or governmental bureaucracies. The examples concern the general tendency of bureaucratic structures to work out an accommodation with influential interests in their immediate environment. Philip Selznick described this situation in his classic study of the Tennessee Valley Authority:

> . . . power in a community is distributed among those who can mobilize resources—organizational, psychological, and economic—and these can effectively shape the character and role of governmental instrumentalities. This has a dual significance. It may result in the perversion of policy determined through representative institutions; and at the same time, this fact offers a tool for ensuring the responsibility of public agencies to their client publics. . . .[54]

The manner in which T.V.A. was created generated many difficulties for its officials. The Authority was the creation of the federal government and not a response to the requests of local citizenry and local groups. To accomplish its primary mission, planning the use and conservation of the region's resources, the T.V.A. depended on the cooperation of important local agencies. Officials developed a "working philosophy," called the grass-roots doctrine, which required agency personnel to seek out the support and participation of local organizations.[55] In exchange for the assistance of the land grant colleges, county agricultural agents and county social associations, T.V.A. executives adopted policies favored by these groups. The Authority assisted the prosperous farmers and neglected the poor, the black farmers and the black colleges.[56]

The farm subsidy program, designed to stabilize the prices of agricultural commodities and conserve the purchasing power of farmers, provides some surprisingly large benefits to a few corporations. In 1967, agricultural subsidies, four billion dollars, were twice the amount spent for the poverty program. Some of the payouts included the following:

> . . . the Hawaiian Commercial and Sugar Corporation received $1,300,000, U.S. Sugar, $1,200,000 and three California operators took in a total of $8,100,000. . . .[57]

These facts support Selznick's contention that government programs tend to aid those groups which have mobilized resources for action. Since the lower class has limited resources and cannot easily be organized for collective action, many of the needs of members are overlooked or met inadequately. The solution, according to the pluralist theory and to Selznick's statement, lies in greater efforts at mobilization and in developing workable strategies for political action.

STRATEGIES FOR POLITICALLY WEAK GROUPS

Groups lacking in resources and political know-how have several strategies for improving their socioeconomic position. One requires fewer resources than needed for a major assault on the Congress. It calls for selecting a branch of government, on any level, which has within its power the ability to accomplish important social changes, and which is influenced not so much by the resources of an interest group but to other less material considerations. The judicial system which exemplifies this type of governmental unity decides cases of considerable importance to interest groups and their constituents on the basis of the persuasiveness and legal correctness of arguments. For more than half a century, the National Association for the Advancement of Colored People has petitioned the courts for equity against statutes which discriminated against black people. Over the years, the NAACP has been able to invalidate many of the statutes which supported the caste system of race relations.[58]

A second approach, which many minority groups have employed, requires formation of a social movement based on the energies of members and tangible support from higher classes. For almost fifteen years the Civil Rights Movement has been a significant political force in America with its major strength in a handful of voluntary associations, such as the Southern Christian Leadership Conference, Congress of Racial Equality, the Urban League, and the Student Nonviolent Coordinating Committee, among others. Demonstrations of the strength of the movement are an important political weapon. Hence the Civil Rights Movement sponsored the freedom rides in 1961, the March on Washington in 1963, the march from Selma to Montgomery, Alabama in 1965 and the Poor Peoples March in 1968. These demonstrations of feeling and commitment, coupled with the reaction of opposing groups, contributed materially to the enactment of civil rights legislation.[59] Unlike the strategy employed by the NAACP, the Civil Rights Movement has focused on a variety of targets, both on the local and the national levels, including private employers, municipal governments, school boards, the White House and the Congress. Many of the demonstrations and protests organized by the movement have sought to create an awareness among the public of the nature of the discrimination to which black Americans customarily have been subjected, and to gain widespread publicity in the mass media and sympathy for their aims.

A third course of action consists of efforts of the lower classes to form coalitions with groups higher in the class system. The superior resources possessed by these groups combined with the numbers of the poor and of certain minority groups could favorably influence legislation and the activities of powerful organizations. One example of such a coalition, even if somewhat formless and based more on common aims than on a central organization, launched a program in 1961 which later became an important feature of two legislative acts. The program had a dual origin in the Ford Foundation and The President's Committee on Juvenile Delinquency. Both agencies sought to control and minimize juvenile delinquency by improving the educational and neighborhood environment in which these youngsters lived. Among the strategies for change utilized by the reformers was a technique which subsequently became known as *community action*, participation in developing and planning of the program by the persons to be helped.[60] In this instance, a wealthy private organization and the executive branch of government took positive action to benefit members of a lower class. This experiment was embodied in legislation to combat poverty and given the name of community action.

The strategy of community action exemplifies the decentralization of power from government to organized groups of citizens, in this instance representing lower and working class people. The legislative program thereby strengthens the political resources of otherwise weak groups. The neighborhood inhabited by poor people plays an active role in efforts to improve the local environment. The board representing the poverty areas often has some powers over budgets and planning, and in some cases plays a role in allocating funds for education.[61]

The poverty program in New York City has a city-wide, elected board, the Council Against Poverty, which operates outside the formal structure of government. The largest bloc on the Council consists of persons elected by the poor from all parts of the city. The Council, which has considerable control over funds, is a major decision-making body and it

> . . . decides priorities and allocates funds to activities such as the organization of parents around the school-decentralization issue and the forming of consumer coops and credit unions. It also finances programs by which tenants are informed of their rights against land-lords and of how to demand code enforcement from city agencies. . . .[62]

Most of the poverty boards have found favor with city officials. This is indicated by the fact that in 1968

. . . 883 of 913 reporting local governments elected to continue the existing Community Action agencies.[63]

The principle of community action also was embodied in the model cities legislation enacted in 1966. Residents of the areas to be redeveloped are required, if the municipality is to receive federal funds, to be represented by a board which participates in the planning of local improvements. In some cities, these boards have funds sufficient to employ a technical staff including such specialists as city planners and architects. These experts assist the board to critically evaluate the program and to recommend changes to municipal officials. Occasionally, members of the technical staff become ardent spokesmen for the interests of the residents of the poverty area.[64]

Establishing boards of local citizens from a poverty area or black neighborhood does not automatically guarantee a better program. In some cases the boards may "rubber-stamp" the plans of city officials and agency executives. Lack of education and experience may compel many board members to rely heavily on the advice of technical experts. The normal demands of earning a living and managing a household may leave board members with too little time for comprehending the complex problems of area redevelopment. An agency that appears to symbolize the decentralization of power, in actuality, may conceal the real locus of power, either in city hall, the technical advisors or both. Nevertheless, as Glazer points out:

. . . The agencies have provided a training ground for large numbers of local black community leaders . . . many of whom are now on the first rungs of careers in electoral politics, and look forward to participating in the system as democratically elected representatives of citizens, rather than tearing it down.[65]

DECENTRALIZATION OF AUTHORITY

Advocates of decentralization generally argue that planners and officials in Washington cannot acquire the knowledge of local affairs necessary for developing effective and acceptable policies. Compelled to supervise programs throughout a region and the nation, government officials endeavor to apply general guidelines to a wide variety of local conditions. Too often the results are the opposite of those intended. The solution, they believe, lies in a greater involvement of local organizations, both private and public. Adherents of these organizations have been heard in Washington. A number of government programs require considerable participation by business firms. These include the "turnkey" program for public housing and the partnership between the government and corporations in manpower retraining.

An important decentralization proposal concerns the sharing of federal revenue with state and local municipalities. This plan would modify the trend cited earlier in the chapter of the increasing proportion of total tax revenues which the federal government has acquired since the thirties. Tax sharing would increase the fiscal resources of local units of government and provide options for action not currently available. Since the states would gain greater decision making powers, more pressure would be exerted on state leaders to cope with local problems. Whatever the merits of this plan, the question has been raised, bearing on the elitist-pluralist controversy, of whether state funds would be allocated to the most serious problem areas or to those constituents that control the legislature. Some city officials have expressed concern that federal revenues turned back to the states would be allocated mainly to rural and suburban communities which dominate many state legislatures. The cities would continue to suffer from a dearth of fiscal resources. Rather than see this happen, many city officials would prefer to take their chances with Washington, perhaps from a conviction that urban forces carry more weight on the federal than on the state level.[66]

Thirty years of experience with the welfare state has raised more questions on effective forms of political and economic organization than existed in the twenties. A ferment of ideas and proposals on social change are discussed in academia and in the executive offices of government and of business.

PLANS FOR DECENTRALIZATION OF AUTHORITY

Robert Levine sees the basic difficulty in federal administration of programs for social change in the shortage of capable executives, due primarily to the rapid growth of these responsibilities.[67] He advocates a method of implementing activities which does not seem to markedly increase the need for executives. He terms this strategy the "less administrative approach." More specifically, Levine favors adoption of those programs which rely on existing organizations and institutions for attainment of objectives, rather than those requiring creation of new government agencies. Government officials should determine the objectives, while implementation should be delegated to organizations in the local community. This approach is exemplified in federal subsidies to businesses which locate plants in the ghetto and to the income maintenance program of family allowances or of the guaranteed annual income. These and similar programs have a far better chance of succeeding, according to Levine, for implementation is in the hands of men who are familiar with local conditions. Government officials in Washington cannot cope with the multiplicity of varied situations which exist throughout the nation.[68]

Another set of critics of the federal government would take issue with Levine's recommendations. Cloward and Piven, in an article concerned mainly with improving conditions of urban Negroes, consider the Levine strategy an example of "centrally programmed decentralization," which would weaken municipal government.[69] Since Negroes soon will comprise the majority of residents in many large cities, their best hope for progress lies in gaining political control of municipal government and using municipal resources to improve neighborhoods and schools. Federal programs which bypass city governments in order to get certain tasks done, in the long run, dissipate the resources for self-improvement available to leaders of the Negro community. Efforts by corporations and businesses to improve the dismal conditions of black ghettos also weaken city government. The authors favor a pluralistic approach based on the growing power of the Negro in city government and reject pluralism based on functional interdependence of federal and local organizations.

Another school of thought argues that corporations and other private organizations should and could assume greater responsibility for disadvantaged groups. These critics argue that business corporations have a social conscience and without sacrificing the profit motive could effectively carry out programs to benefit minority groups. As business groups do more for the poor, for ill-trained workers and for redeveloping slum areas, government will have fewer responsibilities and the impetus for creating federal agencies will be weakened.[70]

Some critics are highly skeptical of this strategy and question the degree to which these corporate efforts will make any substantial dent, for example, in the unemployment rate or in the percent of substandard dwelling units. Despite the arguments expressed by Levine and others, these scholars insist on an expanded effort by federal agencies and on new laws and programs to deal with the varied problems of American society.[71]

CONCLUSION

The nation seems to have come full circle in its thinking about the efficacy of the federal government as an instrument for reorganizing society. In the last third of the nineteenth century, the doctrine of laissez faire dominated the beliefs of most leaders in and out of government. America, they felt, would progress to the degree that economic organizations were left free to respond to market forces; property rights were as or more fundamental than human rights. Many thought that government should be limited to housekeeping activities.

In the decades since the depression, federal agencies have been involved in many programs for improving the condition of the American people. These experiences have generated reservations among both conservatives and liberals as to the efficacy of government for redistributing important values to deprived groups and thereby easing serious social problems. Proposals for reducing the influence of federal agencies and strengthening those on the local level do not indicate a movement to restore laissez faire to its former position of preeminence as a doctrine of societal administration. They signify an effort to discover ways by which a variety of local organizations and groups, which in the past had not taken part in decision making, could be more deeply and effectively involved in efforts at problem solving. At the same time, it must also be recognized that worthy federal programs consistently have received meager financing relative to the scope and severity of the problem. In any event, from the ferment of ideas on these subjects may emerge a broader consensus which could lead to a more successful attack on the nation's social ills during the next decade.

Selected Readings

Bottomore, T. B., *Critics of Society* (New York: Pantheon Books, 1968).

Commager, Henry Steele, *The American Mind* (New Haven: Yale University Press, 1950).

Commager, Henry Steele, ed., *Lester Ward and the Welfare State* (Indianapolis and New York: The Bobbs-Merrill Company, Inc., 1967).

Coser, Lewis A., *Men of Ideas* (New York: The Free Press, 1965).

Dahl, Robert A. and Charles E. Lindblom, *Politics, Economics, and Welfare* (New York: Harper & Row, Torchbook, 1963).

Etzioni, Amitai, ed., *Complex Organizations: A Sociological Reader* (New York: Holt, Rinehart & Winston, 1961).

Gross, Bertram M., *The Managing of Organizations*, 2 Vol., (New York: The Free Press, 1964).

Hofstadter, Richard, *Social Darwinism in American Thought*, Rev. ed., (Boston: The Beacon Press, paperback, 1955).

Mannheim, Karl, *Ideology and Utopia*, Louis Wirth and Edward Shils, trans., (New York: Harcourt, Brace & World, Inc., Harvest Book, n.d.).

Mannheim, Karl, *Man and Society in an Age of Reconstruction* (New York: Harcourt, Brace & World, Inc., Harvest Book, n.d.).

Marsh, David C., *The Future of the Welfare State* (Baltimore: Penguin Books, 1964).

Rose, Arnold M., *The Power Structure* (New York: Oxford University Press, 1967).

Schottland, Charles I., ed., *The Welfare State* (New York: Harper & Row, Torchbook, 1967).

Notes to Chapter 9

[1] Allan J. Topol, "Law and the Nation," *The Saturday Review* (August 3, 1968), p. 49.
[2] *Ibid.*, p. 50.
[3] William E. Leuchtenburg, *Franklin D. Roosevelt and the New Deal, 1932–1940* (New York: Harper & Row, Torchbook, 1963), pp. 89-91. For an account of the collapse of the stock market, see John Kenneth Galbraith, *The Great Crash, 1929* (Boston: Houghton Mifflin Company, Sentry ed., 1961).
[4] W. Lloyd Warner, et. al., *The Emergent American Society*, Vol. 1 (New Haven: Yale University Press, 1967), pp. 562-3.
[5] For an important analysis of the history of the changes in the concept of citizenship in England and the significance of this change for patterns of social stratification, see T. H. Marshall, "Citizenship and Social Class," in *Class, Citizenship, and Social Development* (Garden City, New York: Doubleday & Company, Anchor Book, 1965), pp. 71-134.
[6] Harry K. Girvetz, "Welfare State," *International Encyclopedia of the Social Sciences*, Vol. 16 (New York: Macmillan and The Free Press, 1968), p. 514.
[7] Warner, et al., op. cit., p. 571.
[8] *Ibid.*, p. 600.
[9] This term is used by Bertram M. Gross, *The Managing of Organizations*, Vols. I, II (New York: The Free Press, 1964).

[10] James Burnham, *The Managerial Revolution* (New York: John Day, 1941).

[11] Kenneth E. Boulding, *The Organizational Revolution* (New York: Harper, 1953).

[12] For a summary of the principal issues, see Gross, *op. cit.*, Vol. I., Ch. 4.

[13] The discussion in this section relies heavily on Warner, *et al.*, *op. cit.*, Chapters 14 and 15.

[14] *Ibid.*, pp. 578-9.

[15] *Ibid.*, pp. 603-4.

[16] U.S. Bureau of the Census, *Statistical Abstract of the United States, 1968*, 89th Edition (Washington, D.C.: U.S. Government Printing Office, 1968), pp. 310-97.

[17] *Ibid.*

[18] *Ibid.*, pp. 594-5.

[19] *Ibid.*, pp. 599-600.

[20] U.S. Bureau of the Census, *Statistical Abstract of the United States, 1968*, 89th Edition, *op. cit.*, p. 394.

[21] *Ibid.*, p. 382.

[22] U.S. Bureau of the Census, *Historical Statistics of the United States, Colonial Times to 1957* (Washington, D.C.: U.S. Government Printing Office, 1960), p. 719.

[23] U.S. Bureau of the Census, *Statistical Abstract of the United States, 1968*, 89th Edition, *op. cit.*, p. 377.

[24] Dorothy P. Price and Barbara S. Cooper, "National Health Expenditures, 1950–66" *Social Security Bulletin*, 31 (April, 1968), p. 3.

[25] *Ibid.*, pp. 4-6.

[26] *Politics in America: 1945–1966*, 2 ed. (Washington, D.C.: Congressional Quarterly Service, 1967), p. 62.

[27] *Federal Role in Education*, 2 ed. (Washington, D.C.: Congressional Quarterly Service, 1967), pp. 2-3.

[28] Clark Kerr, "Financing Higher Education: The Distribution of Money and Power," *The Public Interest*, 11 (Spring, 1968), p. 101.

[29] U.S. Bureau of the Census, *Statistical Abstract of the United States, 1968*, 89th Edition, *op. cit.*, p. 379.

[30] For discussions of the relations between ideas and social organization, see the following: Reinhard Bendix, *Work and Authority In Industry* (New York: Harper & Row, Torchbook, 1963), Ch. 7; Zbigniew Brzezinski and Samuel P. Huntington, *Political Power: USA/USSR* (New York: The Viking Press, 1964), Ch. 1; Franz Schurmann, *Ideology and Organization In Communist China* (Berkeley and Los Angeles: University of California Press, 1966); Francis X. Sutton, Seymour E. Harris, Carl Kaysen, James Tobin, *The American Business Creed* (New York: Schocken Books, 1962).

[31] This discussion draws heavily from Clinton Rossiter, *Conservatism in America*, 2 ed. (New York: Random House, Vintage Books, 1962), Chapters V and VI. For a study which deals directly with the influence of Darwinian theory on American social thought, see Richard Hofstadter, *Social Darwinism In America*, Rev. Ed. (Boston: Beacon Press, 1955). See also Pitirim A. Sorokin, *Contemporary Sociological Theories* (New York: Harper & Row, Torchbook, 1964), pp. 214-18.

[32] Reinhard Bendix, "Bureaucracy and the Problem of Power," in Robert K. Merton, *et al.*, eds., *Reader In Bureaucracy* (Glencoe, Illinois: The Free Press, 1952), pp. 114-35.

[33] Henry Steele Commager, *The American Mind* (New Haven: Yale University Press, paperback, 1950), p. 202.

[34] Quoted by Commager, *op. cit.*, p. 202.

[35] *Ibid.*, pp. 203-16. See also Sorokin, *op. cit.*, pp. 640-42, 655.

[36] *Ibid.*, pp. 215-6.

37 Morton White, *Social Thought In America* (Boston: Beacon Press, paperback, 1957), pp. 3-31, 59-75, 103-6.

38 Gompers v. United States, 233 U.S. 604, 610 (1914), Quoted in Felix Frankfurter, *Mr. Justice Holmes and the Supreme Court* (New York: Atheneum, 1965), p. 97.

39 For a pertinent discussion of Holmes' writings, see Commager, *op. cit.*, Ch. XVIII.

40 Morton White, *op. cit.*, pp. 94-106; Commager, *op. cit.*, pp. 92-100.

41 H. H. Gerth and C. Wright Mills, *Trans., From Max Weber: Essays In Sociology* (New York: Oxford University Press, 1946), Ch. VIII; A. M. Henderson and Talcott Parsons, *Trans., Max Weber: The Theory of Social and Economic Organization* (New York: Oxford University Press, 1947), pp. 324-92.

42 Robert Michels, *Political Parties* (New York: Dover Publications, Inc., 1959), Lipset and associates applied the Michels' thesis to an empirical study of the International Typographical Union. See Seymour Martin Lipset, Martin Trow and James Coleman, *Union Democracy* (Garden City, N.Y.: Doubleday Anchor Book, 1962).

43 C. Wright Mills, *The Power Elite* (New York: Oxford University Press, Galaxy Book, 1959).

44 For empirical studies which support Mills' view of power in America, see Floyd Hunter, *Community Power Structure* (Chapel Hill, N.C.: The University of North Carolina Press, 1953); and Floyd Hunter, *Top Leadership, U.S.A.* (Chapel Hill, N.C.: The University of North Carolina Press, 1959). For a critical assessment of community studies purporting to embrace the power elite thesis, see Nelson W. Polsby, *Community Theory and Political Theory* (New Haven: Yale University Press, 1963). For a general critique of the ruling elite theory, see Robert A. Dahl, "A Critique of the Ruling Elite Model," *American Political Science Review*, 52 (June, 1958), pp. 463-9. For critiques of Mills' thesis, see Daniel Bell, "Is There A Ruling Class in America," in *The End of Ideology*, Rev. Ed. (New York: Collier Books, 1962), pp. 47-74; Talcott Parsons, "The Distribution of Power in American Society," in *Structure and Process in Modern Societies* (New York: The Free Press, 1960), pp. 199-225.

45 For two works which examine the theory of political pluralism from different viewpoints, see David B. Truman, *The Governmental Process* (New York: Alfred A. Knopf, 1951); Gabriel A. Almond and Sidney Verba, *Civic Culture* (Boston: Little, Brown and Company, 1965). For a study of leadership in a large city which emphasizes the empirical and theoretical importance of group participation and conflict on major issues see Edward C. Banfield, *Political Influence* (New York: The Free Press, 1961). For a careful critique of the postulates of the pluralist theory, see Robert Presthus, *Men At the Top* (New York: Oxford University Press, 1964), Ch. 1.

46 Gerhard E. Lenski, *Power and Privilege: A Theory of Social Stratification* (New York: McGraw-Hill, 1966).

47 For a study of leadership in an American city which analyzes the historical changes in the position of elites and the masses with the extension of suffrage, see Robert A. Dahl, *Who Governs?* (New Haven: Yale University Press, 1961), Book I.

48 Grant McConnell, *Private Power and American Democracy* (New York: Knopf, 1966), pp. 142-46; Robin M. Williams, Jr., *American Society*, 2nd. ed. (New York: Knopf, 1967), pp. 494-501.

49 In describing this pattern of decision making, Dahl and Lindblom have written: ". . . Many decisions are made by a loose confederacy of giant organizations each with great control over the others. Under these conditions, decisions can be arrived at only through horse trading, bargaining, the negotiation of treaties. . . .government very often turns out to be simply one of the bargain-

ers. . . ." Robert A. Dahl and Charles E. Lindblom, *Politics, Economics, and Welfare* (New York: Harper & Row, Torchbook, 1963, originally published in 1953), p. 498. For the authors' views on pluralism, see pp. 302-09, 333-48.

[50] *Ibid.,* pp. 335-39. For discussions of the pluralist view of leadership see Daniel Bell, *op. cit.,* pp. 47-74; Dahl, "A Critique of the Ruling Elite Model," *op. cit.,* pp. 463-69; Nelson W. Polsby, "Three Problems in the Analysis of Community Power," *American Sociological Review,* 24 (December, 1959), pp. 796-803. For an empirical study of leadership in a city which supports the pluralist view, see Robert A. Dahl, *Who Governs? op. cit.*

[51] Martin Meyerson, "National Urban Policy Appropriate to the American Pattern," Brian J. L. Berry and Jack Metzler, *eds., Goals for Urban America* (Englewood Cliffs, N.J.: Prentice-Hall, Spectrum Book, 1967), p. 75.

[52] Eunice and George Grier, "Equality and Beyond: Housing Segregation in the Great Society," Talcott Parsons and Kenneth B. Clark, eds., *The Negro American* (Boston: Beacon, 1967), pp. 531-32.

[53] "You Can't Get There From Here," *Trans-action,* 6 (April, 1969), p. 5. This article summarizes a larger study of transportation. James W. Whittaker, "An Analysis of the Transportation Requirements of Residents of Poverty Areas in New York City," (New York: New York University Graduate School of Business Administration, 1968).

[54] Philip Selznick, *TVA and The Grass Roots* (New York: Harper & Row, Torchbook, 1966, originally published in 1949), p. 265.

[55] *Ibid.,* pp. 47-59.

[56] *Ibid.,* pp. 262-64.

[57] Michael Harrington, "The Will To Abolish Poverty," *The Saturday Review* (July 27, 1968), p. 11.

[58] Kenneth B. Clark, "The Civil Rights Movement: Momentum and Organization," in Clark and Parsons, eds., *The Negro American, op. cit.,* pp. 604-08.

[59] Daniel C. Thompson, "The Civil Rights Movement-1968," *In Black America-1968* (Washington, D.C.: United Publishing Corporation, 1969), pp. 65-76; Kenneth B. Clark, "The Civil Rights Movement: Momentum and Organization," Parsons and Clark, *eds., The Negro American, op. cit.,* pp. 595-625; Harold C. Fleming, "The Federal Executive and Civil Rights: 1961–1965," Parsons and Clark, *eds., The Negro American, op. cit.,* pp. 391-99; James H. Laue, "The Changing Character of the Negro Protest," *The Annals of the American Academy of Political and Social Science,* 357 (January, 1965), pp. 119-26.

[60] The development and operation of these programs are discussed and evaluated by Peter Marris and Martin Rein, *Dilemmas of Social Reform: Poverty and Community Action in the United States* (New York: Atherton Press, 1967).

[61] Nathan Glazer, "For White and Black, Community Control Is the Issue," *The New York Times Magazine* (April 27, 1969), p. 50.

[62] Nat Hentoff, "Profiles (Mayor John Lindsay—1)," *The New Yorker* (May 3, 1969), p. 85. Hentoff quotes Mitchell R. Ginsberg, head of the Human Resources Administration in the Lindsay administration.

[63] Glazer, *op. cit.*

[64] Information on these matters was provided by Dr. Roland Warren in unpublished address presented at the School of Social Work, University of Alabama, April 22, 1969.

[65] Glazer, *op. cit.*

[66] W. W. Heller, "Should the Government Share Its Tax Take?," *The Saturday Review* (March 22, 1969), pp. 26-9; U.S. Senate, Committee On Government Operations, Subcommittee On Intergovernmental Relations, 90th Congress, First Session, *Periodic Congressional Reassessment Of Federal Grants-In-Aid* (Washington, D.C.: U.S. Government Printing Office, 1967); P. R. Dommel, "Confusion Over Revenue-Sharing," *New Republic,* 159 (November 30, 1968), pp. 12-3; "Should Uncle Share the Wealth?," *Nations Business,* 55 (April, 1967), pp. 35-7.

67 Robert A. Levine, "Rethinking Our Social Strategies," *The Public Interest,* 10 (Winter, 1968), pp. 86-96.

68 *Ibid.,* pp. 89-91.

69 Richard A. Cloward and Francis Fox Piven, "The Urban Crisis and the Consolidation of National Power," in Robert H. Connery, *ed., Urban Riots, Proceedings of the Academy of Political Science,* XXIX, No. 1 (1968), pp. 161-68.

70 Charles E. Lindblom, "The Rediscovery of the Market," *The Public Interest,* 4 (Summer, 1966), pp. 89-101.; Bruce L. R. Smith, "The Future of the Not-For-Profit Corporation," *The Public Interest,* 8 (Summer, 1967), pp. 127-42; Robert C. Albrook, "Business Wrestles With Its Social Conscience," *Fortune* (August, 1968), pp. 88-91, 178.

71 Michael Harrington, *The Accidental Century* (Baltimore: Penguin Books, Inc., 1966); Harold L. Wilensky and Charles N. Lebeaux, *Industrial Society and Social Welfare* (New York: The Free Press, Paperback, 1965), pp. ix-x, xlviii.

CHAPTER TEN

COMMUNICATION AND INFORMATION: INSTRUMENTS FOR PLANNING MANAGEMENT AND PROBLEM

INTRODUCTION

A number of views concerning the relations of the state to society, the degree of the state's responsiveness to a broad or narrow spectrum of interest groups and its capabilities for managing numerous social problems have already been considered. Despite widespread consensus on the principles underlying the welfare state, the responsibilities of public and private organizations for problem management remains a controversial question as efforts to formulate workable programs for combatting the ills of our urban society continue.

Recent developments in the social sciences seem destined to influence the problem-solving capabilities of both governmental and economic organizations. Communication theory, which played a crucial part in the construction of guidance systems for certain types of military weapons, has been applied to the behavior of organizations. The gathering and use of knowledge through communication are basic elements of this theory. The potential of this theory for changing social structure to accord more closely with the basic values of American society is suggested by the following examples, which represent significant chapters in the recent history of this nation.

The Atomic Bomb

In the summer of 1939, several distinguished physical scientists met with one of the best known scientists in the world, Albert Einstein. Physicists throughout the world had become aware, through the results of certain research activities published in scientific journals, of nuclear fission and the applicability of this process to weaponry. Since Einstein had access to President Franklin D. Roosevelt and they did not, the visitors sought his aid as a communication link to the White House.[1] The scientists wished to inform the president of the necessity of changing governmental research activity. If the message was first transmitted to lesser officials, it might be distorted as it moved upward in the chain of command. Since the message might never reach the White House, Einstein's assistance was essential.

The visit culminated in the drafting of a letter, over Einstein's signature, advising President Roosevelt of the scientific knowledge which made the atomic bomb feasible, and recommending that the United States Government initiate procedures to develop this weapon ahead of Germany. The destiny of democratic nations and the future of world history were at stake. The letter was received in October by President Roosevelt, after the Nazis had invaded Poland. Research was initiated in February, 1940, with a grant of $6,000, an amazingly low sum by current

315

standards.[2] The research program expanded in the ensuing months, and in 1942, the Manhattan Project was established. The following year, a site for testing the first atomic weapons was developed in Los Alamos, New Mexico. With the dropping of the atomic bomb on Japanese cities to hasten the end of the war, the nuclear age began.

Controlling the "Boom and Bust" Cycle

A few years prior to the events just mentioned—during and after the depression period—a more complex sequence of events occurred whose consequences were no less significant than the discovery of atomic energy.[3] The adoption of Keynesian economic theory (see below) by top officials of the federal government and by some influential businessmen led to major changes in economic policy and in the role of government. Heretofore, the laissez faire dogma contended that movement of prices and wages, supply and demand in a "free" market, would counteract periods of economic stagnation and of inflation. The theory offered little or no justification for government efforts to boost economic activity during a recession.

The upturn in business, repeatedly predicted since the stock market crash in 1929 by President Hoover and his close advisors, failed to materialize by the time Roosevelt took office in 1933. More than thirteen million adults, many of whom were in the working and middle classes, were unemployed. Both right and left wing radical movements were strident and that of Huey Long was gaining in power. But, traditional economic theory provided no rationale for government action; officials had to wait for market conditions to initiate the upturn in production and employment.

Fortunately for America and for the western world, an unorthodox interpretation of the capitalistic economy had been widely discussed for several years, due in large part to the efforts of a few professors and students at Harvard University. They embraced the theory of John Maynard Keynes, British economist, which differed radically from that of laissez faire. Keynes analyzed the factors preventing the decline in the cost of labor and of capital from inducing businessmen to increase output and employment. For Keynes, aggregate income and purchasing power were the crucial factors in influencing demand for products. Aggregate purchasing power could best be increased by raising government expenditures, by what has become known as *pump priming*. The private economy desperately needed an infusion of capital from the public sector. The balanced budget, which had been a sacred cow of orthodox economists, had to be sacrificed to the principle of deficit financing.

Keynesian theory analyzed the weaknesses of the market system and offered a solution as well as a justification for actions previously thought to be destructive of capitalism, government financed programs. Keynesian theory provided an economic rationale for the adoption of a variety of welfare state programs, such as Social Security and public housing. Galbraith evaluated the adoption of Keynesian theory and the development of public programs based on its propositions by saying:

> By common, if not yet quite universal agreement, the Keynesian revolution was one of the great modern accomplishments in social design. It brought Marxism in the advanced countries to a halt. It led to a level of economic performance that now inspires bitter-end conservatives to panegyrics of unexampled banality. . . .[4]

Unlike the case of the atomic bomb, Keynes' personal effort to explain economic theory to President Roosevelt failed. Instead, the "revolution" was accomplished primarily by men and women who had studied under advocates of Keynesian theory at Harvard and other universities, and who either were at that time or became government officials. Many of these persons held key posts in the top departments of the government, including the Bureau of the Budget, Treasury and Commerce Departments and the Federal Reserve System.[5]

The revolution in economic theory and role of the federal government was furthered by the varied processes of communication between a few learned professors and government officials concerned with developing programs for ending the depression. It was a revolution which was not directed by any power clique. The social changes were made by high office holders who more or less agreed with one another on the causes of the depression and on the means by which economic prosperity could be restored. The process which transformed the economy and government was summed up by Galbraith when he said:

> . . . not often have important new ideas on economics entered a government by way of its central bank. . . .[6]

Both examples, historic events of great importance, illustrate the significance of the exchange of ideas and information. In both instances, communication took place between certain specialists and government policy makers.[7] Government officials used the information they had received to modify the activities of certain federal agencies. In the case of the atomic bomb, the federal government launched a research program to develop a new and more deadly type of weapon. The federal government also accepted a new responsibility, preventing the "boom and bust" cycle, by maintaining a steady rate of economic growth. The information obtained from communication processes led to specific kinds of learning and changes in the activities and structure of the federal government. Both events, winning World War II and maintaining a steady rate of economic growth, will be felt throughout the world for generations.

COMMUNICATION THEORY

For purposes of clarity, we differentiate interpersonal activities involving the exchange of information and the content of the messages. While the "how" and the "what" usually occur together, each phenomenon involves somewhat different problems. The first focuses on those dimensions of interpersonal activity which facilitate or impede the transfer of information. The second concerns the nature of the knowledge transmitted, the specific content and the form in which it is organized. The first category concerns the ways by which social interaction affects the flow of information while the latter stresses the kinds of information of use to an organization or to society.

The basic concepts in communication theory concern "error," "feedback," "learning" and social change. The theory views organizations as goal-oriented since activities are directed at the attainment of particular objectives. The theory assumes that "errors" or dysfunctions are inevitable. Since, in many cases, unexpected events can prevent the attainment of major goals, an organization, to be effective, must be capable of detecting mistakes. The transmission of knowledge on the consequences of activities is a prerequisite for corrective action. The process by which this information is transmitted is termed "feedback," a process of communication whereby an organization obtains information on the results of its activities.[8] Feedback, which suggests the organization is "on target," will lead to the repetition of the behavior which produced this result. Where the information indicates major deviation from the target, or accomplishment of goals with results that reduce the value of this condition, the organization, other things being equal, will modify its policies, its goals, or both. If feedback of these adjustments indicates improved consequences, the organization will record and "remember" that fact and the activities will be repeated. If the modifications still do not provide satisfactory results, additional innovations may be adopted.

Information files or "storage" of knowledge enable an organization to compare present with past performance, the effectiveness of current with previous policies. Thus it can be said that organizations have a "memory." The "memory" capacity enables an organization to combine knowledge of current conditions with knowledge of the results of past practices. In this way the organization strives to maintain a balance between tradition and the flux of contemporary circumstances. It strives to avoid the rigidity of stubborn adherence to orthodox strategies and the anarchy of considering each change in environment as justification for a change in policy.[9]

A stable organization deliberately establishes processes of social interaction which collect and transmit information to executives. Organizations which perform these functions adequately will use knowledge to maintain effectiveness and stability in a variety of social situations. Rapid changes in environment will be accompanied by timely changes in activities. Knowledge is essential for determining which of several proposals will provide the most effective response to environmental change. Leaders who fail to invest adequately in data collection and processing endanger the effectiveness of their organizations.

For instance, the behavior of a golfer as he responds to the challenges of the golf course illustrates these propositions. Our golfer seeks to complete the course with a score not higher than and, where possible, lower than par. Inevitably, as he moves from hole to hole, mistakes will be made. On one occasion he may "top" the ball, on another he may hit under it. He may slice it too far in one direction or another; he may putt the ball too hard, too short, or slap it to the left or right of the cup. An observant golfer will carefully study the results of each swing and consider the degree to which he hit the ball to the desired location. The observant golfer, through the information transmitted by his sensory organs, defines the situation as "on target" or as "error." If the latter, he considers what went wrong and how the previous procedure could be improved. If he topped the ball, he may consciously try to swing under the ball. If the ball veered in the wrong direction, he may alter the position of the club face in relation to the ball. The golfer seeks to correct mistakes by altering behavior. As he persists in this mode of response, he learns how to cope with the game of golf. To assist his memory, the golfer may record each shot, in which case he compiles a "data bank." This information will be most useful if the player can retrieve it rapidly when needed.

This example simplifies reality. It concerns one man against the physical environment and not in direct interaction with other persons. Our golfer has but one important objective, for which he performs a number of different actions of a distinct type—hitting the ball with a club. Hence feedback concerns one goal and actions occurring in one place at a particular time.

The communication problems of organizations are far more complex. They involve all those activities pertaining to a number of objectives, which must be studied simultaneously, although occurring in different places and involving the numerous social units which receive the outputs of the organization. Data must be collected from many different points in space and time about a variety of subjects. Since the activities of the organization occur over a greater period of time than those of our golfer, which cease when the game ends, data acquisition is more or less a continual process. The heterogeneity of social units, subject matter, time and place increases the complexity of information collection and interpretation. The quantity of information collected daily requires facilities for storage. But the information must be processed when placed in storage to facilitate rapid retrieval. Interpersonal relations need to be organized to meet the specifications for information collection and processing. An organization also must have "feedback" on the extent to which its communication network meets these requirements.

Several examples illustrate the importance of feedback for an organization. At the turn of the century, a young naval officer developed a technique for improving the aiming mechanisms of naval guns which constituted, in effect, a critical evaluation of the current performance of naval gunnery. The technology in use up to that time did not permit continuous-aim firing, but allowed guns to fire only when the roll of the ship placed the batteries "on target." Development of technology for aiming guns which corrected for the roll of the ship permitted a considerable increase in firepower, thereby improving the navy's offensive and defensive capabilities, or ability to perform its primary mission.[10] Despite the obvious advantages of the innovation, the admirals did not rush to adopt it. The initial reports submitted to the Ordinance Bureau by the inventor were filed away and forgotten. Only persistent efforts by the officer brought the new procedure to the attention of interested and influential Navy executives. The sources of resistance to the proposal for "continuous-aim firing" reveal some of the obstacles to effective feedback. The officers of the Bureau ignored the reports as it criticized the system of firing then in use which they had developed. Acceptance of the criticism was made more difficult by the obscure and relatively unknown status of the officer who hit on the device for "continuous-aim firing." The higher ranking and more prestigious officers of the Ordinance Bureau hesitated to admit that a person of lesser status had developed such a valuable innovation. This inconsistency between status and role performance came close to reducing the fighting effectiveness of the entire fleet.

Although this event had a "happy ending" due to the communication of vital information to appropriate executives, the examples below indicate the consequences of failure of feedback. In 1966, President Johnson ordered all federal agencies to adopt a revised form of budget evaluation, Program-Planning-Benefit System. This procedure required an analysis of the "cost" and the "benefits" of each program carried out by an agency. It therefore provided a basis for identifying effective and ineffective programs. Once this task had been completed, agency chiefs could either eliminate or modify the least successful programs. However, utilization of this program evaluation procedure required information on both costs and benefits.

The lack of certain facts also prevented adequate evaluation of an Office of Education program for combatting adult illiteracy. The office did not have information on the number of participants who had benefitted from the instruction, nor did it have information on the nature of the gains which beneficiaries had made. Similarly, assessment of the effectiveness of the college student loan program was handicapped by the lack of data on the number of recipients who had and who had not graduated.[11] These information gaps prevented agencies from determining the degree to which major goals had been attained. Inability to differentiate effective from ineffective programs contributes to the retention of activities which produce few tangible benefits but consume valuable resources. Effective goal attainment requires differentiation of relevant from irrelevant information and procedures for communicating the data to policy makers.

SELECTION OF INFORMATION FOR SOCIETAL FEEDBACK

Devising an information system for the total society, which some social scientists term a system of social accounts, and paralleling that used for the economy, represents a seemingly impossible but necessary enterprise. Federal and local units of government cannot be content to evaluate the results of the activities of each of their agencies, but must evaluate also the activities of each of the institutions within their spatial domain. At the same time, this problem should not be delegated solely to governmental agencies but should also concern private research organizations.

Several important implications of data collection activities bear on decisions of the specific social phenomena to be studied by agencies of government. Like all other activities, information collection and processing require the expenditure of scarce resources. Selections should be carefully made, for to do otherwise wastes money and manpower which might have been allocated more profitably for other purposes. Selection procedures which fail to separate irrelevant from relevant information burden processing and storage facilities, create delays, cause poor decisions, and waste resources. Agencies also should be conservative in collecting information on conditions or activities which cannot be changed under existing characteristics of social structure and technology of social change. Data gathering on such matters often creates expectations of change, and failure to follow through generates resentment.[12] On the other hand, executives may err on the side of caution. Changes which are not feasible under certain conditions may become quite practical under other circumstances. Should this occur, the absence of data on the particular condition can hinder change efforts. For example, the difficulties of eliminating air and stream pollution hardly justify the failure to obtain data on the extent to which these resources are contaminated.

The following, tentative proposals illustrate the nature of the decisions involved in selecting information for use in formulating public policy on issues affecting the vitality of American society. This approach blends the functional emphasis on the persistence of society in general[13] and the specific prerequisites of a democratic polity[14] with an effort to approximate a complete social inventory or social accounting system.[15] Data collection also must be oriented to a dominant trend in contemporary America, the emergence of what the political scientist, Robert Lane, labeled the "knowledgeable society," a society in which the production and use of information comes to play an ever wider role in guiding the processes of problem management.[16] In the "knowledgeable society," information becomes an indispensable resource and data must be obtained on the adequacy of its production, distribution and utilization.

Functional Requisites of Society

The initial problem concerns the degree to which the institutions of America fulfill the conditions recognized as essential for the continuity of all societies. It is useful to begin with the distinction between the external and internal environment. The former involves a number of considerations, one pertaining to relationships with foreign nations, the other to the physical environment in which the national society is situated. For the first dimension, matters pertaining to a durable peace and to the prevention of nuclear warfare must have high priorities in information collection, along with data on exchange relationships for economic inputs and outputs. The first set of considerations relate to the survival and well-being of the society and its place in the world community, while the latter concerns the growth and efficiency of an internal institution, the economy. A third feature of the external environment concerns those activities within society which change the physical environment in a way which interferes with or even prohibits normal activity. Pollution of the atmosphere, streams, lakes and rivers, and exhaustion of vital resources such as fertile land and minerals are several commonplace consequences.[17] Advance warning of shortages in vital resources could stimulate research on the development of alternative sources of supply—the use of minerals in and under the ocean.

Internally, the basic requisites of society include the manner in which the kinship institution performs its reproductive, child-rearing and socialization functions. Signs of growing family instability, of steady rise in divorce rates and decline in the rate of remarriage among divorced persons, of parental abuse and neglect of children, and of deepening conflict between the generations would be important symptoms of social disorganization. Failure to correct these conditions undoubtedly would lead to disruptions in the activities of other institutions due largely to widespread deviation in role behavior.

Other basic activities concern the production and distribution of commodities essential for maintaining human existence in a particular physical environment. Mere subsistence hardly suffices, for the economy, in the long run, must provide those products which assure the vitality and vigor of the population. The members of society also must receive training in the language, customs, moralities, and beliefs of the society in order to be in a position to fulfill responsibilities expected of adult members. Beyond this, training also is required for performance of specialized occupations. Some of these educational experiences are provided by the socialization activities of the family, others by an institution intended to serve primarily for transmitting the accumulated knowledge and wisdom of the society.

Given the many sources of conflict within persons, between the pressures of innate drives and external social constraints, and the conflicts between groups deriving from the scarcity of valued resources, mechanisms for orderly resolution of disputes and for maintaining the rules of the social order also are indispensable. Government uses its monopoly of the resources for physical compulsion to enforce legitimate rules of social conduct. It has the capability, without which no society can long exist, to compel recalcitrant and hostile persons to accept and comply with social conventions. Continuity of society does not depend solely on consensus, agreement or friendly persuasion.

At the same time, it is doubtful that any society which relied exclusively on force to uphold rules would have the capacity to endure serious shocks. Commitment to ultimate values on the part of members of society assures the acceptance of obligations in order to fulfill those role responsibilities on which all the institutions of society ultimately depend. No one structure develops and maintains this consensus. The family, religion, education and government can strengthen the belief system of society.

Since these areas of social activity influence the durability of society, serious disturbances in any or many at the same time signifies trouble and the immanence of fundamental changes. The decimation of the population from disease, exhaustion of vital resources required by the economy, and decreasing areas of consensus and increases in conflict over basic values, among others, indicate growing difficulties in the operations of social institutions. Early detection of these and related conditions through processes of collecting and communicating information would improve the opportunity for developing and implementing corrective programs.

Functional Requisites of a Democratic Society

An industrial, democratic society committed to the principles of the welfare state requires vast amounts of information. Maintaining a political system based on the concept of citizen participation creates additional criteria of performance which institutions must meet. These conditions, in turn, require still others, as a certain level of formal education and knowledge of public affairs have to be met. A complex, democratic society imposes, in a sense, functional requirements resembling chinese boxes, one inside the other, in seemingly endless number and with numerous linkages.

A general rule of problem solving in a complex, democratic society may be stated at the outset. The stability and continuity of a democratic polity depends on the degree to which each major functional disorder is resolved satisfactorily prior to the occurrence of the next.[18] A system in which serious operational problems accumulate finds itself in deep trouble. America in the late sixties illustrates this circumstance. The nation was committed to a war in Viet Nam for which billions of dollars were expended and hundreds of thousands of persons were engaged in the fighting while, internally, problems in relations with certain minority groups and the needs of urban communities have been urgent. Either set of problems would have taxed the ingenuity of the nation's leaders and the nation's resources. Taken together, these problems in the external and internal environment intensified cleavage between various classes, strengthening radical political groups and reducing the degree of consensus on democratic values.

The various dimensions of a democratic society about which valid information should be regularly and frequently collected can be expressed in the formula developed by Gross, called P.O.I.S.E., which refers to varying types of involvement of individuals in society. The dimensions are:

1. *Political democracy*, which provides for the participation in the decisions of state agencies by adult members or citizens of the state.

2. *Organizational democracy*, which provides the members of organizations with the opportunity for participation and self-development and recognizes their individual rights and responsibilities.

3. *Individual democracy*, which provides individuals with the rights of juridical self-defense.

4. *Social democracy*, which provides guarantees that political and economic rights shall not be impaired because of a person's color, race, religion, national origin, or sex.

5. *Economic democracy*, which provides full opportunities for useful employment and for at least minimum standards of food, shelter, clothing, medical care, education, and recreation.[19]

The implications of this formula for feedback can be specified briefly. Item 1 requires information on the degree to which specific groups are regularly denied access to decision makers on one or all levels of government. Item 2 requires similar data for participation in voluntary associations, from political parties to country clubs. Infringements of the civil rights of citizens and of those who belong to particular groups are relevant to individual democracy. Item 4 refers to the existence, severity and persistence of discrimination against selected groups. The presence of groups suffering from this type of mistreatment will be reflected in information on each of these three items and on the final item. Economic democracy pertains to many of the conditions previously discussed, especially income, educational opportunities and availability of adequate health facilities.[20]

To select any of the above items as more critical than others is un-
warranted. For purposes of brevity, however, we may focus on the first
item, political democracy, as a key to the others. Where organized
groups representing a particular class or stratum have regular access to
decision makers, the chances are improved for favorable treatment.
Access can be defined broadly in terms of participation,[21] including
voting and other forms of communication between citizen and officials,
and membership in voluntary associations which act in behalf of various
strata. These organizations constitute vital units in the communication
network of society by providing information on the condition, attitudes
and needs of members. Both the information and resources of these
organizations are among the factors which enable policy makers to
recognize the desires of constituents. Remedial actions based on this
information may persuade organization members that tangible gains can
be achieved within the political structure. This belief solidifies attachments to democracy and reduces alienation.

Other forms of communication between groups and leaders also occur
in a democracy. These include voting patterns,[22] public opinion polls,
financial contributions to political parties and election campaigns of
specific candidates, turnouts at political rallies, letters to the editors of
newspapers and magazines, editorials in newspapers and on T.V. and
direct communication between constituents and elected officials in the
form of letters, telegrams, phone calls and conversations. These reactions to government activities must also be evaluated in terms of continuing commitment to democracy or a growing affinity to alien dogmas
and political movements. Growth of this type of sentiment signifies the
dimunition of the legitimacy of the political system and the need for
modification either of governmental policies or of the information available to the citizenry.

The productivity of the economy and effectiveness of government
depends on the growth of organizations devoted to the discovery and
expansion of knowledge, the institution of science and all the organizations involved in knowledge production. These include research bureaus
and laboratories along with centers of higher learning. Information on
the training of experts, on the discovery and cultivation of talent and the
utilization of knowledge have a bearing on the performance of society's
institutions.

Forms of deviant behavior which threaten the effectiveness of institutions also must be watched closely.[23] These include: sexual practices
which provide satisfactions outside the usual family structure and kinship roles; the inducement of mental states by use of drugs and beverages
which render persons incapable of fulfilling role responsibilities and

which increase dependency upon such stimulants; the growth and per-sistence of organizations outside the legitimate economic structures to provide illicit services; and the betrayal of trust by persons holding positions of responsibility in complex organizations. Increases in the prevalence of any or all of these phenomena should be regarded as serious disturbances to a democratic, equalitarian, industrial society.

CHARACTERISTICS OF USEFUL INFORMATION

Establishment of effective channels of communication and selection of the areas of social relations to be scrutinized do not exhaust the problems of achieving effective feedback. An agency must also decide on the type of information which would be most useful. The following list exemplifies the considerations which often determine the usefulness of the information that is collected. These include first, the number of measurements of a social trait, whether one or many; second, whether variables should be measured separately or in interaction. If the latter is preferred, the researchers also may choose to differentiate the more from the less influential factors and assign weights reflecting relative impact. Third, whether variables should be studied at a particular mo-ment in time or over an extended time period and, if the latter, the exact length of time, also are important. Fourth, the level of society for which data are obtained must be chosen, such as the total society, regions, certain size communities, or neighborhoods, and whether data should be obtained for just one or for several levels must be decided.

To measure a specific condition of the people of the United States or even of a city usually requires a vast amount of information. To determine the health of a population, for example, would necessitate collection of data on the incidence of a wide variety of illnesses, past and present, the degree to which the population suffers from illnesses which have not been treated or otherwise brought to the attention of medical practitioners and the prevalence of conditions such as obesity which, while not illnesses, are known to be related to a variety of func-tional disorders. One should also include mental illness in the picture, and perhaps such personality disorders as drug addiction, alcoholism, homosexuality, and many others.

If all areas of social life relevant to the state of the society are as complex as that for health, the task might appear to be hopeless. In recent years, attention has focused on an informational item which simplifies the task of data collection, the concept of social indicator. This term refers to a statistic or set of statistics which summarize a complex set of conditions.²⁴ The death rate, for example, may be selected as an indicator of the general health of the population; for other purposes one might prefer the proportion of population of various age and sex groups which are both underweight and overweight. The number of days per person confined to bed for reasons of poor health during a given time period may also serve as an indicator of the health of a population. In other words, social scientists search for precise and specific statements of a given trait or set of traits which are thought to reflect accurately the character of a given set of more complex conditions. Where indicators reflect accurately these more complex circumstances, feedback on a total society becomes a realistic and practical objective. Selection of indicators thus becomes a crucial step in the measurement process.

In selecting information for orienting decision making, a number of guidelines can be followed. First, *multiple measurements* or *indicators* should be obtained on every condition which the organization seeks to understand.²⁵ Given the complexity of social and economic phenomena, no one measurement by itself will be both accurate and comprehensive. Reliance on a single indicator may provide a distorted picture of reality. The study of income redistribution in America, for example, indicates progress when measured by changes in percent of families in the several income brackets. Little change is evident when families are compared by the share of the total national income possessed by each fifth of the families ranked from top to bottom.²⁶

Relevant features of a variable which are difficult to measure should not be given lower priority than those which are more amenable to measurement. Subjective aspects of behavior, such as attitudes and beliefs, and complex dimensions of social structure as "integration" and "cohesiveness" can be as, if not more, critical than phenomena such as income and years of schooling, which are more amenable to precise assessment. Miller and his associates point out, for example, that poverty involves more than a deficiency of monetary assets, but also a state of mind, a lack of self respect and self confidence, which prevents individuals from taking those actions which could facilitate the climb out of impoverished status.²⁷ Unless such critical factors can be weighed, no matter how imperfectly, decision makers may be unaware of them and plans for change will not take them into account. Such plans may be less effective than those seeking to change attitudes along with other basic conditions of poverty.

Measurements of features of social phenomena also should be oriented toward determining the relative weights of various factors in producing certain events.²⁸ The question of whether or not the educational performance of schools in poverty neighborhoods can be improved most by upgrading physical facilities, the teaching staff or the library, by reducing the teacher-student ratio, or by increasing the heterogeneity of the social classes from which the students come is of more than academic importance. The answer will influence the types of programs to be implemented, the allocation of resources and the degree of improvement achieved by schools serving various minority groups. A recent report on education by Coleman and Associates found that the heterogenity of the class background of the student body appears to have more influence on educational performance of students than expenditures for physical facilities and for staff.[29]

The data often should be arranged in the form of a *time series*, measurements of a specific variable over a given period of time. These data provide information on trends, on whether a certain variable is increasing or decreasing, by how much in a given period of time and the precise moment when a larger than usual change occurred. Each of these factors provides insight into the relative effectiveness of the various programs of particular organizations which have sought to cope with the given problem. Trends on the proportion of families living in poverty or on the proportion of a given age group graduating from elementary or high school indicate the effectiveness of remedial programs. In addition, data on trends assist the researcher to project into the future the probable course of events. These forecasts enable organizations to prepare for changes in their environment. School boards, for example, to provide educational facilities for youngsters, must have reliable estimates of future enrollment. To be unprepared when a large increase in enrollment occurs could lead to a chaotic situation. Moynihan points out that availability of estimates of future rural-urban migration of low income persons and minority group members would be of inestimable assistance to city officials in planning for the provision of housing, education, social welfare and other useful services.[30] This type of advanced planning can forestall a breakdown in social institutions and a buildup of support for forms of government alien to democracy.

The definition and management of social problems discussed in preceding chapters were, within an historical perspective, increasingly dependent upon the availability of a variety of indicators. Some of these indicators are well-developed—a more qualifying term than *exact*—some are inexact and ambiguous, leaving considerable doubt concerning the nature of the problem, the magnitude and direction of change. Statistics on most of the social problems considered in this or any other social problem textbook often are deficient and extremely difficult to interpret. Yet they are the basis of political, social, economic, and community decision and policy making. Inaccurate, misleading data are used frequently to provide both proponents and antagonists with political strength in managing, decision making, and planning for the future. *FAMILY, EDUCATION AND CRIME INDICATORS.*   A number of illustrations are pertinent to an understanding of the importance of well conceived social indicators which are altered and adjusted with changes in social systems. The field of demography provides many of the statistics on the family. However, Donald J. Bogue points out:

> Known weaknesses of the divorce rate as a measure have caused disputes as to whether the incidence of divorce has increased, decreased, or remained the same since 1950.[31]

While there have been many research studies of American family behavior, the majority have been concerned with the middle class family. With the interest in poverty stimulated by the publication of such books as Michael Harrington's *The Other America*[32] and the enactment of the Economic Opportunity Act in 1964, knowledge of some groups of low income families has been added to the literature. We still lack data on the upper class family. In order to assess the status of the American family, patterns and direction of change, the gaps in qualitative and quantitative data for all social classes and distinctive groups—racial, ethnic, rural, suburban, religious—will have to be substantially reduced and the data made more reliable than at present. Educational and religious statistics are deficient. The statistic most frequently used to assess the distribution of knowledge in the United States is the number of years an individual spent as a student within the four walls of a formally organized and recognized school. Yet many educational activities take place in other types of organizations. Adult nondegree educational programs, private instruction in the arts, on-the-job training, education acquired in the armed forces are not included in our educational statistics. When the rapid technological changes which have occured in the last several decades are considered against the backdrop of traditional education patterns in the United States, we soon recognize, for example, that most specialists in the vital computer or aerospace industries were trained outside the conventional school. This may not necessarily be an indictment of public education. It is a plea for a redefinition of education and inclusion, in a set of statistical indicators, of training which takes place outside the formal school system.

Although social scientists and religious leaders consider the church an important institution in American society, measuring the religious commitment of Americans entails many problems as Glock and Stark effectively point out.[33] The items of behavior most frequently used to measure man's commitment to his God are church attendance, church organizational affiliation (such as the Brotherhood, Luther League, parish club), and size and furnishings of church buildings. Etzioni and Lehman suggest that while

> goals like 'salvation' are difficult, if not impossible, to measure, an analyst ought to focus on activities that are as proximate as possible to 'salvation' on a means-ends chain of religious actions. Thus, activities such as regular prayer, having 'religious experiences,' and participating in social action programs motivated by theological considerations appear to be means which are more immediately linked to religious goals, while attending church on Sunday and membership in the parish men's club are more remote.[34]

On the other hand, church membership and attendance may be an important measure of the importance of the church as a social and social class organization. The measures developed must be more rigorous and must be strictly related to particular goals, religious or social.

THE MISINTERPRETATION OF SOCIAL INDICATORS

Since indicators are brief statistical expressions of varied and complicated social conditions, no single indicator can be considered an accurate and complete measuring device. Inevitably the necessity to omit certain kinds of data produces some degree of bias. Recognition of the limitations of an indicator can prevent erroneous conclusions and policy decisions. These circumstances can be illustrated by examining an indicator which has been cited in the mass media again and again, the F.B.I.'s crime index. Examination of this index reveals many of the pitfalls in the construction and use of social indicators.

A high score on the crime index often is equated with deterioration of a particular social environment, usually the ghettos of our larger cities. Whatever the causes of this supposed increase in the incidence of crime, the failure of society to indoctrinate its norms, the ineffectiveness of law and law enforcement agencies, the failure of the family, school, church, or the result of socioeconomic inequality, etc., crime rates arouse general interest. The crime index in the U.S. is prepared by the Federal Bureau of Investigation and published annually in *Uniform Crime Reports for the United States*.[35] The report consists of technical and summary sections. The technical section defines collection restrictions and the crime categories used so that misunderstandings may be limited. The summary section which arouses the interest of citizens and public officials through the publicity given it each year by news media, usually in the summer months, makes sweeping generalizations on the increase in crime. Proposals for major reforms in law, law enforcement and action groups, etc., are made without recognizing the peculiar characteristics and limitations of the crime index. Given the manner in which the index is constructed, it tends to confirm the beliefs of many Americans on the growing lawlessness of certain types of people. At the same time, the index fails to measure some of the most serious and damaging forms of crime. Taken as a whole, the index leads to erroneous conclusions on the crime situation in America.[36]

The crime index measures seven types of crime—criminal homicide, forcible rape, robbery, aggravated assault, burglary, larceny (involving property worth $50 or more), and automobile theft. The index does not include other equally if not more serious types of crime such as embezzlement, forgery, tax and insurance fraud, extortion, prostitution, narcotics violation, kidnapping, arson and other categories of illegal activity. Furthermore, the types of crime committed by members of "crime syndicates" seldom appear in criminal statistics, and hence are not measured by the index. Therefore, the index fails to give any indication of changes in the activity, growth or decline, of organized crime in America, which probably represents one of if not the most significant source of lawless behavior.

In considering the information gains provided by the crime index, one must examine the changes in incidence of the particular types of crime included in the index, and not regard changes in the total index as paralleled by changes in a specific category. Despite the impression of a general rise in all types of serious crimes, the

. . . FBI estimates that the criminal homicide rate is now 40 percent lower for the nation as a whole than it was about thirty years ago. . . .[37]

The situation for forcible rape also is less serious than many people seem to believe, with the rate remaining constant at a relatively low level. Indeed, since crimes against persons represent only 12 percent of the reported crimes measured by the index, changes in the index reveal little about dangers from crimes of violence.[38]

Some of the more salient features of the Crime Index lead to erroneous conclusions on the prevalence of social disorganization. Half of the indexed crimes concern larceny and automobile theft, crimes which tend to increase as the population becomes more affluent and police become more efficient in detecting and reporting crimes. Furthermore, certain demographic features of these two categories of crime also lead to an upward trend, namely the increase in proportion of young people, those most likely to commit larceny and steal an automobile. Given these features of the Crime Index, rates will tend to increase as more people own valuable property and as the police continue to receive better training. These features and the categories of crime omitted by the Index constitute serious sources of bias and reveal the liabilities of permitting an agency responsible for controlling certain forms of conduct to be responsible for measuring their occurrence. Biderman therefore contends that the Index may have little positive value. He wrote:

> The FBI report fosters an image of an uncontrolled surge of crime. Such an image contributes to citizens deserting their cities, streets, and parks. Presumably, it gives comfort to those lawbreakers who conclude that what they do is innocent relative to the type of crimes "everyone else" commits. To my knowledge, no one has investigated whether the image or rapidly and constantly mounting crime contributes more to support of constructive measures against crime than to despair and distrust of the mechanisms for coping with it.

> This raises the question of whether the availability of an inaccurate indicator is better or worse for the society than having no indicator at all.[39]

Biderman's conclusions become quite pertinent to the discussion of urban problems and management of riots considered in Chapters 2 and 8.

In the quest for management and/or solutions to the social problems of this decade and those which will follow, societal leaders must have social as well as economic indicators which accurately determine whether a problem really exists in terms of numbers of people, the social institutions and organizations affected, and the social, economic and political costs to society. It has been expensive developing economic indicators; social indicators which deal frequently with elusive qualitative data will be equally expensive. Since the management of most of the problems we have considered costs enormous sums of money, some societal groups may not wish accurate information. Without accurate information capable of surmounting the arguments of opposing forces, it is difficult to recognize alternative approaches to problem management. Lack of data make the programs and techniques which have been utilized over the years more defensible. Whether the cost of the problem is worth the cost of knowledge on the problem must be answered. Biderman puts the question succinctly:

Whether the candle is worth the cost in this instance is dependent upon how we answer the larger question. . . . How seriously do we want to understand the full consequences of what we are doing?[40]

THE ORGANIZATION OF SOCIETAL FEEDBACK

Types of organizations which could best perform information collection and interpretation activities required for problem management and whether or not existing organizations could perform these functions without organizations being established for this purpose are problems which must be answered soon. Since we are concerned with the application of knowledge to social change, there must be a close relation between the persons responsible for informational activities and those responsible for the formulation of public policy. Unless governmental leaders were under some obligation to incorporate the results of the various studies of American society in legislation proposed for enactment, the studies might have minimal impact or be of interest only to academicians. On the other hand, there are some obvious dangers to entrusting the responsibility for data gathering and analysis to a government bureau, namely that political considerations will dominate scientific interests. Studies which reflect favorably on a current administration may receive priority while those which spotlight serious shortcomings in existing programs may be quietly discarded. For these reasons, reliance should be placed on more than one type of organization. An agency established in the Office of the President would have direct access to the chief executive, to the center of power in the American system of government. An organization of data gathering agencies in and out of universities, staffed primarily by academicians or trained professionals, could produce independent reports which would provide another view of the problem areas studied by a government agency. It would also provide academicians the opportunity to study certain areas which the government agency might not be interested in.

To see how a government agency devoted to the assessment of social problems and the condition of American society would operate, we may consider a similar agency concerned with the study of economic conditions. The Council of Economic Advisors was established by law in 1946 to provide expert advice on economic affairs to the White House and to Congress.[41] The success of the Council in influencing the economic policy of successive presidents, in avoiding major recessions and in promoting sustained growth of the economy can be attributed in part to its relations with the White House and with those government agencies concerned with economic matters. The Council, consisting of three members, a staff of about twenty and several outside consultants, reports directly to the President. The Council is not part of any government agency; it is not dependent for funds and other forms of assistance on these agencies, although it has access to their information files. Most members of the Council have been academicians who did not consider service in government as their primary interest and who returned to the university after the stint with the Council ended. Consequently, the Council and its staff enjoy a substantial measure of autonomy which permits it to adopt positions and recommend programs which may conflict with orthodox views. New programs and theories receive serious and careful examination, and are not dismissed prematurely as unsound or impractical.

The professional advice which the Council gave the President since its inception has made a major contribution to the vigor of the economy. The Council has:

> . . . endorsed an active economic policy for government, the full employment concept of the Employment Act, and an emphasis on fiscal rather than monetary policy—all implying priority for expansion rather than balanced budgets . . .[42]

The concrete policies which embodied these recommendations contributed to continuing increases in Gross National Product and in employment.[43] President Kennedy's success in stimulating a sluggish economy in the early sixties and the failure of Franklin D. Roosevelt to end the recession of 1937-1938 can be attributed to the former's possession and latter's lack of "superior economic knowledge.[44]

Some of the conditions required for success in a similar achievement for managing social problems already exist. A considerable amount of valuable knowledge has been and continues to be gathered regularly. The various reports produced by the C.E.A., notably the Economic Report of the President and the monthly publication, Economic Indicators, contain basic information. The annual budget messages of the president, initiated in 1921, are likewise invaluable. In the area of social institutions, an early effort to examine social change and social problems was initiated by President Hoover's Research Committee on Social Trends, with William F. Ogburn of the University of Chicago as Chairman. The Committee published its report, *Recent Social Trends in the United States,* in 1943. Needless to say, no effort to comprehend the state of American society could dispense with the information compiled and published regularly by the Bureau of the Census. In addition to volumes on population, the Bureau publishes data on Housing, Agriculture, Government, Manufacturing and other business activities, and a wide variety of special reports including such matters as migration and minority groups. Some of the most salient statistics are published annually in *Statistical Abstract of the United States* and less frequently in *Historical Statistics of the United States*. Other government agencies also publish data essential to anyone seeking to understand the severity of various problems and the degree of progress made in coping with these situations, namely the Bureau of Labor Statistics, Social Security Administration and Office of Vital Statistics. Within the last few years, the Department of Health, Education and Welfare took an important step toward accurate assessment of certain problem areas with its monthly publication of HEW *Indicators*.

These efforts call for some type of centralized agency to synthesize this material, examine their adequacy, implement supplementary studies and annually assess social conditions in a report to top policy makers in the nation. The introduction in the Senate during the first session of the 90th Congress of S.843, the Full Opportunity and Social Accounting Act constituted a notable advance, although the measure had not been enacted at the time of writing. This bill sought to achieve in the social sphere what had been accomplished for the economy by establishment of a Council of Economic Advisors. The bill had as its objectives:

> . . . to promote and encourage such conditions as will give every American the opportunity to live in decency and dignity, and to provide a clear and precise picture of whether such conditions are promoted and encouraged in such areas as health, education, and training, rehabilitation, housing, vocational opportunities, the arts and humanities, and special assistance for the mentally ill and retarded, the deprived, the abandoned, and the criminal, and by measuring progress in meeting such needs.[45]

The proposed legislation called for the establishment of a Council of Social Advisors in the Executive Office of the President, which would consist of three members with the authority to employ a staff of specialists. The Council would have the responsibilities of:

1. evaluating the effectiveness of programs of the Federal Government in achieving the objectives listed above;
2. developing priorities for programs for achieving stated goals;
3. making and providing studies concerning social needs and government activities;
4. making recommendations concerning government programs;
5. assisting and advising the President on his annual "social report"

which reviews federal, state and local efforts to achieve the stated objectives of public policy.

While the Council of Social Advisors would have no authority to change the policies of government agencies, its use of highly trained specialists in the social sciences and of sophisticated statistical measures, and its access to the president, the White House staff and Congressional leaders would provide opportunity to influence policy making processes. The President's annual report on the state of American society may develop a public opinion favorable to some of the programs which would effectively manage social problems.

Major advances in assessment and interpretation of conditions in society which anticipate the occurrence of disruptions of the social fabric also can be made by improving the accessibility to scholars of data gathered by social scientists and by various organizations.[46] In many cases, after the mass of information has been collected by the social scientist and he has published his report or completed his analysis the records are placed in an attic or closet. A researcher elsewhere in the country needing some of the information available in these forgotten places may decide to conduct his own field investigation on the assumption that there is no other way to obtain the data. Similarly, a corporation, school or local unit of government generally accumulate in dusty basements the records of past events and operations and the correspondence of various top officials. This problem is not confined to the United States. Important studies are conducted in many parts of the world which culminate in similar circumstances, with the information filed away and forgotten or even discarded. Moreover, information of this type, which permits cross-cultural comparisons on specific variables, is indispensable for formulating and testing hypothesis of general relevance which are not restricted to circumstances in a specific society. The development of general theory, the highest goal of a science, depends on this type of information.

The mass of collected data far exceeds the current technology for making the information available quickly and rapidly to social scientists who need them. Consequently, either research suffers or additional resources are expended to collect data which would have been available had the technology for information storage and retrieval been more advanced. At the present time, considerable thought and effort are devoted to the solution of this problem. The time-shared computer and the development of data archives provide definite hope of greatly improving the flow of data to social scientists. To accomplish these ends, several problems must be overcome. One concerns the indexing of the information available in an archive and keeping the index current as additional files of information are acquired. A second problem refers to "records matching capabilities," which involves data about the same unit obtained by different researchers, generally filed in different locations in such a manner that identification of the units studied is difficult. This leads to a considerable loss of information, for the researcher cannot relate the various sets of data about his unit, *e.g.,* a neighborhood, corporation or person. This situation is prevalent among government agencies, several of which may study the same unit for quite different purposes. A third problem concerns the adoption of a computer language, a communication medium employed by all users, which would permit the rapid retrieval of information. Failure to accomplish this step would necessitate a complex translation process for the information from one data archive to be available to those who rely on archives organized around another language system. The fifth problem concerns the manner in which the various organizations which generate data of value to the social scientists can be organized to permit the preservation, storage and retrieval of information. On a small scale, progress has been made in this direction by the Roper Public Opinion Research Center which is a repository for survey data concerned with public opinion. In the area of political behavior, an inter-university consortium at the University of Michigan provides similar functions, while the Council of Social Science Data Archives presently is organizing feasible data exchange relationships for and between its member organizations.

Nationally, two types of organizations may emerge, one centralized at the federal and possibly also at the state level concerning data generated by government agencies, the other on a decentralized basis concerning data generated by such private organizations as business firms, educational organizations, and voluntary associations. The former would constitute a central data bank, storing the vast amount of information collected daily by government agencies in a form accessible to users. A similar arrangement ought to be possible for agencies of state government, with a central headquarters responsible for indexing all the holdings and referring users to the particular state organization which possesses the information desired. Similar data repositories might be developed for all the business firms in a particular industry and for all the schools in a state or region. A researcher in one part of the country who needed information, for example, on the educational background of the executives of different types of firms, or of the scholarly attainments of top university administrators could easily obtain such information for the units desired, at minimal cost, through telecommunication with the relevant data repository. This type of innovation in processing information undoubtedly will increase considerably both the number of studies and the theoretical understanding of social structure and process. Advances in basic theory will further development of the techniques and strategies of long-run social planning.

SUMMARY: INFORMATION THEORY AND POLITICAL PLURALISM[47]

The theory of pluralism considered in Chapter 9 and the theory of information each provides a strategy for coping with social problems. The former emphasizes the responsiveness of government to the interests of groups organized for political action. Information theory regards knowledge about the condition of society as an indispensable resource for policy making. The impetus for action, for pluralism, comes from organizations representing various blocs of citizens from the local to the governmental level. Government leaders modify a program or enact new legislation when influential groups indicate displeasure with certain features of the social environment. Information theory maintains that action should be based, wherever possible, on comprehensive data for any feature of society indicating that the costs are excessive for its continued existence. Initiative should be taken by public officials on the basis of information, as interpreted by qualified experts, and not delayed until the public has become aroused. Pluralist theory relates governmental action to the opinions of citizens about their living conditions. One theory holds that the *people* are the final arbiter of societal efficiency, and the second places its trust with the knowledge of experts.

Criteria for Determining the Existence of a Problem

For pluralist theory, a problem requiring action exists when the following conditions are met: citizens dissatisfied with some aspect of the social environment have established a group; these groups are committed to using available resources for gaining official approval of a preferred course of action; the groups will use legitimate procedures for preventing public officials from gaining some end which they regard as important if concessions are not forthcoming.

Pluralist theory maintains that a democratic system is highly sensitive to changes in the distribution of power among the groups in society. The mobilization of groups for political action may change the allocation of power, and tends to move society in directions in which these groups wish to go, unless prevented by even more powerful groups which oppose the action.

Accurate and comprehensive data which indicate the existence of an unsatisfactory condition becomes the starting point for action for information theory. The facts may pertain to any condition contrary to the values of society, such as the ill health of a large segment of the population, or the prevalence of poverty. Persons who are highly trained in the particular field, such as demographers, statisticians, public health specialists, are responsible for the collection, analysis and interpretation of the information. These men, who often serve as advisors to public officials, use the information for suggesting the programs which government should enact or modify.

Information Inputs for Decision Making

The pluralist approach requires information on the strength of the various groups and organizations concerned about a particular issue. Officials wish to know which force is stronger—the one for or the one opposed to a particular proposal—which is more skillful in the use of its resources and which can most help and most hinder officials in their efforts to gain desired goals. The politics of power is the strategic consideration in deciding what should be done.

Information theory requires comprehensive data on society as a whole and on its institutions. Data also must be gathered on the various levels of society—neighborhood, municipality, state and region. Knowledge about many aspects of society can be obtained from social indicators, measures of social conditions. Indicators will be most helpful for analysis where they are arranged in a time sequence and where they reveal the causal relationships between a number of variables. Controversy centers on questions of the accuracy and relevancy of the data, for these influence policy decisions. This struggle is called the "politics of statistics."[48]

Lines of Communication

Government leaders can obtain information on interest groups in a number of ways. Usually these groups are eager to communicate with officials where prospects are favorable for influencing policy decisions. The hope for success is a strong inducement for seeking out appropriate officials. Formal legislative procedures, such as congressional hearings, also provide an opportunity for an exchange of views. Where public officials and leaders of interest groups are on friendly terms, informal occasions, such as the cocktail party or a golfing foursome, may provide a convenient opportunity for discussion.

Information theory requires establishment of a communication network between organizations in and out of government and the agencies collecting data. Procedures for the gathering, classification, storage and retrieval of information must operate efficiently, especially at times of emergency, when pertinent data must be made available on demand. These facilities represent a *memory* for society and a basis for *learning* from the *mistakes* of the past. The facilities of these *data banks* enable specialists to analyze social conditions, to prepare reports and to suggest programs to the decision makers.

Process of Decision Making

Selecting a course of action for the pluralist approach requires a complex process of bargaining between rival groups. Leaders function as negotiators in developing a course of action that each group can accept. On occasion recalcitrant groups must be persuaded that the stronger position of its rivals prevents a more favorable settlement. A decision usually is reached after all participating groups consider a specific outcome the best that can be obtained under the prevailing pattern of power distribution.

The information approach relies on knowledge of the degree to which several courses of action can produce the intended result in the desired time period with the resources available. The technical appraisal of *goodness of fit* of means to ends weigh heavily in choosing between alternatives. The reports of specialists on these matters decisively influence the choices leaders make.

Distribution of Rewards

Each group that participates in the effort to influence the deliberations of leaders usually has some of its objectives met. Since a weak group often is able to delay or veto the decision of a majority coalition, some concession may have to be made to gain its acquiescence. This political necessity broadens the allocation of rewards, although the lion's share generally goes to the stronger groups. Where many diverse interests have been represented in the deliberations, a broad spectrum of constituents will receive some benefits from government programs. For this reason decisions made in accordance with social pluralism tend to approximate the public interest.

The information approach seeks to avoid situations where the interests of a particular group can frustrate the carefully prepared plans of the experts. Some groups will experience considerable inconvenience or abridgment of prerogatives to facilitate social reform. In this sense, collective goals prevail over those of special interests.

The specialists consider many important features of the social environment in preparing a plan for change. If the analysis has been accurate, the outcome may come very close to the public interest. If errors have been made, the consequences may "ricochet at high speed throughout the system."[49] Few units of the organization will escape the consequences of poor choices.

OVERVIEW

Pluralist strategy seeks to accomplish change while preserving the cohesiveness of society. It places a premium on retaining the loyalties of interest groups to society. To achieve this end, the strategy calls for a protracted and complicated procedure of negotiating differences between a broad spectrum of interest groups. Careful attention usually is given to the evaluations offered by the leaders of each group on the needs and desires of followers. The preference for basing policy decisions on some modicum of consensus among opposing groups reduces the rate of change. The leaders usually make slight alterations in past policy. This gradualist approach to problem management reduces the costs for those groups which surrender prerogatives and provides time for adjustment. This approach usually is effective if the difficulties are not too serious. Basic weaknesses or disruptions, however, may not be substantially improved by a gradualist approach.

Pluralism also accords with the basic values of democracy. All groups should have the opportunity to participate in decision making processes. The strategy requires public officials at all levels of government to be sensitive to organized elements of the citizenry. To relinquish these privileges and responsibilities of participation to elite groups would transform leadership structure from the pluralist to the monolithic pattern.

The necessity to gain the cooperation of all contending groups can result in a patchwork compromise that cannot cope with the social problem. If organization leaders modify a carefully designed plan whenever a group threatens some type of veto action, the final program may be inadequate. Loyalty of each faction to the organization can be achieved at the expense of effectiveness in goal attainment. A related weakness concerns the tendency to neglect interests which are not represented at the bargaining table. As the national interest seldom has a spokesman, the final agreement may reflect the primacy of narrow interests. Since weak groups seldom ask for a hearing, their needs often are ignored. This circumstance will persist until members of these groups either organize for political action or engage in serious protest.

The informational approach aids the management of social problems in several ways. In contrast to the pluralist approach, it does not rely heavily on the knowledge which citizens have on the social environment. Information strategy provides for a more thorough and systematic examination of society. The approach also requires the use of persons who are highly knowledgeable about various areas and programs. Consequently, the approach permits detection of difficulties or potential troubles which escape the attention of most citizens. Plans for remedial action can be prepared, examined and implemented prior to the occurrence of serious conflict or disorganization. Information strategy improves the anticipatory capabilities of society for preventing a serious buildup in conflict situations. The stability of society can be improved by maintaining a high order of functional effectiveness.

The use of systematic methods of data collection and analysis can increase the strain on the capacities of society to change. The more information which is gathered and the more sophisticated the techniques of analysis become, the greater the ability to detect problems. The information experts will set up an agenda for action which may exceed the available resources. Since most citizens lack the information available to the experts, they will tend, in many cases, to prefer the status quo. The differences between the specialists and the leaders of major interest groups can heighten tensions and exacerbate problems.

The evaluations of various situations by the information analysts should not be accepted uncritically. These members of society also have cultural biases which can lead to serious errors. Several examples of this have been studied in the preceding chapters. A cohesive Italian neighborhood, for instance, was classified as a slum and replaced by an urban renewal project which required the relocation of residents and destruction of the social unit.[50] Sympathy for the underdog leads some analysts to ignore the tendency of lower class life styles to impede upward mobility.[51]

SYNTHESIS

Management of social problems requires both of the strategies we have discussed. "Solving" a social problem, as suggested by the definition in Chapter 1, may require changes in the social structure in order to facilitate an increase in the allocation of resources to various groups. Some groups will be compelled to share prerogatives or to surrender some valuable privilege. Where these types of concessions are demanded repeatedly of specific groups by external agencies, in the absence of legitimate opportunities to express opposition, resistance to change will become intense and could lead to violence. Efforts to change a program after passage of enabling legislation also can be expected. The discussion of the T.V.A. in Chapter 9 suggests how this could be accomplished, by shrewd application of pressure on agency executives responsible for implementing the program. Where such efforts succeed, the results of legislation may differ considerably from those intended by the advocates of the law.

Pluralist strategy takes into account the imperative of every social system for retaining the loyalty of members and their commitment to obey the rules. The basic procedures of decision making provide an important measure of protection to each interest group. Sensitivity to the expressed wishes of every organized group, or delaying a decision until consensus between opposing groups has emerged, protects each group from arbitrary governmental action. Benefits are proportional to the efforts each group makes to influence the decision makers.

The stability of social systems also requires functional effectiveness. Stable societies possess the capacity to achieve basic objectives with the maximum feasible conservation of scarce resources. To modify a carefully designed plan to placate an interest group may perpetuate waste and social conditions which contradict basic values. This circumstance also imposes penalties on certain groups—where economy-minded taxpayers refuse to support a program of compensatory education for deprived children.

Although the pluralist and information strategies for problem management may conflict with each other at various times, both must be used. Society must move in both directions simultaneously for better goal attainment and a high level of citizen loyalty to the polity. To accomplish change while preserving the cohesiveness of society constitutes a difficult and top priority objective.

Selected Readings

Baritz, Loren. *The Servants of Power: A History of the Use of Social Science in American Industry* (Middletown, Conn: Wesleyan University Press, 1960).

Bauer, Raymond A., *ed. Social Indicators* (Cambridge, Mass.: The M.I.T. Press, paperback, 1967).

Crosson, Frederick J. and Kenneth M. Sayre, *eds. Philosophy and Cybernetics* (New York: Simon and Schuster, Clarion Book, 1968).

Dechert, Charles R., *ed. The Social Impact of Cybernetics* (New York: Simon and Schuster, Clarion Book, 1967).

Kochen, Manfred, *ed. The Growth of Knowledge* (New York: John Wiley & Sons, 1967).

March, James G. and Herbert A. Simon. *Organizations* (New York: John Wiley & Sons, 1958).

Merritt, R. L. and Stein Rokkan, *eds. Comparing Nations* (New Haven: Yale University Press, 1966).

Rokkan, Stein, *ed. Data Archives for the Social Sciences* (Paris and the Hague: Mouton & Co., 1966).

Russett, Bruce M., Hayward R. Alker, Jr., Karl W. Deutsch and Harold D. Lasswell. *World Handbook of Political and Social Indicators* (New Haven: Yale University Press, 1964).

Simon, Herbert A. *Administrative Behavior,* 2 ed. (New York: The Free Press, paperback, 1965).

"Social Goals and Indicators for American Society," Vol. I., *The Annals,* 371 (May, 1967).

"Social Goals and Indicators for American Society," Vol. II *The Annals,* 373 (September, 1967).

Wiener, Norbert. *Cybernetics: Or Control and Communication in the Animal and the Machine* (Cambridge, Mass.: The M.I.T. Press, Paper, 1964).

Wilensky, Harold L. *Organizational Intelligence* (New York: Basic Books, 1967).

Notes to Chapter 10

[1] C. P. Snow, *Variety Of Men* (New York: Scribner's, 1967), pp. 118-20.
[2] "The Atomic Bomb Project," *Encyclopaedia Britannica,* Vol. 2 (Chicago: Encyclopaedia Britannica, 1958), p. 649.
[3] The discussion of laissez faire economic theory and of the adoption of Keynesian theory is based on John Kenneth Galbraith, "Came the Revolution," *The New York Times Book Review* (May 16, 1965), pp. 1, 34-36, 38, 39.
[4] *Ibid.,* p. 1.
[5] *Ibid.,* p. 34.
[6] *Ibid.* p. 34.

7 Daniel Bell regards the university as the dominant institution of the post-industrial society. See Daniel Bell, "Notes on the Post-Industrial Society," Part I and Part II. *The Public Interest,* 6 (Winter, 1967), pp. 24-35, 7 (Spring, 1967), pp. 102-18.

8 Karl W. Deutsch, "Toward A Cybernetic Model of Man and Society," in Walter Buckley, *ed., Modern Systems Research For the Behavioral Scientist* (Chicago: Aldine, 1968), pp. 390-1.

9 This viewpoint is emphasized by Karl W. Deutsch, *The Nerves of Government* (New York: The Free Press of Glencoe, 1963), pp. 107-9. For additional studies and essays on communication theory, see the following: Karl W. Deutsch, *Nationalism and Social Communication* (Cambridge: The M.I.T. Press, paperback, 1966); Amitai Etzioni, *The Active Society* (New York: The Free Press, 1968), Chapters 5, 6, 9, 18; Raymond A. Bauer, Ithiel de Sola Pool, Lewis Anthony Dexter, *American Business and Public Policy* (New York: Atherton Press, 1963); Raymond A. Bauer, "Societal Feedback," *The Annals,* 373 (September, 1967), pp. 180-92; E. N. Gilbert, "Information Theory After 18 Years," *Science,* 152 (15 April 1966), pp. 320-6; Charles R. Dechert, "The Development of Cybernetics," *The American Behavioral Scientist,* 8 (June, 1965), pp. 15-20; Mervyn L. Cadwallader, "The Cybernetic Analysis of Change in Complex Social Organizations," in Walter Buckley, *ed., op. cit.,* pp. 437-40; Geoffrey Vickers, "Is Adaptability Enough?" in Walter Buckley, *ed., op. cit.,* pp. 460-473.

10 Summarized from E. E. Morison, "A Case History of Innovation," *Engineering and Science Monthly,* 13 (April, 1950), by Robert A. Rosenthal and Robert S. Weiss, "Problems of Organizational Feedback Processes," in Raymond A. Bauer, ed., *Social Indicators,* (Cambridge, Mass.: The M.I.T. Press, paperback, 1967), pp. 324-5.

11 Elizabeth B. Drew, "HEW Grapples with PPBS," *The Public Interest,* 8 (Summer, 1967), pp. 10-11. For a discussion of this innovation in federal decision making, see *The Public Interest, op. cit.,* pp. 4-48.; See Virginia Held, "PBS Comes to Washington," *The Public Interest,* 4 (Summer, 1966), pp. 102-15.

12 Raymond A. Bauer, "The Nature of the Task," in Raymond A. Bauer, *ed., Social Indicators, op. cit.,* p. 12.

13 Robert K. Merton, "Manifest and Latent Functions," in *Social Theory and Social Structure,* rev. ed., (New York: The Free Press of Glencoe, 1957), pp. 19-84. For additional articles on functionalist theory, see the collection in N. J. Demerath, III and Richard A. Peterson, *eds., System, Change, and Conflict* (New York: The Free Press, 1967).

14 Seymour M. Lipset, *Political Man* (Garden City, N.Y.: Doubleday Anchor Book, 1963), Chaps. 2, 3; "Some Social Requisites of Democracy: Economic Development and Political Legitimacy," *American Political Science Review,* LIII (March, 1959), pp. 69-105.

15 Gross develops a scheme for a "total" information inventory of American society in Bertram M. Gross, "Social System Accounting," in Raymond A. Bauer, *ed., Social Indicators, op. cit.,* pp. 154-271. Gross presents a different set of categories for information selection in Bertram M. Gross and Michael Springer, "A New Orientation in American Government," *The Annals,* 371 (May, 1967), pp. 1-19. See also an expanded version in Bertram M. Gross and Michael Springer, "New Goals For Social Information," *The Annals,* 373 (September, 1967), pp. 208-18.

16 Robert E. Lane, "The Decline of Politics and Ideology in a Knowledgeable Society," *American Sociological Review,* 31 (October, 1966), pp. 649-62.

17 Rachel Carson, *Silent Spring* (Greenwich, Conn.: Fawcett Publications, paperback, 1967).; "America's Changing Environment," *Daedalus,* 96 (Fall, 1967),; *Waste Management and Control* (Washington, D.C.: National Academy of Sciences—National Research Council, Publication 1400, 1966).

18 Lipset, *Political Man, op. cit.,* pp. 70-75.

[19] Bertram M. Gross, "The State of the Nation: Social Systems Accounting," in Raymond A. Bauer, *ed., Social Indicators, op. cit.,* pp. 210-11.

[20] A systematic appraisal of American society, using social indicators, covered the following categories: health, social mobility, the physical environment, income distribution, crime and public safety, learning and the arts, participation in society. U.S. Department of Health, Education, and Welfare, *Toward A Social Report* (Washington, D.C.: U.S. Government Printing Office, 1969).

[21] See Sidney Verba, "Democratic Participation," *The Annals,* 373 (September, 1967), pp. 53-78; Gabriel A. Almond and Sidney Verba, *Civic Culture* (Boston: Little, Brown and Company, paperback, 1965); Lester W. Milbrath, *Political Participation* (Chicago: Rand, McNally, 1965).

[22] For a discussion of the interaction between government and voters through the medium of voting, see Talcott Parsons, "Voting and the Equilibrium of the American Political System," in *Sociological Theory and Modern Society* (New York: The Free Press, 1967), pp. 223-63.

[23] Nathan Goldman discusses various forms of deviancy which fails to meet the functional prerequisites of society. See his article, "Social Breakdown," *The Annals,* 373 (September, 1967), pp. 156-79.

[24] For discussions of the theory of social indicators, see Mancur Olson, Jr., "The Plan and Purpose of a Social Report," *The Public Interest,* 15 (Spring, 1969), pp. 85-97; Albert D. Biderman, "Social Indicators and Goals," in Raymond A. Bauer, *ed., Social Indicators, op. cit.,* pp. 68-107.

[25] Amitai Etzioni and Edward W. Lehman, "Some Dangers in 'Valid' Social Measurement," *The Annals,* 373 (September, 1967), pp. 3-4.

[26] S. M. Miller, Martin Rein, Pamela Roby, and Bertram M. Gross, "Poverty, Inequality, and Conflict," *The Annals,* 373 (September, 1967), pp. 21-22.

[27] *Ibid.,* pp. 46-50.

[28] For a discussion of this characteristic, see Otis Dudley Duncan, "Discrimination Against Negroes," *The Annals,* 371 (May, 1967), pp. 98-102.

[29] James S. Coleman, *et. al., Equality of Educational Opportunity* (Washington: U.S. Government Printing Office, 1966).

[30] Daniel P. Moynihan, "Urban Conditions: General," *The Annals,* 371 (May, 1967), p. 166.

[31] Donald J. Bogue, *The Population of the United States* (Glencoe, Ill.: The Free Press, 1959).

[32] Michael Harrington, *The Other America: Poverty in the United States* (Baltimore: Penguin Books, 1963).

[33] Charles Y. Glock and Rodney Stark, *Religion and Society in Tension* (Chicago: Rand-McNally, 1965).

[34] Etzioni and Lehman, "Some Dangers in 'Valid' Social Measurement," *op. cit.,* p. 6.

[35] *Uniform Crime Reports for the United States* (Washington, D.C.: The U.S. Dept. of Justice, Annual).

[36] Our discussion parallels closely that presented by Albert D. Biderman, "Social Indicators and Goals," in Raymond A. Bauer, *ed., Social Indicators, op. cit.,* pp. 111-129.

[37] *Ibid.,* p. 117.

[38] *Ibid.,* p. 118.

[39] *Ibid.,* pp. 114-5.

[40] Albert D. Biderman, "Anticipatory Studies and Stand-By Research," in Raymond A. Bauer, *ed., op. cit.,* p. 301.

[41] Our discussion draws heavily from the chapter on the CEA in Harold L. Wilensky, *Organizational Intelligence* (New York: Basic Books, 1967), pp. 94-109.

[42] *Ibid.,* p. 104.

[43] *Ibid.,* p. 105.

[44] *Ibid.,* pp. 105-6.

[45] 90th Congress, 1st Session, S. 843, pp. 1-2.

[46] The discussion of improving communication among social scientists draws heavily from a report by the Committee on Information in the Behavioral Sciences of the National Research Council, *Communication Systems and Resources in the Behavioral Sciences* (Washington, D.C.: National Academy of Sciences, Publication 1575, 1967).

[47] The discussion of social pluralism in this section relies on the ideas expressed in the following works: Edward C. Banfield, *Political Influence* (New York: Free Press, 1961), pp. 324-41; Robert A. Dahl and Charles E. Lindblom, *Politics, Economics, and Welfare* (New York: Harper & Row, Torchbook, 1963), pp. 272-365; Gerard Degre, "Freedom and Social Structure," in Logan Wilson and William L. Kolb, *eds., Sociological Analysis* (New York: Harcourt, Brace and Company, 1949), pp. 521-29.

For patterns of decision making related to a pluralistic social structure, see Charles E. Lindblom, *The Intelligence of Democracy* (New York: Free Press, 1965); David Braybrooke and Charles E. Lindblom, *A Strategy of Decision* (New York: Free Press, 1963). For a critical analysis of incremental decision making, see Amitai Etzioni, *The Active Society* (New York: Free Press, 1968), pp. 249-309.

The discussion of the strategy of problem management based on information theory owes much to the works cited in the previous chapter. These include: Raymond A. Bauer, *ed., Social Indicators, op. cit.,* "Social Goals and Indicators for American Society, I, II," *The Annals of the American Academy of Political and Social Science,* 371 (May, 1967), 373 (September, 1967). For a report assessing the social condition of American society based on social indicators, see *Toward A Social Report* (Washington, D.C.: U.S. Government Printing Office, 1969). For articles which discuss the work of the committee responsible for preparing the report, and the theory underlying it, see Daniel Bell, "The Idea of a Social Report," *The Public Interest,* 15 (Spring, 1969), pp. 72-84; Mancur Olson, Jr., "The Purpose and Plan of a Social Report," *The Public Interest,* 15 (Spring, 1969), pp. 85-97.

[48] Alan Altshuler, "The Politics of Full Employment," *Trans-action,* 6 (May, 1969), p. 47.

[49] Harold L. Wilensky, *Organizational Intelligence, op. cit.,* p. 185.

[50] Herbert J. Gans, *The Urban Villagers* (New York: The Free Press, paperback, 1962).

[51] Lewis A. Coser, "Presidential Address: Unanticipated Conservative Consequences of Liberal Theorizing," *Social Problems,* 16 (Winter, 1969), pp. 263-72.

INDEX

349